HARVARD HISTORICAL STUDIES • 186

Published under the auspices
of the Department of History
from the income of the
Paul Revere Frothingham Bequest
Robert Louis Stroock Fund
Henry Warren Torrey Fund

SELLING PARIS

Property and Commercial Culture in the Fin-de-siècle Capital

Alexia M. Yates

Harvard University Press
Cambridge, Massachusetts
London, England
2015

Printed in the United States of America

First Printing

Library of Congress Cataloging-in-Publication Data

Yates, Alexia M., 1980–
Selling Paris : property and commercial culture in the
fin-de-siècle capital / Alexia M. Yates.
pages cm
Includes bibliographical references and index.
ISBN 978-0-674-08821-4 (alk. paper)
1. Real estate development—France—Paris—History—19th century.
2. Real estate business—France—Paris—History—19th century.
3. Real property—France—Paris—History—19th century.
4. City planning—France—Paris—History—19th century.
5. Paris (France)—History—1870–1940. I. Title.
HD650.P3Y37 2015
333.330944'36109034—dc23 2015006315

Contents

Introduction: Selling Paris *1*

1 The Business of the City *22*

2 Seeing Like a Speculator *59*

3 The Problem of Property *98*

4 The Unceasing Marketplace *135*

5 Marketing the Metropolis *174*

6 Districts of the Future *217*

Epilogue: Illicit Speculation and Impossible Markets *256*

Appendix *269*

Notes *273*

Acknowledgments *345*

Index *349*

SELLING PARIS

Introduction

Selling Paris

In 1882 the hill of Montmartre was brimming with building activity. The source of all the hammering wasn't just the Basilica of Sacré Coeur, the expiatory shrine for the sins of the Paris Commune (1871) whose construction had begun in 1875. In fact, at this moment the future of the icon that would one day brood over Paris was uncertain: republican deputies were attempting to stop its construction, challenging the legitimacy of using public powers of expropriation for a religious monument.[1] Past the site of the future basilica, the Société Anonyme (SA) Immobilière de Montmartre, or Montmartre Real Estate Company, had created the largest worksite in the city. In less than two years more than 300 workers would cover 32,000 square meters of (emptied) terrain with three new roads and eighty-eight apartment buildings. Journalists surveying the progress reported on yet another instance of the construction of an entirely new neighborhood in the capital city, with streets and apartment buildings that seemed to appear overnight.[2] It was one of many projects spearheaded by the architect Paul Fouquiau. Before this development was completed, another of Fouquiau's firms, SA des Immeubles de la Rue de Clichy, had begun construction on forty-six apartment houses and two new streets in the nearby neighborhood of La Chapelle.[3] At the same time, his SA Immobilière de l'Hôtel de Ville was driving a street through the populous

4th arrondissement and putting up eight new apartment buildings, his Société Générale Immobilière was building dozens more on new streets in the renovated "Quartier Marbeuf" in the 8th arrondissement, and his SA Immobilière de la Rue des Martyrs and SA Immobilière de la Villa Caprice were constructing still more in the 9th arrondissement and rapidly developing west end.

Fouquiau's name has not come down to posterity. Born in 1855 in La Ferté-Saint-Aubin in the department of Loiret, Paul Casimir Marie Fouquiau entered the workshop of architect Jean-Louis Pascal at the École des Beaux-Arts in 1873.[4] How long he remained there is not known, but his earliest buildings date from 1877 (when he was at the ripe age of twenty-two). Perhaps if his submission for a metal tower at the Universal Exhibition of 1889 had been accepted, his name would now be as familiar to us as Gustave Eiffel's. Fouquiau was prolific, and more than competent as an architect; he catered to wealthy clients (though it was rumored that his designs for a house for Victor Hugo were rejected on grounds of personal dislike), and turned his hand on occasion to the monumental projects common among his Beaux-Arts peers.[5] But his innovations were not the kind favored by the architectural profession. He founded no architectural societies, penned no studies or manifestos, contributed nothing that we know of to the developing urbanist community of the turn of the century. He ran for the municipal council and the national legislature, both unsuccessfully. He received the Legion of Honor, but his file contains letters of complaint alleging that the work for which he was particularly honored (at the Amsterdam Universal Exhibition of 1883) was not even his own.[6] What he did do with unabashed success was make money. The crest emblazoned across his pioneering property-marketing journal in 1877 showed Parisian land divided into streets and sales lots, surrounded by the capitalist credo "Time Is Money" (Figure 0.1). He erected hundreds of apartment houses in speculative projects that spanned the last three decades of the nineteenth century, leaving virtually no district of the city untouched.[7] He used his journal and editorial columns to forge new methods of promoting real estate, and, sensing the opportunities that could arise from increasing pressure on municipal and state officials to intervene in housing provision, actively courted public support for innovative working-class housing developments. He became a millionaire—and a bankrupt—several times over.

Along the way, Fouquiau did business with some of the biggest financial institutions and entrepreneurs in the capital city. His real estate developments

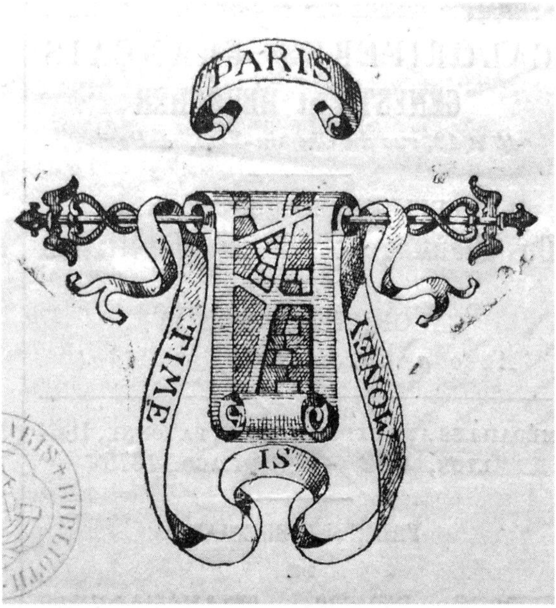

FIGURE 0.1 The crest on the cover of Paul Fouquiau's 1877 journal, the *Indicateur Général des Terrains et Immeubles à Vendre. Source:* Bibliothèque Historique de la Ville de Paris

were one face of a general explosion of financial activity that took place in Paris and other French cities at the end of the 1870s, an effervescence that began screeching to a halt with the crash of the Union Générale bank in January 1882. Fouquiau's name appears alongside some of the most unsavory elements of this boom. He became entangled with the Crédit de Paris, a banking house founded by Édouard-Hippolyte Lepelletier, a financier so disreputable he had to direct his companies in secret. Fouquiau's involvement might appear happenstance but for the narrow escape the architect made from this and a similar venture, the Banque de la Chaussée d'Antin, before both collapsed in the early 1880s. His participation resulted in charges of fraud and other infractions that kept him in court for years.[8] Other indications of a certain ease with illicit methods pepper his career. In 1887 he was implicated in the bribery of a municipal councilor, Paul-Frédéric Lefebvre-Roncier, who received a check for 10,000 francs over his dessert in the glittering Café de la Paix in exchange for a favorable disposition toward an exhibition in which the architect was engaged.[9] In the same year a pamphlet skewered Fouquiau's "notoriously disreputable" operations, including the flagrant overvaluing of his Montmartre development, which he had sold off to a property management corporation called the Rente Foncière, much to its shareholders' discontent.[10] And this company had other reasons to question their affairs with Fouquiau. In the course of a collaboration on the Quartier Marbeuf development, it became apparent that he had appropriated funds from building loans "for his personal use," leaving the Rente Foncière on the hook for a million francs in order to finish the project.[11]

Fouquiau and his counterparts in the building industry took full advantage of the easy credit and flexible business forms available in the Third Republic's (1870–1940) early years—particularly the limited liability joint stock corporation—to bring about the largest building boom of the century. Between 1879 and 1885, more than 13,500 buildings were constructed across Paris, and the rental value of the city's housing stock increased by a quarter. An 1888 municipal report concluded that "in no other period has the dynamic of construction and demolition enacted such significant changes in the condition of land in such a short span of time."[12] Real estate development drew the attention of contemporaries for both its unprecedented production and its ethos: its obsession with profit and its insistence on risk taking and overproduction. In the words of one publication reflecting on the field in 1884, "Builders have become true manufacturers, asking only to produce, produce more, produce forever."[13] In their journals and editorial columns, developers vaunted their flair, self-assurance, and willingness to step up to the demands and opportunities of the moment. One speculator harangued his rather more timid brethren, "When, in the nineteenth century, in a period of complete freedom of action and in the midst of abundant, cheap capital, you decide to play it safe—better to buy a bit of land and grow cabbages and leave your place in the world of business to others."[14]

This is not the familiar story of Parisian development. Most historical accounts focus on the role of state authorities and government institutions in rewriting the capital city, with the renovation of Paris by Georges-Eugène Haussmann and Napoleon III during the Second Empire (1852–1870) dominating the narrative.[15] This view from above has left little room for the endeavors of private enterprise or the everyday urbanism of private property owners, despite their lasting influence on Parisian space. Indeed the networks and tools of knowledge that guide the development decisions of speculative builders are rarely investigated in urban history.[16] Not only are their mechanisms more difficult to grasp than those of public authorities, but developers work hard to naturalize their activities, giving their technical appreciations of a market and a city the appearance of common knowledge. Yet knowing the story of modern Paris requires getting to know its private developers. Private actors like Fouquiau helped establish the systems of property relations that constituted the material conditions of everyday life in the capital of modernity.[17] They were also pivotal agents in the domestication of modern urban culture, a crucial phase of which was unfolding in fin-de-siècle Paris.[18]

Nor does Fouquiau's story sit comfortably with an image of the French entrepreneur and French business as risk-averse and self-limiting.[19] Thanks partly to popular assessments of the French as anticapitalist, this characterization has proven remarkably enduring, despite having been refuted by historians of French business in recent decades. More nuanced treatment of French economic development focuses on the particularities (rather than the inadequacies) of the country's political economy in the modern era, and emphasizes a range of phenomena—from the pronounced role of banks and the state in economic development, to the technocratic nature of business education, to the location of the market in the country's political culture—that explain France's unique embrace of capitalism.[20] Fouquaiu's ventures exemplify an entrepreneurial outlook that combined creative risk taking with acceptance of the enhanced role of the state in economic life. His field was shaped by large financial institutions closely linked to the state, and he made several efforts to translate his business success into political office, following established custom among the French commercial and industrial elite. All the while he championed an American truism—*Time is money,* in English, no less—that brilliantly summarizes the victorious march of the modern economic order, with its imperatives of rationality, efficiency, and total mastery of increasingly compressed space.

But Fouquiau and his ilk are not only vital for illuminating the broad range of actors engaged in city building during a crucial period of urbanization, or the types of entrepreneurial selfhoods that emerged in the context of the Second Industrial Revolution. They are important because their ventures help reveal fundamental reconfigurations in the relations between finance, commerce, and real estate that occurred at the end of the nineteenth century, shaping both the built form and social experience of the modern metropolis. The politics and practices of real estate development—the individuals, institutions, and intellectual labor that established the circuits by which property and people moved (or did not move)—took new form in this period. Certainly, the urban reconstruction of the Second Empire was an important breeding ground for many of the entrepreneurial practices of the early Third Republic. But the political economy of development in the fin-de-siècle capital was profoundly different from that which existed previously, taking shape in reaction to the experience of Haussmannization and the immense political and social upheaval of the Paris Commune in 1871. While the city's economy begged for the employment and tax revenues generated by massive building campaigns, the prospect of "armies" of workers drawn to the city by such projects was, to some, unnerving. Moreover, municipal engagement in urban renovation risked making a new republican city council (now an elected body for the first time in decades) appear to be continuing imperial policies of gentrification and illicit collaboration with real estate interests. The role of speculators in the market was further problematized by the increasing urgency of the social question, which led haltingly to the first steps toward government involvement in housing production, each legislative landmark accompanied by strident debate on the problems and potentials of the private housing marketplace.[21] In short, the end of the century was a period of critical reexamination of the mechanisms and values governing urban real estate.

Real estate speculation and its particular instrument, the société anonyme, concentrated anxieties about what appeared to both Parisian residents and its government as the increasingly elusive possibility of reconciling the political or moral function of the city with its economic identity. The incorporation of sociétés anonymes, or limited liability joint stock companies, was liberalized in 1867. Formerly subject to state authorization and justified as entities contributing to the public good, these companies were henceforth no longer matters of state.[22] Entry into property speculation became significantly easier, particularly for those with little initial capital. Between 1870 and 1900, 253 sociétés anonymes were formed in Paris for the purposes of real estate development (or, as company statutes frequently expressed it, "for the purposes of speculation").[23] The late 1870s also saw the establishment of a comprehensive credit network for the building industry through the coordination of the semipublic mortgage institution the Crédit Foncier (founded in 1852) with the Sous-Comptoir des Entrepreneurs (the traditional lending body of the building industry, created in 1848) and newly formed subsidiary lending and investment institutions the Compagnie Foncière de France (1881) and the Rente Foncière (1879).[24] After the downturn in the building industry, the apartment houses of floundering developers made their way into the portfolios of these same companies. The Compagnie Foncière de France, for instance, acquired 167 apartment buildings within only a few years. By 1910, real estate and insurance corporations owned more than 2,500 buildings across Paris, managing tens of thousands of apartments in the interests of their shareholders. Through the mechanisms of limited liability joint stock companies and the portfolios of property financing firms, property was turning into paper and landlords were dissolving into anonymous corporations.

These companies placed unprecedented emphasis on rational property management and modern advertising. They courted tenants as customers to whom they were accountable; a visit to the Rente Foncière's rental offices, a discussion with its agents, and a perusal of availabilities and floor plans promised "prompt and complete satisfaction." "The easiest, cheapest, and least bothersome way to find an apartment," the firm's advertising proclaimed, "is to turn to a large real estate company."[25] This commercialization of property management depended in part on the services of a newly specialized class of business actors that made its livelihood through the marketing of rental housing, property sales, and property management in the capital. Known as *agents d'affaires,* or estate agents, these intermediaries personified market relations, engaging in a variety of enterprises that bridged the legal, financial, and commercial arenas.[26] They sold stocks and bonds, drew up contracts for corporate arrangements, brokered various forms of merchandise, advised businesspeople on legal matters, and sold commercial and residential properties. All this in addition to their rather more dubious spheres of activity: researching persons of interest for clients, trading in patents, running employment agencies for often desperate job seekers, and brokering marriages.

As they specialized across the nineteenth century, estate agents imposed more aggressively on the professional monopolies of the notaries and solicitors who occupied the realm of property exchange. The highly formalized information networks of these officers of the court constituted the traditional channels of real estate circulation.[27] Estate agents presented competing models of market organization. They proposed their agencies as "real estate exchanges" modeled on other commodity marketplaces, producing volumes of data on property prices and working to build the social spaces of the capital—"publicizing and familiarizing people with the new districts of the city"—as they urged property owners to transition (with their help, of course) from complacent rentiers to "bona fide retailers."[28] Their specialized gazettes, which increased in both number and sophistication from the 1870s onward, joined mainstream papers that began treating real estate as something to write about. *Le Figaro* introduced a weekly column summarizing and analyzing trends in the property market in 1881, *Le Gaulois* did likewise in 1885, and *Le Temps, Le Matin,* and *La Presse* débuted their sections in the early 1890s. The term "marché immobilier" (real estate market) began to appear in national dailies in the same period, closely linked to the creation of large corporations dedicated to property financing, construction, and management whose stocks and bonds traded on the Stock Exchange.

Contemporaries recognized that something new was happening with the city's real estate. A parliamentary commission, convened to survey the industrial crisis in Paris in 1884, addressed the problem directly. Dedicating particular attention to the building industry, it concluded that changes in its practices were deeply implicated in recent market crises. The commission's members observed, "The modern building sector is less industry than it is commerce; transactions are constant, eradicating production, in a manner of speaking." They continued, "For the public at large, the building entrepreneur is a merchant, almost a broker, just like the head of a department store."[29] This was far from an isolated assessment. Two years previously, at the height of the building boom, architectural critic Émile Rivoalen lambasted the banal construction patterns multiplying along Parisian streets, blaming the public's taste for the "ready-made," which led them to approach buildings "as they do goods at the Bon Marché or Belle-Jardinière department stores."[30] Rivoalen's professional disdain notwithstanding, soon individuals really could approach building sales and rentals in a department store setting with the opening of the real estate department in the Grands Magasins Dufayel in 1903 (Figure 0.2). Likewise, when Frédéric Haverkamp, a fictional real estate agent created by author Jules Romains, set up his agency in 1908, he based its organization on the premise that "the properties for sale are your merchandise. It's your job to enable the buyer to circulate easily among them, as he would in the aisles of a department store."[31]

Observations and spaces such as these capture a central transformation in the production and distribution of urban space in late-nineteenth-century Paris: the process by which housing and property came to be considered, and to act, as commercial objects. Establishing equivalence between urban housing and merchandise in a department store was not an automatic or

FIGURE 0.2 Browsing for property: the real estate section of the Dufayel Department Store, from the *Indicateur Dufayel,* 1903.
Source: Bibliothèque Historique de la Ville de Paris

straightforward affair, and required interventions, intentional and otherwise, by a number of agents and institutions. It required the emergence new players, from specialized real estate agents to professionalized property owners to newly abundant limited liability joint stock companies, who approached property development, distribution, and management as a commercial enterprise embedded in a consumer marketplace. It required the development of new credit arrangements and investment norms that facilitated the interpenetration of the stock and property markets by radically transforming expectations with regard to the productivity of money. And it required a political economy of development, shaped in reaction to the political, social, and economic legacies of Haussmannization and the Paris Commune, which carefully guarded the boundaries between private enterprise and public utility. Tracing how real property emerged as a commercial object in the spaces of the city and the portfolios of investors allows us to acknowledge these agents and interventions, opening up the business networks, financial arrangements, and political and social ambitions that structured the production, distribution, and consumption of Parisian property. It demands that we read the commonplace—from boulevards to apartment buildings—in unconventional ways, and add new sources to our pantheon of urban texts: the advertising columns of real estate agents, the annual reports of property management firms, the scribbled surveys of municipal tax assessors. The result is not only a new account of the political and economic stakes (as well as social experience) of city building; it is also an account of real estate as a social product and terrain of contestation that helps trace the changing political economy of capitalism at the turn of the twentieth century.

Property Is a Movable Good

The term "commercial object" serves to distinguish a particular phase in the historically contingent process by which land, property, and housing are rendered amenable to market exchange. Certainly, real estate functioned as a commodity in France (and elsewhere) long before the end of the nineteenth century. The necessary work of establishing a system of goods and equivalences that laid the groundwork for modern economies (as well as modern economics) was in place by the eighteenth century, and the notion that property—particularly urban property—could change hands primarily for its exchange value rather than its use value had a long history. In addition to particularly remarkable moments of market activity, such as the speculation on nationalized lands during and following the French Revolution, vigorous local markets in property whose procedures and norms were not unlike our own were in evidence in the medieval and early modern periods.[32]

Yet the commoditization of real estate is uneven in both time and space, even under advanced capitalism. It is insufficient to take as a given, in the words of one recent study, that "land had become a commodity from an early date onwards."[33] Despite its particular status, real estate, like other commodities, has a social life, a biography that is not exhausted by its "commodity situation."[34] Objects are subject to changing regimes of valuation that define their potential to act as commodities, in accordance with their material characteristics and the cultural framework supporting their conditions of exchange. As a good that is at once immovable, an element of basic necessity (shelter), and particularly freighted with political and affective investment, especially in modern Western democracies, real estate is subject to a complex and contingent moral economy that shapes the process of its marketization. Focusing on the route by which urban real estate becomes and operates as a commercial object lets us reconstruct a particular moment in the evolution of the cultural and institutional supports for its commoditization, as well as the diverse actors and localized circumstances that play a role in establishing the conditions for its exchange.

Real estate, in short, is a social product. Its markets are highly localized, segmented, and subject to a significant degree of informational inequality. Moreover, depending on the historical moment, interested party, and geographic location, as well as the particular contract under consideration, transactions in property markets often remain extremely individualized and personal, a contrast with other investment markets. These conditions ensure that their enmeshment in social networks, political frameworks, and cultural norms—not to mention specific spaces—is especially relevant.[35] Determining the particular means by which these factors contribute to the mechanisms of property production and exchange, however, requires more than simply pursuing the social construction of markets. Rather, this analysis demands unearthing the specific actors at work in the invention of market models and market sites, giving attention to the various kinds of expert and lay knowledge mobilized for this task, as well as accounting for the materiality—or physical, concrete attributes—of both markets themselves and the goods with which they are concerned.[36] This dual emphasis on knowledge and materiality is particularly appropriate for the study of property markets. The resistance of land and buildings to physical relocation has a significant impact on the form of these markets, whose efficiency is dependent on the circulation of representations of land and buildings available for sale or rental.

One of the concerns of this book is to explore the capacity of real property to resist or escape the homogenizing tendencies of capitalism. If a commodity is in part defined as a good whose conditions of exchange have effaced its conditions of production, then land is in some ways a quintessential example. Theorists as different as Karl Marx and Karl Polanyi converge around the complexity of land's position within the political economy of capitalism, deeming land a fictitious commodity (and its income fictitious capital) precisely because its exchange mechanisms erase the fact of its natural origins outside human labor and the market.[37] Yet beneath this veneer of exchangeability, beneath the commodity form granted to land by the market, lies the confounding and constraining obduracy of land, its limited availability, its immovability. Often when real estate is discussed, the objects under consideration—the built structures that are produced by human beings and placed on land—are straightforwardly intended as either a support for social reproduction or as a good directed at a market of buyers and users. In these cases, land's uneasy status as a commodity can generally be put aside. Nevertheless, something of its difficulties in the market is retained in real estate, in the question of location and in quandaries of scarcity, in uncertainty about sources of value. Real property exists both as a material entity and as a right over future revenues; it functions as a store of past wealth and a source of future income. In short, it encapsulates the dynamic between abstraction and materialization that drives the process of capital accumulation. For historical geographer David Harvey, it thus has a particular role to play in the coordination of surplus-value production, helping capital shift between circuits of accumulation.[38] Yet if space is ripe for incorporation into capital's circuits, the forms of labor and types of mechanisms by which that incorporation is attempted remain a contingent part of the process, and its success is by no means preordained. More attention to the legal and political situation of real property is needed to explain how this incorporation occurs, if indeed it does.

The constellation of agents and institutions shaping the marketization of real property in France, while influenced by international trends and models, was unique to that country. Debate on the most appropriate forms for the circulation of property, which raged among jurists, economists, and administrators throughout the nineteenth century, was shaped by the fears and frustrations engendered by Revolutionary experiments with monetizing land and the subsequent perceived inadequacies of the property regime instituted by the Napoleonic Code and its rules of civil procedure. The *assignat,* a circulating monetary instrument based initially on the value of the country's nationalized lands, is only the best known of the many schemes and fantasies of mobilizing land values at the end of the eighteenth century.[39] The Revolutionary era also saw innovations in the seemingly mundane arena of land registration and mortgage reform. Improved registers, national information systems, and notes that could represent property values and endow them with the increases in value that accrued from circulation were proposed and briefly institutionalized in both private banking schemes and a new mortgage regime instituted on 9 messidor Year III (June 27, 1795).[40] The banking schemes were short-lived, and the new Civil Code was shaped by an express desire to restrain the circulation of both physical property and its paper manifestations. It dispensed with the requirement to register most forms of transfers, maintaining the sanctity of private contract in real property transactions. The new legal regime classified real property as a *bien immobilier* subject to civil rather than commercial law, embroiling it in a more cumbersome system of transfer. By ensuring that real estate could not fulfill the critical conditions of *mobilier* goods—namely, the simplicity and rapidity of transfer, based on transparent and publicly-consented-to pricing—this legal framework created conditions that continually justified the exclusion of real property from commerce.

Indeed, for legal thinkers, legislators, economists, and property owners in nineteenth-century France, real estate's defining characteristic was its *inability* to act as merchandise. Although it could certainly be bought and sold, real property's legal definition meant that it could not be an object of commerce. As the proportion of movable assets in French portfolios gained steadily across the century, reaching parity with real property in the 1880s, continued hindrances to the smooth transfer of real estate became one of many points of contestation between advocates of an improved market in land (one that would see property pass easily to "those who can use it most profitably") and those who saw such markets as a threat to family homes and the agricultural traditions of the French nation.[41] Projects to improve the legibility—and consequently, transmissibility—of property were continually scuttled on this divide, even once the acquisition of new colonial territories and a domestic agricultural crisis at the end of the century added new urgency to long-standing debates.[42]

An increasingly thorough interpenetration of urban property markets and the practices and logic of the stock market compelled reflections on the nature and limits of the commercialization of property. As both markets boomed, contemporaries found many occasions to theorize on the relationship between these arenas of investment. Some perceived a pernicious extension of what might be called stock market mentalities to the arena of property transactions. Testifying before the 1884 Parliamentary Commission on Paris's industrial crisis, economist and director of the municipal pawn *(mont-de-piété)* André Cochut directly linked the recent pathologies of the property marketplace to the increasing dominance of the stock market in economic mores. Speculation fueled an "illusion of inexhaustible wealth," fostering visions of a limitless circuit of improvement and ever more diffuse opportunities for profit, leading land to be treated like wheat or corn and the "*marché à terme,*" or forward transactions, to replace the spot market.[43] Yet the bust revealed that the abstract nature of this market had limits. As the stock market eroded in early 1882, champions of the property market, the traditional home of stable investment practices, lauded the security inherent in property ownership. "Real" property was not subject to the falsity that inflated and twisted the movable-asset marketplace. As building entrepreneur Onésime Masselin put it in his series on the stock market and the building sector: "Buildings aren't like rubber, they can't be stretched and multiplied several times in number; Paris contains a certain number of lots and buildings—it isn't possible for anyone to increase its area." This contrasted with the artificial nature of mobile property: "As for stocks, on the other hand, with the help of the stamp duty bureau, Chaix [a publishing house] can produce enormous quantities of them."[44] The real estate firm of John Arthur et Tiffen reacted similarly, advising readers of their gazette that the difference between investments in land and those on the stock market amounted to "the difference between a *real* share and a *fictitious* share." The physicality of real property confronted the fantasy of speculators and refused their efforts to manipulate it: "Shares in real estate are based on buildings or land of incontestable materiality, the numbers of which can be evaluated and which cannot be increased on the whim of *adventurers* [*lanceurs d'affaires*]."[45]

The traditional association of the property market with investment and the stock market with speculation continued to have wide resonance, and was unsurprisingly frequently exploited by estate agents and other brokers dedicated to marketing urban property. These categories were, nevertheless, becoming far more permeable.[46] Investment manuals such as the often reprinted *Art de placer et de gérer sa fortune* (1906) by economist Paul Leroy-Beaulieu advised their readers that property ownership was simply too cumbersome and complicated for the modern investor, and was best left to professional management firms.[47] Indeed, in a stunning reversal from the stance taken on property in the previous century by the French economists known as the Physiocrats, Leroy-Beaulieu advised against investment in land on the basis that such use of capital was sterile and unproductive of interests. Far better to engage in property ownership by means of the increasingly popular société anonyme. It was these firms that worked to progressively enmesh urban property in the norms and practices of the stock market, innovating what would later be known as *papier-pierre,* turning the stones of real property into the paper titles of movable wealth. These new entrepreneurial arrangements, chronicled by financial columnist Alexis Bailleux de Marisy in 1881, "turned land, the construction it supports and the revenues it generates, into paper shares that can be folded and placed in a wallet."[48] They created a new, intermediary form of property that bridged the movable and immovable; "no less serious than real estate," this property adjusted traditional investment practices to new norms of capital circulation.[49] Another contemporary observer, a legal expert reporting to the Société Centrale des Architectes in 1884, declared optimistically that "this may be the future of property."[50]

Property owners could not be unmoved by these developments. The proliferation of market-oriented developers both challenged and redefined the place of individual owners in the urban economy.[51] In 1872, responding to the push of new property taxes and the pull of a cash-strapped municipal administration eager to foster private initiatives, owners founded the Chambre Syndicale des Propriétés Immobilières de la Ville de Paris (currently the Chambre Nationale des Propriétaires). This group turned immediately to securing legal recognition as the representative of a specific economic interest group, as well as to ensuring that urban property owners would be able to take advantage of an 1865 law that allowed rural property owners to form associations to undertake public works. These efforts to claim productive roles in the built and economic landscape of the city were shaped by a number of factors, not least of which was an evolving ecology of investment that destabilized the standing of real property in the nation's political economy. Their quest to establish the means to act collectively as producers of the urban environment failed, the direct result of a commercializing property market that situated owners as agents of distribution rather than production and rendered suspect their capacity to represent the general good.

Paris Is a Movable Feast

The competition and interrelationship between movable and immovable wealth not only constitute the particular double life of property as an asset; they also lie at the heart of the modern metropolis.[52] In the second half of the nineteenth century, many urban centers exhibited impulses toward centralized exchanges intended to integrate property markets with international networks of capital circulation, often building on the examples of other cities.[53] Yet the individuals and institutions that managed the intersection of these forms of wealth were particular to their places and times. Within France, Paris remained the largest property market in the country, and the market mechanisms and agents that emerged there did so in particularly pronounced form. In terms of the number and value of transactions, the capital's market dwarfed those of other urban centers in the country. In 1898, 414.5 million francs of property transactions took place in the department of the Seine, while the next closest department registered a mere 97 million.[54] The interventions of corporations concerned with property development and investment largely or exclusively targeted the Parisian urban landscape, while investment manuals advised that the only sure engagement with urban real estate was that undertaken in the capital city.[55] Furthermore, despite the crash and stagnation of the 1880s, building at the end of the nineteenth century represents the busiest period of development in Paris's history. As the city's population exploded—an increase of a million residents took place between 1872 and 1911—so did its building stock, which forms the core of the Parisian built environment even today.[56]

Anointed as the "capital of the nineteenth century," "capital of modernity," and "capital of the world," Paris has not lacked for chroniclers.[57] In the hands of historians, geographers, and literary scholars, the French capital has enjoyed a privileged relationship to urban modernity, the cradle of an "extroverted urbanism" that helped shape the experience of modern consumer culture.[58] Following the footsteps of the *flâneur* or gaping after the *badaud,* these narratives focus on the spectacle of boulevard life, the crowds that flooded department stores, cinemas, restaurants, and (on quite different occasions) revolutionary barricades.[59] Paris's modernity resides in its distinct publicness, whether in the ways that navigating and narrating the streets of the city helped constitute social imaginaries, or in the way that public authorities rewrote the city and its circulation networks.[60] This publicness helped shape the experience of even the city's putatively private spaces; the Parisian apartment house has been described as a manifestation of "antimodernity," the product of an "interiorization" that accompanied the extroversion of Haussmannization.[61]

The way that real estate—particularly housing—operated within this commercial and consumer culture is equally important to the story of Parisian modernity, and opens a fresh perspective on the influence of consumption on the shape and experience of the urban environment.[62] Yet it also serves to reorient this literature, away from the spectacle of the boulevards, monumental urbanism, and the unmediated march of an almost already postindustrial capitalism to address instead the business networks, legal frameworks, professional statutes, and political and social ambitions that structured the production, distribution, and consumption of Parisian property.[63] In exploring this reorientation, we reveal a number of traditional institutions, such as notaries and individual property owners, that coexist with and help calibrate modernizing institutions, lending modernity a particular and constitutive unevenness.[64]

Paris was home to more than two million individuals at the turn of the twentieth century, and the role of exchange value in the workings of its property market inflected but did not dominate use value. These individuals were, by a large majority, tenants. The previous century had seen the consolidation of the single-floor apartment and the spread of multistory apartment buildings, necessitating the introduction in 1783–1784 of the first ordinances regulating building heights.[65] The vertical density of the city was striking; by the end of the nineteenth century, 48 percent of Paris's buildings were four stories or higher.[66] In 1891 the city's estimated 73,174 residential buildings contained 981,175 separate dwellings, or an average of 13.4 dwellings per building.[67] Although ownership of these buildings was broadly distributed, owner-occupancy was not the norm.[68] At the end of the nineteenth century, only 40 percent of property owners lived in buildings that they owned; when placed in the context of the number of total households in the city, this means that less than 2 percent of households were owner-occupants. Said one architect at the turn of the century, "this trend of living in a collective building, even when one possesses a considerable fortune, is a very characteristic sign of contemporary customs," one that he attributed both to the inexorable increase of land prices and a social revolution that privileged mobility and transience over devotion to the implied permanence of a single-family home.[69] It was also facilitated by a rise in the availability of luxurious apartments; options for the city's wealthier residents diversified as "bourgeois" housing—defined as units with rents in excess of 500 francs in annual rent—increased by 91 percent between 1878 and 1911.[70] Indeed, between 1890 and 1900 the number of the capital's most affordable apartments, those costing less than 300 francs, increased by only 7 percent, while apartments costing more than 2,500 francs increased by 17 percent.[71]

Many reflections on the nature of the fin-de-siècle housing market focused on tenants as frivolous and increasingly imperious consumers. Rivoalen looked dimly upon the expectations of contemporary apartment dwellers, chastising them for being duped by glitzy units that exuded "the appearances of festivity, an approximation of 'style' that grabs the modern tenant and his family, that persuades the buyer in search of a lucrative investment."[72] While this showed deplorable discernment, particularly dangerous in a place and period that elevated taste to a central pillar of national identity, it also spelled disaster for architects forced to bend to the demands of the marketplace: "Comfort is requiring more and more niceties: no one wants to climb or descend a story, elevators are necessary. . . . Tenants refuse to pay unless everything in the building works as if in a fairyland: the temperature must be regulated by central heating or cooling, and in accordance with the tastes and preferences of each individual."[73] In 1899 the industry paper *La Construction Moderne* observed that even the modest tenant was becoming demanding and his situation continued to be aided by the housing market: "Thanks to competition, today it's the property owner who submits and the tenant who threatens to leave."[74] In these descriptions the intense mobility of the capital city was the mobility of tempted and disappointed consumers, who moved like "the Arab in the desert" in search of the better pasturage of "central heating, electric lighting, or an elevator."[75]

Estate agents and other brokers sought to foster these linkages between apartment seeking and other forms of pleasurable consumption. Offering their bureaus as "unceasing marketplaces," they worked to rationalize the presentation of housing supply, designed catalogs and offices that encouraged leisurely browsing, and through innovations such as the introduction of floor plans to property advertising, opened up the domestic interior to the imperatives of circulation that defined the experience of the city's public urban culture. Turning tenants into consumers was an important part of constituting the contours of a commercialized property market. For speculative developers who emphasized the need for their construction to follow rather than lead demand, for observers of the building industry who sought the empirical means to correlate building to population growth, or for corporate owners that eyed building improvements as a means to lure residents from competing landlords, the market operated on the basis of the perceived needs of housing consumers. It is important to remember that the tenants who were relevant to these discussions were the minority of Parisian citizens, those with the means to weigh their options and make decisions on the basis of something other than bare necessity. These were the individuals and families for whom the effort to establish housing as a residential package to be selected from a catalog or gazette had the most resonance, who could most easily accommodate apartment "shopping" within the other elements of "marketplace modernism" that had come to define residential space.[76] The majority of Parisian residents, for whom work and home were more intimately linked and spatial and economic constraints more pressing, played little role in either the self-understanding or development decisions of those in the building industry.

Despite a rhetoric of consumer demand prized by brokers and developers, the degree to which the built environment of the nineteenth-century capital correlated with the desires of its occupants is debatable. Nineteenth-century housing reformers viewed this social landscape with dismay; engineer Émile Cheysson lamented in 1903, "We do nothing but move through hotels, which tell us nothing of our past, promise nothing for our future, and hold no memory of our passing. With each stop, we throw scraps of our identity to the four winds."[77] For commentators of this stripe, the city was a site of collective living that bred collective alienation. Professionals concerned with urban development and the viability of the market, while they generally viewed the consequences of the city's built form as less dire, often had occasion to critique speculative building for ignoring the actual needs of the city and its neighborhoods (the *besoins du quartier*) in favor of invented ones. In building for the average and *en masse,* they neglected the specific requirements of local environments. For Marcel Daly, the son of architectural press magnate César Daly, speculative development led inevitably to the construction of a generalized marketplace: "When a financial company undertakes the construction of entire neighborhoods in large city, because it is undertaking a *business venture* it reduces risks and expenses as much as possible. Thus, somewhat by the nature of things, it is led to establish a small number of models for the operation, which it repeats indefinitely—average models, of a type to satisfy the mass of future clients, models without expression, as they must shock no one."[78]

The result was not necessarily satisfying. One 1885 novelist put the following words into the mouth of his narrator: "Real estate and insurance companies have made building horribly banal. I'm a tenant with International Properties. From my windows, I can see eight identical lodgings, each looking on four identical courtyards, separated by a low wall topped by a fence. It's not complicated to imagine it—just think of cemeteries or barracks."[79] Building entrepreneurs designed and constructed for the market, a market of investors and (indirectly, but importantly) tenants. As vacancies increased (in both bourgeois and working-class dwellings, the former owing to overproduction, the latter to overcrowding in the lowest rent spectrum, creating vacancies in the 100–500 francs range), they struggled to reach, and in some ways create, a market for their product. An anonymous article in the *Revue Générale de l'Architecture* commented that "the builders of these astonishing neighborhoods do not appear to have agreed beforehand on this need to build that drives them so desperately: today they seem to speak a language incomprehensible to housing seekers."[80]

The estate agent was one way this gap of "incomprehensible" language between property producer and property user could be bridged. A biographical approach to the buildings that populated Paris's "districts of the future"—in other words, an approach that studies the creation of these buildings and their evolution in time—reveals other means.[81] Snubbed by contemporary professionals as manufactured products lacking individual character or artistic interest, the speculative apartment building has generally been similarly ignored by historians, despite the fact that such structures constituted the majority of the city's housing stock.[82] By using the portfolios of property investment firms as an archival basis from which to get inside the houses that speculation built, we are able to come nearer to the social experience of the commercialization and financialization of the urban environment. Tax surveys, building permit applications, and annual company reports help track the ways in which corporate owners evaluated and intervened in the Parisian property market, how the imperatives of competitive construction and shareholder returns shaped leasing structures and building maintenance, and the ways occupants fashioned the residential space at their disposal. Boarding and subletting, for example, were surprisingly prominent in the apartments of corporately owned buildings, particularly within middle-class buildings in the new districts of the city. The commercialization of corporate-owned buildings penetrated even to apartment interiors, where tenants became managers versed in the exchange value of their living rooms and bedrooms. This biographical approach not only helps discern the agency of the built environment, but also emphasizes the ways that the durability of that environment—and its unique stickiness as an asset—challenges and forces adaptation from the impulses that governed its creation. By opening up something of the everyday world of the apartment house, we will have a better basis from which to reflect on the way the built environment functioned as a means by which the city continued to make citizens.

Approaching the Parisian real estate market as a social product reveals not only a new range of actors and imperatives at work in remaking the capital of modernity, but also the central role of commercialization and consumerism in elaborating both the modern urban and business cultures of nineteenth-century France. Tracing the manner in which housing and property operated as commercial objects during a crucial period of urbanization, moving between and among the economic activities of investment, speculation, production, and consumption, this book presents an urban history of business and a business history of a city. The dynamics and spaces of this market provided an arena in which the productivity of money and property became a lived reality, and understanding them requires looking as much to Fouquiau and his brethren as to Haussmann.

1

The Business of the City

STONE MASON and republican politician Martin Nadaud addressed the National Assembly in 1850 in a bid to secure government subsidies for public works. He invoked a proverb already familiar to his audience, and with which he would afterward be indelibly associated: "Quand le bâtiment va, tout va"—when construction prospers, everything prospers.[1] The phrase captured the long-standing perception that Paris's economy was entirely reliant on the health and vigor of its building industry. Construction was consistently one of the largest employment sectors in the capital city, with perhaps 10 percent of its residents reliant on the industry throughout the nineteenth century.[2] Then as now, the construction industry was a chief indicator of national economic well-being and public works were an established strategy for economic stimulus (think of the National Workshops in 1848). Yet the sector was not without its downsides. The building industries were important sources of labor for migrant workers, whose presence in Paris was often viewed as a source of social instability, criminality, and even revolution. What is more, if these so-called "dangerous classes" threatened the peace and order of the capital city, the provinces were also suffering as their laborers increasingly opted for permanent installation in Paris as the century progressed.[3] Rural lands lost one-third of their value between 1880 and 1900, and policy makers scrambled to introduce measures that would preserve the country's "traditional" balance between agriculture and industry.[4] As Paris grew, commentators such as municipal administrators and journalists Félix and Louis Lazare worried over "the son of a peasant who abandons the spade for the hammer [and] will never again take up the plow."[5] The alleged need for Paris to build to survive was in constant conflict with the myriad perceived dangers that "armies" of workers assembled in the capital posed to the nation's economic and political life.

Today the notion that cities are entities destined for growth is a commonplace. From the late-nineteenth-century boosters of the American Midwest to the "growth machines" that captured post–World War II urban governance, our moment is heir to a century that has conceptualized and organized cities primarily as sites and engines of economic development.[6] The transatlantic planning communities that emerged at the beginning of the twentieth century were instrumental in establishing an understanding of urban growth as inevitable and potentially beneficial—provided, of course, that it was rationally managed.[7] The acceptance of growth sprang from an emerging perspective that viewed cities as organic entities developing according to natural processes of evolution. In France, Marcel Poëte, an urban historian and administrator who helped found the École des Hautes Études Urbaines in Paris in 1919, filled his foundational texts with biological metaphors, writing of the city as "a collective human being," a "living organism" with functions structured by a "natural zoning" that reflected "the organic needs of a constantly evolving agglomeration."[8] Yet the metaphysical *élan vital* that drove a city's evolution remained chiefly organized by economic imperatives: "Generally speaking, it is commercial and industrial fundamentals that determine the direction in which the city develops." And this growth required that cities abandon enclosures, the fortified walls that "encircle the city and reduce it to living on its own resources," in favor of structures fostering expansion—roads that radiate from the city, carrying the lifeblood of new individuals to its core, without which "a city is doomed to decline."[9] Emerging from international professionalization movements of burgeoning urbanists and municipal administrators, as well as from the experience of wartime planning and needs of postwar reconstruction, the vision of the urban that dominated the early-twentieth-century "science of the city" took the intelligent cultivation of growth as its fundamental principle.

The strength of this consensus should not obscure its novelty. In nineteenth-century France, as in other European countries, the virtues and means of urban growth were by no means settled. Successive governments of the ancien régime had grappled with the dangers and unmanageability of Parisian expansion. While Enlightenment planning ideals favored an open city, no less than thirty-one edicts defining and reinforcing the limits of the capital were issued between 1548 and 1766.[10] The July Monarchy famously re-walled the city in the 1840s, erecting a ring of fortifications that cut through Paris's suburban towns, rewriting the city's physical and imaginary boundaries.[11] Even Prefect of the Seine Baron Georges-Eugène Haussmann, viewed by historians and contemporaries alike as an unmitigated devotee of development, contemplated with trepidation the "Babel" that would result from any administrative expansion of the capital.[12] Indeed, fin-de-siècle urban professionals such as architect Eugène Hénard faulted Haussmann's midcentury renovations specifically for their lack of a coherent growth strategy.[13]

Nevertheless, nineteenth-century legal reforms tended toward greater acceptance of urban expansion. In 1824 King Charles X formally overturned the image of the city as a closed space when he lifted the ban on building outside Paris's tax wall. In the same period, laws requiring that individuals housing visitors in the capital report them to local authorities—even when they were relatives or friends—passed out of use.[14] And the erection of the fortifications in fact facilitated the annexation of those territories that they enclosed.[15] The necessity of dismantling the fortifications was evident from the 1880s, inaugurating a long debate on their destruction and the reuse of their lands.[16] These measures recognized the city as a space of expansion and development, and worked to adjust its administrative practices to economic ideologies that demanded openness and circulation.[17]

Urban growth was a pressing and deeply politicized problem for Paris's administrators at the beginning of the Third Republic. In 1871 the city was granted an elected municipal council with significant authority and regular elections for the first time since the Revolution.[18] Its members inherited the material and social legacies of Haussmannization and the Commune, legacies that had to be managed in accordance with the new republic's political sensibilities. The widespread renovations that characterized Haussmannization not only had fundamentally changed the city's built landscape, but had also altered the relationship between the government and Parisian residents by dramatically imposing central authority over local prerogatives.[19] Critics of the regime's projects spoke and wrote passionately about the danger of dispossession confronting Parisian residents as the city appeared to degenerate from a place of work and production to a "ville-décor" whose only function was to elicit "admiring exclamations from foreigners."[20] New public spaces favored the promenade rather than the workers' commute, and tourist amenities intended for the great showcases of Universal Exhibitions, held in 1855 and 1867, oriented the real estate developments of Second Empire financiers.[21] The urban insurgency known as the Paris Commune (March–May 1871) arose partially in response to these phenomena. Triggered by the experience of wartime defeat, siege, and occupation by the Prussian army, an insurrectionary government and armed citizenry repossessed and repurposed the streets and buildings of Haussmann's Paris before suffering a bloody defeat at the hands of France's new republican government. Exile and executions did away with tens of thousands of the city's residents; shelling and fires ravaged public and private property across the city (Figure 1.1). The nine months of the Prussian siege and Commune took a terrible toll on the city's economy, while the peace conditions imposed upon the French required a massive indemnity payment that drained further resources from investors and governments. Getting Paris back on its feet was, in short, a monumental undertaking that urgently confronted the new administration.

How the city's governors went about this task reveals the particular political economy of urban development that emerged from the revolutionary experiences of the Second Empire and the Commune. The previous regime was by no means excised in 1870–1871. The debts accumulated for its urban projects exerted tremendous pressure on municipal finances; uncompleted projects left outstanding compulsory purchase orders and truncated streets that required completion; Haussmann's collaborator and former director of parks Adolphe Alphand was appointed the city's director of works in 1871 (and held the position until his death in 1891); Haussmann himself became, for a time, director of the Rente Foncière and the Crédit Mobilier, important financing companies closely linked to the real estate speculations of the Second Empire. Yet it was clear that the business of the city—and business in the city—could not proceed upon its former foundations. As the initial work of reconstruction was followed rapidly by a significant building boom and bust, Paris's appointed and elected representatives joined observers from building trades, property owner associations, and national politicians in fiercely debating the virtues and vices of state-sponsored public

FIGURE 1.1 The ruin of the Hôtel de Ville, Paris's City Hall, 1871. The Council resumed sessions in the reconstructed building in 1882. *Source:* Charles Deering McCormick Library of Special Collections, Northwestern University Library

works, attempting to work out the proper relationship between public authority and private enterprise. The building question—which encompassed matters ranging from immigrant labor and workers' housing to state ownership of land and public debt—consistently confronted the new city government, forcing combative articulation of the political and economic principles shaping municipal development policy. The republican majority was strongly opposed to policies that appeared to continue those of the Second Empire, rejecting (at least initially) public borrowing that fueled "exaggerated" building campaigns that flooded the city with "unlucky emigrants," "a plague for true Parisians."[22] In interrogating the agents, form, and impact of urban development, the new municipality attempted to find a politically and fiscally acceptable balance of public utility and private profit in the wake of Second Empire urbanism.

The municipal government was also concerned with establishing itself as the representative of the general interest of the city, imbued with expertise and obligations that distinguished its sphere of action from that of private pursuits. The April 14, 1871 law on municipal elections restored Paris's elected city government, yet the city's dual status as locality and national capital dictated a special regime. Its administration remained divided between state-appointed prefects—the prefect of the Seine and the prefect of police, whose offices employed a combined staff of nearly 28,000 at an annual cost of almost 50 million francs—and the eighty-member city council.[23] The council was subordinate to the prefectures; it enjoyed the power to initiate debates and deliberate on a multitude of questions, but executive authority remained with the Prefecture of the Seine. Despite the limitations on its powers, the council was the chief site of debate for all issues relating to local administration, and its commissions and deliberations bore particular weight in the realm of urbanism. The city's public works constituted the single largest expense of the municipal budget after the annual cost of the debt, and municipal property management was one of the most important areas of autonomy enjoyed by the council.[24] The business of city government, then, was worked out largely in the arenas of property administration and development. Rather than a simple platform for preexisting dispositions, navigating the building question was a process through which the economic ideologies and "dreams of commerce" of the Third Republic took shape, inscribed not only in political discourse but in the avenues and building sites of the French capital.[25]

The Building Question

The neighborhood known in the 1870s as the Quartier Marbeuf was a low-lying area sandwiched between the Champs-Élysées and the Seine. Previous public works—the development of the monumental promenade of the Champs under the first Empire, then those of Avenue de l'Alma (today's Avenue George V) under the Second—had left the district several meters lower than its surrounds, its streets reduced to "absolute cesspits," "horrible worms on the beautiful fruit" of the Champs-Élysées.[26] Residents petitioned and complained to authorities for decades for improvement.[27] The municipal government recognized the need to elevate the district but balked at the cost. The area concerned was large, approximately 70,000 square meters, and its location in the otherwise ritzy west end of the city was so obviously destined for luxury development that property owners drove hard bargains with the city's agents; some estimates placed the net cost for expropriations and road-works as high as 8 million francs.[28] Luckily for some the area's development potential also attracted private enterprise. In the late 1870s the city considered proposals from several groups of financiers and developers, each offering to renovate the neighborhood in exchange for various subsidies and concessions from the city. One scheme, from a group led by the architect Henri Blondel, appealed to both the council's commission on roadways and the city's director of works. Under the negotiated conditions, the city would concede some municipal land in the zone and provide a subsidy of 3.3 million francs, dispensed in exchange for 13,000 square meters of road works, a developed lot for a school, and the obligation that the company build up the area within three years. The gains it stood to collect from taxes on property and imported building materials further sweetened the deal.

Yet the arrangement was far from popular with everyone on the municipal council. It was less than ten years since the fall of the Second Empire, and here seemed a replica of the sort of backdoor dealing and insider brokering that typified imperial development practices. Jules Ferry, a prominent republican and opponent of Napoleon III's regime, had castigated Haussmann for handing out development contracts "under the table, by the hundreds of millions; the principle of public auction, and of competition, was banished to the myths of the distant past."[29] Proponents of the deal knew enough to offer the contract for public tender rather than grant it to Blondel outright, but critics pointed out that the developer had already assembled contracts on half of the land in the area, making him practically the only viable bidder. Councilors Jacques Songeon and Louis-Léger Vauthier—the former an ardent republican who sat with those dedicated to municipal autonomy, the latter an engineer on the left of the council—dismissed the tender as "a heavily subsidized, *direct concession* to a financial company," and "a return, by an elected municipal council, to a system condemned since the fall of the Empire."[30] The concession included not only municipal land and a subsidy, but a delegation of the city's public powers of expropriation. The official declaration of public utility for the project was issued on July 28, 1881, and immediately conceded to Blondel and his Société Anonyme du Quartier Marbeuf a limited liability joint stock company founded in 1880 with a capital of 10 million francs.[31] The company, rather than the city, would embody the public utility that constituted one of the only acceptable limitations on the right of private property in modern France.[32] It would do so, moreover, for a project most observers qualified as luxurious rather than useful. In light of these objections, the deal passed the council by only the slimmest of majorities.[33]

That Blondel and his associates had been among those who profited from concessions under Haussmann did not endear him to many in the late 1870s.[34] He embodied the long shadow of the Empire's projects, whose infrastructural demands and financial burden constrained the city government well into the 1890s.[35] The controversy surrounding Blondel's proposal was part of a debate on the virtues and means of carrying out public works that commenced as soon as the new municipal council was instituted. No less a proponent of public works than Louis Lazare was forced to adjust his opinions in light of the bloodshed of Paris's transition to the Third Republic, concluding that for all the improvements Haussmann brought to Paris, the city "underwent a monstrous increase in its population, which was enlarged and disturbed by more than three hundred thousand provincials, for the most part needy or second class, irresistibly drawn to Paris's exaggerated public works campaign, to the great detriment of the Capital and the peace of France."[36] The basic sin of imperial building policy was "exaggeration"—works that cost too much, happened too fast, required too many workers, and made luxurious monuments rather than useful amenities. In the mouths of municipal councilors, criticism of exaggeration in public spending signified a rejection of imperial excess in favor of republican restraint. With an eye to proving the capacity of the city to reliably self-administrate, the new council took responsible financial governance as its primary raison d'être.[37] The conditions of the city's coffers, as well as a desire to put distance between new city policies and those of its authoritarian predecessor, militated against measures that appeared to follow in the footsteps of the imperial regime. The sentiment was broadly shared. Prompted by the Quartier Marbeuf project, a writer in the liberal *Économiste Français* remarked that "the means and methods of the future cannot be those of the past; we have air and luxury, now we must be patient and build physical and moral hygiene."[38]

Nevertheless, calls for a complete halt to public works in the capital city, such as those of the new prefect of the Seine and future minister of finances, economist Léon Say, were rare.[39] The fact that earlier projects had been exaggerated, proponents argued, did not remove the responsibility for the current government to find reasonable and balanced solutions to the city's problems. The path forward could be found by delineating between works of genuine public utility, for which municipal monies could be fruitfully engaged, and those benefiting private interests, which lay outside the realm of public support. Public scrutiny of this division began early in the new council's existence. In 1872 Jules Delahaye, director of one of the building industry's leading journals, *La Réforme du Bâtiment,* argued forcefully against a proposal by two developers to overhaul the Place du Château d'Eau (currently the Place de la République). He accused the builders of "exploiting the same kinds of promises and spiels that were used so widely by speculators during the Empire." Thankfully, he continued, "the public is not so stupid as to believe that this is an operation of public utility, and sees it for what it is, which is to say, a large business venture, of a type not possible under a self-respecting government." In order to ensure municipal stewardship of common resources and the protection of the public interest, Delahaye suggested key safeguards. "Expropriation for reasons of public utility," he wrote, "cannot be put at the disposal of individuals in pursuit of their own interests"; in addition, "municipal lands can only be sold through public auction."[40] Municipal projects and business should stay as far apart as possible.

The concessionary practices of the Second Empire had turned real estate companies, which had long been valued auxiliaries in urban development, into bogeymen, speculators on dispossession and profiteers on public monies. At the outset of the new regime in 1852, important urban affairs newspapers like the *Gazette Municipale* had championed public-private coordination, calling on the city "to summon private capital to the service of Paris's material regeneration and to support the formation of Companies." The more numerous the companies, the more competition would reduce city expenditures, and the more efficient development would become—after all, the gazette added, "for them, time is money."[41] But the dominance of large financial interests, particularly superstar development companies like the Compagnie Immobilière, which failed spectacularly at the end of the Second Empire, had soured this vision. The emergence of expropriation agents, middlemen who found profit in assisting owners and commercial tenants facing compulsory purchase, further signaled the corruption of public powers of expropriation into a private business.[42] It was common knowledge that the juries charged with assigning indemnities in cases of compulsory purchase awarded higher sums to dispossessed owners when the purchase powers were wielded by a private company rather than the city, an opportunism that not only raised costs but spoke to a general impression of the procedure's illegitimacy.[43] A more responsible government, accountable to a democratic electorate, required vigilance against capture by business interests, whose private ends may prove incompatible with general needs. To reinvigorate the building industry while maintaining a republican solicitude for the public good, in the 1870s *La Réforme du Bâtiment* campaigned persistently for a public works program led and funded by the municipality rather than by private companies.

Consequently the dominant trend on the council throughout the 1870s and 1880s favored the direct management of the city's development projects. Boulevard Henri IV, for example, as well as Avenue de l'Opéra and the completion of Boulevard Saint-Germain were all executed in this fashion. Certainly private enterprise had its place. Councilor François Cantagrel, arguing successfully in favor of offering works for Rue Vieux-Columbier and Rue du Four for public tender in 1875, advised his colleagues "not to speak poorly of building companies; they render valuable services."[44] In debating the undertaking of the Bourse de Commerce ten years later, Narcisse Leven stressed to his fellow councilors that business interests themselves weren't the problem. That an aspiring concessionary (Henri Blondel, once again) had presented a project favorable to himself and risky to the city was understandable: "That's his job, he's speculating and wants to make a profit; I can't fault him for that." But for the city to take direction on these matters from a self-interested entrepreneur, rather than enforcing its own priorities, was an abdication of its duties.[45] And while the council and administration sought for years to find sufficient and reliable sources of funding for public works—debating tax increases, national subsidies, and most importantly, loans—no one believed it possible or preferable to dispense with private coordination completely. The city's limited ability to appropriate betterment values from properties adjoining its projects could force it to work with developers when the resale of lots was necessary to the viability of a project. Even *La Réforme du Bâtiment* admitted that in instances such as the Quartier Marbeuf enterprise, if the city didn't want to find itself "spending a lot of money to develop a district whose property owners would then sell at an immense profit," the project "had to be a business deal."[46]

Avoiding dependence on unscrupulous concessionary companies or the degradation of municipal projects into business schemes required financial resources. In 1875 the city issued a highly successful loan to consolidate debt inherited from the previous regime. When it sought to repeat the venture the following year, this time to fund projects related to the upcoming Universal Exhibition, the specter of Haussmannian excess and financial impropriety reared its head. Arguing for the necessity of the loan to support a more ambitious program of public works, leftist councilor Ernest Lefèvre assured his fellow officials that the borrowing practices he was defending would have nothing in common with the covert policies of the previous regime: "You will not imitate the Empire, when you reject private concessions, intermediaries, and disguised borrowing, instead seeking the funds you need by openly, honestly, and directly addressing the public, which has already been the most liberal and eager of lenders, and which generously couples its financial backing with the precious contribution of its moral support."[47] The unmediated cooperation of the urban citizenry and its elected representatives would ensure the direct translation of public utility onto the urban fabric. Moreover, he justified the "luxurious" elements of the projected works—particularly the monumental Avenue de l'Opéra—as a tactic ensuring that the building campaign would not draw unduly on workers from outside the city. The particular work demanded for luxury developments would slant employment in favor of "those in the Parisian industries, painters, decorators, upholsterers, gilders, decorative woodworkers, etc.," while the provincial or foreign workers of rougher trades "will carry out only the smallest portion of the proposed works."[48]

Haussmann's example was never far from the lips of those opposing expansive borrowing and building campaigns, but reluctance to increase the municipal debt stemmed from a number of sources. The question of city borrowing brought to the fore the council's role as the steward of public wealth. Its responsibilities toward the city's domain, a domain that would long outlive the council's temporary investiture, saw councilors groping for management models to govern their decisions. In the context of debates on the loan of 1886—which allocated approximately 170 million out of 250 million francs to road works and architectural projects—members of the council hesitated before the burdens that long-term loan structures imposed on future municipal governments. Radical councilor Henri Michelin expressly rejected loans as the recourse of monarchs, of rulers neglectful of the future in the style of Louis XV's "*Après nous le déluge*" (which he quoted in council).[49] He proposed tax reforms as a republican means of supporting public works. The responsibility of the current council to the future city was just as binding as the obligations connecting it to past regimes. When Radical councilor Camille Dreyfus observed wryly that "we'll be dead" by the time Michelin's project eradicated the city's debt in 1950, Michelin replied with solemnity: "The City of Paris does not die."[50]

In the same debate Vauthier opposed municipal borrowing on the basis that loans were a measure suited to commercial actors with whom it was inappropriate and dangerous to compare an entity like the city of Paris. The city's task as a manager of public resources bore no resemblance to that of a business actor: "A factory owner who borrows in order to improve his equipment and reduce his production costs can increase the resources he will leave to his children and can make a good business decision; but do we, the City of Paris, carry out public works in order to increase the return they give us?"[51] The director of works, agitating in favor of the loan, disagreed. While the city should not, perhaps, be cast in the role of a profit-driven entrepreneur, he suggested that the problem of returns on capital was precisely the quandary that confronted the city. "The city," he said, "must do today what any property owner who wants to develop his property must do"; it had to study the practical consequences of its works, "examine if the direct and indirect benefits will or will not exceed the sacrifices a loan requires. If the projects won't return a sum superior to that borrowed, it mustn't borrow."[52] A fatuous recommendation—Alphand certainly recognized the impossibility of measuring the benefits of a street opening so as to place them on a balance sheet—but one that spoke to the effort to discern a mode of urban governance from the norms and needs of property management.

One particular regulatory tool, which the city wielded in its role as "a property owner, negotiating with workers and building entrepreneurs," was the municipal price series for building works.[53] This was an official list of customary or normal prices for work and materials involved in construction.[54] It originated in the 1830s, a period of standardization in the processes of government procurement, as a mechanism to facilitate the operations of public officials charged with establishing and evaluating budgets for building projects.[55] From stonework and carpentry to tiling, glasswork, and parquetry, from road pavement to sewer construction, from the placement of trellises and lightning rods to the installation of doorbells, the series evaluated material expenses by the centimeter and the meter (linear, squared, or cubed), by kilogram, by piece, and by type; it priced labor by the day or by the hour, daytime or nighttime, overtime or regular shift, with or without apprentices. Initially for internal use only, the series began being published by an employee of the Ministry of Public Works, one Morel, in 1839. This *Série Morel* subsequently appeared throughout the end of the July Monarchy and Second Empire, while the Parisian administration began publishing its own price series in the 1850s.[56] Despite assertions from administrators that these prices were in no way binding on private contracts, the series was increasingly used by architects and the building trades to arbitrate the prices of their materials and labor, as well as the wages of workers.

The authority of the series increased with changes introduced by the prefecture and council in 1871–1872. Previously municipal prices had been determined by government administrators, bureaucrats employed in the Prefecture of the Seine. For the 1872 revision, however, representatives of private industry, including workers and building entrepreneurs, petitioned for inclusion and were admitted to the process.[57] Alphand noted, "It is particularly important, especially in our current moment, that the administration listens to the interests of the working classes and works to promote conciliation and social peace."[58] The price series, the director of works implied, was a political and moral tool, a sign and mode of good governance, as much as it was an accounting device. Yet the scope of its influence presented problems. Cloaked in the endorsement of the municipal government, the series had become an authoritative document in the contractual relations of the building industry. Workers petitioning the city in 1872 protested the delay in fixing the new series, describing it as "the law of their industry," whose absence threw business into disarray.[59] In 1879 Alphand complained of the general tendency, on the part of both workers and entrepreneurs, to "turn the series into an official regulation governing relations between parties," while Prefect of the Seine Ferdinand Hérold criticized it for encouraging incessant demands for higher wages.[60] Turning the question of its continued existence over to the city's elected representatives, he pronounced it "one of the most serious questions that the Council has ever had to resolve."[61]

Between 1879 and 1882, a period of increasing labor mobilization among the building trades, the council frequently revisited the price series, debating the terms of its publication, the frequency of revision, and the composition of the revision committee. Most of those involved agreed that the series had become so embedded in the practices of the building trades that it could not be eliminated. Indeed, Councilor Léopold-Camille Cernesson, himself an architect, argued that the free laws of supply and demand could not operate in a sector as complicated as the building industry, where projects required a multiplicity of trades and types of work, and where prices for works and materials had to be determined far in advance of their completion or procurement. The mediation of the municipal price series was thus basic to the industry's ability to function.[62] Others foregrounded the moral economy within which the city was obliged to operate. Councilor Charles Amouroux, a former Communard and representative of the extreme Left, observed in 1882 that he would have preferred that the series never existed, that the city had retained "the full freedom of negotiating its prices." However, he continued, "the City's prices have become law, so much so that they are used even in the provinces. . . . Eliminating this base will throw contracts between individuals and workers into complete disarray, and deliver workers, bound hand and foot, to building entrepreneurs." In a similar vein, councilor, liberal economist, and future minister of public works Yves Guyot regretted that workers "have become convinced that it is up to the City to raise their salaries" but acknowledged that until workers and their employers were placed on more equal footing by the new law on trade unions, slated for 1884, the laws of supply and demand required another arbitrating force.[63]

Despite some expressions of consternation, the Radical council of the 1880s generally viewed the price series as an important tool of social harmony. Councilor Ernest Deligny, an engineer and independent republican, embraced the municipal government's responsibility for the interests of the working classes, explaining that it was precisely this responsibility that allowed the price series to work as it did: "The city's price series has risen in prominence and authority because the administration responsible for it is seen by those who use it not as a simple property owner looking to save as much money as possible, but as a unique type of property owner who, while seeking to spend modestly, also wants to tend to the interests of the workers he employs."[64] For Deligny, the logical consequence of this moral responsibility was that the council, rather than the administration, should oversee the establishment of the price series. Elected representatives, Lamouroux agreed, would better mediate between workers and bosses than appointed administrators. The majority did not agree that their obligation extended that far, however, likely reasoning that the council's intervention would further politicize an already contentious labor sector (building entrepreneurs, exasperated with the demands of workers, pulled out of the series revision committee after 1882). The series was maintained, but placed under administrative oversight.

In deflecting responsibility for the series, councilors asserted that their obligations were to defend the interests of the city, not those of any particular corps of workers—even one that generated as much as 400 million francs annually for the city's economy and employed tens of thousands of voters. Yet it remained a key tool of official intervention and patronage. The council made efforts throughout the 1880s to impose the price series on all municipal contracts, briefly succeeding in 1888 only to have the policy overturned by an 1890 ruling of the Conseil d'État, which judged it a violation of freedom of competition in municipal tenders. The principle eventually enjoyed success on the national level, informing the 1899 law that allowed municipalities to set work and wage conditions on their public contracts.[65] In a similar fashion, Paris's support for workers' associations predated the 1884 law on trade unions. The formulation of the price series took their existence for granted, and measures were introduced in 1882 that facilitated the participation of workers' associations in public works tenders.[66] In its negotiations with the city's large utilities such as the Compagnie Parisienne de Gaz—the ninth largest enterprise in the country in 1885—the council actively supported union movements.[67] Progressive labor innovations at the local level, such as the generous work contracts for the Paris Métropolitain that garnered international attention at the end of the century, were important sites of experimentation for national policies of social conciliation and solidarity.[68]

Lest these policies appear as a peculiarly French negotiation of the imperatives of capitalism, they should be placed in the larger context of international efforts to establish the "self-owned city" at the turn of the twentieth century.[69] This was a progressive movement to reconfigure and expand the bundle of services for which the urban collective was responsible, one in which Paris's showing is generally held to have been lackluster. The city did lag in terms of utility ownership. When Glasgow was municipalizing tramways and London was establishing its own public works force, Paris's gas, electricity, and public transport services remained chiefly in private hands, despite much liberal handwaving at "the socialist fantasies of our municipal leaders" and left-wing outrage at the scandals of private monopolies.[70] Nevertheless, adding the employment measures described above (measures that were not reversed when the composition of the city council shifted rightward in 1900) to the city's already significant municipal domain presents a different picture of the Parisian experience with municipalization. Although split between the appointed and elected, as well as the departmental and municipal, authorities, the assets of the entity known as Paris were extensive. In addition to its parks, streets, street furniture, underground infrastructure, administrative buildings, and churches, Paris owned and managed canals, public markets, slaughterhouses, warehouses, theaters, the Stock Exchange, the Merchandise Exchange, a new Labor Exchange, and sundry other sites and services. Some, such as canals, were acquired in the 1860s as part of imperial centralization, while the Stock Exchange was older and the Labor Exchange brand new (it opened in 1886). The slice of assets that counted as the city's "domain" generated approximately 72 million francs a year in 1900.[71]

Cities in Third Republic France were complex legal and political entities. The law on municipalities of April 5, 1884, regularized the election and attributions of municipal councils and mayors, but reinforced their administrative rather than political status. Councils were not empowered to issue political statements, for instance, or to engage in communication with one another.[72] It has been suggested that municipal governments were political only in form, and economic in nature; under the tutelage of the state, they were the temporary shepherds of the goods of the commune and the wealth of its residents.[73] As illustrated by the Paris council's frequent expressions of concern for posterity, there was potent consciousness of the contingent and particular nature of these entities in contrast to the enduring political community. But they were certainly not ordinary economic agents. Their difficult position vis-à-vis betterment values illustrates the point. With the exception of the early years of the Second Empire, Paris was almost never successful in reclaiming costs from the improvements that issued from public works, despite the legal ability to do so.[74] In contrast, German cities made broad use of this power, engaging on an entrepreneurial footing in transactions with urban residents. The limited political nature of French cities helps explain the paradox that the increasing persuasive power of public utility in the nineteenth century was accompanied by the transfer of (public) gains to private property.[75]

Yet if cities had limited representative capacities, their managerial and administrative powers had important political effects. In delineating their policies on the public works that would develop and embellish the city's domain, councilors drew the public interest of the city closer to that of the working classes while trying to maintain firmer divisions between the city and private (often corporate, as we shall see later in this chapter) development ventures. Inevitably such a division was frequently elusive, and the council's decisions could be contradictory and inconsistent. It was, after all, operating in a complex social landscape. Organized trade groups exerted pressure on the council, property owners pushed expropriation juries for indemnities that heightened the costs of public works, and private developers unleashed construction projects across the city that ran ahead of municipal planning, establishing the built environment and business culture in which the city maneuvered to foreground its priorities. The council's encounter with real estate speculation and the passions it produced in the late 1870s placed the problem of profit in urban development front and center in its debates, obliging the city's governors to reckon with the market in land and housing and adjudicate on the potential scope for intervention in its functioning.

The Political Economy of Speculation

The building boom in Paris in the late 1870s and early 1880s was the most significant of the century, surpassing even the most flourishing moments of the Second Empire. The ten years from 1876 to 1885 saw nearly 25 billion francs' worth of real estate transactions in the country, the vast majority in Paris and its environs, and the value of annual property sales reached the century's highest point in 1881.[76] During the peak of the boom, from 1879 to 1884, developers in Paris produced nearly 12,000 new buildings (approximately 16 percent of the city's building stock). Buildings became taller; whereas 186 apartment houses with six stories above the ground floor (the highest buildings possible in Paris at this time) were approved by the municipality for construction in 1877, 403 were authorized in 1880 and 422 in the first three quarters of 1881. In 1881, permits for six-story buildings constituted over a third of all those issued in the city.[77] Construction took place across the city as a whole, but the most spectacular impact was made on the city's western and northwestern districts, where the availability of land and Paris's long-standing population drift to these more comfortable and increasingly fashionable regions ensured favorable conditions for developers looking to erect entirely new neighborhoods.[78]

The Parisian populace and members of the municipal administration regarded the changes in the city with mystification. Police commissioners, particularly from the city's poorer quarters, reported on a housing situation they viewed as inexplicably unbalanced—how was it, one marveled, that rents could go up while building was incessant? This was "in strict contradiction with the laws of supply and demand."[79] This irrationality became even more evident when the stock market crash in 1882 revealed the building boom to be a bubble. Luxury construction suffered earliest, but by 1884 all sectors of the building industry were in crisis. Gone were the heady days of 1879 when building entrepreneurs impatiently awaited masons from the countryside, "going even into boarding houses to find them and waiting at the train stations to meet them coming from the Creuse and Haute Vienne departments."[80] The mass unemployment of 1884 prompted the national government to convene a parliamentary commission to study the country's economic situation.[81] As credit dried up and investors withdrew from the property market, builders and developers began to confront the realities of overproduction. The daily newspaper *Le Temps* reported in 1884 that the newly developed districts of the city were virtual deserts: "From the Trocadéro to the Parc Monceau, one can travel entire streets that are never disturbed by the footstep of a single visitor . . . the monotony of endless perspectives, where the same building repeats itself in a line of fifty examples on either side, is broken only by signs reading: 'For Rent, water and gas on all floors.' "[82]

The development boom was driven by many factors. Public works provoked heightened building activity; the opening of Avenue de l'Opéra saw large swaths of building land offered for auction in 1876, part of the flurry of activity that accompanied the 1878 Universal Exhibition in the capital. The avenue was a tremendous success for the city, costing less than estimated and encouraging investors buoyed by a rocketing stock market to look again at

Table 1.1 Value of annual loans issued by the Crédit Foncier in the Paris region

1874: 17 million francs	1879: 40 million
1875: 36 million	1880: 151 million
1876: 35 million	1881: 153 million
1877: 31 million	1882: 179 million
1878: 43 million	1883: 134 million

Source: Commission d'Enquête sur la Situation des Ouvriers de l'Industrie et de l'Agriculture en France, *Déposition de M. Albert Christophle, député, gouverneur du Crédit Foncier de France* (Paris: Paul Dupont, 1884), 10.

real estate development. The city's population increased dramatically between 1876 and 1881, with workers swelling the ranks of both those producing and those seeking housing. Innovative financial and business practices were also crucial. Easy credit, flexible business forms, and a speculative imperative that permeated the investment arena fueled the boom, which focused overmuch on residential construction for the middle and upper classes. The figures on loans provided by the Crédit Foncier and the Sous-Comptoir des Entrepreneurs (SCE), two of the building industry's most important financing bodies, offer a staggering image of the upsurge in credit to building entrepreneurs (Tables 1.1 and 1.2).

This credit was also changing. From mid-1877 the Crédit Foncier began issuing loans in cash rather than in negotiable bonds, increasing their appeal to developers and giving an immediate lift to its transactions.[83] New institutions were created that expanded access to credit throughout the construction process. The Crédit Foncier and the SCE had been coordinating their operations since 1860. Builders received credit from the SCE—up to 60 percent of the value of their land and constructions—as stories were raised. They converted this short-term credit to long-term mortgages with the Crédit Foncier upon completion of their projects. The Crédit Foncier was a parapublic institution financed by bonds that it was uniquely authorized to issue; it had a monopoly on annuity-based mortgages, which it provided at favorable rates, though by statute it could lend only on the value of revenue-generating properties—buildings or farms rather than empty urban land. It was limited, moreover, to loans of up to half of a property's estimated value. In order to circumvent the regulations and oversight that restricted their activities, as well as to stave off challenges from financial interests angling for

Table 1.2 Value of annual loans authorized by the Sous-Comptoir des Entrepreneurs

1878–1879: 10 million francs
1879–1880: 25 million
1880–1881: 68 million
1881–1882: 93 million
1882–1883: 54 million

Source: "Déposition de M. Robinot, directeur du Sous-Comptoir des Entrepreneurs: Séance du 23 février 1884," in Chambre des Députés, "Procès-verbaux de la commission chargée de faire une enquête sur la situation des ouvriers de l'industrie et de l'agriculture en France et de présenter un premier rapport sur la crise industrielle à Paris," *Annales de la Chambre des Députés, Documents Parlementaires,* 12 (Paris, 1884), 62.

a piece of the mortgage industry pie, the Crédit Foncier and SCE created affiliated corporations that played important roles in the building boom: the Rente Foncière, founded in 1879, and the Compagnie Foncière de France, founded in 1881. The Compagnie Foncière acquired land that it rented to developers, providing the basis upon which they could borrow from the SCE. The Rente Foncière was the consumption element of the production line, designed to purchase completed buildings.[84] Studying the system, financial commentator Alexis Bailleux de Marisy declared that "no arrangement has, in recent times, done more to facilitate the construction of buildings in Paris, to increase their price and returns, to develop a considerable level of transactions."[85] The efficacy and blinding speed of the system led one hostile pamphleteer to compare it to "those prodigious Chicago machines where pigs enter alive and exit, a few hours later, as hocks and blood sausage." The SCE, Crédit Foncier, and Compagnie Foncière swept land and entrepreneurs into a dismembering machine, while the Rente Foncière waited at the other end, "to receive them as they exit the operation, ruined, expropriated, and bankrupt."[86]

Within this new financial landscape, Parisian developers continued some of the trends that began under the Second Empire.[87] There were certainly continuities between the activities of the famous Second Empire speculators, Émile and Isaac Pereire, and those of the Third Republic—not least of which was the fact that the Rente Foncière incorporated many of the interests and assets of their former Compagnie Immobilière. Yet there were also crucial differences. The liberalization of the limited liability joint stock company in 1867 opened access to this important mechanism for mobilizing both financial capital and land, allowing for the emergence of newly influential intermediaries in the housing market, namely development companies formed by architects and building tradesmen. The development patterns of these groups shared little with those of their predecessors; they spread throughout the city rather than concentrating in the core, and engaged in projects in a diverse array of neighborhoods. They also tackled developments on all scales, from the individual building to multiple city blocks. Municipal initiative continued to be important, and developers worked hard to keep their fingers on the pulse of projected public works, but the city's influence on construction patterns was more indirect than under the holistic (if not harmonious) vision of the imperial administration. The Third Republic saw a proliferation of privately designed, privately executed projects that built up the city's infrastructure and residential fabric (Figure 1.2).

Much of this development process had become routine by the 1870s. Building entrepreneurs and officials operated within a framework of shared expectations and recognized conventions that smoothed and even reduced consultations with municipal authorities.[88] Projects undertaken by speculator Paul Fouquiau give an idea of typical methods of proceeding. When Fouquiau embarked on the construction of eighty-eight apartment houses and three new streets in the Montmartre neighborhood in 1880, for example, he followed established protocol by contacting the city with an *engagement,* or official proposal for the development, in March 1881.[89] Yet his new streets had already been laid out in February, and no report on the proposal was produced until October of that year, by which point construction was already under way.[90] Sewers and lighting, each requiring coordination with municipal agents, were completed with minimal discussion in March 1883.[91] In contrast to streets opened by the city for reasons of public utility, which were subject to a prior public inquiry and consultation, the new Rue Simart, Rue Eugène Sue, and Rue Flocon underwent such an inquiry only in late 1883, when the completed streets were entering the public domain.[92] By then the report from the local property owner charged with overseeing the public process concluded sanguinely that the absence of commentary "can be interpreted as a statement of complete support for the project."[93] Fouquiau's three new streets, equipped to municipal standards and bordered by dozens of new apartment houses, entered the public domain on Christmas Eve 1884. Developers operating on this scale were capable of reliably anticipating official reaction, moving forward with assurance when authorizations lagged, and

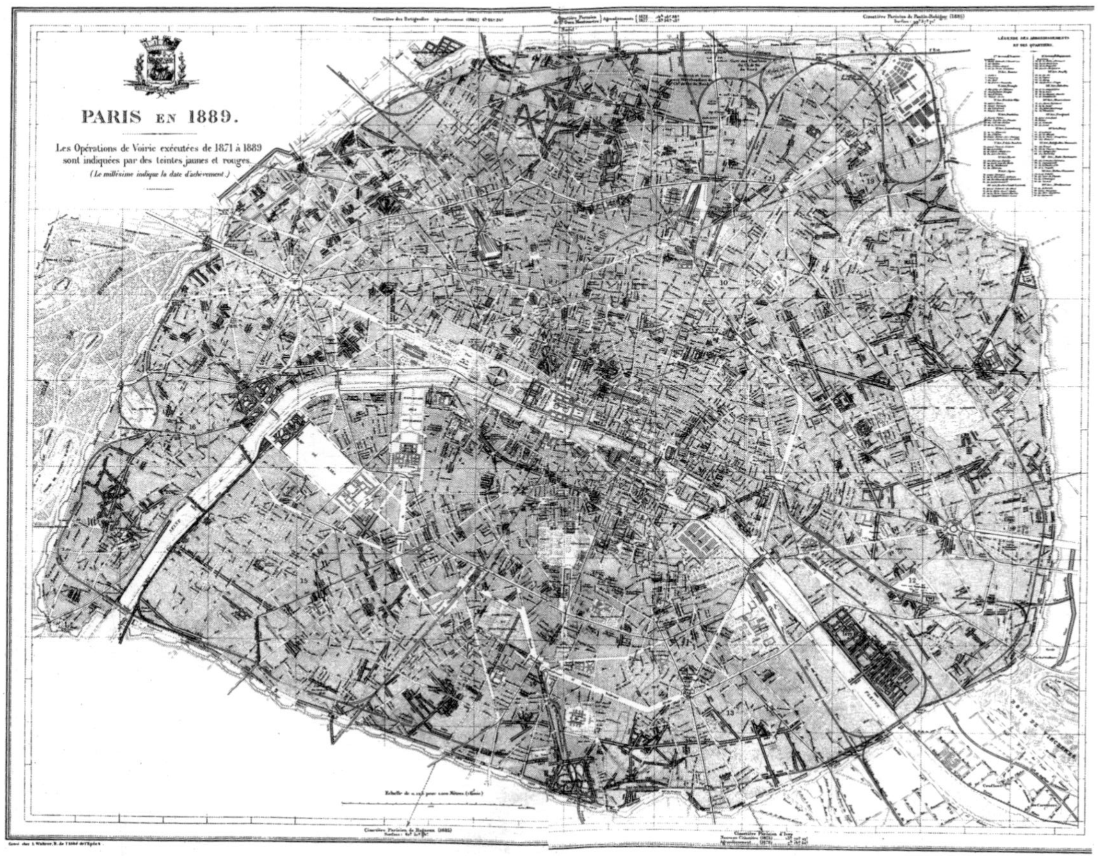

FIGURE 1.2 Map showing public and private development in the city between 1871 and 1889. *Atlas des travaux de Paris* (Paris: Imprimerie Nationale, 1889). *Source:* Loeb Library Special Collections, Harvard University

even ultimately pushing authorities toward regulatory change. For example, in the late 1870s administrators charged with assessing development applications were increasingly confronted with requests to exceed height limitations, contributing to the revision of building codes in 1884 in order to allow for higher buildings containing more habitable floors.[94]

In his Montmartre development, Fouquiau engaged in rather more negotiation with the city than might otherwise have been the case, as the full elaboration of his project required some parcels of city land. It also involved the widening of a road that bordered a municipal property and was intended to open access to a new public school, a task Fouquiau argued was a work of public utility deserving of concessions. Proposals for road developments claiming to serve the needs of the city and seeking public subsidy, tax exemptions, or concessions of public land required the opinion of the council and abound in the minutes of its meetings. Most, having passed first through the evaluation of administrators and engineers at the Prefecture of the Seine, were forwarded by the council to be studied in its third commission, which dealt with roadway matters. From there, they were returned to the council with a recommendation for further action. Each instance involved a decision weighing the venture's particular mixture of public utility and private profit.

In Fouquiau's case, what was under review was the value of the city's land and the cost of some lost fees *relative to the improvements promised by the developer.* The city already had experience considering development projects on this particular site. Among its previous owners were the Lebaudy family, wealthy sugar refiners who on numerous occasions had attempted to secure land swaps and buyouts from the city, as well as one Charles Nolle and a family named Dupin, who teamed up in the 1870s to lobby for the fulfillment of a decree of public utility dating from June 8, 1858, that called for the extension of Rue Simart (a project that would greatly improve the development potential of their lands).[95] Their requests fell on deaf ears. By the time of the Third Republic, officials believed that the completion of alternative projects in the area had reduced the utility of the requested extension. An engineer from the Bureau of Works concluded that "the operation is of little utility to the City, but indispensable for the subdivision and sale of the vast lands owned by these two proprietors"; as a consequence, "it would not be just for the City to support this venture by subsidizing part of the costs of the road opening by ceding municipal lands." As it failed to meet the conditions of general utility, his report continued, this particular development would have to be undertaken as a private enterprise, and the addition of any new roadways to the municipal domain would be subject to the usual conditions: the property owners involved must "cede their lands to the City at no cost, and agree to carry out all development works—provisioning services, lighting, and sewers—at their expense and under the supervision of municipal engineers."[96]

When Fouquiau took over the development, then, the city's position on the project was well established. Yet his intervention changed the rules of the game in important ways. First, it radically transformed the scale and speed of projected developments; the speculator united contiguous properties into a vast lot of 32,000 square meters, secured millions in financing through a nested series of corporate bodies, and arranged for the sale of the finished buildings before construction had even begun (Figure 1.3). Second, his involvement meant that the city found itself negotiating with a generously financed and impatient speculator rather than with a number of local property owners. Corporate real estate development operated on a short time horizon; loans to developers were normally three years, and fast turnarounds were imperative to success. Officials within the prefecture's Bureau of Municipal Affairs argued that "Mr. Fouquiau's plans would have been completely paralyzed" without the concession of city land, placing them in a position to extract a higher price for its lots than that negotiated by officials in the Bureau of Works.[97] Fouquiau eventually consented to pay a higher price for the land "after strong opposition," though he pushed "the other advantages that the City has, or will, obtain from the creation of an entirely new neighborhood" in order to maintain other portions of the agreement.[98]

The particular nature of this neighborhood was the third factor that influenced the city's evaluation of the project. While Municipal Affairs held simply that "that new streets opened by Mr. Fouquiau are subdividing streets intended to develop the vast properties he has acquired and brought into the Montmartre Real Estate Company," the city's works administration recognized that "he is building houses in which workers and modest employees will find hygienic, well laid-out, and affordable housing, [and] it is clear that the City stands to garner both material and moral advantage from accepting the proposal."[99] The Montmartre development was in fact intended as a model housing development for the city's working classes. It contained more than 3,000 apartments and 184 shops, capable of housing more than 10,000 people at modest rents in buildings that nevertheless featured pivotal hallmarks of bourgeois residences: cut stone façades, worked metal balconies, gas-lit

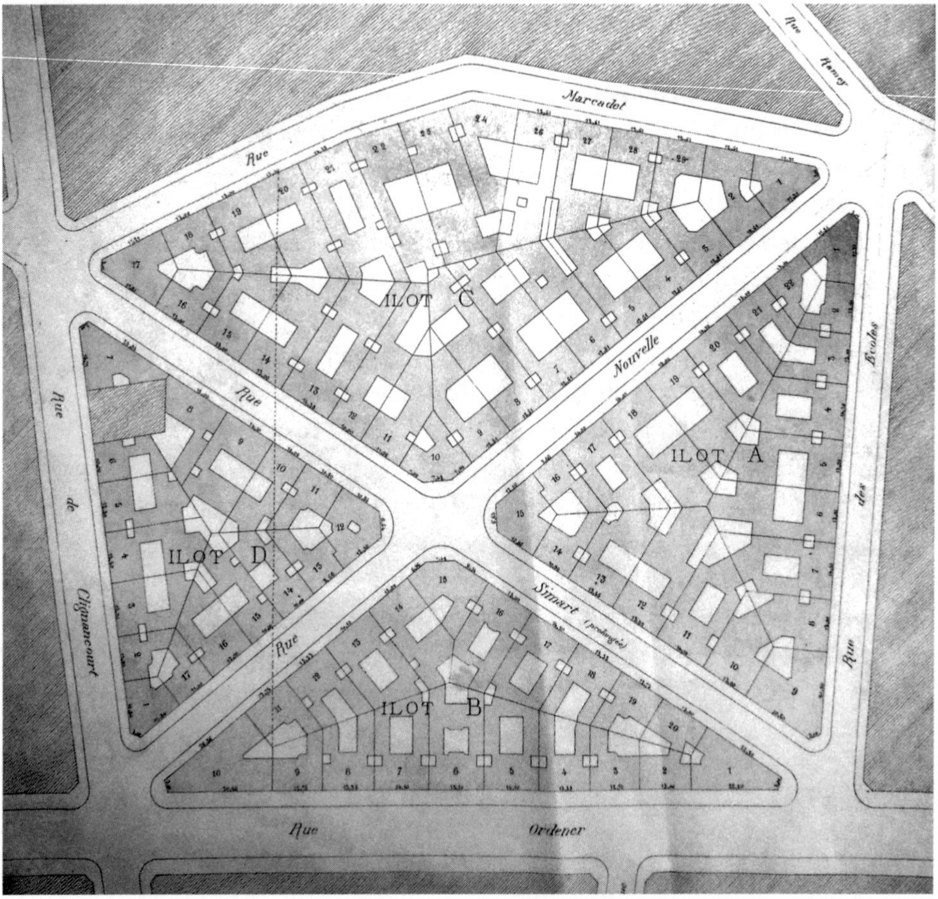

FIGURE 1.3 Overview of Paul Fouquiau's Montmartre development (South at top). *Source:* Archives de Paris, Atlas 96 (SA Immobilière de Montmartre, G. [*sic*] Fouquiau, 1881)

stairwells, and apartments with separate kitchens and private bathrooms—some even included salons.[100] It was the stone and plaster embodiment of the ambitions of the Third Republic liberal housing reform movement, a network of individuals and organizations committed to improving the housing conditions of the city's lower classes through private initiative.[101] The chair of Political Economy at the Collège de France, Paul Leroy-Beaulieu, declared himself "enchanted" with the buildings before they were even finished, and the Société d'Économie Politique, a bastion of liberal economic thought in France, canonized it as a testament to private sector capabilities in the arena of working-class housing.[102] When the Rente Foncière purchased the entire development in 1882, its director, Baron Haussmann, enlightened shareholders with the buildings' political message: "that in order to satisfy the genuine needs [of the people], public intervention is unnecessary; the free application of the fruitful principle of supply and demand suffices."[103] The particular qualities of the housing that Fouquiau constructed encouraged the municipality to deviate from its conventional practice and exempt the developer from some of the costs attendant to his road works.

As this particular case begins to demonstrate, the boom and bust presented Paris's governors with a number of opportunities and challenges. Under the pressure of unrestrained speculative development, the building question took on the additional weight of the rent question and the housing question. Rents had been rising in the city since the 1878 Exhibition, and the spectacle of new streets filled with middle- and upper-class apartments while the vast majority of the city lived in inadequate, overcrowded dwellings—as many as 10 percent of Paris's residents were living in the city's network of furnished boardinghouses in 1882—generated a wave of tenant and activist protest.[104] Proliferating meetings called for rent strikes, petitioners demanded the taxation of vacant apartments and empty land, and proposals for affordable housing schemes flooded the council.[105] In meeting rooms across the city, residents called into question the actions of their elected representatives, complaining that "the municipal council is just copying the Empire, demolishing for the sake of rebuilding," generating more debt in three years than the Empire did in twenty.[106] And while speculation, "the gangrene of our age," was surely to blame for the disequilibria, so too were the city's public works, "which bizarrely enough, are paid for by workers, but only benefit property owners."[107] The congruence of powerful grassroots mobilization with the increasing presence of socialists on the municipal council led to the first serious steps by that body toward facilitating the construction of working-class housing in the city. If these were ultimately unproductive in the short term, part of the explanation lies in the fact that the crisis of unemployment generated by the slump in 1883–1884 reinforced old fears about the unwholesome relationship between construction, public expenditures, imperial excess, and masses of troublesome workers.

Two of Fouquiau's later projects help illuminate the intersection of development and these political priorities. In 1884 Fouquiau once more garnered attention for a vast housing development scheme. As the massive building boom in which he had so eagerly and profitably participated unraveled, the developer approached the city government with a project that promised both employment and housing to the city's working classes. He solicited public support for the construction of more than 400 socially mixed apartment houses, containing a planned 12,000 "ordinary" apartments and 15,000 units costing less than 300 francs a year, which he proposed to build in diverse neighborhoods throughout the city. The project was conceived in collaboration with trade associations in the building industry, whom Fouquiau proposed to gather as associates in a massive limited liability joint stock company. For the workers who penned petitions of support, the project was a solution to the housing crisis as well as a timely response to the desperate situation of the Parisian building industry. "Mr. Fouquiau met with us several times," one wrote; "we established an agreement on the prices and method of payment, with conditions that are favorable for us, and which guarantee us all the work that we can undertake in this important project. It's a collaborative project, for half of the Parisian building industry workers."[108] In this instance, the developer aimed to engage the municipality directly. He petitioned the city to provide the guarantees that private lenders and property owners often provided in order for entrepreneurs to gain access to credit. Fouquiau estimated the costs of his constructions at 700 francs per square meter (200 francs per square meter less than his Montmartre constructions), and solicited a mortgage guarantee that amounted to 78 million francs for loans from the Crédit Foncier. In addition to the loan support, Fouquiau sought exoneration from the municipal and state taxes and fees that applied to new constructions.

The plan was a vast extension of the *société anonyme,* or limited liability joint stock company. Fouquiau was a master of this business form; he had founded more than a dozen such companies in the span of a few years, continually rolling the interests of one firm into the next, always with a profit for himself as founder.[109] Where he normally filled his companies with individual tradespeople, each contributing a different service to a construction project, here entire trade associations would act as shareholder-participants. With the addition of the "moral" support of the city, the scheme envisioned a melding of public and private modes of intervention in urban space, enclosing the municipality within the corporate model. Shocked at the transformation of the city into a business partner, *La Réforme du Bâtiment* derided Fouquiau and his supporters for "having come up with the idea of speculating with the benevolent support of the City."[110] The council recommended the project for further study, but was wary of an inappropriate intermingling of public and private interests. It had rejected an earlier proposal for working-class housing construction by Fouquiau's prospective collaborator, an architect named Olivier, with the comment that "such speculative operations are a private sector issue; the city of Paris should neither encourage nor discourage them, it must abstain."[111]

While both the council and the prefect were generally sympathetic to the proposal, the prefect decided that it could not be pursued until the city government had clarified its intentions regarding an affordable housing agreement with the Crédit Foncier. Fouquiau's project was tabled in the midst of negotiations with this institution for a deal that would see the city act as guarantor for loans to building entrepreneurs who committed to constructing buildings dedicated in part to housing for the lower classes and constructed in agreement with hygienic regulations. In exchange for the city's guarantee for annuities totaling 50 million francs, the Crédit Foncier would lend more than its usual percentage—up to 65 percent of the value of the building—at favorable rates with a seventy-five-year amortization.[112]

The experience of the building boom weighed heavily on the council's discussions of the merits of the agreement. Numerous councilors saw the deal as an invitation that would unleash speculators on all housing, rich and poor. Several were particularly concerned that easy credit, made still easier with the benefit of municipal guarantees, would further stimulate the formation of corporate development firms dedicated to speculative ventures. Even the firmest supporter of the arrangement, Charles Amouroux (Radical Republican), admitted, "As for the accusation leveled against us of dealing with financial companies, I reply that it is an unavoidable necessity; in politics, we have already seen the most moderate and well-established newspapers fall into commercialism and be forced to accept the laws of the Stock Exchange."[113] However inevitable this collaboration may have been, it was distinctly problematic for many on the council. Socialist Jules Joffrin was convinced that "speculators were only awaiting your decision to pounce like crows on the prey you offered them . . . they know the credit of the City is solid. . . . But should it be put at the service of speculators? Should you support or encourage speculative manipulations?"[114] Narcisse Leven (Radical Republican) was certain that the deal would profit only speculators and "the kind of risky builders we've seen so many of," who would no longer be content with limiting their activities to wealthy neighborhoods, but would spread their speculative fever to even the poorest districts.[115]

Alongside objections that dealt with the principle of municipal housing provision, another category of concern sprang directly from the boom and addressed the difficulties the city would encounter if and when builders defaulted, leaving the city responsible for apartment houses and tenants just like a private property owner or institution. Frédéric Sauton (Independent Republican) put it plainly: "What will happen if you give your guarantee? No matter what you do, you'll find yourself dealing with limited liability companies where no individual is responsible. You'll be presented with overvalued lands, exaggerated estimates, building entrepreneurs will be paid partly in shares, profits will be made on the loans you approve. Once the hand is dealt, if you forgive the expression, the company will declare bankruptcy and the City will find itself with mostly poorly constructed buildings on its hands that it will have to take over and manage on its own."[116] The intangibility of the société anonyme, as well as its tendency toward fraudulent undertakings, comprised one of the distasteful and dangerous elements of the potential agreement; the other was that the city would end up with rafts of hastily constructed building stock, finding itself transformed from a financing to a managing institution, much like the Compagnie Foncière de France or other investment bodies involved in the building boom. Speculation tainted the municipality, threatening the moral and physical fabric of the city. When the agreement was scuttled, a member of the Société d'Économie Politique attributed the failure to "the unremitting animosity of an entire subset of the municipal council toward large financial corporations."[117]

This animosity fed from broader concerns regarding the nature of the société anonyme and the power of associated capital, concerns that were felt acutely in the wake of the crash of the Union Générale in 1882—a bank collapse that affected an unprecedented number of investors from across the country—and the subsequent instabilities of the financial and industrial sectors. When combined with easy credit, the limited liability of the société anonyme allowed unprepared individuals to form commercial enterprises with little difficulty and undertake operations wildly out of proportion with the nominal capital available to the company. Even the director of the SCE acknowledged that the company's policy of lending on the value of land rather than on the standing of the entrepreneur meant that "credit was widely offered to people who did not know how to use it."[118] Workers who had been left in the lurch when real estate companies folded loudly condemned what they saw to be both immoral and possibly illegal business operations. A representative from the Société Égalitaire des Maçons du 14e Arrondissement (Egalitarian Society of Masons of the 14th Arrondissement) reported to the Parliamentary Commission convened to study the status of industry and commerce in 1884 that he was currently engaged in judicial proceedings against one such company, whose capital of 100,000 francs (a figure the witness claimed to be largely fictional, in any case) "is little enough . . . to undertake 10 million in works." He continued, "I say it's a swindle to have a company undertake works without having a penny to finish them."[119] In another instance, police had to intervene when a "scandalous scene" erupted outside the house of an architect named Cronimus, who "found his resources, some honest and others less so, principally by founding the Société de Constructions de la Seine, of which he had himself named director, gathering around him people without any commercial stature." The limited liability company had been paying its subcontractors in shares, expecting them to shoulder the burden of paying workers *à la tâche,* or per completed task. When workers threatened to quit, or did quit, they were simply replaced, a setup that soon led the subcontractor Génin to the front of the director's house, where he threatened to kill the architect and was arrested.[120]

The testimony of trade and workers' associations, as well as that of parliamentarians, at the 1884 Parliamentary Commission returned often to the problems workers faced as both individual and collective actors in a marketplace of increasingly amalgamated capital. Deputy Georges Brialou, a former worker who sat on the extreme left in the Chamber of Deputies, traced the problem back to the abolition of trade corporations in the French Revolution, as a consequence of which "all capital grouped together and outrageously exploitative companies were formed." In fact, the construction trades had been among the first to overturn injunctions against trade-based associations.[121] Nevertheless, throughout the nineteenth century capital enjoyed more freedom to associate than labor did. The société anonyme was a particular innovation on this basic tendency, dehumanizing relations between capital and workers: "In the limited liability company, individuals disappear; there are no longer any names, there are only shares and bonds which are made to return as much as possible."[122] Another worker and activist who would himself become a deputy for the Seine-Inférieure (Union Républicaine) in 1885, André Lyonnais, similarly viewed the société anonyme as a danger to healthy relations between owners and workers. He lamented the loss of personal responsibility that accompanied the innovation of anonymous associations of capitalists. With individual honor no longer at stake, he argued, the state had a particular responsibility to review the conditions regulating these firms.[123] Dr. Paul Dubuisson, a reformer concerned with industrial working conditions, expressed dire fears for the fate of the working classes in a market dominated by anonymous firms. He impressed upon the Commission that "the limited liability corporation no longer has anything human. It's an impersonal being that can't be touched." The boss's legal responsibility to the abstract entity of the company severely limited his ability to deal compassionately with his workers. As a result, "relations between capital and labor take on a character that is increasingly merciless and disastrous. Economic laws rule absolutely. Between them and the worker, there is nothing to absorb the shock. The worker is crushed."[124]

These experiences of the urban economy were crucial to how Parisians and their politicians came to view the speculator as a moral and economic actor, and to understand the conflicts between public and private interest. Echoing popular opinion, contributors to the council's debates agreed that the construction boom was unduly focused on luxury building. The accusatory thrust of the distinction between "luxurious" or extravagant and "useful" works that had become a mainstay of criticism of Haussmannization was heightened. When a financial company calling itself the Caisse Centrale du Travail et de l'Épargne asked the city in 1882 for a subsidy of 7 million francs in exchange for completing Rue Réaumur, the councilors studying the proposal not only dismissed the request as unreasonable (and beneath the dignity of the city to haggle over), but also irately informed their colleagues that "the company has presented its proposals uniquely in its own interests," planning to erect a "palace" to advertise its financial prowess at the new intersection. "But gentlemen," the commission's reporter continued, "our job is not to turn Paris into a copy of Florence under the Medicis."[125] The same hesitations led many councilors to resist an 1883 proposal by the Bank of France to expand its premises with the help of a municipal subsidy. Categorizing a project as a mere "embellishment," a work of ornament or extravagance, had remarkable powers of excision. Councilor Yves Guyot even worried that it had become a justification for inaction, a prop for a politics of status quo that could endanger the city's development.[126]

The dislocations and imbalances occasioned by the building boom served to reaffirm the majority belief among councilors that public authorities had no place intervening in the private property market. Even as a housing crisis created unprecedented mobilization among tenants and activists in favor of intervention in housing provision, the council as a whole remained convinced that as direct builders their constructions would compete with and depreciate existing properties, while as subsidy providers they risked stimulating unhealthy speculation. Failed development and management companies provided demonstrations of the unreliability of real estate investments and the futility of attempting to master an entity as complex as the capital city's property market. In the midst of the boom, liberal economist Leroy-Beaulieu held these ruined enterprises up as examples of the fate that awaited an interventionist city government. "It is not at all desirable," he wrote in his influential *Essai sur la répartition des richesses,* "for the state or municipalities to be transformed into giant real estate companies. . . . If experience has shown us anything, it is that real estate companies are exposed to huge risks and most of them fail within a couple of years."[127]

The question of publicly owned lands in the city's domain posed this problem of property management distinctly.[128] On these lots, the tensions between public and private development confronted each other directly, as this final project of Fouquiau's demonstrates. In November 1882 Fouquiau collaborated with property speculator Albert Laubière and architect Ferdinand Bal to purchase lands in the 11th arrondissement put up for auction by the city's Bureau of Public Assistance. They paid 1,611,000 francs for the properties at the intersection of Rue de la Roquette and Rue Saint-Maur and proceeded to parcel out the approximately 20,000 square meters of land into lots, which they rented with purchase options to builders.[129] The developers stood to make a fortune from the project; the land was purchased at approximately 80 francs per square meter, and purchase options signed with builders valued the subdivided lots at 200 francs per square meter.[130]

This alienation of municipal lands for private development immediately generated considerable opposition, both within the council and without. In response to press reports in early 1883 that the lands sold by the Bureau of Public Assistance had already been resold at a huge profit, the Bureau's director was forced to accede to an inquiry into its sales. He pointed out that the lands in question had not, in fact, been resold; rather, the buyers had leased them with purchase options and transfers of mortgage priority. These arrangements were speculators' preferred mechanisms of property acquisition during the boom. By renting land whose owner agreed to cede his or her privileged position as first creditor on the property, a developer was able to borrow from institutions that would only lend in that secure first position. A property owner became a collaborator in development, giving developers access to building credit and taking on elevated risk in exchange for high rents.[131] The director (correctly) described these agreements as "very risky, and hence prohibited to Public Assistance . . . if it fails, the seller can lose everything, the price of the sale and even the land itself."[132] Even so, the editors of *La Réforme du Bâtiment* observed that even though it was certainly not appropriate for public bodies to engage in such enterprises, "it is nevertheless certain that they can sell their lands in thirty or forty lots, instead of eight, in order to make them accessible to all investors."[133] As Councilor Guillaume Maillard, a leftist and member of the faction committed to municipal autonomy, remarked disapprovingly, "the administration must have known that, by making lots of 2,000 or 3,000 square meters, they were placing the property at the mercy of the two or three finance companies with significant capital."[134]

In their investigations of the matter, members of the municipal council inquired particularly into the boundaries of the city's entrepreneurial activity. Councilor Joseph Manier (a "républicain communaliste," or a republican sympathetic to the political program of the Commune) insisted on knowing why the administration could not have carried out a more profitable subdivision of the property, on the model of that undertaken by the eventual purchasers, or better yet, have retained the land in order to build affordable housing.[135] The director's replies centered on the particular obligations the bureau faced as the manager of the domain of the poor. Direct building was impossible, for instance, because Public Assistance could never act as an "ordinary property owner," expelling poor tenants who would inevitably fail to pay their rent.[136] Yet the sale was itself required because the agency "could not leave the property of the poor unproductive."[137] Development was imperative, but the public authority was limited in the means of achieving it. The director concluded that dividing the land into large blocks had ensured that the sales would be carried out quickly, and that the eventual buyers would have sufficient scope to undertake wholesale improvement of a district described as dangerous and unhealthy. As a result of this scandal, the council decreed that in the future all projects for land divisions for the Bureau of Public Assistance be approved by the municipal council before proceeding to sale.[138]

The council had been seeking more precise information on public lands since at least early 1882, when councilor Abel Hovelacque submitted a request for a map of municipal lands, including those belonging to Public Assistance, in order to allow councilors to evaluate development projects with reference to the entire municipal domain.[139] Councilors proposed measures that would increase oversight of alienations of the public domain; Jules Joffrin, opposed to the interests of speculative companies who sought "nothing less than the expropriation of the City," pushed his fellow councilors (unsuccessfully) to impose conditions on purchasers that would require the construction of affordable housing.[140] Manier's proposals were among the more radical; since his election in 1879, he brought forward repeated propositions for the municipalization of all urban land.[141] Although his calls for mass expropriation had little chance of success, they tapped in to the discontent undergirding less revolutionary schemes, such as the appropriation of property surplus values and the taxation of empty lands and apartments, which also aimed to realign private profit and public good.[142] As in the case of long-term borrowing, the stewardship of municipal lands forced the council to reckon with its obligations to future generations. In 1886 councilor and socialist Édouard Vaillant proposed that future alienations of the municipal domain be banned, on the basis that "one generation cannot pledge and sacrifice future generations without usurpation." In place of sales, Vaillant proposed long-term leases of municipal land, which would allow for development while retaining profit and control for the common wealth.[143]

These proposals were part of a prolonged discussion on the most just division of profits from urban property. Every development project debated by the municipal administration hung on this fundamental problem of determining and allocating potential profits as weighed against present and future costs. Fouquiau's venture on public lands was one instance where administrative decisions fostered speculation—the land allotments were such that only large-scale developers had the means to engage with the project. As the resulting backlash indicates, real estate speculation occupied a particularly contentious place in the decision-making procedures of municipal administrators. The status of housing as a commercial good was problematized by the agitation of housing reformers of a variety of stripes, and the politics of its provision was embroiled in suspicions of the morality of the société anonyme and uncertainty regarding the appropriateness (and effectiveness) of public intervention in what appeared to be an unmasterable domain. As debates surrounding the possible agreement with the Crédit Foncier reveal, the ambiguous status of speculation in the metropolis could result in crucial missed opportunities for a more humane path of urban development.

Although it was a perennial concern of municipal governance, the relationship between Paris and its building industry was perhaps never as fraught as in the years following Haussmannization and the Paris Commune. The social and political legacies of these revolutionary urban phenomena were the testing ground for a municipal council concerned with exploring and shaping the boundaries of its new authority and abilities. Imperial excess was imprinted on the capital's monumental streets, in its municipal accounts, and, more menacingly, in the ruins from 1870–1871 that dotted the landscape of the republican city—the burned-out shell of the Tuileries, for example, loomed over passersby until 1883. Answering this exaggeration, the republican council took up the mantle of utility, casting its projects (when it undertook them) as succor for the working classes rather than embellishments for the bourgeoisie. Attitudes toward urban development and perspectives on the city's role as a market actor were more than a rejection of the speculative follies of the Second Empire; they were also responses to the dramatic changes occurring in the production and financial organization of the building industry in the 1870s and 1880s. The diffusion of sociétés anonymes gave a new face to city building and required a considered response from those appointed stewards of the public domain.

The gyrations of the building industry in the early Third Republic called into question its unique relationship to the city's economic prosperity. Surveying the struggling industry and the chaotic housing market, participants at one of the city's many rent meetings in 1883 penned a letter to Jules Ferry, président du conseil and minister of public instruction, asking, "How is it that we have come to think that overproduction of this type of work is the express condition of the capital's prosperity and the keystone of its economic system?" The letter explained that government had to radically reconsider its relation to the building sector. "Never, in any time or in any place, has government created or maintained industry. . . . Rather industry has emerged, consolidated, and developed on its own, spontaneously, springing from the necessity of providing satisfaction [for needs]. How is it, then," the authors continued, "that for so many people and for the government itself the building industry appears to be an exception to this great natural law?"[144] The letter not only asked the state to abandon its policies of public works, but also requested that it pay to return all non-Parisian workers to their provincial and foreign homes, alleviating the competition for jobs and the pressure on rents.

Councilors were distinctly aware that when it came to development, they were not free to operate under conditions of their own choosing. Debating the 1886 loan, Cernesson pointed out that for all the benefits of Haussmann's renovations, they had hamstrung the current council; by borrowing to undertake more, it was perpetuating a "vicious cycle" that guaranteed a similarly intractable and even violent situation (Remember 1871!) for its successors.[145] Yet public works continued to exhaust the municipal response to an entire range of urban issues. The city's director of works reminded councilors in 1886 that the last elections had seen the Parisian populace express a desire for initiatives "that simultaneously answer the needs of the city's roadways, its hygiene, its food supply, and the reinvigoration of its building industry." What besides public building projects, he continued, could possibly fulfill all these goals?[146] If development was indeed inescapable, then perhaps, some reasoned, the benefits of these projects could at least be limited to *true Parisians,* the class of rooted and respectable workers that Haussmann himself had deemed most worthy of municipal solicitude. A restrained expenditure of 35 or 40 million francs on public works per year, councilor Paul Strauss suggested, could support the building industry without creating so much activity that rural migrants would be lured to the city.[147]

As the letter from the rental meeting indicates, the problem of growth remained a social and political as well as economic issue. The permanently urbanized provincial was a specter haunting discussions of the capital's political economy. (Perhaps most worryingly for authorities, the amnesty granted former Communards in 1879–1880 meant that many of the "newcomers" to the capital in those years were both agents and reminders of urban revolution.) Following the suggestions of several trade groups, the forty-four deputies sitting on the 1884 Parliamentary Commission recommended that measures be taken in the localities to discourage migration to the capital, as well as in Paris itself, in order to encourage provincial workers, "drawn by the hope of higher earnings, but who sometimes—indeed, often—find only disappointment," to leave the city.[148] In trying to constrain the growth of the capital city, the commission was moved not only by economic motivations, but also by a vision of the city as a site of citizen-making whose limited resources could not accommodate all fortune seekers. Development policies that continued to privilege cosmopolitanism over community increasingly strained the city's social and political capacities. Testimony from M. Finance of the Syndicat des Ouvriers Peintres en Bâtiment (House Painters' Syndicate), for example, contended that the flurry of building in recent years had completely overturned Parisian daily life, aggravating urban nomadism and eroding community relations. He reported, "At the moment there are no longer any Parisians in Paris. You are in one neighborhood today, another tomorrow"; given the resulting anonymity, it was impossible to ensure mutual aid or fraternalism among the working classes.[149] Other workers testifying before the Commission concurred, lamenting that "instead of being a home for Parisians, Paris has become habitable only by rentiers and rich foreigners."[150] Gripped by such concerns, the council remained skeptical of growth for growth's sake.

Reconciling an urban political economy understood to be dependent on development with a vision of the city as a place for civic engagement proved persistently difficult. As an 1883 election poster from the 16th arrondissement—a district overrun with construction—proclaimed, the task of elected representatives was to maintain harmony between the constitutive aspects of modern Paris, "at once a city of work and a city of luxury."[151] This challenge, of managing the tensions between the city as a place of residence and life-making and the city as a place of capital exchange, between the city as a site of flow and the city as agglomeration, embroiled speculative architects, ambitious councilors, banking professionals, and tenants and their activists in long-standing quandaries of urban governance. As the city's governors navigated the terrain of the building question—debating the municipal price series for building works, negotiating with development companies, and evaluating the role of public monies and lands in urban development—they were guided by an effort to distinguish between public interest and private profit in the name of a republican municipality. Real estate speculation was an affair of the private domain, and—unfortunately, for those advocating a more progressive path—that's where the betterment values it generated remained.

2

Seeing Like a Speculator

WITH HIS 1909 treatise on expropriation and land values in Paris, sociologist Maurice Halbwachs sought an explanation for the patterns and forms of urban development in the French capital. Halbwachs rejected both the overly deterministic, ahistorical models of classical economists, whereby land values were the result of a tautological coordination of supply and demand, as well as overly individualist journalistic or historical accounts that attributed development patterns to the heroic action of individual entrepreneurs and administrators. Instead he identified the urban collectivity itself as the source of its own expansion patterns. New streets and the houses that bordered them, he argued, were manifestations of already existing "social needs," felt, more or less consciously, by the mass of inhabitants.[1] In this model, the city was an organic entity that flowed in accordance with profound (if often confused) collective desires. The activities of municipal planners or individual speculators, far from imposing themselves unnaturally upon this movement, were in fact the product of these needs, and in turn served to typify, magnify, and expand them. Halbwachs wrote: "Far from interfering with the natural laws [of development], speculators are themselves natural forces, created by a specific society that itself could not exist without them."[2]

Halbwachs's treatise is one of the few works in early sociology to consider the role of speculators in urban development, and helps introduce a consideration of the multiple institutions, agencies, and individuals engaged in constructing markets for real property. When Halbwachs was writing, Paris was in the early stages of another phenomenal building boom, approaching the formerly unprecedented heights of 1878–1884. These bursts of activity inherent in the building cycle routinely drew observations—some awe-filled, some outraged—about the capriciousness of development. As hosts of buildings appeared to spring fully formed from the city's soil, commentators marveled at the "magic wands of our architects," gripped in a frenzy of "speculative madness," which laid Paris open "to an enchanted spectacle of districts of forty or eighty buildings appearing all at once, as if by magic."[3] Developers—individuals who make a living by arranging and transforming land and financial capital into real estate merchandise—played a role in perpetuating such discourse, justifying their activities with reference to the driving forces of consumer demand and the unalterable pressures of Parisian growth.[4] Yet such descriptions elide the elaborate—if not always successful or beneficial—work of generating and managing knowledge about the city and its real estate that private development involved, and tend to discourage analysis of the practices and norms governing the allegedly impenetrable forces behind a building "fever."[5] Understanding the city's development requires approaching speculative builders as purposive actors in urban land-use decisions and drawing out their role as generators of common knowledge about how cities and markets should function.

Subject to intense contemporary dissection, the early Third Republic building boom laid bare the ambitions of a heterogeneous group of urban renovators, highlighting the limits and obstacles to their models of urban growth. It amplified preexisting tendencies in the building industry and urban development—namely, the dissociation of ownership and development capital—and magnified their consequences.[6] It also influenced subsequent patterns of urban development, encouraging a different approach to financing within credit institutions, and introducing a leap in the scale of corporate ownership of the city's residential property. Importantly, it was a catalyst for new ways of thinking about the city's real estate. For the first time, discussions of market phenomena at play in the changing aspects of real property began to cohere; phrases like "land market," "market for buildings," and, occasionally, "real estate market," started to feature in press accounts in the

1880s and 1890s. (The real estate columns in which they appeared were also new additions to the daily roster of news reports.)[7] Statisticians and economists took an interest in the city's real property, dedicating studies to prices and their geographic distribution.[8] A new object of analysis was coming into being, though its rules and boundaries remained indistinct. Developers were operating with a particular model of real estate dynamics in mind, one laden with the economic mechanisms of supply and demand and increasingly dependent on the authority of prices, but also populated by the particular concerns of local market participants and situated in a specific and structured urban space. While one could increasingly speak of real estate *markets*, "the market" as a self-contained and autonomous arena of exchange whose rules dictated the conduct of those it engaged was not as yet a hegemonic mode of understanding the economic life of real property.[9]

Moving land and constructions toward a regime of abstract exchangeability requires confronting and overcoming the embeddedness of property relations. This is a powerful and, arguably, necessary tendency within capitalism, but this tendency should not be mistaken for its realization.[10] Real estate remained a political matter, a family affair, and above all, in this context, an immovable good; its spheres of exchange are not only geographically constrained but also (and importantly) geographically constituted. Seeing like a speculator means reconstructing the motives and means of those entrepreneurs engaged in this task of mobilizing and transforming real estate in urban development. But it also means more. Following the work of anthropologist James C. Scott, it means analyzing the particular characteristics of real estate as a commercial good in order to emphasize countertendencies inherent in the rationalizing impulses of both state and capitalism.[11] By focusing on the dynamic of abstraction and territorialization so visibly at work in the marketization of real estate, we can explore the persistent entanglements that stymie and shape the calculative practices that define economic objects.[12] In this chapter we will see how producers of the urban environment understood this changing arena; in Chapters 4 and 5, we will see how those concerned with real estate distribution grappled with framing the same dynamics.

The Speculative Builders of Paris

From Blondel's sprawling concessions and Fouquiau's vast building enterprises to the dubious ventures of small-time operators like Cronimus, architects were leading participants in the entrepreneurial explosion that transformed the capital at the end of the nineteenth century. Their numbers had expanded significantly during the Second Empire, and Paris's rebuilding formed a training ground for "a particular class of architects," "intense, bold, committed, skilled in business, working for themselves and not afraid to risk their own capital."[13] The availability of the société anonyme business form in the 1870s opened new possibilities for a sector whose immense capital needs otherwise depended entirely on reputation, trust, and personal connections for their satisfaction.[14] Shares in companies and cash bonuses accrued handsomely to architects who founded and collaborated in these ventures. When the architect Henri Fernoux founded the SA Paris Nouveau in 1881, he received thirty shares valued at 500 francs apiece (an amount totaling one-tenth of the firm's total capital) in exchange for purchase options he secured on lands in the 16th arrondissement as well as for his studies and plans and "the benefit of support that he secured from financiers and builders."[15] Crisscrossing the city in pursuit of profit, dragging capital in their wake, architects sought out land, negotiated with owners and agents, drew up development plans, secured financing—all efforts for which they exacted compensation before construction even began. By his own account, Fernoux thus contributed to the construction of more than 200 apartment buildings in the capital between 1879 and 1884.[16]

These commercial successes did not always align easily with the field's professional and artistic aspirations. Throughout the nineteenth century, professionalizing architects used their associations and journals and the practices of their own agencies to distinguish their liberal pursuits from both the mechanical work of the engineer and the commercial endeavors of the building entrepreneur.[17] The Revolution's abolition of the guilds had opened architecture to all comers, while the Napoleonic tax regime identified it as a commercial undertaking, requiring that architects pay the *patente* or business tax like other market participants. Overturning this classification and reasserting the distinction between creative and commercial labor that had defined the field under the Old Regime was one of the chief motivations behind the formation of the Société Centrale des Architectes in 1840. They achieved their aim only four years later; the property sales journal *Le Plan* applauded the legal reform that removed the obligation to pay the patente as having "definitely reestablished the natural distinction between the artist and the tradesman."[18]

Yet business was an unavoidable terrain for most individuals calling themselves architects, and tensions regarding the parameters of commercial and professional activity persisted. Appraisals of the entrepreneurial aspects of architectural work from within the profession highlight some of the complexities of the sector's commercialization in the late nineteenth century. The first national congress of the Société Centrale des Architectes, held in 1873, specifically tackled the problem of "architect-entrepreneurs." In his address to the congress, Achille Hermant, architect for the city of Paris and instructor at the École des Beaux-Arts, distinguished the architect and the building entrepreneur on the basis of their relationship to commerce. He insisted that "the architect, as we all understand him, can have no part in the commercial transaction that takes place between the property owner and the building entrepreneur." The mercantile aspect of the industry was indelibly corrupting of artistic endeavor; an architect who stooped to carrying out construction and building sales would be degraded, de facto, into a building entrepreneur. (And there was no joy for a building entrepreneur who also composed plans for construction; his place in the world of trade could not be renounced.) Hermant concluded, "An architect remains apart from all venal affairs; he designs, he directs, but he does not traffic."[19] When in 1892 the city of Lorient addressed a call for tenders for a new municipal construction to both architects and building entrepreneurs, provincial architects were outraged at this "confusion of professions, as bizarre as it is regrettable," and the Société Centrale called on its members to boycott the competition.[20]

The building boom in the late 1870s and early 1880s was a particular challenge to the field. Architect and critic Émile Rivoalen complained that the boom revealed increasing preference for the services of building entrepreneurs over those of architects, which he attributed to modern desires for finished products and fast turnaround: "Since a taste for the 'ready-made' has become part of everyday life, smart building entrepreneurs are fabricating myriad, easy-to-sell *hôtels* and middle-class houses in advance—a net profit for the seller, a turnkey operation free of worries for the buyer . . . therein lies the appeal of this kind of architecture for the buying public."[21] The artistic collaboration between client and architect-artist had been abandoned, he maintained, in favor of the simple and predictable output of the building entrepreneur. Especially worrying were signs of a growing tendency among architects to abandon their artistic standards and dive into commercial enterprise themselves. In an 1882 contribution to César Daly's *Revue Générale de l'Architecture et des Travaux Publics,* Rivoalen regretfully remarked, "You all know that today *speculation* is the only career option for some of our colleagues in Paris."[22] Art was caving to the pressure of enterprise, vocation losing out to industry.[23] In an 1886 article in the *Forum Artistique,* we read: "As for architects themselves, it must be admitted that there are many who see in their profession only the builder, the businessman," a job taken up "merely on the advice of their parents, so as to have an honorable and profitable position."[24]

Criticism and handwringing aside, speculative building was in fact rising in esteem at the end of the nineteenth century. The description of building entrepreneurs offered in the 1880 edition of Édouard Charton's popular career guide registers a dramatic shift from that included in the book's first edition in 1842. In the earlier printing the building entrepreneur garnered barely two pages, with no discussion of the educational qualities or aptitudes necessary for the field; he is described as "an individual whose trade and profession it is to build houses without being commissioned, seeking a profit by then selling them to individuals."[25] The building entrepreneur resorts to the services of an (underpaid) architect merely for matters of superficial decoration and "art," relying on his own experience of day-to-day building affairs to oversee projects. Consequently, Charton explains, "The chances of those who buy such a construction are not entirely good," and eager purchasers are often robbed of their investment by the premature degradation of shoddy constructions.[26] Thankfully, the author admits, there are a few practitioners who rise above the lucre of the field and "seeing this kind of work as more than a way to make money" are able to perform great services, particularly in urban centers.[27]

By 1880, however, the opinion of the guide had evolved significantly. Building entrepreneurs—having now earned an eight-page discussion—are recommended to a variety of practical and theoretical training programs, and the field is described as "one of the most favored at the moment."[28] The "ready-made" houses produced by these businessmen, once an object of suspicion, now appear as trustworthy, efficacious, and even occasionally preferable to directly contracted buildings:

> Certain building entrepreneurs understood well the profits that could be made from this kind of construction. In some cases, when they enjoyed sufficient capital, they constructed buildings for themselves that they then rented out. Alternatively, they built multi-story buildings or small houses that they resold with significant gains. This last system presents marked

> advantages for both the builder and the buyer. The builder can do as he likes, exploiting all his skills without being inhibited by anyone. The buyer acquires a specific building at a price he negotiates or at auctions; if he isn't pleased with the layout or doesn't find it sufficiently well-constructed, he doesn't have to raise his bid. He knows what's on offer, because he was able to inform himself. Above all, he knows what he will pay, thus avoiding the all too frequent risk confronting those who build their own houses, who have an unpleasant surprise when the final bill far surpasses initial estimates.[29]

Here the market, with its range of goods and its reliable price signals, is the favored source for property acquisition. While savviness and well-informed selection is required of buyers, their intellectual exertion is dedicated to consumption rather than production. Returning to the shape of the profession, Charton presents the architect and entrepreneur as faithful collaborators, with no hint of previous accusations of one poaching on the territory of the other. As building entrepreneurs have accommodated themselves to the naturally superior position of the architect—or, as indignant employers in the city's painting trades put it, had found themselves "the underlings of architects or property managers, sometimes of both"—Charton could report peaceable relations between the two professions.[30] The entrepreneurial companies founded in the early Third Republic were indeed characterized by the dominance of the architect over the building tradesmen, an arrangement that testified to the increased confidence of architects in the commercial realm, as well as to the new organizational possibilities offered by the société anonyme.[31]

Depictions of architects as aggressive, ambitious, and intelligent businessmen emerge from the editorials and guides of developer Onésime Masselin, a public works contractor and author of numerous technical and legal works concerning the building industry in the 1880s and 1890s. For Masselin, "speculation, well understood, demands intense observational skill, continual contacts with individuals specializing in these sorts of affairs . . . it is the constant subject of deep reflection."[32] He was convinced that a risk-taking developer lay hidden under the skin of all architects, desperate to join the ranks of those amassing fortunes in real estate. Their prospects of success grew rosier thanks to the société anonyme, whose features Masselin aimed to demystify in an 1880 manual. He stressed that these ventures required care and attention, but that they could be mastered with proper guidance. They involved managing multiple variables, aligning divergent interests, assembling appropriate resources, and the possession of expertise in a number of sectors: the ability to understand the requirements of construction, familiarity with the workings of credit networks, experience with the municipal bureaucracy, and a grasp of the legal formalities that encumbered the procedure. "If some architects or building entrepreneurs are not producing [along these lines]," he explained, "it is because of the obligation to perfectly fulfill all of these conditions. The desire to do as everyone else isn't lacking, the urge is there, the ambition is just as cherished, fortune is smiled at as often, the need to produce is just as urgent, plans are just as grand."[33] Writing at the height of the boom, Masselin trumpeted speculative building as the core of the profession; architects too antiquated or timorous to understand this had best move aside, and certainly had no right to begrudge the risk to those who were dependent on such business for their livelihoods.

Masselin's instructions and recommendations point to the importance of collaboration in the work of development. In the rare instances when speculative building appears in historical urban studies, it generally figures as an uncoordinated venture whose operations—because they are often small-scale, fleeting, and poorly documented, and because they seem to respond so straightforwardly to market incentives—give little traction to scholarly inquiry.[34] Certainly, building in late-nineteenth-century Paris remained an affair of traditional small-scale enterprises even as the imaginary of its operations became dominated by sprawling corporate ventures. Most borrowers availing themselves of the Crédit Foncier and Sous-Comptoir des Entrepreneurs continued to be individuals rather than corporate entities, and the majority of the Crédit Foncier's loans were for sums of less than 50,000 francs. (To put this in perspective, the cheapest buildings outlined by Masselin's manuals cost 212,500 francs to build, plus land costs.)[35] At the height of the boom, the Crédit Foncier may have been lending the most money in the commercial center and expanding bourgeois districts of the west end of the city, but its highest *number* of loans was issued in the working-class 18th arrondissement, where smaller operations were the norm.[36] Yet aside from one-off projects undertaken by owners, builders, and others who recognized likely opportunities, working in the highly segmented world of professional development was far from solitary or spontaneous. It relied on ties of collaboration and information-sharing mediated by personal contacts, property professionals (such as notaries and lending companies), and even specialized publications. While valorizing the ambitions of heroic architect-developers, Masselin's recommendations to budding entrepreneurs revolve around the formation of a professional community dedicated to speculative enterprise—even if only on the porous and limited scale of the seven collaborators required for the formation of a société anonyme. As they assembled the numerous trades that participated in building construction into cohesive companies (Table 2.1), these associations gave corporate form to the personal and professional connections upon which real estate development depended. For the increasing numbers of developers that were building simultaneously in multiple districts, who approached the city as a whole as their terrain of operation, their ventures were facilitated and shaped by overlapping groups of associates, intertwined development projects, and citywide credit networks. Even financing institutions such as the Compagnie Foncière de France, the Société des Immeubles de France, and the Rente Foncière can be said to have assembled their own types of development communities: shareholders and bondholders whose individual commitments amalgamated to form a new propertied interest.

Preexisting social and professional groups were undoubtedly important sources of business relationships and likely contributed significantly to an operator's success. Blondel, for instance, continued to work with some of the same financial entities that had supported his operations under the Second Empire. Yet the upswing in building and company formation also generated its own dynamics. For many of the most prominent architects involved, this was the period in which their careers began. Fouquiau was barely out of his twenties when he founded his first real estate development firm, and François Dauby, another active architect-developer, was just thirty; Fernoux and Albert Laubière, a frequent collaborator of Fouquiau's, were older, having just reached forty, but were young by the standards of the occupation.[37] Once a company was founded, it provided a forum in which those with both the skills and the means to carry out further ventures could meet and establish working relationships. After all, though a société anonyme was formally an association of capital, in practice it was an association of people. Its mechanisms facilitated collaboration by providing flexibility: when a building entrepreneur or development company got into difficulty, or sought to expand, they could cede their interests to other parties, add associates, or form a new company. Architects frequently re-formed and moved between companies in rapid succession. One of Fernoux's companies, for instance, the SA des Nouveaux

Table 2.1 Associates and shares in the Société Anonyme des Terrains et Constructions de la Place d'Italie (1882)

Name	Occupation	Shares (500 fr each)
Théodore Lautier	Architect	80
Hippolyte-Constant Dupont	Merchant	80
Joseph-Adolphe Mignaton	Masonry contractor	58
Auguste-Théodore Baudrit	Locksmithing/Ironwork	15
Claude-François Rigoulot	Cabinetry/Woodworking	10
Émile-Ferdinand Raronnet and Jules-Vincent de Baleine	Carpentry	6
Auguste-Désiré Belloir	Plumbing	6
Louis-Joseph-Victor Larcher	Heating	4
Jean-Baptiste Vert	Painting	6
Jean-Baptiste Aubrun	Water and Sewer	4
Louis-Auguste-Victor Mérigot	Ornamental sculpting	1
Total		**270**

Source: ANMT 65 AQ I 142, SA des Terrains et Constructions de la Place d'Italie, Statuts, 1882.

Quartiers de Paris, was founded in 1878 as the continuation of an older firm, the SA le Quartier Neuf du Faubourg Saint Denis.[38] Sometimes in succession, sometimes simultaneously, François Dauby was part of the SA de Construction de Passy (November 1880), the SA de Construction de la Chapelle (February 1881), the SA Immobilière des Terrains et Constructions des Ternes (August 1881), the SA Immobilière de la Rue Vaneau and the SA des Terrains et Constructions du Faubourg du Temple (both founded November 1881), as well as the Société de Construction de la Rue Littré (January 1882) and the SA Immobilière des Terrains et Constructions de la Rue Cardinet (February–March 1882).

Notaries also occupied an important place in the business networks of property development. These were public officials responsible for establishing and maintaining the authenticity of private contracts throughout France. Their offices housed the legal footprint of a family's wealth, storing the wills, marriage contracts, and property deeds that ensured the preservation of patrimony. From this privileged vantage point, notaries were important agents of property circulation in France. The parameters of this position had been evolving for some time, however. Legislation in 1843 had banned notaries from engaging in speculative building operations, and the growth of the Crédit Foncier had significantly reconfigured their role in the mortgage markets over which they once held sway.[39]

A survey of the notaries associated with real estate development companies as recorded in the *Journal des Sociétés Civiles et Commerciales* for the boom period of 1880–1882 reveals that some played an important role in facilitating the formation and operations of limited liability development companies. A total of thirty-nine different notaries appeared for the 125 cases where a name is provided.[40] Several of these appear only once or in a few instances; Maître Massion, for example, appears three times, but each case concerns the same firm (the Comptoir Foncier, founded by ex-prefect Haussmann and eventually folded into the management firm Rente Foncière). On the other hand, some stand out as more broadly engaged with the new enterprises. Maître Dufour oversaw the constitution of four limited liability joint stock development companies between June 1880 and December 1881, and drafted modified statutes for the Société des Nouveaux Quartiers de Paris (a firm whose stock capital was valued at nearly 10 million francs) on at least three occasions. Between September 1880 and February 1882, Maître Latapie de Gerval authenticated the constitution of seven property development firms, with stock capital ranging from 50,000 francs to 6 million francs. Six of these ventures were speculative firms founded under the aegis of Fouquiau, indicating a close working relationship between the two men. (This relationship is all the more noteworthy given that Latapie de Gerval's office was located in the 15th arrondissement, far from the bustling business center of the 2nd, 8th, and 9th arrondissements, where the vast majority of the other notaries were concentrated.) The precise connection between the two is unknown, but it seems clear that Fouquiau's ventures determined the form of Latapie de Gerval's involvement with speculative property firms, as in this period they constitute the bulk of the notary's activities in this arena, whereas Fouquiau himself worked with other notaries as needed.[41]

Despite their official status as passive actors in the realm of contract law, some notaries used their own networks of intermediaries to become active participants in the business of development. From his office on Rue des Pyramides in the 1st arrondissement, Maître Pinguet had a hand in the constitution of no fewer than eighteen property development firms, all limited liability joint stock firms, over the nearly two-year period between July 1880 and June 1882. Of these eighteen, five are listed at the same address (18 Rue Clapeyron, in the 8th arrondissement), and three others at 14 Rue Saint-Lazare, indicating some probable overlap of clients. The majority of the firms were founded with short incorporation periods (as low as three years, with a maximum of ten) and relatively low capital (stock capital of 25,000 francs in at least three cases, and 20,000 francs in one), and were clearly intended as rapid speculative endeavors. Among small-scale developers, Pinguet's office may have served as an important information node, procuring credit, properties, or associates for their ventures. Even so, many of his clients also did business with other notaries, limiting their reliance on a particular legal professional and indicating broader networks of contacts.

Publicity journals and advertising columns were another resource for speculators interested in finding associates and drumming up business opportunities. These ranged from classified-style ads in which investors or agencies proposed capital for building ventures (though surely not all followed through on their glowing promises) to more professional publications established by developers themselves with the goal of advancing operations in which they or their associates had an interest. Fouquiau's *Indicateur Général des Terrains et Immeubles à Vendre,* a journal he founded in 1877, exemplifies the latter. A pioneering and ambitious compendium serving the interests of a broadly defined development community, the journal was quickly taken over and much enhanced by Laubière, who renamed it *Le Foncier* in 1879 and advertised a readership of nearly 20,000.[42] Laubière advertised land available for builders in several arrondissements in the city, including diagrams of the lot(s) and information on how much the owner was willing to authorize in loans for construction. He ran ads for building lots on the same development repeatedly, using parcel plans to show the progression of sales with each passing week and to impress upon interested parties the fleeting nature of opportunities. The journal produced a visual corollary of the construction fever sweeping the city (Figure 2.1). In addition, it provided Laubière with a venue in which to narrate the state of the Parisian property market, including short editorials—many by Masselin—that explained the nature of property development and speculation as the developers themselves understood it, while also providing information on property sales,

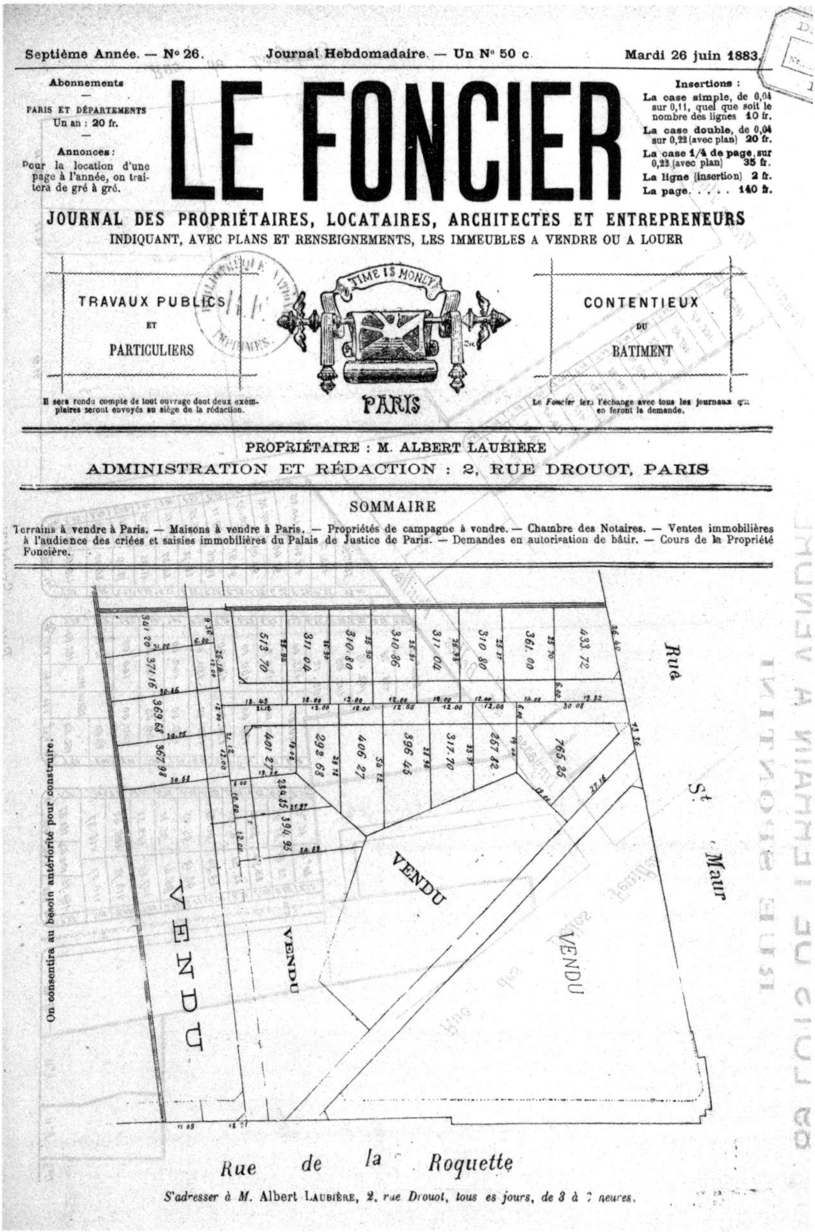

Septième Année. — N° 26. Journal Hebdomadaire. — Un N° 50 c. Mardi 26 juin 1883.

Abonnements
—
PARIS ET DÉPARTEMENTS
Un an : 20 fr.
—
Annonces :
Pour la location d'une page à l'année, on traitera de gré à gré.

LE FONCIER

Insertions :
La case simple, de 0,04 sur 0,11, quel que soit le nombre des lignes 10 fr.
La case double, de 0,04 sur 0,22 (avec plan) 20 fr.
La case 1/4 de page, sur 0,22 (avec plan) 35 fr.
La ligne (insertion) 2 fr.
La page. . . . . 140 fr.

JOURNAL DES PROPRIÉTAIRES, LOCATAIRES, ARCHITECTES ET ENTREPRENEURS
INDIQUANT, AVEC PLANS ET RENSEIGNEMENTS, LES IMMEUBLES A VENDRE OU A LOUER

TRAVAUX PUBLICS ET PARTICULIERS

TIME IS MONEY
PARIS

CONTENTIEUX DU BATIMENT

Il sera rendu compte de tout ouvrage dont deux exemplaires seront envoyés au siège de la rédaction.

Le Foncier fera l'échange avec tous les journaux qui en feront la demande.

PROPRIÉTAIRE : M. ALBERT LAUBIÈRE
ADMINISTRATION ET RÉDACTION : 2, RUE DROUOT, PARIS

SOMMAIRE

Terrains à vendre à Paris. — Maisons à vendre à Paris. — Propriétés de campagne à vendre. — Chambre des Notaires. — Ventes immobilières à l'audience des criées et saisies immobilières du Palais de Justice de Paris. — Demandes en autorisation de bâtir. — Cours de la Propriété Foncière.

S'adresser à M. Albert LAUBIÈRE, 2, rue Drouot, tous les jours, de 3 à 7 heures.

FIGURE 2.1 Advertisement showing the sales progress on Albert Laubière's development, *Le Foncier,* June 26, 1883. *Source:* Bibliothèque Nationale de France

public auctions of real estate, and advertising for building entrepreneurs and services. Such publications, along with the types of property manuals and guides discussed below, constituted the information networks through which property was mobilized and a vision of Parisian growth was constructed.

The agents at work in Paris's speculative boom were a diverse lot, born of the opportunities for easy money that real estate development seemed suddenly to present. New sources of gain were created in the gap between property ownership and development capital. Analyzing the market failure in 1884, *Le Temps* argued that the whole episode had above all been an affair of middlemen: "Who profited? Speculators; a few property owners, but above all, a number of intermediaries who bought, resold, repurchased, and so forth, each time taking a slice."[43] The commercial culture fueling and transforming development practices was evident in the commentary elicited by architects whose enterprises evoked long-standing tensions between profiteering and professional identity; in the special attention some notaries dedicated to developers and their businesses; in the eager deployment of the société anonyme as a tool for mobilizing capital and associates by builders, property owners, and others. Masselin's guide to speculative development offers a glimpse of the attitudes and emotions animating this enthusiasm for real estate. His eager but frustrated developers-in-waiting see the fortunes accumulating around them and yearn for their part of the pie. He rebukes those who preferred to hold themselves aloft from speculative enterprise, valorizing instead the architect capable of rising to the opportunities of the moment. Even if the boom were to come to a close, he explains, "that would be no reason for someone who needs some business to balk at the trends of modern ideas. *Better to follow the current than to try to swim against it.*"[44] This notion of sticking with the current recalls the image used by English economist Frederick Lavington some decades later to explain irrational market behavior. In bubbles, Lavington analogized, entrepreneurs are like skaters on a frozen pond; they gain confidence from the increasing presence of other skaters, which encourages them to continue or even increase their activity, rather than drawing the logical conclusion that the group's accumulating weight is a danger.[45] A direct path leads from Masselin's advice to market overcrowding and overproduction. Nevertheless, these links of professional collaboration, financial interdependency, and occupational self-promotion helped arrange the city's geography into a terrain of development whose consequences outlived this plunge through thin ice.

The Paris of Speculative Builders

The development journals introduced above were a remarkable component of the late-nineteenth-century building industry. Amid the construction of apartment houses and new city streets, developers produced writings about their projects, publishing specialized periodicals, tracts, and newspaper columns that discussed the practices and (more rarely) ambitions of urban development. The fact that such writings exist is itself noteworthy, testimony to a new promotional culture that was increasingly important to development activities. Testimony also, on occasion, to developers' pleased acknowledgment of their role in shaping the environment and economy of the city. "We are all in the building industry, here," wrote Lucien de la Saigne in an 1879 issue of *Le Foncier.* "It is time to hoist our flag high and strong, wrapping it proudly about us. Everything works when building works! Yes! It is life, it is activity that we lavish on the city; it is work for unoccupied arms, tranquility in the home, comfort and ease, even wealth!"[46] (De la Saigne was one of the principal investors in Fouquiau's Société Foncière Parisienne, a company heavily involved in the Quartier Marbeuf operation.)[47] The alternatives to prosperity—inactivity, unemployment, poverty—did not need to be directly invoked for readers to understand the building industry as a defense against discontent of the sort that produced the horrors of the Commune.[48] In the pages of these publications we find evaluations and justifications that developers and their brethren alternately exploited and felt compelled to deploy in the course of their business operations. In particular, they provide indications of the visions of urban growth and the social life of real estate that undergirded development activity in this period. While concerned commentators and municipal administrators were formulating their diagnoses and proposals for reckoning with urban growth, the property developers whose works were adding to the built and social landscape of the city were operating according to their own analyses of Paris's evolution.

The new cadre of developers that fanned across the city in the late 1870s focused their public pronouncements on the happy inevitability of Paris's growth, growth that was ensured by the city's particular attributes as a magnet for wealthy foreigners and evidenced, they believed, in the steady improvement in its property values. At the end of 1881, when rumblings were beginning to cast doubt on the sustainability of Paris's building boom, *Le Foncier* defended continued investment in land and construction on the basis of an unending demand for improved housing in the capital. The population of Paris continued to expand, and at the same time "large hotels are multiplying without being able to keep up with the number of foreigners who make up Paris's floating population—yet another reason for the creation of new neighborhoods." Demolitions in the city center, as well as the expansion of commercial premises in the same area, displaced people who then sought more modern and comfortable housing in replacement. The article went on: "These families will now look for their housing precisely in these new districts, which they'll seek out even more once they find well-ventilated and much more spacious apartments for the same price. We're no longer content with these so-called 'apartments' where air barely circulates. Well-being has become general, and the worker who lives in a hovel on the Butte des Moineaux wants a clean and healthful apartment."[49] This infinite demand was what gave Parisian real estate its security and infallible surplus value, negating the possibility of any crisis, at least from the perspective of the investor. The Société des Immeubles de Paris, a real estate development and investment company founded in 1879, explained to its shareholders that "the incessant movement concentrating an ever more numerous population in Paris, the developing taste for well-being that manifests itself in the search for dwellings as in other forms of luxury, the increasing ease of communication, all mean that the increase in value of Parisian buildings is a foreordained rule."[50]

Even once the crash had definitively begun and the penury of tenants and buyers for expensive buildings was obvious, *Le Foncier* preached the long-term viability of Parisian properties, confident in the unique qualities of its market: "Because Paris has an extraordinary intensity of energy; because it is an exceptional city in terms of all kinds of needs and resources; because its geographic placement puts it at the head of the various railway lines of Europe; . . . because Paris is a haven for the idle, who find all sorts of pleasures and distractions here, an incredible field of activity for businessmen, an incomparable center for literary, artistic, and scholarly production, and finally, because Paris is a refuge for the *déclassés* of the provinces and beyond. In Paris, this cosmopolitan city *par excellence*, an average of two hundred new individuals in search of housing has arrived every day for five years."[51] The buoyant faith of speculative builders found reinforcement in the discourse and analyses of professional economists. The city's real estate demanded such attention in this period that Paul Leroy-Beaulieu introduced a column accounting for its workings in his weekly *Économiste Français* in 1882.

He agreed with the vision of urban growth that underlay real estate boosterism but nevertheless predicted a temporary decline in rents in the most expensive categories of apartments. Paraphrasing building entrepreneurs and speculators, he acknowledged "that the wealthy classes grow unceasingly in a city such as Paris; that well-off provincials increasingly abandon the provinces; that foreign 'nabobs' come in greater numbers each day to live in our happy capital. . . . All this is true." Moreover, he added, commercial needs were expanding, and "each day more clubs, meeting groups, [and] corporate bodies are created that need large premises and establish themselves in apartments originally intended as residences."[52] Once the extent of the sector's problems began coming to light, Leroy-Beaulieu remained optimistic, citing the progressive filtering of urban tenants as a guarantee of the capital's property values: "The ever increasing preference for abandoning the center of the city for the outskirts will prevent the troubles of the land market from degenerating into a deep crisis. Provided that prices are dropped, in the end the new districts will gain tenants at the expense of the old."[53] The market mechanism could be relied on to align supply and demand.

The Paris of speculative developers was perpetually expanding, not only in numbers but also in needs. The city's housing filtered from rich to poor as increasingly exigent consumer demand drove new development.[54] The architect Fernoux captured part of the process when he observed that changes in taste and values meant that "old buildings are abandoned in favor of new ones with better layouts, more conveniently arranged, with light and large courtyards. . . . Buildings like those on Rue de Rivoli, considered smart when they were built thirty years ago, strike us now as poor buildings that we wouldn't enjoy living in."[55] Developers insisted they were following the lead of a steadily growing urban population with democratized desires for fashionable modern housing and its attendant amenities. The urban resident that mattered to developers was a competitive housing consumer, provided with the means and the desires to obtain improved and more appealing lodgings. Catering to these impulses freed older, more central housing, which by implication became available for those other urban residents, passed over in silence, who could not afford or were not inclined to operate competitively in the housing market. They were left to "cram into the buildings that the bourgeoisie has discarded, buildings that are older and often unhealthy."[56]

For developers the imagined attitudes and aspirations of occupants were mediated by the perceived concerns of another, equally important demographic: property investors. The early Third Republic boom was distinctive for its traffic in buildings rather than lots. These buildings were intended for a market of investors who approached property ownership as one element of a strategy of wealth management. Property ownership remained diffuse in Paris in this period, though it was more concentrated among wealthier individuals than at previous points in the century; for the majority of owners, who did not use their buildings as residences despite remaining within the city, real estate was purchased as an addition to a portfolio of investments.[57] While contemporaries decried builders' focus on high-end building as irrational in terms of the overall housing needs of the city, speculators grasped that contemporary buyers had little interest in owning and managing working-class buildings. Once more Leroy-Beaulieu confirmed their intuitions, acknowledging a desire among the upper classes to restrict their economic affairs to people of their own social class. After all, these affairs placed the reputation and dignity of the capitalist at stake; as he wrote in 1882, "a sensitive man doesn't enjoy throwing his tenants in the street." Bourgeois and luxury housing, on the other hand, provided "much more peace of mind; it's a much more agreeable job, and, if we can use the word, more decent. [Owners] are not bothered every moment by claims or complaints; they deal only with people of their own social world." Even if rates of return from older working-class housing exceeded those of new construction (primarily owing to the proportionately higher rents, both as percentages of their income and percentages of the building and land's value, to which the working classes were subject), buyers flocked to the upper segments of the market because "they value their peace of mind, their reputation, their dignity."[58] Other qualities viewed as particular to working-class buildings, such as increased tenant turnover and the need for more frequent repairs, increased the perception of risk and dissuaded investors. The SA Constructions Rationnelles, a builder of three working-class apartment houses in 1880, explained to shareholders who complained of excessive maintenance costs, "We carry out no superfluous works; we owe this great cost to the transient nature of our clientele. If we had more stable tenants, we would certainly see the category of 'expenses' diminish significantly."[59] The sales pattern of the buildings that were erected during the 1880s confirms the popularity of luxurious buildings among investors. Of the buildings that were acquired from failed developers by the Compagnie Foncière de France, those that the firm could sell most quickly were located in the more exclusive neighborhoods (chiefly the 16th arrondissement) and in general comprised only one apartment per floor, the interior arrangement that characterized upper-class housing.[60]

Guided by a fundamental faith in the unending growth of the capital and its particular attributes as a magnet for wealthy foreigners, developers generated a remarkable consensus on the form and location that speculative development should take in the city. Credit structures and lending norms both informed and reinforced this consensus, framing the conditions of possibility for real estate enterprise. Auguste Fougerousse, a public works entrepreneur and activist in the workers' cooperative movement, explained the workings of the industry's credit system to readers of the *Économiste Français* in 1883. He wrote: "Institutions loaned about half of the value of land and the future construction; the more expensive the land, the higher the loan. Because you weren't paying for the land and building costs are about the same price everywhere, it was in your interest to build in wealthy districts."[61] Building on rented lands obtained with the transfer of mortgage priority—a process we encountered in Chapter 1—led to an inflation of land prices wherever speculators engaged, as owners who let lands in this fashion charged a premium to compensate for the risks entailed in abandoning their privileges. Some contemporaries estimated that land could reach as high as double its normal value under this regime.[62] These financing practices had two important consequences. First, they encouraged developers with little capital to construct on more expensive lands (in order to secure higher loans), a choice that in turn required building for the middle and upper classes in order to recoup on the expenditure. Second, they facilitated an abstraction and commercialization of property. Purchase options sliced into the absolute condition of ownership, creating new kinds of marketable property rights. Critics scorned them as dubious paper values dissociated from the actual practices and security of property ownership as it was conventionally understood. The testimony of André Cochut, economist and head of Paris's Municipal Pawn *(Mont-de-piété),* before the 1884 Parliamentary Commission captured these anxieties eloquently when he described a real estate market captured by the practices and mentality of the stock market: "What happened in the wheat trade happened to land: pledges for future deliveries traded from hand to hand, through networks," ensuring that "an empty parcel of land, to which the seller's privilege was naturally attached, thus became an exchangeable stock."[63]

Cochut's criticisms captured a discomfort with the way development practices were aligning the movable and immovable elements of real estate. Real property gained its value from the promise of future returns; transferable options trafficked in this futurity, exposing the intangible elements of property and its value. The material aspects of real property seemed to be effaced as these instruments circulated on the basis of an imagined speculative landscape of homogenous lots. Yet the reduction of real estate to a perfectly exchangeable commodity is a difficult and perpetually incomplete process. In his study of Parisian land values, Halbwachs summarized the problem succinctly. Houses, he explained, would approach the interchangeability of any other industrial product if they were freely transportable over unlimited space. But the reality was that "they have to group together in a relatively tight area, sticking one against the other, adopting a location vis-à-vis neighboring buildings (and, via this location, vis-à-vis the entirety of buildings) that will not change and that will be easily discernible, and hence an integral part of the house itself." As a consequence, a city was composed of a limited number of houses but a nearly infinite number of locations, each with their ineffable and irreproducible "originality."[64]

Advertisements for building land during the boom bear out the impossibility of detaching projected buildings completely from their particular physical surroundings. Lots advertised by Albert Laubière in his *Indicateur Illustré des Appartements à Louer* in 1880, for example, are compressed into a collage of floating parcels, but these remain linked to the specific roadways and neighboring buildings of each site. The names of adjoining property owners are advertised, inscribing the lots for sale within the spaces constituted by individual and identifiable property rights. In fact, these claims served to establish the boundaries of the sites for sale as much as did the delineation of their surface area (Figure 2.2). Advertisements included maps that highlighted distinguishing features of particular localities, such as factories or markets, and showed the variation in prices of lots relative to such amenities. These ads certainly presented the city as a site for the circulation and consumption of property, but also educated viewers in the subtle differentiation of seemingly similar items of exchange. Developers looking to exchange plots of land for different interests in property development companies, or simply seeking expensive lots from which to garner larger credits from lending bodies, were navigating the reality of an already deeply structured urban environment. The tendencies toward abstraction that produced

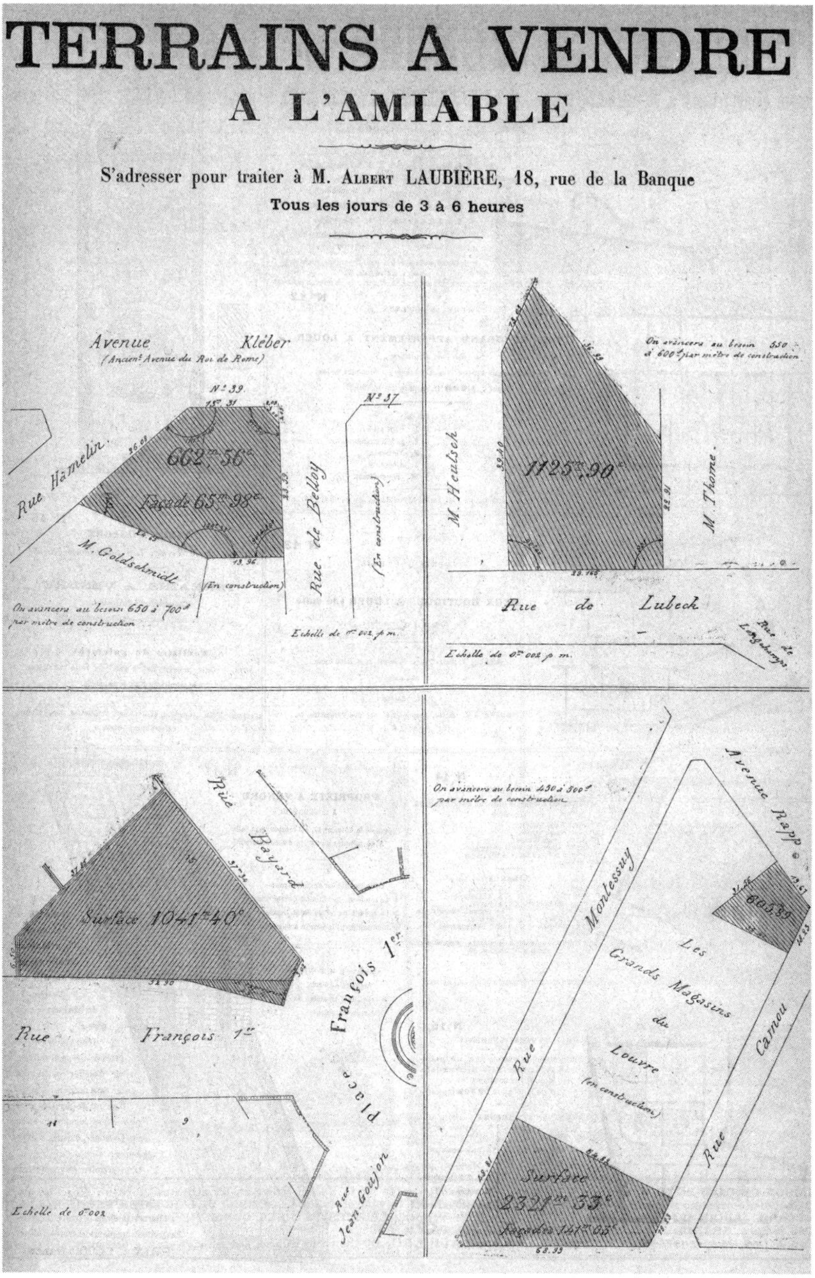

FIGURE 2.2 Advertisement for building lots in the *Indicateur Illustré des Appartements à Louer,* August 10, 1880. *Source:* Bibliothèque Nationale de France

profound anxieties for many contemporary observers of real estate—and had important consequences for the built landscape of the city—encountered, in practice, persistent friction. This friction between *immobilier* and *mobilier* was an inescapable and defining characteristic of real estate's commercialization; managing it was the task of the devices and information that framed the arena in which speculators operated.

An 1879 article published in Laubière's *Le Foncier* helps introduce the priorities, principles, and tools that shaped the activities of developers. The anonymous author who penned "Comment on fait un bon placement immobilier" ("How to make a good real estate investment") addressed those "who share the desire, common to many at the moment, to find a great deal." It offered general advice for both investors and speculators, implying they shared similar logic and interests. Of utmost and fundamental concern was the selection of the property. The writer warned hasty purchasers that "buying land—*without choosing it*—is one of those irreparable and clumsy errors whose consequences, sooner or later, can bring about the ruin of the purchaser." "To know how to choose from hundreds of offers that which supplies the most advantages for the present, and above all, for the future," the author explained, was "a prime duty of all heads of households"—a contention that constituted an impressively broad public for real estate affairs. Speculators, the author continued, "even the most practiced, reflect long and hard before buying a piece of land, examining the pros and the cons of the orientation of the street and the neighborhood, inquiring, above all, into the revenues of neighboring buildings and the rental opportunities."[65] The speculator is a cautious and thorough entrepreneur, governed by reason rather than intuition. His research focuses on the character of the local neighborhood, the standing of specific streets and nearby buildings, as communicated chiefly through the economic indicators of rent and net returns.

The information that helped define a building's niche in the city's ecology was not always easy to obtain. Chronic variability in prices sprang from the deeply localized, unreproducible character of real property, meaning that data on neighboring properties was never perfectly transferable, even if readily available. Architect M. Blottas wrote a guide to property evaluation in 1856 in which he acknowledged that "today there are very remarkable fluctuations and differences in rent prices, even within the same city, the same neighborhood, the same street, and for rentals that are entirely similar and perfectly comparable."[66] There was a fundamental unpredictability to a real estate price that resolved itself only in a sales or rental transaction. Yet, as other advisors recognized, this contingency told only part of the story, and efforts multiplied to improve precision and educate readers in reliable indicators of value.

A lengthy investment manual penned in 1863 by André Haussmann (uncle of the city's prefect) took a geographic approach to the problem of property price, dividing the capital into thirteen concentric zones radiating outward from the city center. Real estate in these rings declined in value as distance from the center increased, without this general tendency "being reducible to a metric simplicity."[67] (Exceptional factors, such as the popularity of some suburban regions as destinations for weekend excursions, accounted for deviations in the pattern.) The zone governed property values completely; the author noted that the best-quality street of one zone, for example, might be a third-category street in another, with the attendant decrease in value despite an identity of objective characteristics. Within zones, prices reflected a combination of "permanent" elements, such as road quality, sidewalks, sewers, street lighting, and public transportation lines (a walk of 500 meters to an omnibus stop was considered normal, a walk of one kilometer translated into a loss in value of 2 to 4 percent), and of "transitory" elements, localized in nature, such as the construction of a new boulevard or the presence of a large amount of property on the market. Although important to consider, these transitory phenomena, temporary and unpredictable, were momentary influences on the more substantive, fundamental components of a property's value. They helped shape how property acted in the marketplace but did not significantly alter its use value. Haussmann's tables and tips for reckoning property values comprised a few hundred pages; nevertheless, he indicated that these were merely general prescriptions, desiring to stave off any impression that he had "presumed to fix something as uncertain as the price of land in Paris."[68] Indeed, the percentages he indicated were all relative to one another, creating an interdependent landscape of value that was precisely the opposite of fixity.

It is important to consider for a moment the use and understanding of the terms "price" and "value" in such treatments of urban real estate. Writers and advisers on real estate were well aware that value and price exerted influence on one another without being identical, even if the terms were often used interchangeably in both popular and more specialized forums. There were careful distinctions between the types of values that could be assigned to a property. Common practice in the nineteenth century dictated that the value of a piece of real estate could be determined by capitalizing its revenues at 5 percent. Thus an apartment house that garnered 10,000 francs net in yearly revenues would result in an evaluation of the property's worth as 200,000 francs. This 5 percent rate was a rough and ready figure that could be raised or lowered depending on the particular circumstances of the building in question. (In 1901 the average gross return on real property in Paris was in fact 6.63 percent, very close to the 5 percent net figure.)[69] It reflected the opinion that real property should give the same return as the *rente* or national debt (which was also a form of real property) and had a remarkable longevity; in the old regime, it was known as the "denier vingt," a multiplier used to transform revenues into building values.[70] The value of land and built property, then, was distilled from the income received in exchange for their products and services. This led to difficulties in assigning value to owner-occupied urban houses, which did not register income. In part to help with such instances, a second method of estimation was also frequently deployed, one that calculated a "*valeur intrinsèque*," or value in capital. This combined the cost of the materials and labor employed in a building's construction with the value of the land on which it stood, subtracting a certain amount to account for the age and depreciation of the structure. Estimations from municipal expropriation procedures, from decennial tax evaluations, and from the mortgage assessments of the Crédit Foncier's agents show that both methods were commonly deployed, with an assignment of value normally falling between the two figures, as determined by the judgment of the evaluator.[71]

Still, neither the revenue value nor the capital value of the building necessarily aligned with its sales value *(valeur vénale),* understood as the amount a property could be expected to garner in a normal sales transaction. This value was determined chiefly through comparison with similar properties in the locality, and was thus dependent on the characteristics of the local market. Finally, this normal sales value could easily differ from a property's sales *price,* which sprang from the particular and isolated circumstances of the sale, such as the availability of properties at a specific moment, the inclinations of the seller and buyer, even the competitive frenzy of an individual auction. The possibility that the price of real property could diverge significantly from its value lay behind the Civil Code's perpetuation of the old regime's practice of requiring restitution for *lésion d'outre-moitié,* in which a freely contracted agreement between a buyer and seller could be nullified (or restitution paid) if the seller consented to a price that represented less than seven-twelfths of the value of their real estate.[72] The value of real property, in other words, had sources exogenous to the marketplace transaction.

Entities concerned with calculating rental and sales values ranged from insurance companies, mortgage lenders, and tax and public works administrations, to professionals such as architects, notaries, and property owners themselves. To the types of values outlined above would have to be added still other examples, such as the *valeur locative* upon which property taxes were based (rental revenues minus a quarter for residential buildings), or the reconstruction value upon which insurance policies were based. Tax evaluators could be stymied by the diversity of Parisian buildings and the impact of small differences of location or building type on property revenues.[73] Assessment had to be particular to each building; in 1888–1889, state evaluators abandoned a plan to determine a range of "types" into which Parisian properties could be sorted and quickly assessed, concluding that this method, "no doubt excellent for smaller centers," had serious shortcomings in Paris, "where rental values vary significantly not only from one neighborhood to another, but even from street to street, and between houses on the same street."[74] Expropriation indemnities, assigned by juries of local proprietors, were arrived at through evaluations of the properties in question, the status of their owners, the proposals of the administration, and other difficult-to-document and idiosyncratic impulses among jury members. It was a legal rather than technical procedure; when the municipal council debated employing property specialists—rather than legal professionals—as its representatives in expropriation procedures in 1886, councilors reasoned that technical precision could not avail against the subjective modes of constituting and allocating value that reigned in the jury.[75] There was much debate, both professional and popular, about what these sums should represent, whether they should be understood as payments for a sale or compensations for a prejudice, whether they should integrate amounts for intangible losses or, as was legally stipulated, suffer reduction in recognition of the surplus values generated by public works. Uncertainties aside, published maps of expropriation zones and tables of offers, demands, and indemnities were among the most common representations of Parisian property in circulation.

The local and unreproducible characteristics of real estate, combined with the multiplicity of types of valuation, meant that assessments of worth involved a high degree of subjective interpretation. In his guide André Haussmann described his method as scientific, likening himself at different moments to a chemist, an agronomist, and a naturalist interested in isolating a system's constitutive elements and establishing methodical classifications. Yet this scientific endeavor had distinct limits. "Although this classification takes care and attention," Haussmann wrote, "it presents no serious difficulties. Retailers routinely sort through their merchandise and make a similar ranking, easily designating a first, second, and third choice and setting prices accordingly."[76] Common sense, rules of thumb, and even intuition (born of experience) were an unavoidable part of the process. The indications he offered were ultimately a general guide to the dynamics of property, subject, like other merchandise, to the unpredictable conditions of particular times and spaces, and to the interpretations of informed intermediaries.

As a representation of real estate patterns, Haussmann's efforts were a vague application of the concentric model of von Thünen's isolated state to the urban setting.[77] His precisely defined zones followed Paris's annular topography, defined by its *grands boulevards,* its ring of fortifications, and the snail-shell coil of its administrative districts. He stretched his zones east and west—shaping them more like rectangles with rounded ends than circles—in order to account for other key dynamics, such as the deeply engrained sociogeographic divisions between the eastern and western portions of the city, and recent experiences of the "displacements" of commercial centers toward the northwest (the center of Haussmann's map was, tellingly, the Stock Exchange).[78] Aligning his zones with the city's form also allowed him to contain his analysis to its boundaries. The concentric circles that were deployed with gusto by Chicago's boosters in the same period, for instance, stretched purposefully into endless hinterlands in order to broadcast the limitless promise of Chicago's expansion; in later years such maps would inform the influential concentric zone theory of urban growth pioneered by Ernest Burgess of the Chicago School of Sociology.[79] Haussmann's system was more concerned with ordering the new geography of a capital that had recently annexed its suburbs than it was with predicting future patterns of development. His discussion about the relationship between distance and land use is limited to the recommendation to build in the city center, where higher rents promised better returns. His was an investment guide, not a study of the urban organism. Its advice and omissions both reflected and reinforced well-established residential trends: an urban center favored by the city's more privileged residents, and a periphery dominated by the households of the less well off, whose future as a profitable development zone lay some decades in the future.[80]

In the Third Republic, information on Parisian real estate became increasingly abundant and its representations more diverse. The statistical services that flourished within the municipal administration gathered impressive amounts of data on the conditions of property in the city, its rate of construction, sale, and revenues, as well as the amount and geography of debt accumulated upon it. The Service de la Statistique Municipale de la Ville de Paris, overseen in turn by father and son statisticians Louis-Adolphe and Jacques Bertillon, published its first annual compilation of municipal statistics in 1880. It presented summaries of property values, sales, and construction in tabular form, following the administrative divisions of arrondissement and *quartier*.[81] Jacques Bertillon was a pioneer in graphical statistics, but in these works graphic elements were reserved for mapping and measuring the more "natural" urban phenomena of death by typhoid, precipitation, or the flow of water through the city. The city's real estate received more vivid treatment in the maps of average rental costs and property values that appeared in the Department of the Seine's tax evaluations, published in 1891, 1900–1901, and 1911 (Figure 2.3).[82] In these graphics the city's districts are colored to designate average prices and values, creating a pixilated landscape of discrete price areas. Known as choropleth maps, they effectively visualize variability across a region, emphasizing contrasts and discontinuities. The eye is pulled toward the densely colored areas of higher value concentration in the city's northwest, away from the pale deserts of low revenues.

The maps devised by the architect Paul Planat, published in *La Semaine des Constructeurs* in March 1884, provided a different basis for appreciating and assessing the situation of the city's real estate (Figures 2.4 and 2.5). In this case Planat was not mapping property values, but instead was attempting to track the nature of development in the city in a more dynamic manner. He used data on changes in neighborhood population and construction levels between 1876 and 1881 to chart the degree of correlation between the two, testing whether the demands of the population for housing, and the demands of housing for tenants, were in geographic harmony. Without abandoning the administrative boundaries of the city's neighborhoods, he superimposed contour lines that followed the changes in population and building much more

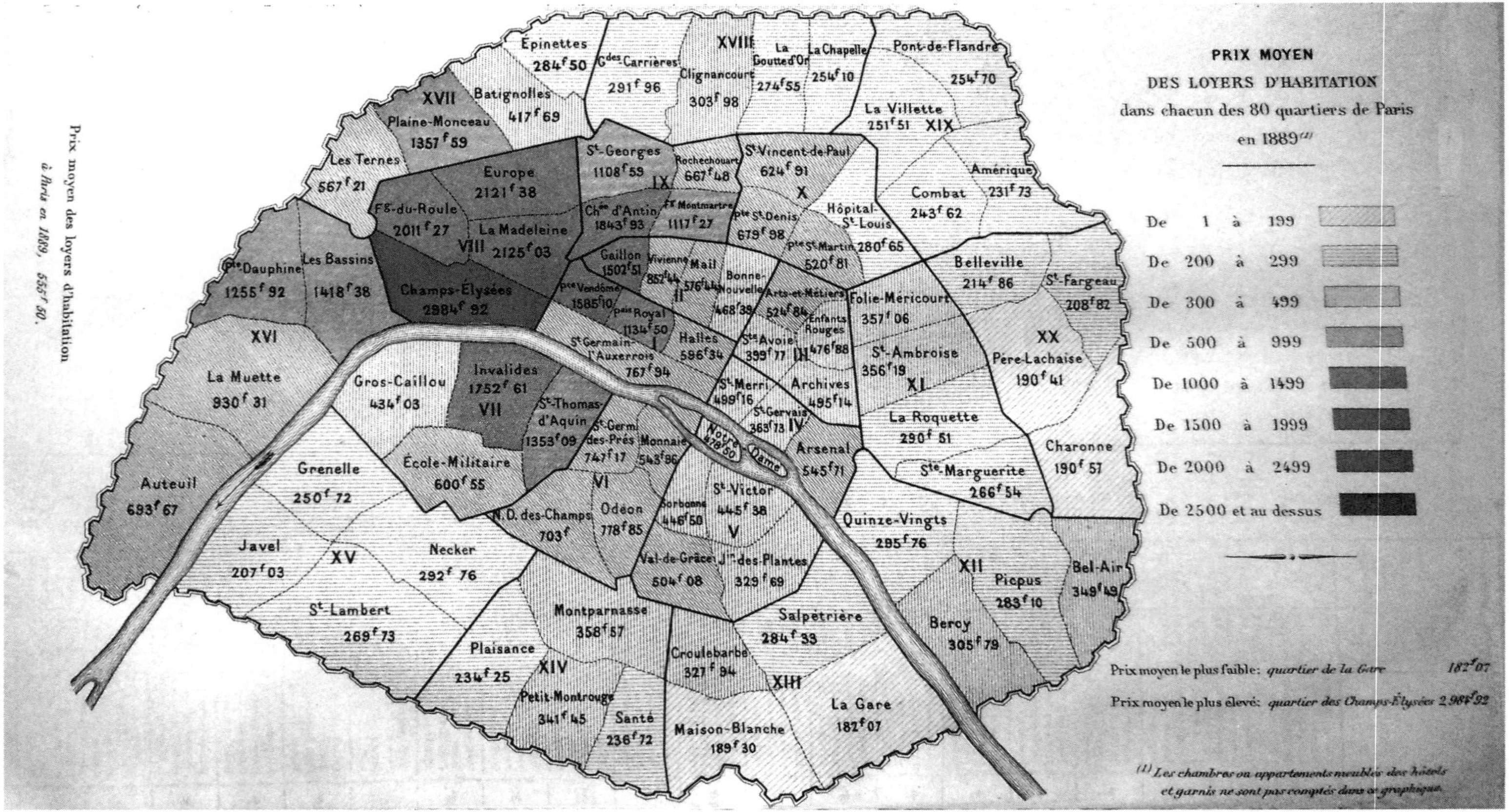

FIGURE 2.3 Average rental rates of each of Paris's 80 *quartiers* in 1889. From Préfecture de la Seine, Direction des Finances, Service des Contributions Directes, *Les propriétés bâties de la ville de Paris en 1889 et en 1890* (Paris: Imprimerie Nationale, 1890). *Source:* Bibliothèque Historique de la Ville de Paris

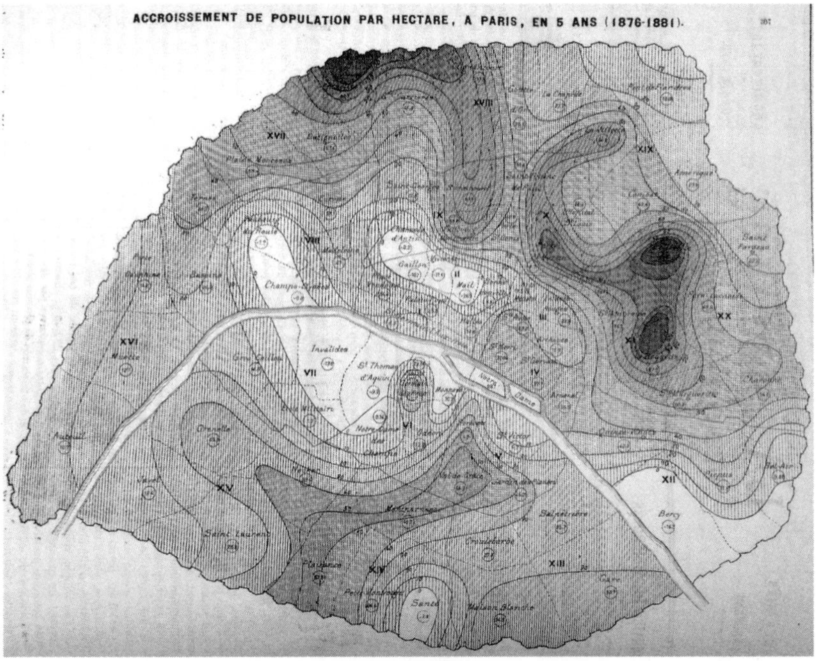
ACCROISSEMENT DE POPULATION PAR HECTARE, A PARIS, EN 5 ANS (1876-1881).

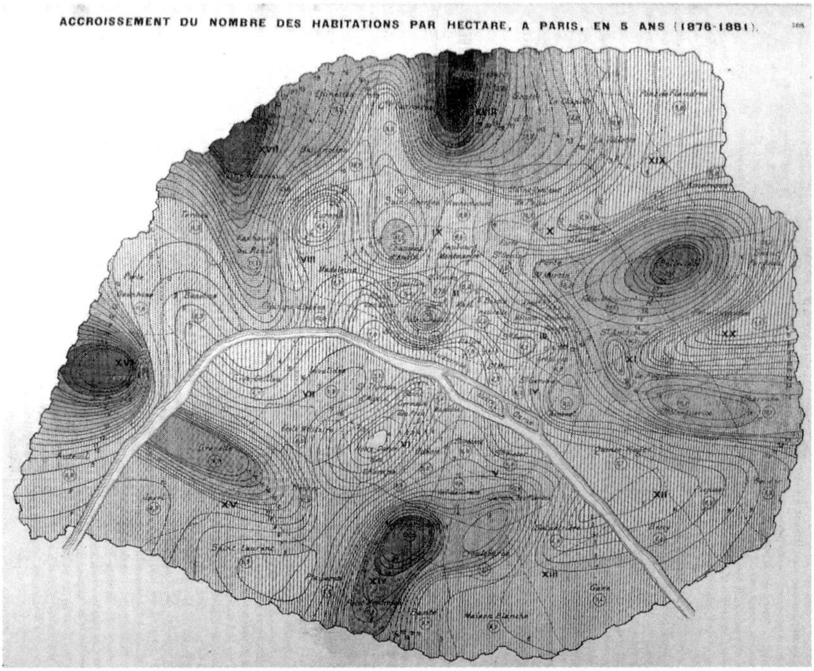
ACCROISSEMENT DU NOMBRE DES HABITATIONS PAR HECTARE, A PARIS, EN 5 ANS (1876-1881).

FIGURES 2.4 AND 2.5 Maps by Paul Planat indicating the movements of population (above) and the diffusion of new construction (below) in Paris, 1876–1881. *La Semaine des Constructeurs,* March 22, 1884. *Source:* Loeb Library Special Collections, Harvard University

minutely, creating what he called a "statistical landscape" that threw into more precise relief the gradations of increase and decrease in each.[83] This was a novel technique; it had been only a few years since engineer (and Parisian municipal councilor) Louis-Léger Vauthier had used contour lines in an 1874 map to represent Paris's population, a recognized innovation in statistical mapping.[84] Planat's maps highlighted the multinodal nature of Paris's growth. Zones of heightened development were located on the outer boundary of the city, designated by lines that condensed before spilling fluidly in different directions, swirling through nearby neighborhoods and altering course around the smaller ripples of development stemming from other nodes. The administrative districts serve to orient the reader in this sea of movement, rather than provide the analytic framework for data. Planat, a building industry insider, privileged the patterns generated by construction over those defined by the administration, generating an image that more closely reflected the impact of developers on the city's landscape.

Capturing the disjuncture between the production of developers and the movements of population that issued from the construction boom, Planat's maps reveal and insist upon the divergences between the real city—its geographies, its demographics—and the speculative city of developers. This mismatch is all the more remarkable given the frequency with which builders invoked, as a guiding principle of development, the phrase "besoins du quartier" or "needs of the neighborhood," recognizing that construction should respond to preexisting desires and necessities. Yet they appeared to have misjudged these needs, at least in the short term. Certainly the logic of the *besoins du quartier* required better information on patterns of urban development than was available to building entrepreneurs and speculative architects in the early 1880s. When Fouquiau introduced his journal in 1877, he stressed the industry's need for a type of "real estate archive" that would respond to glaring informational inadequacies, while later diagnoses of the crisis in the property market frequently laid blame on a woeful lack of clarity about housing demand and land prices in the metropolis.[85] Surveying a crumbling industry in 1883, *La Réforme du Bâtiment* demanded that the city publish an accurate accounting of the housing needs of each district in the city, a statistical survey that would "inform speculators on the needs of the [city's] population" and so allow them to fruitfully orient their production.[86] Similarly, when the daily newspaper *Le Matin* introduced its regular real estate column in 1885, it deplored the fact that "if an architect, building entrepreneur, or property owner wants to learn the value of land in a given neighborhood in Paris, it is currently nearly impossible for him to do so," and proposed the publication of an "Annuaire Foncier du Départment de la Seine."[87] When the municipality did publish the statistical volumes on rent, land, and property values described above, they were greeted with enthusiasm by commentators in *La Construction Moderne,* who observed that "[these volumes] have a real utility for architects, insofar as they give precise information on the income levels of residents of each neighborhood, and so help indicate how expensive a building one should reasonably build there."[88] (The journal said nothing of the fact that there was a gap of two years between the years covered in the city's statistical works and their dates of publication.)

Yet better information would have done little to resolve some of the fundamental difficulties that arose from the key mechanism by which both developers and lenders functioned during the fin de siècle: organizing development primarily on the basis of the price of land. The second part of the anonymous investment advice article in *Le Foncier* shows this mechanism in operation, presenting the case in favor of expensive lands as preferred sites for profit making:

> In the first place, since construction costs as much on land found at the farthest outskirts of Paris—Montrouge, Belleville, La Chapelle, etc.—as on land found in the center of the city, it follows that owing to the lower rents in the outer regions than in the center of any city, revenues will be less in the suburbs than in the center.
>
> But surely, you protest, the cheapness of land on the periphery will compensate? Compensation doesn't exist: it is only imaginary, one of those fallacies that many people share.

Expensive lot or cheap, "foundations, iron joists, floors, flooring, doors, windows, roofing and many other elements are necessarily the same," while "eliminating luxurious elements" such as gilded locks, painted ceilings, or expensive wall decoration "amounts to an extremely small reduction in costs, as savings apply only on accessories, not on the principal portion of expenses." Most importantly, readers learned, the seller's price has taken into account development potential. In his example, the more expensive lot is located on a wider street, which allows for a higher building. Land takes its value from the revenues it can produce, making its price a transparent and reliable indicator of development potential. This is what the author means when he insists that "compensation doesn't exist"; cheap land can only mean one thing: low returns. The author calculates the more luxurious building's return at 7.9 percent, and that of the more modest at only 5.4 percent.[89]

In part the role played by price is a predictable ancillary of the progressive separation of land ownership and development capital in the nineteenth century. But new types of property guides that appeared in the latter decades of the century suggest that readers—from developers and buyers to owners and lenders—were expecting more information from prices than may have previously been the case. These guides consisted chiefly of real estate sales figures gathered from transactions from across the city. One of the first such compilations was Maxime Maucorps's *Annuaire de la propriété foncière de Paris* (Paris Land Directory), which appeared in four volumes between 1867 and 1870. Maucorps was a property specialist whose price chronicles appeared in several publications.[90] His series compiled information on land and building sales, expropriations, and development in the capital city, and sought to allow owners, buyers, and developers to determine the value of land on the basis of data on comparable transactions. Previous to this point, guides to property for both investors and developers were purely descriptive; they discussed the legal aspects of land ownership and exchange, addressed the characteristics of a piece of real estate that ought to be of concern to purchasers, and offered advice on ideal investments, but actual data on market activity was not included.[91] Even André Haussmann's extensive guide to valuing Parisian real estate prices did not employ real prices, instead delineating relative rates of value increases and decreases whose application ultimately depended on the common knowledge of "specialized individuals." Nevertheless he acknowledged an increasing demand for broader access to the raw materials of property assessment; whereas previous generations had been satisfied with the opinions of authorities such as the *intendants* who administered aristocratic domains, when it came to evaluating property, the current era was the "century of *accounting*, of *distrust*, in which everything is communicated in numbers, numbers that must be seen and understood so that they can be verified."[92]

Price reportage dominated columns and guides to Parisian real estate in the Third Republic. Among the most prominent works was the *Guide foncier* or "Land Guide" published by the real estate agency of John Arthur et Tiffen in 1886. This volume drew its information on twenty years' worth of property sales in the Paris region from the operations of the Crédit Foncier.

The authors promised that if carefully studied, the guide provided all the information necessary for calculating the precise value of a piece of land on a given street.[93] (Indeed, it was one of the main data sources for sociologist Maurice Halbwachs's 1909 study of Parisian land values.) Another real estate company, Maublanc et Fils, published their *Aide-mémoire foncier de l'architecte et du propriétaire* (Land Aide-Memoire for Architects and Property Owners) in 1893, which also listed all property sold in Paris over the past twenty years.[94] Over at the Foncière Immobilière Parisienne, the agency of architect Maxime Petibon, a number of such compilations were published: the *Indicateur foncière de la ville de Paris* (Land Guide for the City of Paris) appeared under various titles in the 1880s, while the *Manuel officiel des affaires immobilières et foncières de la ville de Paris* (Official Guide to Paris's Real Estate and Property Market) was published annually in 1899–1903 (Figure 2.6).[95] In the *Indicateur*, streets were listed alphabetically for easy reference, each with short summaries of their defining characteristics. In 1887, for instance, one could read that Rue de l'Abbaye in the 6th arrondissement was "generally bordered by handsome buildings, quiet, beautifully situated; considering their location, rents are cheap." Of Rue Abbé Grégoire, one learned that the street, "lined with new houses on the upper part and older ones on the lower . . . is gloomy because of the collège Saint-Nicolas; on the other hand, the market lends occasional animation to the street, and it is well enough populated, in general the rents are not too high."[96] Petibon boasted that his work was the first to combine the history of Parisian streets with their real estate statistics, establishing an entirely new framework for describing and discerning the city's development landscape. Deploying qualitative and quantitative indicators to establish a context for a property, he confirmed the central tenets of property investment: that "a building must be located in a good area and be in keeping with the neighborhood," with rents "in line with (and even lower than) the means of the neighborhood's residents."[97]

The appearance of such compilations is important to understanding the market for property in the capital city. On the face of it these guides had a straightforward, practical goal—to provide the data necessary for determining average values through informed comparison. As guides to the entire city, they posed a spatial solution to the geographic disconnect demonstrated by Planat's maps. Accumulating citywide information into one resource, they offered a bridge from the local expertise of builders to a wider terrain of

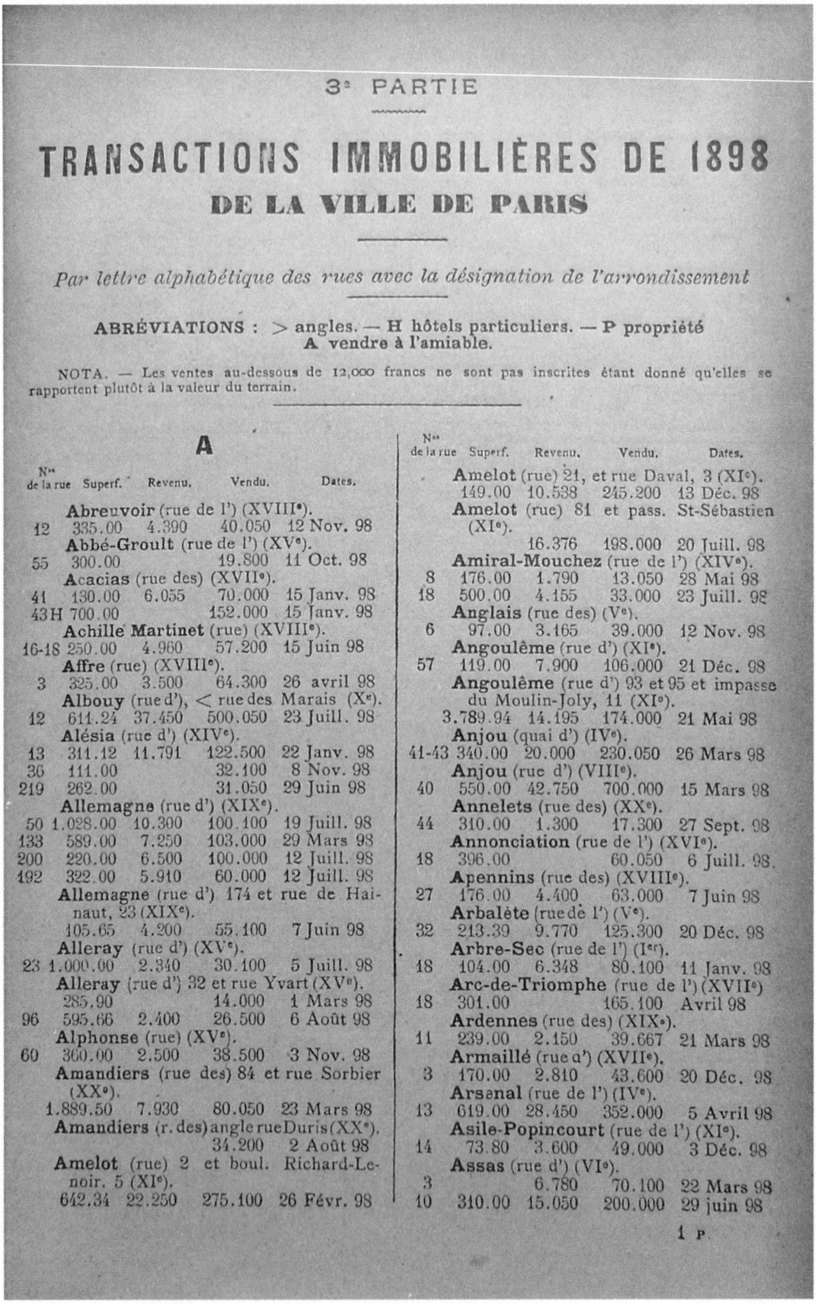

3e PARTIE

TRANSACTIONS IMMOBILIÈRES DE 1898

DE LA VILLE DE PARIS

Par lettre alphabétique des rues avec la désignation de l'arrondissement

ABRÉVIATIONS : > angles. — H hôtels particuliers. — P propriété A vendre à l'amiable.

NOTA. — Les ventes au-dessous de 12,000 francs ne sont pas inscrites étant donné qu'elles se rapportent plutôt à la valeur du terrain.

A

Nos de la rue	Superf.	Revenu.	Vendu.	Dates.
Abreuvoir (rue de l') (XVIIIe).				
12	335.00	4.390	40.050	12 Nov. 98
Abbé-Groult (rue de l') (XVe).				
55	300.00		19.800	11 Oct. 98
Acacias (rue des) (XVIIe).				
41	130.00	6.055	70.000	15 Janv. 98
43H	700.00		152.000	15 Janv. 98
Achille Martinet (rue) (XVIIIe).				
16-18	250.00	4.960	57.200	15 Juin 98
Affre (rue) (XVIIIe).				
3	325.00	3.500	64.300	26 avril 98
Albouy (rue d'), < rue des Marais (Xe).				
12	611.24	37.450	500.050	23 Juill. 98
Alésia (rue d') (XIVe).				
13	311.12	11.791	122.500	22 Janv. 98
36	111.00		32.100	8 Nov. 98
219	262.00		31.050	29 Juin 98
Allemagne (rue d') (XIXe).				
50	1.028.00	10.300	100.100	19 Juill. 98
133	589.00	7.250	103.000	29 Mars 98
200	220.00	6.500	100.000	12 Juill. 98
192	322.00	5.910	60.000	12 Juill. 98
Allemagne (rue d') 174 et rue de Hainaut, 23 (XIXe).				
	105.65	4.200	55.100	7 Juin 98
Alleray (rue d') (XVe).				
23	1.000.00	2.340	30.100	5 Juill. 98
Alleray (rue d') 32 et rue Yvart (XVe).				
	285.90		14.000	1 Mars 98
96	595.66	2.400	26.500	6 Août 98
Alphonse (rue) (XVe).				
60	360.00	2.500	38.500	3 Nov. 98
Amandiers (rue des) 84 et rue Sorbier (XXe).				
	1.889.50	7.930	80.050	23 Mars 98
Amandiers (r. des) angle rue Duris (XXe).				
			34.200	2 Août 98
Amelot (rue) 2 et boul. Richard-Lenoir, 5 (XIe).				
	642.34	22.250	275.100	26 Févr. 98
Amelot (rue) 21, et rue Daval, 3 (XIe).				
	149.00	10.538	245.200	13 Déc. 98
Amelot (rue) 81 et pass. St-Sébastien (XIe).				
		16.376	198.000	20 Juill. 98
Amiral-Mouchez (rue de l') (XIVe).				
8	176.00	1.790	13.050	28 Mai 98
18	500.00	4.155	33.000	23 Juill. 98
Anglais (rue des) (Ve).				
6	97.00	3.165	39.000	12 Nov. 98
Angoulême (rue d') (XIe).				
57	119.00	7.900	106.000	21 Déc. 98
Angoulême (rue d') 93 et 95 et impasse du Moulin-Joly, 11 (XIe).				
	3.789.94	14.195	174.000	21 Mai 98
Anjou (quai d') (IVe).				
41-43	340.00	20.000	230.050	26 Mars 98
Anjou (rue d') (VIIIe).				
40	550.00	42.750	700.000	15 Mars 98
Annelets (rue des) (XXe).				
44	310.00	1.300	17.300	27 Sept. 98
Annonciation (rue de l') (XVIe).				
18	396.00		60.050	6 Juill. 98
Apennins (rue des) (XVIIIe).				
27	176.00	4.400	63.000	7 Juin 98
Arbalète (rue de l') (Ve).				
32	213.39	9.770	125.300	20 Déc. 98
Arbre-Sec (rue de l') (Ier).				
18	104.00	6.348	80.100	11 Janv. 98
Arc-de-Triomphe (rue de l') (XVIIe)				
18	301.00		165.100	Avril 98
Ardennes (rue des) (XIXe).				
11	239.00	2.150	39.667	21 Mars 98
Armaillé (rue d') (XVIIe).				
3	170.00	2.810	43.600	20 Déc. 98
Arsenal (rue de l') (IVe).				
13	619.00	28.450	352.000	5 Avril 98
Asile-Popincourt (rue de l') (XIe).				
14	73.80	3.600	49.000	3 Déc. 98
Assas (rue d') (VIe).				
3		6.780	70.100	22 Mars 98
10	310.00	15.050	200.000	29 juin 98

1 P.

FIGURE 2.6 Page from Maxime Petibon's 1899 *Manuel officiel des affaires immobilières. Source:* Bibliothèque Historique de la Ville de Paris

operation, assembling all of Paris into a single development space. Yet their existence and organizational form also had a more fundamental impact. In the pages of these volumes, the incomparable became comparable, and the disparate transactions of dissimilar goods congealed into a market. Exchange appeared constant and goods readily marketable. Price guides established records of market activity, granting the market a diachronic existence, and reinforced an understanding of property prices as relative and historical rather than intrinsic. Although the natural qualities of a lot (such as the nature of its soil or the length of its façade) remained important in determining value, these guides illustrated the conviction that urban property was in general only as valuable as the properties that bounded it—a rule that the maxim "Needs of the neighborhood" applied even more strongly to built property.[98] They also supplied the information necessary to compose readers into the calculative actors demanded by a marketplace. Alongside the appearance of daily newspaper columns tracking real estate transactions and chronicling an entity called "the real estate market," these guides brought awareness of property prices to a broader public, knitting them into a self-referential system. Already in 1863 André Haussmann's guide to Parisian real estate had hinted at the potential importance of access to this sort of information, noting that two new kinds of publicity—advertising, and a recent law on property registration (1855)—would increase the likelihood that even small numbers of transactions could "strike the imagination" of owners and buyers and set the rates for the market.[99]

At the same time as these paper anthologies proposed an unprecedented transparency and regularity for the multitude of transactions that might comprise the city's real estate market, contemporaries disputed their ability to adequately capture the rapid and fluctuating dynamics they illuminated. A dispute in the municipal council surrounding the adoption of the John Arthur et Tiffen company's *Guide Foncier* illustrates these tensions vividly. A council commission reviewed a proposal that the city subscribe to the volume, and recommended purchasing one hundred copies (at a cost of ten francs each), putting one each at the disposal of various administrators, councilors, commissions, and libraries. Supporters of the purchase foregrounded the council's desperate situation when it came to knowledge about the city's real estate prices, and argued that its ignorance placed the elected body at a disadvantage when evaluating the administration's proposals. Alexandre Paulard, a new socialist councilor from the 19th arrondissement, backed the subscription because he believed the volume provided proof of the inexorable increase in the city's property values, increases that were illicitly appropriated by property owners by virtue of their monopoly. Nevertheless, several councilors took affront at the expense to taxpayers; others were skeptical of a volume compiled by a real estate agency, for which a municipal subscription would be a publicity boon. To make matters worse, as councilor Léopold Hervieux pointed out to general laughter, the agency in question "is currently run by a woman."[100] Some detractors were willing to acknowledge the value of the book as a statistical study, but their arguments made clear that its very nature as a sort of archive signaled its incapacity to operate usefully in an arena characterized by flux, sudden alterations, and rapid trend reversals. Councilor Léon Donnat complained that a book would become out of date within a year, and recommended that council instead have recourse to the constantly refreshed data available in the weekly sales tabulations that appeared in specialized gazettes. Athanase Bassinet added that real estate prices "vary from day to day," depending on "changes in neighboring properties." His words no doubt carrying the weight of his experience as a journeyman mason and entrepreneur of public works, he continued, "The value of land is fluctuating by nature."[101]

Aside from revealing the council's rather remarkable lack of resources or agreed-upon procedures for assessing property values, this debate opposed two narratives of the behavior of real estate in a market. The first described a good about which information was perfectible, particularly through a historical approach, permitting increasingly accurate interpretations of future value. The second depicted a market being constantly reborn, where new transactions set rates independent of past tendencies, and whose workings inevitably eluded technologies of predictability. As with the guidance on property evaluation offered by specialized publications, efforts to formalize assessment along more standardized and objective lines ran up against the necessity of subjective judgment and local circumstance. This "localness" meant not only a spatial specificity, but also a temporal specificity; the moment of a transaction was, in important respects, ahistorical. Councilors that opposed the adoption of John Arthur et Tiffen's *Guide Foncier* were skeptical of a narration of the property market that depended on past experience as a frame for future action. Their market had no memory. Nor would the council; it purchased the one hundred volumes, but declined to subscribe to subsequent updated editions. In vital ways, real estate remained unknowable.

The ways developers narrated and quantified the city helped to constitute the real estate market in which they operated. Through their information channels, market diagnoses, and development tools, they worked to establish conditions for the profitable production, distribution, and consumption of built property as a commercial good. As speculators made decisions about what land to develop and what types of properties to produce, foremost in their minds was the need to appeal to buyers increasingly habituated to the easy productivity of money and the rapid circulation of wealth. Their efforts belied the "magical" effect of their production, as much as they challenged Halbwachs's notion that the speculator was called forth by the urban collectivity "as, according to one school of biologists, a need creates the organ."[102]

Publicly, speculators were ambivalent about their agency. Such ambivalence was, and is, an important component of establishing a market that appears to operate in a dispassionate and depersonalized manner, independent of the actions of any particular participant. By stressing their dependence on demand and their adherence to the already existing socioeconomic geography of the city, speculators naturalized their interventions in the urban landscape, giving their material and intellectual labor the appearance of common knowledge. Many of the tools at their disposal emphasized the imperative of crafting housing to match or follow the character of its surroundings; the evaluation manuals discussed above were one such tool, as were the compilations of property values that demonstrated the localized, embedded nature of property values. The weight of locality was inescapable. As Onésime Masselin turned reluctantly in early 1882 to exploring possible reasons for a developer's failure, he focused on the importance of addressing neighborhood requirements: "When you draw up a speculative project for a somewhat large piece of land, you must first of all look into the essential question of the *needs of the neighborhood,* putting nothing on paper before having thoroughly studied, in all its aspects, the opportunities for rental, the nature of rentals that are in demand, the level of rents, the possible demands and needs of future tenants, etc., etc. . . . Always build with an eye to the *needs of the neighborhood,* that's the key."[103]

Yet some of the most trenchant criticism of the operations of early Third Republic developers was that they were undertaken with seeming disregard for these "needs of the neighborhood," or *besoins du quartier.* As Planat's maps tried to relate, divergences between production and consumption, between the city of developers and the city of Parisian residents, were significant. To some, the source of the fault line was obvious. As a delegate from the Union Amicale des Maîtres Compagnons et Appareilleurs (Friendly Society of Master Journeymen and Stone Cutters) observed wryly of the building boom in 1884, "from every angle, they tried to do something that would make money."[104] Similarly, the real estate agency of John Arthur et Tiffen wrote in the same year: "Construction was no longer a goal, it was a means. . . . One called oneself a building entrepreneur in order to obtain credit."[105] The resulting constructions were, at their core, senseless; architectural critic Émile Rivoalen dismissed the buildings of the Trocadéro district for their utter lack of real utility: "Life is missing from these symmetrical heaps of brick, by which I mean a *raison d'être,* a proven and recognized *need.*"[106] Guided by an understanding of the city based on future limitless growth rather than expressed and current needs, speculators filled empty spaces with space that remained empty.

Invocations of the "besoins du quartier" expressed an understanding of urban space as a material and historical force that impressed upon and remained ungovernable by speculative interventions. The realities of use value—meaning the requirements of the city's population with regard to housing, as well as the inherited built environments of its neighborhoods—were seen to have the potential to stymie models of development based on exchange value. The city was not subsumed to the market, and speculators could get it wrong. Lenders seemed to think this a lesson worth paying attention to. In the aftermath of the boom, the director of the Sous-Comptoir des Entrepreneurs stressed that his institution would no longer support massive efforts to rewrite the urban fabric, singling out his company's involvement with projects such as the eighty-eight-building development by Fouquiau in Montmartre as a venture that would not be repeated. Rather than financing builders operating in new, empty regions, their operations of choice, he reported, would be "those in existing neighborhoods, which involve tearing down a ramshackle building and replacing it with one in the latest style."[107] These were impulses that Halbwachs would easily recognize: speculators were to follow rather than attempt to lead the city's natural development.

It is an indication of the contested status of real property as a commercial good that this crisis was conceptualized according to a politics of place rather than of the market. As important as economic mechanisms were to their models and behavior, speculators spoke of the city and its dynamics rather than those of "the market." Yet the point is that speculators were neither unconscious mediums for the organic evolution of the city nor the powerless intermediaries of supply and demand. Their practices and beliefs—as well as specific social spaces in which they operated—were responsible for the formatting of land and built property as commercial goods, a formatting that at the end of the nineteenth century was recognized as decidedly polyvalent and thoroughly social.

3

The Problem of Property

IN 1898 the city of Paris contained 1,432 streets classified as private roadways.[1] Opened on private lands by one or more property owners, these streets ranged from exclusive aristocratic enclaves such as the Villa Montmorency in the 16th arrondissement, to putrid laneways less than a meter-and-a-half wide in the poor, working-class districts of the city. They were core tools of urban development, often evolving from access roads, and were open to varying degrees of public circulation. While frequently turned over to municipal administration, the traces of these private contributions can be read in the landscape of the contemporary city. They constitute the everyday residential networks of *rues, villas, passages, impasses,* and *cités* that fill the interstices of Paris's monumental spaces, often visible today as much by their distinctive forms as by the names of their owners and developers.[2] Writing in 1873, Louis Lazare referred to them as "hermaphroditic streets," juridical and physical anomalies that posed moral and aesthetic challenges to the solidarity of the city.[3] Their barriers and gates, unstandardized lighting, and irregular paving were reminders of the multiplicity of interests engaged in constructing the urban landscape and the uneven process by which informal spaces were made visible and amenable to public governance.

Paris's private roadways are more than routes to the variegated spaces subsumed in the spectacle of the capital of urban icons.[4] They are paths to the physical, legal, and economic spaces available to private property owners as they undertook to define roles for themselves as agents in both urban development and the urban economy. The obscure byways of private streets prove a remarkably illuminating vantage point from which to discern the evolving relationship between the city and the owners of its real estate. Increasingly subject to municipal regulations adjudicating their form and amenities, private roadways no longer offered property owners the autonomy they once had by the time of the Great War. Yet they formed the seeding ground for forms of collective organization that seemed for a time to hold out the possibility of enhanced engagement of property owners in the public works that were reshaping the capital city.

We have seen that the political economy of urban development in early Third Republic Paris was characterized by consistent efforts to delineate the spaces and relations of public authority and private initiative. Property owners had particular roles to play in this context, roles they both demanded and were assigned as they asserted their development priorities. From the early 1850s calls had been heard encouraging property owner participation in the city's renovation. In the pages of *La Revue Municipale,* a consistent chronicler of the patterns and politics of Parisian development, a vision emerged of a network of property owner associations that would replace speculative capital, forming "one great Parisian association, funded by the capital of these same property owners, who will have every interest in making the company work because its success means the renovation of their neighborhoods and an increase in their fortunes."[5] But it was the political and financial circumstances of the 1870s that provided the requisite impetus for such a scheme. The Third Republic's first prefect of the Seine, the economist and later minister of finances Léon Say, disappointed those expecting a resumed public works campaign by advocating for complete abstention from state-sponsored urbanism, turning instead toward a reinvigoration of private initiative, particularly in the form of property owner associations. Say demanded that property owners take responsibility—and bear much of the cost—for projects that stood to improve their properties and their revenues. As partners with the city, owners were also advised to discontinue the habit of exorbitant indemnity demands that had developed in expropriation procedures during the latter years of the Second Empire. The city warned that such demands would no longer be considered, and could in fact provoke the city to drop a development project entirely.[6]

These impulses in the municipal government contributed to a political awakening for urban property owners.[7] Property relations in the capital city were strained in the wake of the siege and Commune. Rental contracts between landlords and tenants had been central points of contention during this tumultuous period, and for more than a year following the return to order, the cost of housing remained a contested issue subject to the intermediation of special rental tribunals.[8] Moreover, significant portions of Paris's built property had been damaged or destroyed. Much of the immediate reaction of returnees to the newly "liberated" capital expressed outrage and grief on behalf of its devastated landmarks. The urban landscape quickly became a nostalgic frontier, with photographs and tours of the ruins narrating the events as a tragedy of property rather than of people.[9] Not only did urban property thus acquire a new valence in the aftermath of the Commune, it was also quickly subjected to new taxes intended to ease the financial burden of reconstruction and the liberation of the country from the occupying Prussian army.

In response to these developments, in 1872 concerned property owners formed the Chambre Syndicale de la Mutualité des Propriétés Immobilières du XIe Arrondissement de la Ville de Paris, the city's most influential and longest-lasting property owner association.[10] With its membership booming from an original 108 to 8,585 members by 1900 (estimates place the total number of individual property owners in Paris at the turn of the century at around 48,000), this association constructed a new image for the modern urban property owner, crafting an understanding of the occupation as a *métier* requiring application and contributing significantly to the social and economic whole. It also dedicated considerable attention to formalizing the capabilities of property owners as agents of urban development. Much of the association's early lobbying efforts focused on extending an 1865 law on rural landowner associations to the urban setting, establishing a framework for the coordinated action of urban property owners in the arena of public works. They achieved this reform in 1888, though in application it departed significantly from the aspirations of its supporters, serving to further advance government authority over private initiative rather than empower private interests.

The mobilization of Parisian property owners (followed swiftly by those in other major urban centers) was also a response to broader economic transformations.[11] Despite the fundamental security of their juridical status across the political upheavals of the nineteenth century, urban property owners experienced great fluctuation in their social and economic positions. Parisian property became progressively concentrated in the hands of an increasingly professionalized property-owning class (that is, those who defined their occupation simply as property owner) between 1848 and 1880.[12] When editorialists and popular writers referred to these landlords as *Monsieur Vautour*—Mr. Vulture—they were attacking owners as simultaneously voracious and unproductive. Perceived in some circles as squatting on land and buildings that accumulated value and generated revenue even in the absence of their personal effort, property owners found it increasingly difficult to justify their profits and position within a political economy that supposed labor as the source of value. Luckily for owners, economic theories were shifting in the mid to late nineteenth centuries; utility was coming to be seen as an alternative source for the value assigned to a commodity. While they certainly did not neglect to foreground the work involved in property management, property owners benefited from the availability of competing models of economic value as another avenue of justifying their revenues. When the delegates meeting at the International Congress of Built Property (1900) sought to define and defend their interests, the meeting's Parisian president found it helpful to characterize property not as a status or right (though certainly it was also both), but as a market relationship and an exchange of services, its economic capacity more closely linked to social reproduction and distribution than to production.[13] Value came from the market itself, arising from the interplay of supply and demand.

An evolving investment environment, in which landed and built property faced increasing competition for middle-class savings from progressively more accessible and diverse investment options, shaped the place of property owners and their assets in the national economy. Movable assets—investments in traditional "movables" such as furniture and jewelry, as well as comparatively newer assets such as stocks and bonds—equaled immovable assets in the portfolios of French investors by the 1880s, and surpassed them by the period of the Great War.[14] In distinction to the dynamic world of the stock exchange, where fortunes appeared to be made and lost overnight and scandals routinely rocked the confidence and savings of investors, real estate's immovability stood out as a haven of stability: "What is there that is more solid, more tangible, more plain to the eye and more deserving of confidence than real estate investment, than stone and iron?"[15] Yet it also offered a frontier to be conquered by new kinds of commercial practice and financial experimentation. Real estate investment companies, whose shares "each represent a portion of real property," and thus, "by their nature, offer complete security, the certainty of profitable returns, and the probability of appreciation," represented the latest interpretation of the long-standing dream of mobilizing land values, a dream that wound through the financial projects of agricultural reformers, politicians, and economists from at least the eighteenth century.[16] Both economic theory and France's legal frameworks encountered difficulty in integrating real estate and its exchangeability into their concepts and procedures. The former took diverse and occasionally contradictory positions on the place of land in economic production, while the latter, in the form of the Napoleonic Code, excluded real estate and transactions upon it from the commercial sphere.[17] Organized property owners found their ability to mobilize and the scope of action available for their interventions determined to a significant degree by these wider transformations in the culture and practices of economic life. By illuminating the spaces and means available to private property owners in the urban development regime of the fin-de-siècle metropolis, we can recover a particular story of more general impulses toward the commercialization of property.

Private Streets and Public Interest

Paris's streets have for centuries been administered under legal regimes particular to the capital city. Most important among ancien régime legislation was the royal declaration of April 10, 1783. This regulation subjected the streets of Paris to the stipulations of the February 27, 1765, *arrêt du Conseil,* which applied to roadways maintained by the state and required builders to obtain official notification of the *alignement,* or building line, before undertaking construction.[18] In essence this obligated builders to obtain a form of building permit. The letters patent of August 25, 1784, followed on the tail of this legislation, regulating building heights in the city in relation to street widths. The 1783–1784 legislation coincided with Louis XVI's commission of Edme Verniquet's famous map of the capital city, and was intended to mitigate the densification that resulted from the midcentury emergence of the modern apartment house. Henceforth, it decreed, "no new roads may be opened or formed, for whatever reason, in the city and suburbs of Paris without authorization granted to this effect in the form of letters patent."[19] The size of new streets was also regulated and a minimum width of thirty feet was imposed. Other cities in the realm would not see their private street development subjected to the need for official authorization until 1807.

The particular Parisian regime of street governance continued to develop throughout the century, and had important implications for construction. Throughout the country, building on streets other than public roads required no authorization and was subject to none of the stipulations that regulated construction and building forms on the *voie publique,* or public way.[20] Instructions to provincial prefects in 1862 stressed that "if the area on which one wants to build or the building that one wants to repair does not abut the current public thoroughfare, an authorization is not necessary." Even if the lands in question "are intended as the site of a new or extended public thoroughfare," unless the process of legal expropriation is undertaken, "the owner ought to experience no hindrance in the legal exercise of his property rights."[21] In Paris, however, this particular element of the free disposal of private property was curtailed by the decree of March 26, 1852. This legislation formed the base of imperial urban policy; in addition to considerably expanding the state's powers of expropriation, it required all potential builders to submit detailed architectural plans in order to receive permission to begin their works. The centuries-old distinction between building on public and private streets was abandoned.

In principle the streets of the capital were thus made uniformly visible to the municipal administration. In practice, however, much confusion remained about the policing of construction on private streets. In fact, the status of those buildings not *directly* facing public roadways, such as constructions in courtyards (an extremely common building practice for both residential and industrial construction) was also murky. Regulation of building heights, for example, referred always to the façade height facing the public street, leaving the height of those buildings with their façades facing interior courts unpoliced. The Parisian practice of making the street the basic unit of urban development, rather than parcels of land or individual buildings, was responsible for the incredible interior densification of properties. Only with the increasing power of hygienic laws would regulation move from the façade and the street to address the private spaces lurking behind uniform building frontages.[22] The most important legislation in this respect was the 1884 regulations on building heights and courtyard sizes. This legislation also extended, for the first time, to specifically address properties comprising private streets, fixing their heights in a manner similar to those on public thoroughfares.[23]

Obstacles to the application of this legislation persisted, however. A letter from Paris's director of works to the director of public roads and walkways in 1888 reported that justices of the peace "often hesitate to pass judgments against property owners and entrepreneurs taken to court for having undertaken construction works in interior spaces without authorization." This hesitation, he explained, sprang "from the fact that the Decree of March 26, 1852, is entitled 'Decree relating to the streets of Paris' and also that the word 'authorization' doesn't appear in the text."[24] The dominance of streets both as the terminology and the target of official oversight limited the reach of the administration into interior—or interiorized—spaces. When the prefect consulted with a Réunion Générale des Architectes (General Council of Architects) on proposed changes to building height regulations in 1881, they spoke strongly against a perceived extension of administrative authority into the interior of property parcels, describing the measure as "a completely modern invention, which has been introduced illegally into practice and jurisprudence." Public hygiene laws, the council concluded, were being exploited in order to arbitrarily constrain the rights of property owners and builders: "By an incredibly elastic and entirely bureaucratic interpretation of the *repressive* law of 1850, the Prefecture of the Seine has assimilated interior constructions to constructions on the public way."[25]

Judicial authorities continued to be puzzled by the exact parameters of public authority over constructions on private streets well after the obligation to obtain a building permit was established in 1852.[26] Imposing on a property owner's right to freely dispose of their property—in this case, the right to build on it whenever desired—infringed on individual and social rights foundational to all regimes that governed France throughout the nineteenth century. It required serious legal consideration and accommodation. The 1852 decree that instituted authorizations for private building attended to the natural rights of proprietors when it designed the procedure for authorization requests. Once an owner had submitted all the appropriate documentation—namely, fully labeled and numbered architectural drawings and a request for the official street alignment and grade—they were able to begin construction within twenty days, providing the Prefecture did not issue a prohibition. This formula was established in order to respect a proprietor's freedom to build on their land by granting the municipality only a narrow window of time in which to move to restrict this right. As the Cour de Cassation cited in a decision in 1889, "art. 4 § 2 of the decree, as it is written, grants the Administration only a veto power, not the power to grant authorization."[27] It was not within the power of the municipality to *grant* a right, held by a property holder as a right of ownership, but only to *limit* the exercise of this right. And as legislators reflected elsewhere, even this power was strictly circumscribed; deciding on whether the prefect retained the authority to prohibit a construction after the expiration of the twenty-day delay, a decision of the Conseil d'État in 1906 responded in the negative, noting that "in effect, the regulatory provisions limiting the right to build are exceptional and extreme provisions; they restrain the property owner in the name of public utility, [and] must be interpreted in a narrow sense."[28]

Fundamental ambiguities in the character of the private street accentuated the potential for confused and irregular imposition of municipal regulations. It has been noted that authorization for new street development was required from the late eighteenth century. Yet this principle was moderated depending on the intentions of the developer. Streets opened by property owners with the intent of turning them over to public authorities required not only authorization, but also that developers fulfilled various conditions in their construction, such as maintaining minimum widths, establishing paving, lighting, and drainage systems in accordance with municipal standards, and allowing the whole to be supervised by an agent of the city. Once these works were completed, the private street could be classed as a public thoroughfare and its maintenance ceded to the municipality. Approximately fifty streets had been opened or extended by private individuals in the nearly two decades between 1830–1848; these numbers expanded greatly by the end of the century, as property owners, encouraged by the projects undertaken in the Second Empire and after, undertook "to find a better employment of their real estate assets by opening new streets that allow a profitable subdivision."[29] In the ten-year period between 1886 and 1896 approximately eighty such streets were opened and turned over to public administration.[30]

Yet it was not always the intention of a street's developers that the newly opened roadway end up in the public domain, a decision that could entirely change the regulations applicable to its construction. Owners that did not apply for the classification of their streets as public roads might face no conditions as to their form or amenities. The housing established on these passages was subject to the law on unsanitary dwellings of April 13, 1850, but the street itself faced no such sanctions, particularly when it remained closed to general circulation by gates or other devices. On the other hand, jurisprudence agreed that the absence of these gates constituted a tacit agreement on the part of the proprietor(s) to ensure safe and peaceable use of the thoroughfare, and an order of the Prefect of Police in 1888 made various hygienic measures obligatory in private roadways that were open to general circulation.[31] Failure to adhere to these measures, which included adequate lighting, maintenance of the roadway, freedom from encumbrances, and, in some cases, the addition of sidewalks, could result in authorities blocking access to the street.

Both property owners and the municipal administration could use a street's private status to their advantage. Private streets could act as a refuge from the increasingly stringent requirements of municipal policing, a way for owners to develop land while remaining, if not completely out of reach of administrative protocols, at least in a zone of heightened uncertainty with regard to the proper scope of governmental action. Even streets opened with the intention of being turned over to the city could capitalize on their private status in order to elude administrative oversight. In 1882 the Société des Immeubles du Faubourg Saint-Honoré opened Rue Saint-Philippe du Roule in the 8th arrondissement and let the administration know that while it would ultimately seek to turn the street over to municipal jurisdiction, the company would not request its classification as a public roadway until all works had been completed. As one of the city's engineers reported: "The goal of this manner of operating can only be to avoid the administration's oversight in order to save some money at the expense of well-executed works." As long as the road remained private, however, the city's intervention was limited.[32]

Owners might use private status to establish an elite enclave, but it was more often the case that a street's closure allowed for underserviced (if still socially and economically vibrant) zones of work and home for the city's more vulnerable residents.[33] In his study of Paris's working-class eastern districts, Louis Lazare chronicled the decrepit private streets and dank passages that wound through these regions.[34] In 1874 he wrote in *Le Courrier Municipal* of the dangerous privileges the physical and juridical cloak of the private roadway accorded to unscrupulous owners. He acknowledged that those roads that were opened with the intention of being handed over to the municipality were sufficiently regulated to satisfy the general interest. Yet avoidance of these regulations was far too easy: "If the owner of these same lands has the idea that his venture would be even more profitable if he opened only a *private passage,* or a *cité,* three or four meters wide, legislation is powerless [to stop him]. . . . He contents himself by executing the roadwork requirements that govern *only* the entrance of his passage or *villa* on the public thoroughfare. After that, on the inside [of the development], he can do as he likes."[35] While the police could ensure minimal levels of hygiene and safety on the street, they lacked the authority to demolish it or change its form. From this Lazare concluded that "there should be no such things as *private* streets in Paris."[36] Putting rental housing on a street and opening it to general pedestrian and vehicular traffic should terminate rights to private governorship of its spaces. The public life of the city must always trump the private interests of individual property owners. Lazare emphasized his point (and further illustrated the confusion that persisted regarding the right to build in the capital city) by insisting that "no house should be constructed in Paris, either abutting public roadways or on the interior of building lots, without authorization from the City."[37] Even buildings intended for the sole occupancy of their owner ought to be subject to these conditions, given the disjuncture between an individual's temporary tenure and a building's long-term impact on the landscape and collective life of a city.

For its part the city could use its refusal to accept streets as public thoroughfares as a stick to force builders to upgrade their properties, though this tactic was effective only with owners of some financial means. Once its owners officially requested public status, Rue du Saint-Philippe du Roule was forced to undergo many improvements before it was finally accepted in 1890. When builders of a new road in the 11th arrondissement approached the city to facilitate the joining of their property—which remained private—to the public way in 1884, an initial municipal engineer's survey was favorable, reporting that "the newly opened street is of sufficient importance that there is reason to remove the depression by which it currently connects to the public street." Moreover, the builders had agreed to pay for the operation, and to "accept in perpetuity all waters originating with the drainage gutter of Rue du Faubourg du Temple, regardless of future increases in the volume and composition of these waters." Unhindered access to the public way was a benefit for which property owners were willing to negotiate. Upon review, however, the head engineer denied the request and the bargaining of the petitioners, stressing that "as long as the owners of a private street show no intention of bearing the costs necessary in order to obtain its classification as a public street, the City has no interest in facilitating access to it." He thought it more appropriate that, until formally received by the city, the street maintain a visible sign of its private status.[38]

Even when property owners and builders gained approval for a street opening, this authorization did not guarantee that the city would assume control of the street upon its completion. Development standards played into the decision, as did the broader public interests of the city as a whole: "In effect, in addition to the free concession of the land and a perfect state of development, a street must respond to a collective utility sufficient to justify the expense that its maintenance will incur. In this respect, authorization [to open the street] is issued to property owners at their own risks."[39] The possible gains of this approach—namely, a more uniform urban fabric, standardized infrastructure, and development that effectively responded to the needs of the city—had to be balanced against the dangers of unregulated expansion of the type denounced by Lazare. A municipal engineer reporting in 1872 on the development progress of Rue d'Uzès—a street opened in the 2nd arrondissement on lands belonging to the Delessert family—rejected closing the street despite its dangerous condition, as such a move "will only advantage the builders, who would thus be complete masters of the terrain."[40]

The legislative warren and practical uncertainties surrounding private streets motivated some of the most significant legislative innovations in the realm of urbanism. Senator Paul Strauss complained in 1900 that "one *arrêt* classifies a private roadway as part of a building, while another refuses to consider it as part of the houses bordering it. As a result, in all cities, private roadways almost completely escape administrative intervention."[41] He was instrumental in establishing the February 15, 1902, law on public health (supplemented by the June 22, 1904, sanitary regulations for the city of Paris, which would act as the dominant piece of urban legislation for the city of Paris into the post–World War II period) as well as the July 22, 1912, law on sanitation of private roadways.[42] The municipality was dogged in its ambitions to minimize the elusive spaces within its jurisdiction. Where legal ambiguities remained, or where the Conseil d'État showed itself committed to defending the prerogatives of private property owners, the municipality responded with new regulations upholding uniform oversight over the city's streets.[43] Steadily the envelope for free or informal use of space was diminishing. Nevertheless, flexibility remained in both the framework and the application of the law, and thus in the forms of urban space populating the regimented boulevards and avenues of Haussmannian and post-Haussmannian urbanism.

The regimes governing Paris's roadways indicate the daily complexity of public-private coordination in the construction of urban space. They also introduce a key quandary confronting urban property owners at the end of the nineteenth century: the problem of association. In order to assert their privileges over the urban landscape, property owners under the Third Republic sought to formalize their role as agents of urban transformation through the establishment of official associations sanctioned to undertake public works. For more than a decade, representatives of Paris's property-owning class lobbied to extend to the urban setting the right to form associations in order to carry out projects of public utility, finally achieving their goal with the law of December 22, 1888. In practice (and despite the broader ambitions of the legislation), these associations were closely linked to the spaces of private roadways. Indeed, the modus operandi of Strauss's 1912 legislation built on the 1888 framework by enabling authorities to compel the formation of property owner associations for the improvement of private streets. These obligatory associations functioned by disassembling common property in the street: owners were required to quantify the extent of their individual interests and contribute accordingly to the shared cost of necessary renovations. From this perspective, these efforts to reform the condition and status of private roadways were part of a much more general discomfort with intermediary (or, to recall Lazare's term, "hermaphroditic") forms of proprietorship, a discomfort that echoed throughout academic, economic, and political discourse on property at the end of the nineteenth century.[44]

"The City Helps Those Who Help Themselves": Private Property and Association

Preoccupied with managing public finances and eager to distinguish their policies from the authoritarian practices of the Second Empire, municipal administrators willingly embraced the possibility of Paris's property owners forming associations in order to undertake public works and street development. In 1871 Prefect of the Seine Léon Say suggested that property owners, grouped in associations, might fruitfully replace exhausted public initiative.[45]

Following him, in 1872 municipal councilor Jules Léveillé proposed using property owner associations as agents of development that mediated between the corrupt concessionary politics of Haussmann and Say's abstentionist doctrines. These associations, Léveillé explained, "would be corporate bodies, working in coordination with the City, carrying out expropriations in their own names."[46] These entities would act in a manner similar to the private companies who had treated with the city under the previous regime, but they would be property owners investing in their own neighborhoods for long-term benefit, rather than speculators intervening for quick returns. Organized property owners, then, could act as a rejection of both authoritarian administration and unbridled corporate greed, reclaiming the urban landscape in the name of its inhabitants. The Council of the Seine embraced the proposal, declaring: "Considering the state of public finances, which are crushed under the weight of past commitments, all obstacles hindering individual or collective initiative should be removed so that individuals involved in a particular project can replace the State, the Department, and the City as broadly and as often as possible."[47]

A more active and proprietary stance toward urban projects was a particular aim of the newly formed Chambre Syndicale de la Mutualité des Propriétés Immobilières du XIe Arrondissement (hereafter simply the Chambre des Propriétés). The group propounded the virtues and utility of association, a concept central to Third Republic politics as it mediated the tensions between liberal individualism and socialist collectivism. The group enjoined property owners with "a well-known reputation of honorability," "the most complete and absolute disinterestedness," and "a common spirit of unity and accord" to second the efforts of other professional associations, making common cause to further the progress and salvation of the nation.[48] Association would counter "the natural tendency among property owners toward a certain indifference and isolation," reorienting their atomized habits toward collective action without effacing the sacrosanct principle of individual, private property.[49] This political message had a spatial corollary; as the group expanded across the city, the collective voice of "Paris's real estate interests" emerged to translate local into general interests.[50] The Chambre des Propriétés embraced Léveillé's report on proprietor associations immediately; it declared its willingness to take up the task of municipal development and expressed support for "truly conservative and socially minded ventures," such as the opening of roadways "that are useful rather than ostentatious, that are supported by the Parisian population, and that facilitate and increase the work of the building sector, the keystone of all industries."[51] The group's statutes noted the prefect's encouragement of property owner associations as one of its inspirations, and among its earliest stated goals was the facilitation of the administration's works on Boulevard Voltaire, an important artery located in the district from which the group originated.[52]

While the Chambre des Propriétés represented a new kind of property owner association, one that would quickly become the dominant voice of the capital city's propertied class, it was not the first property owner grouping to appear in the city. On the privately developed streets discussed above, associations formed by the owners of adjoining properties were occasionally constituted as a means of administering common spaces. In the 1840s, for example, when a property owner named Vincent Poncet collaborated with the Société des Nu-Propriétaires to create the "Nouveau Quartier des Martyrs" in the northwest of the city, proprietors on the Passage des Martyrs were automatically members of the property owner association.[53] The Société des Propriétaires Réunis de la Rue Neuve des Martyrs, dite "Passage des Martyrs" was responsible for the maintenance and policing of the street in the place of public authorities. In general assemblies every five years, an executive commission was established to oversee annual contributions for lighting, paving, clearing, and maintaining the street and its gates, as well for the wages and lodging of the passage's watchman.[54] Its governing power was demonstrated in 1854 when it successfully sued two individual owners for refusing to contribute their share toward the maintenance of the common roadways. As their lawyer argued, this street, constituting a community of interest, "is nothing but an association"; supporting the rights of one owner to extract herself from the rules common to all "would mean the destruction of contracts and the ruin of the development."[55]

Such associations were an important precedent for the types of associations under discussion at the beginning of the Third Republic. But as a rule these earlier groups were far more concerned with maintaining their private properties than with seconding the administration in development projects. They tended to be conservative institutions, their rules and obligations built into their acts of sale and their existence determined by the private status of the street. Moreover, the phenomenon was not widespread. A study of over one hundred private developments in Paris's 20th arrondissement in the nineteenth century returned only ten that provided for annual general assemblies of new owners.[56] Lobbyers for the promotion of property owner associations in the early 1870s were seeking a form of association that was explicitly public, oriented toward the general rather than the particular, and available to owners without any contractual basis for cooperation.

The key precedent for a new type of property owner grouping was the 1865 law on rural property owner associations, which allowed rural proprietors to form associations in order to undertake public works of collective interest.[57] It was the hope of municipal and state proponents of property owner associations, as well as of the Chambre des Propriétés, that a reworking of the law would allow its application in cities. Once modified, the law would not only grant urban property holders legal rights to collectively undertake development projects, it would also extend the rights of the majority of those owners in the face of intransigent individuals. Léveillé's report described the measure as a progressive reform, imposing new obligations to the collective interest on private ownership.[58] Associations would act as intermediaries between the individual and the state, merging the local and the citywide; the prefect would need to evaluate a project's general utility, yet the costs for these projects were to be underwritten by those likely to derive the most direct benefit. The city would promote works in those areas where property owners showed themselves willing to second their efforts.[59] As Léveillé concluded, "In short, we are telling each neighborhood: the City helps those who help themselves!"[60]

Yet to some the fracturing of the city in this manner represented a fundamental misreading of the nature of urban development. The rural law did not map identically onto the metropolitan landscape. The purpose of the 1865 law had been to recognize a type of interest, namely collective interest, that existed in an intermediary zone between the public and the individual, providing a framework for projects that did not meet the standards of public interest but were of significant importance to a group of individuals.[61] This intermediary interest was productive in rural settings, but it was deemed challenging, even dangerous, for the urban environment, where development undertaken by competing groups could dissolve into contradictory battles for local interests. An 1888 commentator on the law's proposed extension worried that "the creation of associations might necessarily lead to the division of the city and the elimination of its unity . . . it directly threatens one of the principles of our public law: municipal law and administration."[62] Municipal governance as the embodiment of public interests threatened to evaporate in the face of an assemblage of intermediary bodies; localities would replace the city. The newness of Paris's council made this an even more potent risk. As a direct consequence of these concerns, the "collective interest" of the 1865 law would later be excised from legislative proposals, replaced by the "public interest" of the city as a whole, an adjustment that radically shifted the scale of reference by which projects were to be conceived and approved.[63]

Other critics insisted that the nature of the urban environment itself defied a development approach premised on easily identifiable and localized returns on investment. A study on the financing of public works that appeared in 1873 faulted the proposed associations for a narrow conception of the relationships governing urban growth. Allegedly penned by Émile-Justin Ménier, an industrialist and member of both the Chamber of Commerce of Paris and of the Conseil Général of the bordering Seine-et-Marne department, the work was likely authored by Yves Guyot, a journalist, economist, and future Parisian municipal councilor and deputy who published several volumes on behalf of Ménier.[64] It was simply untrue, the book argued, that property owners and tenants in the immediate vicinity of a development project necessarily reaped the greatest benefit: "In a city like Paris, the advantages of completing works radiate outward in every direction . . . and it is possible that the inhabitants located on the edge of the city feel their effects as much as those situated in the center." The urban setting, in this vision, was a complicated and interdependent network, so complicated that the effects of a particular project were impossible to predict, and might take years to manifest. For this reason, allocating financial responsibility on the basis of geography could never accurately account for the range of costs and benefits entailed in modern metropolitan development. The author concluded, "In my opinion, the entire city forms a vast association. The interests of all those who live there are tangled and combined in a thousand ways."[65] Applying the logic of the property owner association on a citywide scale, Ménier/Guyot suggested an alternate program of financing public improvement schemes through a tax on wealth, distributed across the capital and its different branches of activity.

This discussion of the spatial and legal boundaries of the responsibilities of private (urban) property was informed by decades of legislative debate and political economic thought. The law of September 16, 1807, on wetland drainage was a key precedent for the 1865 law and an essential touchstone for reflection on the allocation of financial responsibility in urban development.[66] It provided the legal foundation for the state or municipality to recover a portion of the increase in property values that accrued to property owners following public works. These "indirect surpluses"—so called because they accrued to individuals other than those who had directly paid for the works and because property value increases were not themselves the primary goal of the works—were subject to public appropriation in order to ensure that expenses born by the community did not unduly benefit a handful of individuals.[67] Because land, a uniquely monopolizable and irreproducible good, was placed seemingly at random in the path of public works, value surpluses could not be credibly connected to the labor of owners. They stemmed rather from the efforts of the state, acting on behalf of the general public, which consequently, the reasoning went, enjoyed a legitimate claim on them. The law allowed for public authorities to recover as much as half of the property value increases stemming from their projects in the form of an indemnity imposed on owners. Unsurprisingly, the difficulty of determining what portion of an increase in value could be accorded to specific projects, and what the geographic range of implicated properties might be, was quickly apparent. As late as 1886 government jurists found themselves without any method of distinguishing between definite property value increases and mere "advantages" that accrued to properties as a result of their embeddedness in a "social milieu," in which public works were but one element influencing value.[68] No legal standard emerged, and individual cases were generally decided on their particular circumstances.

Although the 1807 law was rarely deployed by nineteenth-century administrations, it inaugurated the dream of self-financing development projects. The law gained new relevance at the end of the nineteenth century in the context of an international debate on the "land question," and the proliferation in a number of countries of state and municipal projects for the appropriation of increases in property values.[69] The economic rather than legal basis of these projects was found in the principle of the "unearned increment," theorized by James Mill and John Stuart Mill, and popularized internationally at the end of the century by American land reformer Henry George.[70]

A modification of Ricardo's theories of ground rent, the unearned increment refers to the inevitable growth in land values that occurs as a consequence of the endeavors of the collectivity and without the necessary contribution of the property owner, but from which the property owner alone benefits by virtue of his monopolistic right. It was an extremely thorny problem in political economy. By providing a way to distinguish between those portions of land's returns that legitimately inhered in the labor of the owner and those that did not, it simultaneously reinforced the labor theory of private property and introduced limitations on property rights. It was consequently subject to a range of political interpretations, and authors from widely differing perspectives debated the possibility and appropriate means of allocating these increments to social use. In France, liberal economist and mathematician Léon Walras sought to provide a sound mathematical basis for state appropriation of future land rent increases while maintaining the legitimacy and sanctity of private property. Similarly, progressive economist Charles Gide argued for the legitimate claims of owners to rent increases, but was intrigued by the possibility of applying George's single-tax reforms to "new" and "unoccupied" territories. Supporters of more thoroughgoing forms of appropriation included sociologist Maurice Halbwachs, who claimed that the perpetual nature of property ownership constituted a "hoarding" of land rent—most blatant in the practices of land speculators—that demanded "socialization" in the name of protecting the poor.[71] In the early 1880s, these debates inspired Parisian municipal councilor Joseph Manier to put forward repeated proposals for the municipalization of Parisian land, citing the precedent of the 1807 law and insisting to his fellow councilors that land values belonged to society and the city, not private companies or individuals: "Was it members of a real estate company who sowed the ground with five franc pieces? No. The City undertook everything."[72]

The experience of land organization in "new countries" at the end of the nineteenth century stimulated debate on the fundaments of private ownership in property and provided striking illustrations of the social production of land values.[73] James Mill had initially illustrated the principle of the taxation of the unearned increment with reference to the economic organization necessary to the peopling of new countries.[74] Yet if the transformation of alternative property regimes into regimes of private appropriation—the conversion of collective, common, or waste lands, as they were encountered and classified in the colonial setting, into private property—invoked the familiar problem of transforming nature into property, in the metropolitan context it was urban land, already long transformed by labor, that raised the question of the necessarily collective nature of property values.[75]

In his 1881 *Essai sur la répartition des richesses,* liberal economist Paul Leroy-Beaulieu wrote that urban property, even more so than rural holdings, posed a problem to a theory of proprietorship based on the value-producing power of labor. Of course, he asserted, urban property owners performed important tasks. The simple act of private appropriation served a vital role in shaping the urban setting, taming disorderly and unpleasant metropolitan environments through the sorting power of prices and rents. Moreover, he argued, this role was an inherently risky one; far from automatic and ensured increases in values (of the kind described in the theory of the unearned increment), urban property owners had to plan, strategize, and ultimately hazard their fortunes in their endeavors.[76] Despite this, Leroy-Beaulieu acknowledged, popular opinion held "that there is no inactivity so complete as that of the urban property owner," an inactivity that still manages to be "more richly rewarded than the most clever and energetic labor."[77] While chiding such characterizations, Leroy-Beaulieu was forced to admit that labor was an inadequate justification for the soaring property values of late-nineteenth-century cities. "What human labor," he wrote, "can justify prices of 200, 500, 1000, or even 2000 francs a meter for land in a large city?" The theories of value and land rent devised by midcentury classical economists—Leroy-Beaulieu singled out those of Frédéric Bastiat in particular—were untenable in the face of such realities. Instead, he conceded, the source of urban land values had to be found in the market, "in a set of exterior circumstances" that acted without the owner's participation.[78] Acknowledging the social elements of property's economic life, Leroy-Beaulieu shared conceptual ground with critics of the private appropriation of urban rents, echoing the observations of those such as Halbwachs, for whom "a profound solidarity" existed between the individual property owner and urban development: "Owners on a given street or in a neighborhood can be perfectly unknown to one another, but they will benefit as a group from everything that makes the street livelier, that brings wealthier inhabitants to the neighborhood."[79] The nature of cities transformed isolated owners into a de facto collective.

In providing a framework to facilitate the initiation of public works by urban property owner associations, modification to the 1865 law would arrange public and private contributions to the urban fabric to more accurately reflect the social nature of land values. It would provide individual owners, hitherto condemned to the inefficacy of isolation, with the conceptual and practical framework for collective action. Simultaneously, of course—and made explicit in the discussions of the municipal councilors to whom the law appealed—it imposed the cost of urban renovation on landowners themselves, a fact that makes the support of organized property owners somewhat surprising. Yet for more than a decade the Chambre des Propriétés and a core group of legislators lobbied to achieve the desired legislative reform. In 1875 the association's vice president, Léon Cochegrus, reminded its members that the contributions of private property to the urban collective remained inhibited: "When it comes to undertaking works of collective interest in common, urban property is condemned to a certain isolation, its full development along these lines often impeded by individual liberties."[80] In 1876 the Chambre des Propriétés sent a petition to the Chamber of Deputies and the Ministry of Justice requesting the opportunity to organize under the privileges of the 1865 law in order to "support the general and particular well-being of the country." Explaining its request, the Chambre drew upon familiar praise for the virtues of association. More particularly, the petition's authors directed attention to the benefits of urbanism organized and directed at the local scale, a kind of initiative from below that would compensate for the blind spots of administrators and negligence of large-scale speculators, thus "shortly bringing to distant and disadvantaged neighborhoods and cities the same benefits that central districts have had the good fortune to enjoy for quite some time."[81]

This emphasis on the virtues of the local was perhaps a strategic error. Elected officials were consistently skeptical of the ability of particular owners to represent general interests, and of local concerns to reflect public utility. The 1876 petition was rejected as dangerous in a city such as Paris, and the fourth parliamentary commission to which it was referred asserted that such associations "will never have a character of public interest sufficient to and prescribed by the law in question."[82] Undeterred, the Chambre des Propriétés collaborated with republican deputies Charles Floquet and Martin Nadaud to present a *projet de loi* to the Chamber of Deputies on March 1, 1877.[83] The memo sent by the association in support of the measure emphasized that support for urbanism directed by property owners would signal a return to liberal policies, empowering private initiative and rejecting the "long series of excessive loans" that characterized imperial practices and unfairly burdened the taxpayer. At the same time, however, the association insisted that individualist private property could adjust itself to the needs and rights of the collective: "It must be acknowledged that where public welfare is concerned, property rights can be negotiated."[84]

After several attempts and extensive discussion of the mechanisms that would delineate and represent the multiple interests involved in public works, the law of 1865 was successfully modified on December 22, 1888, allowing urban property owners to form associations with the goal of carrying out public works.[85] Projects would require the approval of the municipal council, followed by the authorization of the prefect—which kept the declaration of public interest in the hands of official representatives. In the case of only a majority of owners agreeing to the project, the minority could be expropriated once the project was authorized by a decree of public utility. As the law was making its way toward official status, members of Paris's municipal council began expressing hopes that property owner associations would submit plans for specific projects under discussion. In early 1887, nearly two years before the law became official, councilor Léon Donnat proposed that the council set aside 2.5 million francs as subsidies for these groups, citing their capacity to provide employment for Parisian workers while relieving pressure on municipal expenses. Not only could these groups operate in a more permanent fashion than necessarily intermittent public works projects, but by supporting them the council would "succeed in making those property owners who stood to profit from a project pay for it, rather than distributing the burden across the entirety of taxpayers and consumers."[86] Modifying the stance of his earlier writings on associations, Guyot, now sitting in the Chamber of Deputies as reporter for the budget commission, issued a report that enjoined municipal administrations to take advantage of the new law and invite property owners to contribute portions of their property value increases as "a kind of voluntary tax" to support public works.[87]

The practical impact of the law, however, fell far short of these aspirations, and it appears to have had a limited influence on the manner in which private property intervened in public development in Paris. The necessary regulations specifying the manner in which associations should be formed did not come until March 9, 1894, and it was not until 1897 that the first association authorized under the 1888 legislation appeared in the capital.[88] The second such association, founded in 1900, was in fact instituted by the Compagnie Foncière de France, a large property investment and management company, for the purposes of governing its private street development, Cité Vaneau, in the 7th arrondissement.[89] Between 1897 and 1914, nineteen associations were formed under the aegis of the 1888 law, and all targeted private roads and passages. In other words, these associations looked very much like the previous, contractual associations that managed private developments in the capital, and showed little sign of a progressive participation with regard to Parisian urbanism.

The lasting practical innovation of the 1888 legislation was the introduction of what were termed *syndicats autorisés*. The law not only gave property owners the right to form associations when unanimity was achieved among those concerned, it also authorized the formation of associations by administrative intervention when merely the majority of owners—defined by the size of properties and the amount of property tax—sought to cooperate. Of the nineteen associations formed between 1897 and 1914, eight took the form of authorized associations.[90] These authorized associations could be founded on the initiative of property owners, or the municipal administration could begin the process by calling the property owners of a given area into assembly. Yet this second path to authorized association, not attempted before 1900, was rarely successful. A 1914 legal study on private roadways noted that "despite persistent efforts, the prefect of the Seine and his administration have not succeeded in constituting the owners of a Parisian private street in this sort of group."[91] Even when the majority was interested in cooperating with municipal plans for their properties, their financial means were generally insufficient to permit significant undertakings, and often contributions were not forthcoming.[92] The associations of Boulevard Chauvelot and Rue Jean-Vaury, both founded in 1910, were subject to decrees naming officers to recover taxes that had not been paid in 1914 and 1913, respectively.[93] The inadequacy of the 1888 legislation, with regard to both the lack of subsequent private initiative and the difficulties that remained in the path of administrative intervention, would lead to the law of July 22, 1912, a hygienic measure applying to private roadways that introduced the *syndicat obligatoire*, an associative form that dispensed even with the necessity of the majority consent of concerned land owners. Henceforth the city could force owners of private streets to finance and maintain hygienic standards on their properties, obliging their spatial practices to fall into step with Parisian urbanism.

The campaign for the passage of the 1888 law was a specific permutation of the long-standing problem of delineating and allocating responsibility for urban improvements. Betterment values—the increases in property values at the heart of the 1807 and 1865 legislation on property owner associations and rural improvements—had been central to Haussmann's development policies. He successfully appropriated portions of them for the first six years of his projects, and once he lost easy access to them in 1858, he continued to finance his undertakings through concessionary companies that acquired these values for themselves. The 1888 legislation represented a new iteration of these methods. From some perspectives it can be seen as a type of "Haussmannization from below," wherein the public utility of the city was for sale to owners with the resources to collaborate and undertake developments. The city's political role as the adjudicator of public interest risked being ceded to the economic interests of a small group.[94] Yet state actors remained suspicious of the unstructured role of private property in the metropolis. This law subjected property owners to multiple administrative procedures, rejected any room for a collective interest specific to a group of proprietors, and placed on them instead the onus to prove the value of their proposed works to the public interest of the city. The form of the 1888 legislation highlights the dominance of public interest, ambiguously defined but certainly scaled to the level of the city as a whole and its expanding grasp on the production of urban space.

Property and the World of Commerce

The campaign for the passage of the 1888 law was an effort by property owners to lay claim to authority as producers of urban space and representatives of public interest. It was also an attempt to consolidate their position in a changing political economy. Sociologist Hélène Michel has noted that the last decades of the nineteenth century saw property owners relocated in the state recordkeeping apparatus from the "active" to the "inactive" population. Classified with liberal professionals before 1856, then grouped as "individuals without profession," in 1896 they found themselves categorized along with rentiers as those making a living from their investments, and placed among the inactive population. Michel explains this shift as a marginalization attributable to the growing social status of work or labor as the source of national wealth.[95] It is not obvious that this recategorization represented the drastic shift—or associated marginalization—that Michel contends, but it is clear from their own activities that property owners found themselves grappling with the issue of defining their place in the national economy. Property owner associations spread across the country, adopting a discourse of vocation, professionalization, and specialization that not only asserted the particular status of the occupation but valorized its contribution to the general (moral and economic) welfare. When the Chambre Syndicale des Propriétaires d'Amiens began its biweekly journal in 1891, it introduced its first issue with a description of the role of the property owner that was characteristic of this discourse: "The profession of property owner consists of employing building entrepreneurs, workers, buying materials, etc. The property owner is an industrialist: he produces and he maintains, and it is his duty to see to the defense of his economic and material interests by supporting the national labor effort."[96] Emphasizing at once specialization, industrial contribution, and commitment to the nation, these depictions claimed a place for the property owner among the country's most important producers and managers of wealth.

Although the debate on the nature of real property and its revenues was international, in France the country's legal code provided a particularly robust framework for situating real estate relative to the market. With clear distinctions between the civil realm, to which real estate belonged, and the commercial sphere, the question of commercializing real property—of rendering it an object of commerce—had a unique tangibility in the French case. As one legal student of the question opined, "Legal history teaches us that, in all times and in all places, real and personal property have followed diametrically opposed paths. . . . More than anywhere else, France demonstrates the spectacle of this grand rivalry in its most dramatic form, in all its fascinating twists and turns."[97] The relationship of real property to the world of commerce provided property owners with a particular set of tools and constraints as they sought to establish a clear position for the modern property owner in the nation's political economy.

Once the 1884 law on associations permitted—for the first time since 1791—associations of individuals for economic, commercial, industrial, or agricultural interests, the Paris Chambre des Propriétés seized the opportunity to assert its members' shared economic status by constituting itself as a syndicate under the aegis of this law. Yet they soon found their right to organize on this basis challenged. In January 1892 the group's president, Boucher d'Argis, received a letter from the Procureur de la République ordering the association to disband within three weeks. The basis for the directive was that the 1884 law could not be applied to property owners, as they did not constitute an economic interest group. Boucher d'Argis protested, defending the right of property owners to claim an economic identity and organize in its support, drawing a contrast with rural property holders and assimilating the activities of the urban property owner to those of the commercial tradesman and the professional property developer. Where the farmer merely maintains what has been provided by nature, he wrote, the urban proprietor creates as well as maintains, generating wealth where none had previously existed. Furthermore, he argued, no one took issue with the idea that corporations founded for the construction and management of urban property—here Boucher d'Argis cited specifically the Compagnie Foncière de France, the Société du Quartier Marbeuf, and the Société des Immeubles de France—were commercial entities with distinct and legitimate economic interests. It was impossible, he continued, that a distinction as to one's profession could be drawn merely on the basis of scale, when all property owners were engaged in risking capital and managing property. An urban property owner was as much a productive, enterprising force as the sprawling corporate organizations that were coming to dominate and define the Parisian property market.[98]

It is telling that the association's president chose to identify the contemporary property owner with the new joint stock companies rather than the more familiar figure of the professional hotelier. The distinction between the (commercial) hotelier and the (civil) owner of an apartment building had been hashed out in decades of legal and legislative proceedings.[99] Yet it was also important for the group to associate itself with the modern interests that were reshaping the networks of housing production and management in the capital. The promotional materials of the numerous real estate agencies expanding across Paris in precisely this period reinforced (and capitalized on) this association. Advertising its services to the capital's property holders, the real estate agency of John Arthur et Tiffen wrote in 1884: "Renting is a trade, especially since the market has been changed by the competition of large insurance and financial companies, well-established in the construction of large apartment houses." In a diagnosis of the property owner's professional status that ran directly contrary to the statistical categories employed by the national census, the article continued: "Property owners, who were previously mostly rentiers receiving steady income from their rents, are today true tradesmen."[100] As an increasingly commercialized actor operating in a competitive marketplace, Boucher d'Argis pronounced, the property owner "runs the same risks as the industrialist and the merchant."[101]

The idea of risk was central to the definition of an occupation, or a transaction, as a commercial one. Speculation and hope of profit, with the attendant risks they implied, were the constitutive attributes of a commercial act under France's legal codes, and thus formed the legal, moral, and economic essence of commerce.[102] The freedom of commerce instituted by the Décret d'Allarde (1791) and the constitution of 1793 rested on an identification of commercial actors as, in the words of one historian, "taking deliberate risks, voluntarily engaging in commercial acts and accepting of their own free will the vagaries of prices, of free competition, the risks of bankruptcy and of trade."[103] The parameters of "good" and "bad" speculation established over the course of the nineteenth century hinged on their treatments of risk. Good speculation was that which did not interfere with free competition and freedom of trade, and remained unimpeachable as the motor of the market; bad speculation, in contrast, reduced risk by illicit means, by monopoly and hoarding, an infraction with which speculation was closely connected in the criminal code.[104] Risk thus served as a measure that distinguished between legitimate and illegitimate forms of economic practice. It separated safe investment from foolish speculation, and provided a means of evaluating balance and fairness in commercial exchange. Hence its utility to property owners seeking a justification for the profits derived from their industry.

Yet the "business" of property ownership often failed on precisely this front, appearing instead as a monopolistic and risk-free venture. An 1860 pamphlet penned by journalist Alexandre Weill puzzled over the nature of urban proprietorship, expelling the property owner from economic relevance on the basis of the security of his investment: "There is no way in which the property owner can be considered as a laborer. Neither can he be compared to a silent partner [*commanditaire*] nor to a merchant, because *he never risks his capital*."[105] Weill referred specifically to privileges such as payment of rents in advance and insurance against property damage that insulated owners from the dangers faced by capital ventured in other spheres. Indeed, the majority of property owners in the city of Paris were engaging in traditional investment practices. They owned, on average, between one and two buildings (a number that declined slightly from midcentury to the end), and in most cases were not owner-occupiers, a status limited to the very rich and the very poor. As the prices of buildings increased across the century, ownership became the prerogative of an increasingly professionalized property-owning class whose members purchased and retained, rather than resold, their buildings.[106] Even as housing production became increasingly speculative, property owners consumed housing as a ready-made good and did not tend to resell. The apartment buildings constructed by developer Albert Laubière and several of his collaborators in the 1880s and 1890s on Rues Pétion, Pache, and Camille Desmoulins in the 11th arrondissement, for instance, were very rarely resold by their initial buyers (and only once was a building alienated in less than ten years from the date of acquisition).[107] These buildings were purchased as investments and were not intended for occupancy by their owners. Only two buildings on Rue Pétion, one on Rue Pache, and none on Rue Camille Desmoulins were home to owner-occupants.[108] Approximately one in four buildings in Paris housed its owner at the turn of the century, but the geography of this distribution was far from even, and significant portions of the city—evidence such as this suggests regions of speculatively developed housing, in particular—were devoid of owners drawing use value from their properties.

The character of this investment was determined by a ground shift occurring in the national financial landscape. Whereas real estate had once dominated the portfolios of French investors, it was steadily diminishing in significance in the second half of the nineteenth century. The profusion of savings banks and popular credit institutions such as the *caisses d'épargne*, the multiplication of financial circulars—from 39 in 1873 to 242 by 1904—and the steady diversification of instruments and securities supplied by the Paris Bourse and its unofficial corollaries spread the idea and mechanisms of savings and investment throughout early Third Republic France.[109] In his series on the country's "financial mores," economic commentator Alexis Bailleux de Marisy contended that ownership of stocks and bonds was more democratized in France than in any other country in the world, while the prolific turn-of-the-century statistical studies of Alfred Neymarck, member of the Society of Political Economy and editor of the journal *Rentier*, seemed to confirm these impressions.[110]

This evolution had consequences for real estate investment beyond a reduction in potential capital. Not only did the sociétés anonymes that engaged in real estate development and management establish new modes of investing in real property, but the broadening of participation in financial markets increasingly normalized the productivity of money and resituated the place of property management in the economic landscape. Even though property owners' claims to be engaging in risk-laden industrial pursuits may have become increasingly untenable in comparison to the booms and busts of the stock market, the apparent ease with which securities produced returns for their owners underscored the time and labor—the work—required of property ownership. Belle époque guides to wealth management in fact often rejected property investment as too tedious and demanding for the modern investor.[111] Gazettes dedicated to property sales at the turn of the century never failed to recommend real property as the safest and most respectable employment for accumulated capital, but even they could not avoid the reality that such investments required more care and attention than others. A column that appeared in the wake of the 1882 stock market crash in the real estate circular *Le Foncier* reminded readers of the reliability of the property market, a reliability that indeed demanded more personal attention: "Certainly, a purchased building doesn't appear in black and white in the daily listings of the Stock Exchange, like the Union Générale [bank]. And yes, the management of a building requires more effort than clipping coupons [from a bond]; it requires repairs, putting up with tenants, responding to concierges, etc. . . . But surely this is slight compared to the ruins accumulated at the Exchange."[112] The work of property management contrasted with the ease of accumulation—and ease of loss—of movable assets.

Uncertainty regarding the economic position of the property owner as the century drew to a close can also be linked to the conflicted status of property as a merchandise or an object of commerce. France's legal framing of the commercial sphere drew important distinctions between the realms of real property *(biens immobiliers)* and that of personal property *(biens mobiliers)*. The architects of France's legal codes were concerned with property as patrimony rather than as exchangeable good; Napoleon himself insisted that the state found its advantage "in the stability of property within the same families."[113] The Napoleonic Code perpetuated associations between landed proprietorship, nobility, and social order; its treatment of real estate was tinged with an anticommercial ethos that found little value in facilitating the expansion of credit and debt. Real estate and its transactions were thus not included in the realm of commercial law; while not explicitly excluded from the legal category of merchandise (article 632 of the new commercial code), *biens immobiliers* were omitted from discussions of the jurisdictions of commercial courts, which referred only to *meubles* or *biens mobiliers*.[114] Real estate served as the conceptual Other of the commercial realm, a realm of enforced durability, reliability, even obscurity that paralleled the fugitive, fluctuating, and transparently priced sphere of commercial exchange. The natural attributes of immovable and movable goods served as the foundation for defined realms of society and market.

Nevertheless, real estate's status as a merchandise was persistently tested throughout the century. If jurisprudence generally held to an interpretation of real estate and those dealing in it as civil entities, there were frequent instances of lower courts and juridical debate endorsing contrary judgments.[115] The Tribunal de Commerce of Poitiers admitted real estate speculation as a commercial act in 1850, suggesting that the definition of merchandise crafted by the Commercial Code no longer suited conditions of modern exchange: "What reason is there to maintain real estate speculations carried out with the sole goal of generating profits outside the realm of commercial operations, given that the term 'merchandise' is currently routinely applied to purely intellectual goods, such as an author's property rights over their literary, artistic, and scientific productions?"[116] Similarly, in 1868 the Tribunal de Commerce de la Seine argued that in the hands of certain enterprises, real estate in fact becomes "a means, an instrument of work, an object of commerce." More importantly, the court added, the formation of stock companies engaged in the production and management of apartment buildings eliminated the "natural" immobility of real property by creating shares that "effectively transform their real assets into easily transmissible movables" circulating "from hand to hand," in perfect accordance with the commercial code's definition of merchandise.[117] In both cases, the Cour de Cassation overturned the lower rulings, upholding the noncommerciality of property transactions. However, as the editors of the Dalloz series of jurisprudence noted in 1882, a number of jurists, including eminent figures such Raymond-Théodore Troplong, had acknowledged the need for the legislature to admit the possibility that buildings and other real assets could be considered objects of speculation, even if only in those instances in which transactions occurred between reputed commercial actors.[118]

Real estate's legal standing certainly influenced the conditions of its production and distribution. Yet the range of actors and interests that converged around the business of real estate ensured that its commercialization proceeded apace. The development of sociétés anonymes that owned and constructed buildings, particularly in the capital city, steadily challenged the "natural" immobility of built property. The building booms they spurred helped create an image of real estate as an easily exchangeable material good. Speaking to the first International Congress of Built Property, held in Paris in 1900, lawyer André Jacquemont observed that "speculation on buildings has taken on such proportions that one wonders whether the word 'merchandise' from article 632 of our commercial code might not also refer to buildings."[119] Jacquemont went on to insist that the only way to successfully speculate in built property was to treat it as a merchandise like any other, subject to the laws of supply and demand: "One must begin from the principle that because the house is *merchandise* it must find a taker."[120] But the liberalization of the société anonyme not only established new models for understanding the treatment of property as a physical good. It also accelerated and diversified real estate's translation into movable forms, abstracting the material—a particular group of buildings with a specific location and attributes—into transferable shares priced on the stock exchange. Shares in such companies could be assimilated to stones in a building, benefiting both from the stability of this immovable property and the ease of transaction of paper wealth.

These developments were sufficient to force accommodation from the legal arena, accommodation that amounted to nothing less than the commercialization of elements of the civil code.[121] Most importantly, an 1893 law sought to end the ambiguity hounding corporate involvement in property development by automatically qualifying all limited liability joint stock companies as commercial entities. Henceforth, real estate development and investment companies that mobilized millions of francs of property, shares, and bonds, and that had nevertheless been treated as civil entities—companies as huge and consequential as the Panama Canal Company, the failure of which was rocking political and economic circles in the early 1890s—would be recognized as commercial ventures. This law was formulated in response to the quandary that such enterprises presented to commonsense understandings of market activities, offering a route to facilitate their business endeavors while avoiding the far more revolutionary act of redefining the status of property itself as merchandise (which would occur in 1967).[122]

New possibilities of real estate investment via the ownership of shares in sociétés anonymes represented a marriage of *mobilier* and *immobilier* that was viewed favorably by many fin-de-siècle commentators. It dovetailed with a range of contemporary efforts to experiment with shareholding as a path to proprietorship for the lower classes.[123] As a financial advice and advertisement journal of the early twentieth century noted, "The high prices of buildings render them inaccessible to modest purses," while "the difficulty of liquidating a property also dissuades middling investors." Fractional ownership, in the form of investment in a recommended property firm, could provide both the social benefits of ownership and the financial benefit of easy mobilization, bridging the "ancient divide between movable and immovable assets [that] has survived in some forms down to the present day."[124] From its founding in 1852, the Crédit Foncier, the country's central mortgage bank, had familiarized an increasingly broad demographic with the revenue-generating potential of real estate thanks to the huge numbers of bonds it issued in order to support its lending activities. By 1890, the company had placed more than 2 billion francs worth of mortgage instruments among savers.[125] The turn of the century saw the formation of property investment firms aimed specifically at the working classes, such as the Fourmi Immobilière (founded 1899), a company that entertained its shareholders in 1911 with a story of a young boy asking his grandfather to "buy me a hundred francs worth of house."[126] These enterprises sought to mobilize property through mechanisms perfected in stock exchange. Real estate man J.-B. Boisselot called his business La Mobilisation Foncière and offered clients "real estate investments accessible for everyone," explaining that "mobilization is achieved by constituting a stock or ownership interest company *for each building,* with the particular goal of acquiring, owning, and administrating this building and of dividing net revenues among the shareholders or associates."[127] Reporting on this endeavor, the Chambre des Propriétés applauded what they saw as "the *democratization of real estate investment,* allowing modest rentiers and capitalists, even employees, workers, and any laborer that has some savings, to engage in investment in apartment buildings."[128] This broadening of property's appeal, they reasoned, could only serve to bolster the position and strength of property owners vis-à-vis the demands of the state, engaging increasing numbers of citizens in the tasks and interests of proprietorship.

Yet this mobilization of property—a term of art in the nineteenth century—was by no means uncontroversial. When administrative proposals appeared near the end of the century for the compilation of a *livre foncier,* a government register of the country's property titles modeled on registry systems in Germany and Australia, commentators recognized that its goal was to render property transactions more reliable, potentially encouraging the circulation of property.[129] A prolonged discussion on the livre foncier occurred at France's first Congress of Built Property, held in Lyon in 1894. Lawyer and political economist Charles Brouilhet spoke in defense of the registry. Property values, he observed, were approximate and opaque; the livre foncier would provide the legibility necessary to generate confidence and contribute to the fluidity and simplicity of transactions. While acknowledging that "some will likely object that the ancient hearth should not become an ordinary article of merchandise," these individuals were woefully out of date—"a few hundred years ago," he quipped, "this objection would have had some basis." Given the current economic climate, "it is absolutely necessary that a serious commercial dynamism form around urban buildings."[130] He went even further, praising the system for offering the basis upon which titles could be created that could be used both as bills of exchange and as bearer bonds, opening the commercial sphere to property owners. But the majority opinion, heartily applauded by the congress, was expressed by Georges Deloison, former legal counsel to the Parisian Chambre des Propriétés and president of the Union of Built Property Associations of France, founded in 1892–1893. Deloison vehemently opposed the livre foncier. After enumerating the logistical and logical impediments to the functioning of such a registry, he attacked what he perceived as its moral danger: the abstraction of landed property into ephemeral paper wealth. The goal of this project, he wrote, "all obstacles overcome, all sacrifices made, all the principles of our law and all previously sacred interests abandoned, aims at replacing land by a negotiable share, like a bearer bond." Such a transformation not only raised the danger of speculation and economic destabilization. It posed a threat to the moral economy of the nation, encouraging people to view land not as an inalienable component of the homeland, but as a venal commodity. Substituting the "nobility" of land for a "simple exchange value" would lead inexorably "not only to the *mobilization* but also to the *demoralization of land*."[131]

Broad social and political opposition to the depopulation of the countryside hobbled partisans of property mobilization. Making it easier for property to be transferred, either through sales or transmissible credit notes backed on land, would, it was feared, make it easier for rural landholders to leave or be deprived of their properties. The last decades of the nineteenth century saw increasing focus on the plight of the rural landholder and the social and economic perils of the *déracinement* (uprooting) of peasants. At the very moment when the first Congress of Built Property was being held in France, Deputy Jules Léveillé—the former municipal councilor so enthused about the contributions of property owner associations to public works—was presenting a proposal to import to France an American law on the inviolability of the family home. Termed the "homestead law" (though it differed considerably from its American namesake), this reform was intended to preserve a debtor's family property from his creditors, and thus to limit property mobilization and increase the stability of the rural population.[132] One historian has noted that the French homestead law specifically aimed to minimize the marketplace involvement of rural citizens.[133]

At the 1900 International Congress of Built Property, the danger of the livre foncier as a tool for property mobilization and an incentive to rural depopulation again took center stage. The nearly alchemical power of the proposed land registry system was described as follows: "And *voilà,* all at once, the property right represented as a security ceases to be connected to the material object to which it refers and becomes an immaterial good. . . . Rather than an object of exclusive, material appropriation, or of purely individual use value, property has become a true instrument of exchange and circulation."[134] This abstraction, signaling a shift in power from landholders to financiers, as well as from the individual to the collective, was also conceived of in spatial terms, as a realignment of sites of influence in the national economy. Reports at the Congress continued on the specific dangers of rural depopulation: "Is this really the moment to turn the eyes of the peasant away from the lands he tends, accustoming him instead to seeing only the easily negotiable security that will allow him to capitalize on them in the city?"[135] Even if peasants did not sell off and move, land mobilization would elevate the Stock Exchange over the village square, securing the victory of urban speculation over agriculture.

Mechanisms and imperatives that increased the traffic between real estate's movable and immovable aspects shaped the world of property investment in the nineteenth century. Innovations in the business of real estate, from the transferable shares of the société anonyme to the bonds of the Crédit Foncier, were important in this regard. So, too, was the long reach of international political economy and the reinvigorated colonial expansion of the turn of the century. The acquisition and occupation of colonial territories obliged the imposition of land registry systems that served simultaneously to secure property rights and to establish the means of depriving (indigenous) people of them.[136] Supporters of the French "homestead act" perceived this threat, and it is likely that the self-appointed representatives of property owners who gathered at repeated congresses, consistently opposing state efforts to improve the transparency of France's property system, grasped it as well. Indeed, it explains their enthusiasm for the application of the livre foncier in Algeria, Tunisia, or Madagascar.

Property owners who disdained the application of the livre foncier in France availed themselves of arguments dating from at least the mid-eighteenth century that prescribed a particular, irreplaceable role for land and real estate in national political and economic life. Along with the effort to disband the Chambre des Propriétés on the ground that its interests were not sufficiently economic, these instances highlight the contradictory impulses buffeting property owners as their patrimonies seemed to be losing out in the competition for fortune and prestige. Ultimately the 1892 request that the Chambre des Propriétés disband as a professional syndicate was abandoned. The Paris association secured the support of Pierre Waldeck-Rousseau, author of the 1884 law on associations under which they had organized. The deputy advocated for an inclusive interpretation of the law and asserted the professional status of the urban property owner, emphasizing their position as wealth-producers and employers. Unlike rentiers, he explained, "an urban building does not generate its own income. Revenues result only from continual efforts. Making it run requires employing workers, often permanent employees. The owner has to work his house. Thus, he exercises a profession."[137] Just as with the defenses offered by property owner organizations themselves, the source of wealth was not to be found in built property itself and automatic, unearned increments, but rather in the labor of the owner, a labor that constituted the owner as an active economic agent and justified his proprietorship.[138]

Property owner associations continued to operate in a legal grey zone until a new law on associations was passed in 1901. This law provided a less explicitly commercial mode of representation—signaled in the abandonment of the term "syndicate"—and the Paris Chambre des Propriétés quickly reconstituted itself under this form. Organized property owners continued to evidence difficulty with the economic definition of their activities. Increasing pressures for the commercialization of real estate threatened the particular place of property in the nation's moral economy, a matter of no small concern to a group preoccupied with its social status. Yet it also provided them with the means to assert their utility and relevance. The organization's presidential address of 1905 combined these impulses, invoking Auguste Comte and observing approvingly that soon citizens would have but one right, "that of freely fulfilling his role or social duty." For property owners, this social role was conceptualized in terms of ethical commercial exchange: to provide housing that was hygienic, spacious, and well-aerated, and to do so in exchange for a reasonable rent. Apartment buildings, president and law professor Léon Duguit continued, were not elements of production, but rather, in the words of political economist Charles Gide, "objects of consumption, since like clothing or food, they are end-user products and are actually used for the needs of those that inhabit them."[139] The self-appointed representatives of urban property owners increasingly explained their contributions to national economy by emphasizing the productive role of the distribution and consumption (rather than production) of urban space.[140]

Individual proprietors were the norm in late-nineteenth- and early-twentieth-century Paris, but they did not have a monopoly on defining marketplace relations or the status of housing in the urban economy. The landscape in which their buildings were located was also subject to the activities of speculative builders and the investment practices of corporations that reshaped the nature of ownership. In a remark that overestimated the numerical presence of corporate owners in the Paris housing market but accurately captured their qualitative influence, *Le Temps* could report in 1912 that the "the hard heart of M. Vautour" had been replaced by a new owner, "most often a limited liability company whose shares are dispersed among thousands of shareholders."[141] The proliferation of these new actors was accompanied by a diversification of property-owning practices—such as the rental arrangements with speculative builders discussed in previous chapters—that blurred the line between ownership and entrepreneurialism, between investment and speculation. At the same time the economic landscape that defined real estate ownership was evolving. The rise of securities investment simultaneously encouraged the commercialization of property and its particularization as an embedded asset. On the one hand, turning property into shares seemed to open new avenues of wealth production, challenging any juridical or administrative categorization of real estate as an inactive element of national wealth. Similarly, proponents of improved land registration, both at home and abroad, sought new means to mobilize land values and increase the security, rapidity, and quantity of property transactions. On the other hand, mobilization and commercialization remained dependent on real estate's status as an ontologically different sort of good, one whose finite, immovable, and monopolizable elements guaranteed stability for both individual investors and the national economy.

The built and business environment of the late-nineteenth-century capital thus provided organized property owners with multiple but ultimately contradictory tools with which to promote their particular interests. The demands of property owners for more involvement in the patterns and methods of the capital's development, manifested in the campaign for the extension of the 1865 law to the metropolitan setting, was a response to their exclusion from the realm of production of the urban fabric, an exclusion perpetuated both by Haussmann's centralized development scheme and by the steadily growing array of "urbanism professionals" such as architects, engineers, and public works entrepreneurs. It was also part of an effort by urban property owners to assert their role in the national economy as productive actors capable of mobilizing and contributing to the public welfare.

Only the strength of these impulses seems to explain how organized property owners apparently failed to grasp that the economic and political goals of the 1888 law were at odds with their own conception of their role in the city. This contradiction emerges clearly when that law is read alongside the evolution of the regulatory framework structuring private roadways, a framework whose mechanisms were closely linked with the associations legalized in 1888. Both the attempt to master the spaces of the private roadway and the law on development associations followed the same priorities: devolving the cost of urban development to those understood as its most direct beneficiaries. Both foregrounded the social and collective elements of urban proprietorship and privileged the general interest of the municipality over the particular interest of the individual owner. In the case of private roadways, the move to sanitize particular streets emerged as a planning priority thanks to a hygienic vision of the city in which blighted areas increasingly posed threats to their unblighted surrounds.[142] Roping private streets into a common administrative vision meant threatening owners with expensive repairs and maintenance while progressively stripping them of their "privilege to be masters at home," as lawyer Henri Talamon put it to assembled owners at the National Congress of Built Property in Nice in 1911. Soon "owners on private streets will find no further advantages in their property, but rather a quantity of burdens."[143] As for urban development associations, their legal precedents were firmly rooted in an understanding of land values as socially produced, divorced from the labor of the property owner and hence open to redistribution. While the Chambre des Propriétés was eager to prove conciliatory to the public interest, the purpose of forming interest groups and promoting a discourse of professionalism and expertise was specifically to avoid giving ground before such claims of justified expropriation. Neither were lawmakers exempt from miscalculation with regard to this legislation. The state and municipal authorities who promoted the 1888 law did not see that its attention to private property as a producer of urban space was out of step with the new role of urban property owners in the distribution and consumption of space. For all these reasons, the law on urban development associations was a failure.

Some of the changes to the status and nature of property and property owning in the urban context were the result of transformations that were national, even transnational, in scope: the *embourgeoisement* of the property-owning class, the increasing relevance of collective or amalgamated capital (namely, corporate interests) in property development and management, evolving attitudes toward wealth and its production, and international examination of (and experimentation with) systems of property ownership and distribution. These transformations made the alignment of private proprietorship with the general rather than particular interest increasingly difficult. More than ever, urban proprietorship seemed the territory of an elite, and one dedicated increasingly overtly to profit through enhanced methods of commercialization. Yet these transformations were anchored in the specific material and political context of fin-de-siècle Paris, contexts that determined the conditions of possibility for the behavior of private property owners as they set about promoting claims to economic citizenship and urban governorship. The contrast between the hopes and realities engendered by the 1888 law suggests the limitations of the local with regard to Parisian urbanism in this period. Despite the persuasiveness of the ideal of locally organized interventions in the urban fabric, the limited successes of associations, soon followed by the withdrawal of organized property from discussions of the proprietor's role in the production of urban space, illustrates the difficulties in rendering localized efforts intelligible in the generalized space of the city. As owners became market actors, their role as urban actors became less intelligible and the spaces—physical and juridical—for collective action more constrained.

4

The Unceasing Marketplace

Estate agent A. Thibou's 1880 advertisement for his "Commercial, Industrial, and Financial Agency" in France's business directory, the *Annuaire Didot-Bottin,* proposed a staggering breadth of services to the public:

> Purchases, sales, and management of estates, commercial properties, and industrial establishments. Litigation, collection of annuities, rents, and credits, commercial information. Drafting of private agreements, associations, financial partnerships, stock flotation. Accounting; opening, adjusting, and updating entries; inventories, balance sheets, trade-offs, consultations, liquidations, private arrangements, debt compositions. Capital investments, loans, advances on stock/bond deposits, mortgages, stock orders. Purchase and sale of all merchandise on commission. Acceptance of invention patents, registration of designs and trademarks, representation at expositions, publicity in France and abroad.[1]

All of these and more were activities undertaken by the typical *homme d'affaires* or *agent d'affaires* in Third Republic France. Closely related to the legal profession, these individuals took advantage of regulations prohibiting officers of the court from engaging in commercial activity in order to develop all manner of enterprises requiring legal and commercial expertise. Defining themselves variously as representatives, intermediaries, brokers, and advisors mediating the affairs of buyers and sellers, they exemplified the increasing importance of distribution, marketing, and consumption with regard to production in the latter decades of the nineteenth century.[2] Contemporaries viewed them as the quintessential expression of commercial society. A demonstration of "the principle that need creates the organism," as one student of the sector put it, agents found their niche "as economic transformations make people increasingly strangers to one another even as they are increasingly dependent on one another." Indeed, they were so closely tied to the flux of commercial activity that an enumeration of the field, "supposing it was exact today, would be lacking or completely inaccurate tomorrow, given the ebb and flow of economic imperatives."[3]

Agents d'affaires are particularly important figures in the history of Paris's real estate market. Property business figured prominently in their activities; management and rent collection, drawing up acts of sale, brokering mortgages, and coordinating real estate transactions were key aspects of their expertise, and areas in which they sought to challenge other individuals, chiefly the notary public, for clientele. While involved in the capital's real estate market from the early nineteenth century, agents dedicating themselves exclusively to property transactions were few in number before that century's final decades. The specialized real estate agent emerged from the ranks of the hommes d'affaires in steadily increasing numbers from the 1870s; by the turn of the century professional organizations began to appear, assembling agents who trafficked in buildings, commercial sales, and apartment rentals.[4] The pages of the *Annuaire Didot-Bottin* testify to property brokerage's rapid expansion. In 1855 the directory listed 249 agents d'affaires in the capital city under the heading "Estate Agencies and Commercial and Property Sales." In 1862 this group had grown to more than 350. In addition there appeared a new category, "Apartment and Property Rental Agencies." From 1870 the general listing of agents d'affaires diminished as it was hollowed out in favor of more specialized vocations. In addition to rental agencies (a listing that continued to grow throughout the final decades of the century), others such as property managers, commercial property brokers, and the entire heading "Buildings, Sale and Purchase of" were introduced for the first time in the 1880s and 1890s. The category "Hommes d'Affaires" appeared following the formation of the Compagnie des Hommes d'Affaires du Département de la Seine in 1876, an association of agents d'affaires who identified themselves closely with the legal profession and who discarded the commercially inflected term "agent" in order to signal a certain professional distinction. Between 1899 and 1902 Maxime Petibon's annual *Manuel Officiel des Affaires Immobilières et Foncières de la Ville de Paris* listed 125 substantial real estate agencies in the capital city, while the official census of professions in 1896 recorded 807 individuals—including 141 women—working in property sales and rental agencies in Paris and a further 75 in the immediate suburbs.[5]

At precisely the moment when property owners and developers, industry observers, and legal commentators were debating the legal framing of property as a merchandise and raising the (political, economic, and social) question of its most appropriate forms of circulation, the specialized estate agent began to formulate a distinct professional identity based on their role as mediators in urban property markets. Parisian estate agents formulated projects to equalize marketplace information, such as centralized exchanges comparable to those already in existence for stocks, bonds, and commodities, and attempted to develop systems of mandate- and commission-sharing similar to the multiple-listing services (MLS) that were being pioneered in the United States in the same period. These systems, composed of paper registers, professional membership cards, and centralized market sites, sought to coordinate competition and provide more perfect access to market information, thus establishing the necessary distributive networks to improve the liquidity of real estate.[6] Formulated alongside and in competition with other models of marketplace organization, they were a key part of urban property's processes of marketization.

Their efforts also show what it was like to be a businessman in Third Republic France. As the social life of real property was constituted in and across the market/society divide, the agents involved in its circulation faced similar tensions between professional identity and marketplace activity. Their associational and regulatory efforts aimed to police the morality of their occupation and limit competition by imposing a model of professionalism upon the commercial realm.[7] The opposition they encountered came not only from the field itself—as motley an assemblage of practitioners as ever there was—but also from competitors protected by state monopolies, from economic liberals opposed to association in the marketplace, and from a political culture traditionally ambivalent with regard to the public expression of marketplace identities. Yet by the turn of the century, commerce enjoyed more credibility as a source of national vigor and an arena for the cultivation of modern citizens. In a 1902 career guide, politician and historian Gabriel

Hanotaux praised commerce as the valiant helpmeet of production and a worthy outlet for the energies of the nation's youth: "If there is a career that demands initiative, perseverance, the capacity for instant evaluation, self-possession, in a word a powerful and resourceful character, it is certainly the commercial career."[8] The estate agent opens a window on the conditions and practices of commercial self-making, on the spaces afforded to the self-styled entrepreneur, in the political economy of fin-de-siècle France.

Notaries, Auctions, and the Circulation of Property

The drama driving Henri Becque's 1882 play *Les Corbeaux* comes from the agents, interests, and anxieties that circled around Parisian real estate at the end of the nineteenth century. In "The Crows," the death of middle-class businessman Vigneron leaves his family at the mercy of individuals seeking to profit from his estate. Teissier, Vigneron's former business partner, illicitly appropriates the bulk of the dead man's interests, taking advantage of the ignorance and inexperience of his female heirs. He colludes with the unscrupulous family notary, Maître Bourdon, to obtain some lands belonging to the estate in the vicinity of a Parisian railway station. These properties pose a particular problem to the widow. Soon after her husband's death, Mme Vigneron receives the architect he had hired to build apartment houses on the lots in question. From these houses, Vigneron had hoped to generate the rents that would allow him to "live without having to work," once he had safely established his children and given up his factory. The architect, Lefort, reveals to the widow that the purchase of these lands had been a bad business affair for the deceased, one engineered irresponsibly by his notary. There were several characteristics of the lots that made them difficult to resell, and building on them was the only way the family could hope to pull any benefit from the transaction. Portraying himself as an urban expert of the type encountered in previous chapters, Lefort dismisses Bourdon's glowing assertions of the value of the lands: "Don't try to tell me about buildings, I know Paris's market from A to Z."[9] He warns the widow of the machinations that will likely be undertaken by the individual charged with the sale of the lands, the efforts that will be exerted to lower the price and ensure their acquisition by a preselected client (in this case, Teissier). Bourdon is outraged by the accusations against his position, turning on Lefort: "You are casually attacking the most respectable corporation that I know. You are throwing suspicion on the law itself by impugning those charged with carrying it out. If it were possible, sir, you are doing even worse than that: you are violating the security of families."[10] Still uncertain, Mme Vigneron considers handing her affairs over to another intermediary, an agent d'affaires named Lebrasseux.[11] In response the notary terrifies the widow with dire illuminations: "[Lebrasseux] is a former solicitor who had to give up his office because of embezzlement. You are probably not aware that black sheep are ruthlessly expelled from the order of solicitors just as they are from the corporation of notaries. After this misadventure, Lebrasseux set up an agency near the Palais-de-Justice. What goes on there, I can't tell you, but you can report back to me in a little while."[12] By the end of the play, the notary and Teissier have successfully appropriated the entire estate, and would have reduced the family to a state of destitution but for the fact that Teissier marries one of the daughters, who acquiesces to his proposal for the sake of her family.

Suspicion of the notary as a self-interested and sometimes criminal intermediary had a well-established pedigree. Notaries appear often in the caricatures of Honoré Daumier, and Balzac included a chapter entitled "A Treatise on the Danger Money Runs in Notary Offices" in his 1825 *Code des gens honnêtes ou l'art de ne pas être dupe des fripons* (Handbook for Honest Folk, or the Art of Not Being Duped by Scoundrels).[13] These earlier satirical portraits, drawing on themes of overindulgence, illicit second households, and other questionable personal practices, were, in the early Third Republic, accompanied by a significant increase in actual criminality and a widespread perception of a "notarial crisis."[14] The particular anxieties of this crisis originated not only in the very real crimes that notaries committed in the execution of their offices, but in the fact that they maintained a powerful and esteemed position as advisors on all matters of family law, particularly succession.[15] As Maître Bourdon pronounced self-righteously to the architect Lefort, the notary was not only the representative of the law, but also, and more importantly, the guardian of family security. Indeed, historian Jean-Paul Poisson has characterized the notary's office as a *lieu de mémoire,* a site that embodied the desire for family stability and endurance in the face of the necessary transience of individual existences.[16]

The notary came to embody this permanence through his involvement in the constitution and consolidation of family landed wealth. As key advisors and managers of patrimony, notaries and their offices acted as intermediaries for all sorts of property transactions. French law assigned them a particular role in contracts involving real estate. While property sales were legal and complete when carried out by private contract between two legally empowered individuals, they were "opposable aux tiers," or legally binding on third parties, only when transcribed at the Conservation des Hypothèques. This process was often carried out by a notary pursuant to his authentication of the contract of sale.[17] Real estate sales represented a moderate portion of a notary's overall activities, which focused more on matters of family law and, importantly, various kinds of credit transactions. Studies by Poisson have shown that while attention to property sales increased over the course of the nineteenth century—as did the total volume of all acts carried out by Parisian notaries—they represented less than a fifth of transactions in offices he studied.[18] Real estate matters came to dominate the affairs of notaries only after the passage of legislation requiring their intermediation post–World War II.[19] Nevertheless, the weekly auction sales held by the Chamber of Notaries were prominent public instantiations of a real estate market, as were those held by the *avoués,* or solicitors, who carried out real property auctions at the Palais de Justice. The mandate of this group included the sale of property seized by judicial proceedings (such as those initiated in bankruptcy) and properties shared *indivisum* by heirs. Through the centralization of information on these sales at the Civil Tribunal of the Seine, this profession had established "a kind of property marketplace," praised by some as more efficient than wandering through the 122 notary offices that dotted the capital.[20] Statistics published in the city of Paris's *Annuaire Statistique* from 1880 reveal an average of 318 annual sales of land and buildings at the Chamber of Notaries auctions for the period 1880–1914, while figures for the Civil Tribunal (supplied for 1904–1914) put its annual average at 410 (Graph 4.1).[21]

These officials constituted the traditional world of property circulation, representing between them the conventional movement of land through family circuits (notably the episodes of marriage and inheritance), as well as the more mobile elements of real estate implicated in credit networks through mortgages and liens and subject to seizure by commercial creditors and others. This circulation network was certainly not without dynamism or the capacity for innovation. The affairs of notaries could result in the accumulation of large sums of money in the care of their offices and kept them close to a wide variety of economic and commercial activities. The involvement of notaries—and the funds of their clients—in an array of investment and speculative enterprises, and a spate of bankruptcies that resulted, led to the introduction of legislation

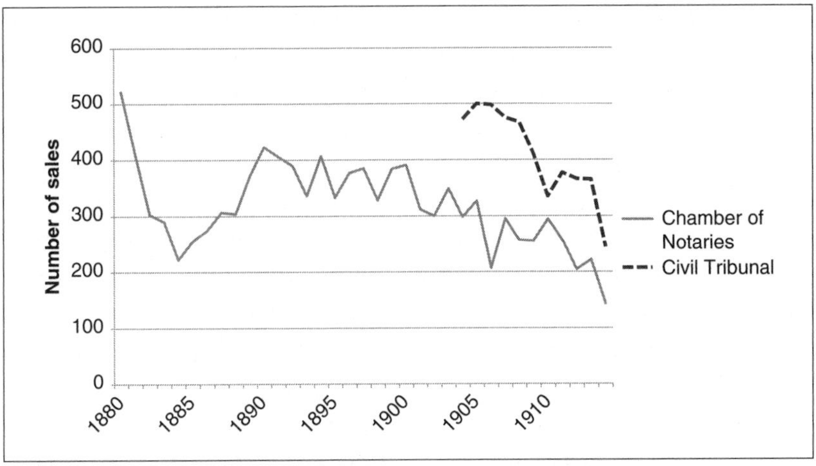

GRAPH 4.1 Total land and building sales by auction, 1880–1914. *Source: Annuaire Statistique de la Ville de Paris*

in 1843 barring notaries from commercial activities.[22] These regulations were intended to limit competition between the banking and notarial sectors, as well as to further insulate family patrimonies from unwarranted circulation, asserting a distinction between the realms of stable investment and unreliable speculation.[23] Thanks to such legislation, as well as to the diversification and democratization of information networks more generally, notaries found their role in both credit and property markets evolving as the century progressed, particularly in the competitive marketplace of Paris. For example, the best study of Paris's notaries has revealed how the expansion of the Crédit Foncier's activities in Paris, an expansion that was enabled by the reestablishment of a public lien registry in 1855, displaced notaries as prime agents in the mortgage lending market. Notaries took up lucrative roles as scriveners for the company's loans, but they no longer enjoyed their previous standing as privileged mediators in the arrangement and distribution of mortgages.[24]

As for property sales, a notary undertook them in one of two ways. In those instances when he was aware of a client or fellow official interested in the purchase or sale of a property whose availability had come to his attention, a private sale might be arranged. Alternatively, properties were sold through public auctions. Parisian notaries established an auction room for real property by a decision taken on 25 prairial an XII (June 14, 1804), slightly preceding a similar decision by the Company of Auctioneers *(commissaires-priseurs),* the public officials charged with the sale of movable goods.[25] They also anticipated by a few years the founding of London's Auction Mart, a site that would become a headquarters of real property auctioneering in England in the nineteenth century, and were decades in advance of both Manhattan's Exchange Salesroom (later the Real Estate Exchange and Auction Room) as well as auction rooms in other French urban centers.[26] In contrast to their official brethren in the realm of movables, notaries did not function as price setters and were not legally bound to any estimates that they helped establish. Nor did they enjoy a privilege in the realm of public real property auctions comparable to that of the commissaire-priseur, who had a monopoly on public sales of personal property. Reflecting the gravity with which the prerogatives of real property owners were treated, owners themselves, as well as any other duly designated agent, could engage in auctions freely, provided they did not undertake to impersonate the office of the notary (an infraction known as *immixtion*).[27]

The auction was a well-established legal form that served simultaneously to establish markets and to effect the distribution of goods. When carried out by officers of the court, their judicial standing meant that the publicity, schedule, and form of real property auctions remained largely consistent from the eighteenth through to the twentieth century. Advertising was highly standardized; posters for weekly sales were affixed at designated locations across the city and notices were inserted in a limited number of official publications. For court-ordered sales—*adjudications judiciaires,* such as sales of seized properties or sales of properties belonging to a minor—advertising was tightly controlled; the number of flyers printed per sale, the number of journals in which a sale might be publicized, and the nature of the information conveyed was all determined by statute.[28] Volontary sales—*adjudications volontaires,* in which sellers enjoyed full command of their rights and privileges—could summon more robust advertising campaigns, including flyers, mailings, and more elaborate posters, though publicity often followed the model of judicial forms. The Chamber of Notaries reminded its members in 1848 that notices and posters should be "as uniform as possible; they constitute our pledge to the public," an expression of "all that is serious and sincere" in the affair.[29] Precision and consistency in the advertising and procedures of auctions ensured the validity of the market they brought into being. If the mechanisms of the auction were followed faithfully, the conditions of transparent information and perfect competition that reigned in the auction hall would generate the *juste prix,* or fair price. These conditions ensured that auctions acted as "the most sincere expression and the most precise thermometer of property values," guaranteeing the interests of all involved.[30]

Auctions, in short, were performative, bringing into being the very market that they claimed to express or represent.[31] Rather than a voluminous and abstract space encompassing the widest possible sphere of exchange, the market constituted by the auction was intensely localized and ephemeral, assembled in the office, public hall, or café that housed the sale, for the few moments it took for three candles—the mechanism used to time final bids—to burn and extinguish themselves. Participants in the sale were (theoretically) unknown to one another; the auction replaced the personal networks of a seller with a market of anonymous buyers united through the goods on offer. By virtue of drafting conditions of sale, sellers entered into contingent contracts with parties as yet unknown to them; these contracts would be fulfilled upon the emergence of a suitable price from the back-and-forth of the salesroom. Auctions were thus also performative in another sense. They were the site of rites whose performance granted legal form to the acts they accomplished. The contingent contracts of sellers took the form of a sale by virtue of the authority vested in the adjudicating power of the notary. The importance of the forms surrounding these sales—from the sparks on the end of candlewicks to the hallowed pronouncements of the notary—was such that mimicking them was a serious infraction, injurious to the public and the notarial profession, regardless of the fact that the adoption of the forms of the sale did not impart similar legal authority to its agents.[32]

Notaries enacted a number of regulations to ensure the emergence and governance of this perfect marketplace.[33] Rules adopted by the Chamber in 1846 required that its members use the auction room for all sales other than those specifically ordered to occur elsewhere by court decision. By forbidding dummy bidding and limiting the right of owners to withdraw their properties from auctions, they sought to encourage serious competition and bolster the reliability of transactions.[34] By restricting attendance at auctions to accredited legal officials hired to represent their clients, the Chamber hoped to guarantee both the identity and solvability of bidders, matters that the size of the city of Paris and the tumult of the auction room obscured.[35] A solicitor or notary attending an auction had to produce proof of his mandate on behalf of a client, and bore instructions on the maximum bid he was permitted to offer. The *chaleur des enchères* (auction frenzy) would thus be inflected by the rational study of the serious buyer. Representation was also thought to bring about perfectly fair competition by eliminating the intimidation and aggressive passions that could materialize in the auction room when individuals were known to one another.[36] Nevertheless, repeated censures issued by the Chamber and the Ministry of Justice regarding the traditional practice of drinking during auctions (and of holding sales in cafés and cabarets when auction houses weren't available) give the flavor of these potentially unruly events.[37]

Although contemporary accounts attest to the marvelous effects of the auction room on the volume of property transactions, these auctions accounted for only a portion of total property sales in Paris.[38] Real estate columns that began appearing in the daily press in the last decades of the nineteenth century routinely chronicled the sales at the Chamber of Notaries and the Civil Tribunal, but also remarked on the inadequacy of these sites to capture the entirety of the thing called the property market. An 1893 contribution to the weekly "Chronique Foncière" published in *Le XIXe Siècle* observed that auctions remained important "even though the sales at the Chamber of Notaries are no longer considered the true criterion of prices."[39] Not only did many sales escape its mediation, but public knowledge about these transactions was limited. Contemporaries widely acknowledged the lack of transparency in the real property market, and the failure of those charged with sales and purchases to provide better illumination seemed particularly puzzling. Certainly notaries gathered their own information on the activities of their auction house. In 1841 the Chamber issued a circular asking notaries to track and report their sales; in 1845–1846, it undertook a study of the impact of eliminating dummy bidding on overall sales and prices.[40] But until they consented in 1882 to a request from the Prefecture of the Seine that they share information with the city's statistical services, this data was not presented synthetically to the public.[41] One of *Le Matin*'s weekly "Chronique Immobilière" installments complained in 1893 that the paucity of publicly available information about sales at the Chamber of Notaries made it nearly impossible "for buyers or sellers to stay regularly informed on the fluctuations in rates on the property market." While the Chamber of Notaries could easily act as the Chamber of Stock Brokers did and establish an official price list for properties, notaries instead "remained mute, closed to any official communication of price fluctuations."[42] Indeed, the same column had previously announced its intention to "fill a gap" and improve conditions for real estate investment by "creating the most complete information bulletin possible," ending the closed market that made investment so difficult. Real estate columns such as these, the anonymous writer concluded, were "destined to become the bulletin of the property market, like the bulletin of the Stock Exchange can be for the securities market."[43]

These persistent and persuasive comparisons between property and securities markets shed light on some of the Chamber's reluctance to further centralize and publicize the information stemming from notaries' position as intermediaries. Public officials maintained a complex relationship to the commercial sphere. Legal manuals frequently referred to the dual nature of the notary, as part officer of the court and part commercial intermediary, recommending that the dignity of the office required abandoning any activities that threatened to emphasize the latter.[44] Thus many notaries, "guided by sentiments that we cannot impugn . . . have allowed auxiliaries to set themselves up alongside them," estate agents who take on the brokerage elements of property affairs and "restrain the notary to the legal role initially assigned him."[45] When in 1881 a company calling itself Le Notariat proposed to establish a central bureau in Paris, assembling the supply and demand stemming from the city's multiple notarial offices, critics of the venture focused on the confusion between commercial operations and notarial functions that would undoubtedly arise from such a "Bourse." Assimilating their transactions to those undertaken with commodities and stocks would "distort this institution"; "in order to be honored and respected as they ought to be, notaries must endeavor to remain within the parameters of their occupation as delineated by the law. . . . They most avoid allowing themselves to be confused with estate agents."[46] (Indeed, notaries did not establish an information-sharing service for their clients' private sales until 1919.)[47] This distinction not only shaped the form of the property market that emerged from the auction room of the Chamber of Notaries, it also provided space for a range of intermediaries to position themselves in the distribution networks of the capital city.

As estate agents intervened more aggressively in the arena of property sales, they banked on providing an improved market model to that guarded by notaries. This aim did not necessarily require supplanting notaries. In 1874 an estate agency calling itself the Mandataire du Notariat proposed its services as a national publicity venue for notaries, centralizing information while retaining the privacy and prerogatives of the notarial profession. Collaboration between commercial agents and public officials would relieve notaries of "the restraint that their office places upon them, and especially the restricted circle in which they are obliged to operate," producing a market for real property capable of competing with the increasingly popular securities market.[48] In this particular case, the editors of the journal claimed to have originated in the lower ranks of the notarial profession itself. This was a common training ground for estate agents. The bevy of clerks and minor legal trainees who assisted public officials frequently found their promotion within the field blocked by the prohibitive costs of notarial offices (which reached well into the hundreds of thousands of francs at the end of the century); to make a living, they turned to auxiliary activities.[49] The founders of the Mandataire du Notariat presented their exclusion from the uppermost echelons of the field as a virtue; because "nothing hindered the freedom of action" of its agents, they could grease the wheels of commerce and "encourage all nature of transactions."[50]

Collaboration on equal footing with notaries was a particular goal of the first professional association of estate agents, the Compagnie des Hommes d'Affaires du Département de la Seine, founded in 1876. The group's statutes asserted, "In their relations with public officials, members are required to express all consideration due to these individuals, and to assume the role of useful and devoted auxiliaries."[51] The organization's founders—a group that included many former public officials—expressed confidence that the business opportunities of the capital city were sufficient to ensure that estate agents could earn honorable and useful livings "without at all intruding on the prerogatives of public officials."[52] Notaries, on the other hand, took a more hostile view of the occupation's formalization and its challenge to their potential monopoly on property transfers. From the mid-nineteenth century, they asserted and sought to extend their privileges, defending an allegedly exclusive right to perform public auctions and lobbying to increase the kinds of contracts that would require notary authentication.[53] By the time the Syndicat Professionnel des Hommes d'Affaires de France et des Colonies (Professional Estate Agents' Union of France and Its Colonies), the occupation's first national association, was founded in 1898, the relationship between the two fields was openly antagonistic. In 1907 the Compagnie des Hommes d'Affaires and the Syndicat Professionnel collaborated to draft a report supporting government regulation of their profession, emphasizing their superiority over the protected legal practitioners. Public officials, the report insisted, "confined as they are within narrow rules, and because of their monopoly, are alien to the emulation born of individual initiative, and fail to render all the services for which they were created." The authors continued frankly: "These organizations, venerable by virtue of their age, no longer fit with the intensity of modern activity."[54] Estate agents proposed a market based on transparent information networks, one they considered better adjusted to the needs of contemporary property circulation and antipathetic to the requirements, practices, and often, the inclinations, of the notarial profession.

"A Means and Not an End": The Agent d'Affaires

As agents d'affaires worked to establish a position in the Parisian property market, they also carved out a professional standing in the rapidly changing commercial sphere. While a variety of people referred to themselves as "businessmen" in addition to their trade-specific designation, for those claiming "homme d'affaires" or "agent d'affaires" as their defining occupation *tout court,* the title referred simply—and broadly—to someone who makes a living managing the affairs of others. It had some roots in the old regime position of the *intendant,* the estate manager who administered properties on behalf of absentee aristocratic landowners.[55] By the 1830s the homme d'affaires had moved decidedly into the commercial realm, with dictionaries identifying its more modern manifestation, the agent d'affaires.[56] These agents exploited the expanding array of nineteenth-century consumer demands, presenting themselves as invaluable guides to the unfamiliar worlds of commercialized leisure (travel agents, publicity agents), urban social networks (employment and marriage brokers), anonymous financial relationships (investment advisors, loan brokers, corporate partnership facilitators), commercial legal systems (court representatives and advisors, contract negotiators), innovation (patent registries), and property acquisition and management (real estate agents, property managers). They embodied market relations; when career guide author Édouard Charton described the field disparagingly in 1842, he referred to them as the "living incarnation" of publicity journals.[57]

As intermediaries charged with a host of diverse tasks, the agent d'affaires held a maddeningly imprecise occupation. An 1898 law thesis admitted that "the word 'business' [*affaires*] is one of those which defies analysis . . . in a word, it is the play of interests." As a consequence, "the estate agency appears as a sort of vague territory into which we can place all speculations which are not otherwise designated by the Commercial Code, and which have as their goal the performance of some type of service and the satisfaction of the most diverse interests."[58] The legal and fiscal categorization of their activities proved problematic for decades. Legal scholars debated the estate agent's position relative to his clients, arguing about whether they ought to be considered mandated representatives—which involved christening a new legal type, the salaried representative, as a mandate was conventionally a service provided for free—or as engaging in a hire of services. These categories had important ramifications for tax obligations and commission structures, and frequent divergences in jurisprudence left everyday business practices uncertain. By the interwar period, even the basic legal classification of the agent as a *commerçant,* a designation attributed to them by Article 632 of the 1807 commercial code, came into question, particularly as the occupation branched off into specializations whose members often contested a characterization of their activities as "merely" commercial.[59]

A negative image pursued the occupation from its inception.[60] Balzac, for example, dedicated large sections of his 1825 *L'Art de ne pas être dupe des fripons* to the machinations of agents d'affaires, while criminal-turned-police agent Eugène Vidocq's 1837 physiognomy of thieves used the example of the estate agent to illustrate the meaning of the term *escroc* or swindler.[61] Édouard Charton presented a long picture of the field in his 1842 career guide, *Guide pour le choix d'un état,* noting that "a discredit, certainly too general to be always fair, clings to the very title of estate agent." Charton describes the occupation as particularly urban, above all a specialty of Paris, and divides it into three types, reserving the name of pure agent d'affaires for those brokers who "peddle notes of businesses and properties to sell or acquire, of capital to borrow or invest, etc." While they have the potential to do great service, their field is overrun with disreputables, "recruited particularly from among the crowd of men who can succeed in nothing, either from lack of talent, or because of their laziness or misdeeds." Moreover, market competition is such that agents are required to undertake a detestable variety of ruses in order to secure and keep clients. In the witty portrait of the agent provided in the 1840 compendium of Parisian physiognomies *Les Français peints par eux-mêmes,* the agent is adept at social passing and maintaining the appearance of thriving business. Not only is his office full of empty folders (testifying to the "importance" of the agency), but his private life is similarly orchestrated, with an apartment near the Stock Exchange selected to suggest booming affairs (Figure 4.1).[62] Charton found these behaviors

FIGURE 4.1 The "living incarnation" of advertising gazettes: An agent d'affaires posts notices for an investment opportunity in *Les français peints par eux-mêmes* (1840). *Source:* John Hay Library, Brown University Library

innately debasing: "The secrecy and the intrigues which [the position] obliges, the humiliations it forces him to suffer, repel any self-respecting man." As a consequence, the position "is not one of those that we recommend to the choice of our readers."[63]

Charton touched on the principal obstacles to professional (self-)respect that would haunt the field throughout the century, namely, the range of affairs with which it dealt, the ease of entry owing to a lack of precise qualifications, and the dubiousness attached to the commercial nature of its pursuits. In popular understanding, the profession remained one of last resort. Journalist Aurélien Scholl commented in an 1885 portrait of the agent d'affaires, "I've never heard a single middle- or lower-middle class man say: 'I'm going to make my son an estate agent.' And yet, there are a great number of estate agents." As for their origins, Scholl characterized them thusly: "The estate agent belongs to the great family of social dropouts. These are the losers in the battle of life. They are those who weren't meant to be notaries, or lawyers, or solicitors, or bailiffs, or court clerks, or auctioneers. There you find unlucky students, unpublished poets, solicitors' clerks who pined uselessly after a dowry and an office, ruined notaries, stammering lawyers, all people who have to gain their daily bread by their wits rather than their inheritances." Scholl was not without admiration for a field in which individuals were reliant on their flair and gumption to make a living. Success depended on voracious and unyielding effort: "Few professions require as many skills as that of the estate agent: knowledge of the human heart, daring, swiftness, shrewdness, aplomb; all these are indispensable. Above him he has privilege, around him endless competition. If he slackens for an hour, misery is waiting to catch him." Scholl focused on the legal aspects of the field, and indicated that the occupation's lack of definition was responsible for its low esteem: "If one day all offices and privilege are eliminated, the estate agent will find himself with a well-defined profession. In an instant he'll move up ten notches on the social ladder."[64]

Conquering a specified and defined place in the marketplace was the goal of the organizational and professionalization efforts that agents d'affaires undertook in the early Third Republic. Beginning from 1876 with the formation of the Compagnie des Hommes d'Affaires du Département de la Seine, occupational self-government was facilitated by the 1884 law on professional associations.. Seeking to establish an occupational monopoly and achieve social distinction, agents d'affaires crafted a model of association that aimed at ensuring individuality in an anonymous marketplace, proposing a method for members of their occupation to secure a respectable commercial selfhood based on responsibility, restraint, and skill.

A great deal can be learned about fin-de-siècle attitudes toward and understandings of the commercial realm by exploring the difficulties these intermediaries encountered in defining and policing their occupational boundaries. The received narrative of the Malthusian and risk-averse French entrepreneur can no longer be credited in light of new historiography on both economic development and business history in France, but the late nineteenth century was nevertheless characterized by persistent ambivalence about the relationship between private profit and public interest.[65] Historian Sarah Maza has argued that such outlooks were deeply embedded in traditional understandings of the social order that precluded the equation of citizenship and commercial endeavor. Suspicion of the self-interest thought to lie at the heart of economic undertakings, she speculates, suggested an alternate figure, the *fonctionnaire* or state bureaucrat, as the ideal model of civic identity.[66] Yet France was also a country in which economic liberalism had entered firmly into the discourse of commercial actors and public officials, and changes in the second half of the nineteenth century encourage a reconsideration of the presumed limitations of positively valued market-based identities.[67] The Third Republic, described by some as a "republic of businessmen," was deeply permeated with liberal economic ideals, despite a dedication to a balanced economy that necessitated accommodation with protectionist impulses.[68] Liberal doctrines played a powerful role in retarding the development of state-mandated social programs, for example.[69] In significant ways, the hand of the state on business activity was lighter than ever. The last years of the Second Empire saw both the liberalization of the limited liability joint stock company and the abolition of debt imprisonment, or *contrainte par corps*. An 1885 law regularized various stock market transactions that had previously been legally classified as gambling, and 1889 saw legislative reforms that eased the process of declaring bankruptcy and enabled the quick recommencement of commercial activity. The 1884 law on associations, meanwhile, was an acknowledgment of economic interests that transcended the individual and provided an institutionalized mode for presenting oneself in the public sphere as an economic agent.

Yet this new realm of commercial assertion was not a free-for-all of competitive individuals; it was a site for the articulation of collective identities based on the demonstration of specialization and expertise. The recognition of the validity of occupational groupings was part of a broader republican project to enable democratic participation in public life, of which the universalization of education and its attendant promise of social mobility constituted an important part. One of the many consequences of the new weight placed on education was an obsession with careerism, marked by a proliferation of guides and advice manuals specifying the myriad ways by which the young could make their way in the world, and the type of social status they could expect upon arriving at their goal.[70] These guides covered a diverse array of occupations, including manual and commercial trades, and strongly emphasized educational requirements. Social mobility was bound up with a culture of expertise and specialized training.[71] Association and education were two key measures aiming to harmonize economic interests with social needs and political imperatives. Both worked to create and represent expertise as a critical mode of establishing occupational identities compatible with virtuous self-making in the marketplace. Indeed, legally speaking, all commerçants were required to be experts in their particular trade, which explains the persistence of topics like chemistry and law in commercial education and popular works for businesspeople at the turn of the century.[72]

The emphasis on specialized knowledge in commerce served to adapt traditional norms (artisanal modes of production structured in corporative forms) to modern business conditions, rationalizing the chaotic affairs of the marketplace. So long as expertise did not serve as an argument for monopoly, specialization ensured accountability, proficiency, and transparency in the marketplace. Yet if specialist status was applicable to the most diverse occupations, it posed a problem for those whose "specialty" lay in intermediation, in filling the gaps between other specialist fields. Estate agents experienced this difficulty individually, as members of an occupation whose poor repute was attributable precisely to its fuzzy boundaries and questionable utility, and as a professional grouping in search of official status and representation for what outsiders considered an unspecialized pursuit. When the Compagnie des Hommes d'Affaires assembled in 1876, its members' chief complaint was the low status of the occupation, blamed on its unpoliced boundaries. Its organizing report commented: "Because anything that can be the object of a mandate is part of its domain, this profession is open and nearly limitless. As a result, no industry presents a wider or more varied range in the position of its practitioners."[73] This boundless field gave an impression of vagueness, damning to any professionalization project, and particularly crippling in the context of an economic imaginary prizing specialization. Furthermore, as the Compagnie readily admitted, it eased the entry of "those whom misfortune, and sometimes disciplinary measures, have excluded from other professions."[74]

Indeed, there was more than a difference in scales of operation between the estate agents who came together to form the Compagnie and the vast majority of entrepreneurs in the field. The forty-six initial members of this syndicate all came from the ranks of the legal profession: former notaries, bailiffs, solicitors, and clerks of varying levels in these establishments. They celebrated this professional background as a marker of competence, morality, and disinterestedness. In contrast, the sorts of individuals and infractions that permeated the field and so troubled the Compagnie's founders are illuminated by bankruptcy dossiers from the period.[75] Some operators came from positions as unrelated to the task of the commercial intermediary as tailoring and dairymen.[76] One Claude Moreau sent a letter soliciting clients for his property sales services that he signed "Ex-secretary of the Parisian Hairdresser's Union."[77] Eighteen out of a total twenty-six agents whose criminal dossiers were included in their bankruptcy files had previous convictions, for infractions ranging from defamation and attacks on police or other state agents to evading military service. Commercial violations—fraudulent bankruptcy, swindling, selling tampered products, or running a gambling house—were most prominent. Fully a third of this group would not have met the Compagnie's entrance requirements.

Bankruptcy dossiers also bear out the Compagnie's fears about the ease of entry to their field. One of its most attractive features, in fact, was that the work could be undertaken with very little start-up capital—which likely explains many an individual's failure, at the same time as it promised rewards for the industrious but underfunded. For example, when Claude Nicolin, director of the Comptoir Central des Ventes de Fonds de Commerce, was declared bankrupt (for a third time) in 1868, the trustee attributed his failure to "the total absence of sufficient resources to found his agency, to some losses, and to his general costs and the cost of publicity he was obliged to carry out."[78] The lack of capital could be made up for in many ways, often exploiting the flexible business structures available under French commercial law.[79] Paul Malric, who was declared bankrupt and condemned to two years in prison after fleeing his creditors in 1877, opened his apartment rental agency the year before at the age of twenty-five. His investment partner, Levesque, was to provide the entire start-up capital of 75,000 francs, the majority of which went unpaid. Within two months the company had taken the form of a cooperative enterprise; thanks to a wide publicity campaign, Malric et Cie attracted a number of employees who received shares in the enterprise's profits on the basis of the amounts they invested, ranging from 500 to 3,000 francs. The trustee reports that "in a short time, Malric et Cie. took on the appearance of a first-rate establishment" and the inventory reveals a handsomely appointed agency covering two floors on the prestigious Rue Royale, the heart of Right Bank business affairs. Within weeks, however, the demands of his employees for payment provoked Malric's flight and subsequent conviction as a fraudulent bankrupt.[80] In a similar, though not duplicitous, vein, Georges Woitier sold interests in his business to new associates on no fewer than five occasions between 1887 and 1890 when his need for capital grew pressing or his partners withdrew their shares. Investors for this genre of business seemed abundant but, in light of the risks they were running, necessarily exigent; his twenty-one creditors received a total reimbursement of only 2.28 percent on their combined loans of 22,541.71 francs.[81] The ready availability of malleable business forms enabled individuals to enter the occupation easily and build large concerns rapidly.

Informal practices of self-policing were one way agents attempted to discipline their field and protect themselves from cutthroat competition. It was not uncommon for real property agents, for example, to have employees sign contracts prohibiting them from going into the same business within a certain amount of time after leaving their current employment. Their employers could thus be assured that expanding their business would not mean training their competition.[82] Yet such measures could be received poorly in the commercial courts, as they were considered a violation of the principle of freedom of enterprise. Generally speaking, judicial support for estate agents was unreliable. Their commissions were vulnerable to reduction at the discretion of the courts, reflecting both their unusual legal status as paid representatives and a general disinclination to attribute significant value to their services. A glance at the legal sections of commercial publications—as well as at editorials penned by concerned agents—indicates that commission reductions were routinely imposed; even on the rare occasion that a written contract between client and agent was available, a tribunal could still judge the remuneration excessive for the services rendered and order a reduction.[83]

The Compagnie des Hommes d'Affaires hoped that occupational self-government would help resolve this ignoble subordination to the whims of clients, colleagues, and jurists. A formalized disciplinary body, it argued, would prove to all and sundry that the position of homme d'affaires was an honorable one, composed of individuals "voluntarily submitting themselves to well-defined duties and obligations," and would begin the work of regularizing their status vis-à-vis competing professionals and a wary clientele.[84] More specifically, professional association was thought to provide a means of mastering the market not only through the force of collective organization, but through a particular cultivation of individuality and autonomy. Henceforth, the organizers of the Compagnie des Hommes d'Affaires insisted, estate agents would be divided into two camps: "on the one hand, those who have the required talent and morality to be part of such a corporation, and on the other, those lost in the crowd without anything to recommend them"[85] Professional association allowed the business agent to rise above the nameless mass that crowded the field's ranks. They continued: "Public esteem, the respect to which all honest men have the right, will return to true estate agents; no longer will they be confused with the first comer that takes up the title, and this last will be able to abuse only the simple-minded, as he will be an individual adrift, and his misdeeds will not be able to reflect on a serious and honest corporation."[86] Without an associative body enabling the complete expression of selfhood through a voluntary submission to disciplinary structures, the agent is incapable of purposeful action in the marketplace. Or, more suggestively, the uncorporatized homme d'affaires would be *merely* an individual, lost in a sea of other individuals. These prognoses recall the description of the agent d'affaires offered by Scholl, who ended his 1885 account of the occupation with a depiction of its daily, grueling battles for survival: "A few agents succeed and swim in the open waters, but the majority wades, sometimes above, sometimes below the tides, trying to evade the current that drags so many poor devils into the dregs of Parisian life."[87] For the businessmen of the Compagnie des Hommes d'Affaires, association would help overcome the fracturing of the marketplace that threatened to erode autonomy. The limits of the "self-made man" are clear; in this particular configuration of economic individualism, independence hits the obstacles of both competing monopolies and the absolute leveling of democratized commercial pursuit. It can be achieved only through establishing a community capable of defining legitimate business behavior and thus distinguishing oneself from those who are abandoned to commercial gales.

This search for autonomy in the market should not, however, be confused with autonomy *from* the market. Professionalization is fundamentally a project of market closure and status seeking.[88] Professional organization was as much a business strategy for the hommes d'affaires as it was a campaign for improved social esteem. Control of members' moral standing and competence was aimed at improving their public image and drawing a broader clientele to their offices. Member agents were forbidden to use general titles for their offices, but rather were required to identify themselves by their personal name, a mark of accountability and transparency as the agent linked his enterprise with his individual character. At the same time, competition between members was regulated, with the association's statutes warning adherents that, "in their relations with each other, the greatest brotherhood must always exist between them, and be maintained by the honesty of their methods."[89] Business ties with individuals who did not meet conditions for membership in the Compagnie were prohibited. Despite the many backward-looking aspects of their professionalizing project—repeated references to "corporations"; the choice of one of the ancien régime's most prestigious organizational designations, "compagnie," for their title; the effort to restrict entry to the occupation—the modern commercial nature of their occupation was impossible to deny. In 1885 the group constituted itself as a professional union—and hence by definition a body dedicated to economic interests—and did not abandon this status even when noncommercial modes of representation became available with the 1901 law on associations.[90]

Achieving the recognized boundaries and delineated barriers to entry that would distinguish the occupation as a specialist pursuit ultimately required state intervention. Beginning in the mid-1880s, legislators also turned their gaze to the agent d'affaires, tabling a succession of proposals to regulate a field deemed a danger to both incautious clients and established professionals. The estate agent's role as a manager of household wealth garnered increasing concern in the context of a rapidly expanding and commercializing financial arena. A stock market boom in the early 1880s placed finance at the heart of the spectacle of Parisian life. In 1882 the middle-class weekly *L'Illustration* ridiculed the way the city must appear to tourists: "A foreigner visiting Paris could note the following impressions in their notebook: 'The appearance of the capital of France: a wine merchant. A banking house. A tobacconist. A credit bureau. A panorama. A café. Another wine merchant. Another financial house . . . voilà Paris!' "[91] The subsequent crash, devastating the savings of small investors across the country, shifted finance to the foreground of the political agenda as well. The moment was thus well suited to efforts to secure the privileges of established professions in the name of protecting family patrimonies. For a number of reasons, licensing proposals that appeared in parliament in 1886, 1898, and 1913 were not debated in the Chamber. (Neither, indeed, were those that followed in 1925, 1930, and 1935. Agents waited until 1970 to receive a professional status.)[92] Nevertheless, the content of the regulations and the motivations behind them shed light on the role and place of estate agents in the commercial sphere, and reveal the ways in which local interests and national political cultures shape the application of free-market principles.

The licensing schema proposed in the Chamber of Deputies in 1886 was authored almost wholly by members who themselves hailed from the professional sector. Deputy Léon Borie was an industrialist, but his colleagues included three doctors—one the son of a notary—as well as one notary and lawyer.[93] The proposal was informed by the efforts of the Compagnie des Hommes d'Affaires, and inspired by reforms passed in 1884 by the new German government in Alsace, which barred "unsuitable" practitioners from acting as intermediaries in real estate transactions, loans, and marriage brokerage. The system proposed in France in 1886 was a much more complex affair. It depicted estate agents as illegible operatives whose background, competence, and morality were both questionable and unverifiable. Their clients were portrayed as unwary and inexperienced, prone to the seduction of gleaming signs and promises of gain even as they treated matters that engaged "the fortune, position, future, even honor" of themselves and their families.[94] For the good of the state, the national treasury, the public, and "true" hommes d'affaires themselves, the bill would create and regulate no fewer than fourteen categories of agent d'affaires. Reflecting the background of its drafters, the most stringent conditions were applied to legal intermediaries, but property managers, accountants, patent brokers, loan negotiators, commercial information firms, and real estate agents would all need to provide various proofs of competency, as well as evidence of French citizenship and full enjoyment of political and civil rights. (These stipulations immediately excluded women and non-naturalized immigrants from the profession.)[95] While never discussed in the Chamber, judicial commentary on the project was critical of its rigidity and infringement on freedom of enterprise.

Efforts for regulation of the occupation continued, however. By the end of the century, real estate agents were at the head of the community's organizational labors. The Syndicat Professionnel des Hommes d'Affaires de France et des Colonies was formed in 1898 by a commercial property agent from Clermont-Ferrand, and quickly taken over by Antoine Jauffret, a real estate broker from Nîmes who relocated to Paris in the early twentieth century.[96] Jauffret was the founder and editor of *La France Immobilière,* a real estate publication intended to function as both an advertising venue and a professional soapbox. It became the official mouthpiece of the national union in 1899 and acted as a booster for the social position and business affairs of the field. From 1901 it hosted the Bureau Centralisateur, a service that brought together the sales and purchase demands of members in exchange for a portion of the commission in the event that its intermediation led to a successful transaction. By 1904 the Bureau became a commercial enterprise distinct from the professional organization. The commissions it generated increased from only 742 francs in its first year to 71,166 francs in 1907.[97] Assuming a commission of 3 to 5 percent, this last figure reflects property sales worth between about 1.4 and 2.4 million francs, an amount that pales beside the more than 31 million francs generated in auctions at the Parisian Chamber of Notaries in the same year, but which nevertheless potentially represents a large number of transactions in a country where the vast majority of sales concerned properties valued at less than 5,000 francs. Running until the Great War, the journal published articles on the dignity of the occupation, compiled legal rulings in an effort to create "a *specific jurisprudence* for our profession," and publicized reports from annual assemblies and congresses.[98] Its most important theme was professional licensing, projects for which permeate both its pages and the association's annual meetings.

Subsequent regulatory proposals granted greater respect to both freedom of enterprise and existing practitioners than had the 1886 project. Thus while lamenting that "the first huckster off the street, without supplying a single reference, without proving any capacity, can take the title of homme d'affaires," the Syndicat Professionnel drafted a proposal for regulation of the field in 1899 that declared as its first principle, "The profession of homme d'affaires is open and may be practiced by any person providing evidence of known honorability and morality."[99] Choosing character over competency as the standard for licit practice, estate agents acknowledged the practical character of their occupation while refusing to accept its more dubious practitioners as permanent colleagues. In 1907 the Compagnie des Hommes d'Affaires and the Syndicat Professionnel joined forces to lobby for the regulation of their profession.[100] Their joint effort sought "a sort of regeneration" for honorable agents d'affaires, who would prosper when the prejudices surrounding the field—namely, "that the profession of agent d'affaires is a means and not an end, that it is the profession of those who no longer have one"—were eliminated.[101] In contrast to the self-interest associated with their position as businessmen, agents argued for their profession's utility and dedication to public service.[102] They foregrounded their specialized knowledge and training and emphasized their proximity to established legal professionals, while deploying free-market ideals in order to distinguish their special contributions. As competitive entrepreneurs, unprotected by monopoly or the privilege of birth (common criticism of the notarial profession held that it had degenerated into an inherited office), they argued that hommes d'affaires were obliged to stay in tune with the needs and desires of modern society. All they were asking, the report stressed, was "a regulation of their profession that would allow them to exercise it freely."[103]

The real property agent served professionalizing estate agents as a key example of the economic and commercial advantages of the (regulated) agent d'affaires. Efficient intermediaries maximizing the return on the time and money invested by their clients, property agents were vital nodes in the informational network on which real estate exchange depended. The 1907 report claimed that property agents helped interested parties "find solutions in a couple of hours or a few days, solutions which would demand much more time—time wasted for the interest of capital as well as for the improvement of personal situations—without an agency serving as a point of contact."[104] The ideal agent d'affaires, "a steadfast man, capable and discreet," would operate as a nearly unseen regulatory force, bringing harmony and balance to otherwise cumbersome and irksome transactions (Figure 4.2). The repeated invocation of the term "intermediary," stressing an agent's position linking actors in an anonymous commercial sphere, implied a new position of independence and assertiveness vis-à-vis the client, supplementing that of trusted council and mandated representative. As a consequence, the real estate agency "truly becomes a neutral terrain, an unofficial, unceasing marketplace."[105]

Their assertions that licensing would support a flourishing market, one that maximized production, free of the inconvenient and outdated impositions of entrenched corporations, seemed nevertheless at odds with estate agents' efforts to limit access to their occupation. The associations disseminated their project to the nation's Chambers of Commerce, and although it gained the approbation of twenty-four, including those in Tours, Rouen, Nîmes, and Dijon, the support of the larger commercial centers—Lyon, Marseilles, and Paris—was notably absent. The Chamber of Commerce of Beauvais and l'Oise, a city and department northwest of Paris, rejected the project as a plan for "a sort of investiture," the establishment of a monopoly for members of the organizations concerned. The Chamber suspected that licensing "would create a new privilege and suppress the right and freedom to set up business which currently exists for anyone who would like to open an estate agency."[106] While a regulatory proposal based closely on the 1907 joint report was put forward in the Chamber of Deputies by Jules Brunet in

FIGURE 4.2 Steadfast, capable, and discreet: Advertising template for real estate agencies, ca. 1910. *Source:* Personal collection, Jean-Marc Levet. Used with permission

1913, it is likely that opposition of this nature would have scuttled the effort, even had the proposal not been buried in committee at the outbreak of the war.[107] A new monopoly in the realm of commerce offended liberal sensibilities and threatened the position of existing professionals, leaving estate agents pedaling between privilege and relentless competition.

"An Unceasing Marketplace": The Estate Agent and the Property Market

In the absence of day-to-day records of real estate agencies from this period, an understanding of the business practices of real estate—of how far the imperatives of commercial specialization and organization discussed above may have permeated or reflected contemporary behaviors—must draw on sources such as literary depictions, publicity practices, and bankruptcy records. The latter have been touched on briefly, and the property press of this period is the subject of Chapter 5. Placing the career of Frédéric Haverkamp, a fin-de-siècle real estate agent and developer created by novelist Jules Romains, alongside other contemporary sources, we can explore the ways estate agents set about establishing agencies, constituting a model of market organization in which their place as centralizers and rationalizers made a particular contribution to the national economy. In particular, this examination illuminates the role of estate agents as generators, purveyors, and managers of information on Paris's real estate market.

Jules Romains's twenty-seven-volume novel *Les hommes de bonne bolonté* (published between 1932 and 1946) contains one of the most sustained depictions of a Parisian real estate agent. With this work, Romains sought to reestablish the narratives of urban social life characteristic of Balzac and Zola. Yet rather than follow a single character or family, he favored continuous addition and simultaneity, joining new personages, scenes, and plots to the previous without building a coherent narrative. In this way he sought to capture collective life as it really was: an assemblage without necessary personal connections, but unified nonetheless. The action begins in 1908, and the first several volumes introduce the character of Frédéric Haverkamp, a real estate agent destined to rise to great financial heights. He leases a small office on Boulevard du Palais (the exact heart of the city), installs a brass plaque reading "Agence immobilière," hires a promising young man, Wazemmes, as an assistant, and sets about dissecting the city of Paris.

Haverkamp comes to real estate trafficking without any previous experience ("In sum, I knew nothing of my new career. I had absolutely everything to learn") and reflects often on the nature of his chosen field. Just as the professionalizing agents of the fin de siècle did, he embraces specialization; in choosing to reject brokering commercial properties early in his career, he observes that "it is better to specialize outright. An agency that messes about with a little of everything will never find its place."[108] In his early thirties, he is described as visionary, methodical, brilliant, and active, a man whose faculties need only the right project through which to reach their fullest expression. Paris will be the field for the development of his person and his fortune. Haverkamp dreams of the capital rewritten under his hands:

> Suddenly he sees roads, intersections, between the enclosures of empty lots . . . mounds cleared, an entire district cropping up. And at the same time, at the other end of Paris, [he sees] a part of the plain crisscrossed by new streets, and lands below the Seine covered in tall grass, and at the same time, in a very old neighborhood, shacks leaning one upon the other. And he, Haverkamp, is part of all this, present in all this. He moves through the new streets, between the lot enclosures. He works the land, he clears the hillocks. He is the substance that uproots districts—he crumbles piles of hovels, he takes encrusted tenants with tweezers and puts them down further away. Thrusting his concrete feet into the ground, Haverkamp the building climbs to the sky. Haverkamp buildings rise in blocks, making triangles, quadrilaterals. He sees Paris attacked from the periphery, from the center; land devoured step by step. He sees the Haverkamp enterprise seep in and spread over Paris like a glorious plague.[109]

His visions of a transformed city are reminiscent of those that haunted Zola's Aristide Saccard, the hero of *La curée* and *L'argent,* but are more controlled; where Saccard is prey to his passions, Haverkamp keeps them tightly restrained, indulging in such fantasies in rare moments of relaxation. As Romains writes, "visions never overwhelmed calculations."

In preparation for his endeavors, Haverkamp spends several weeks touring real estate agencies in the capital, posing as a potential buyer or an agent with interested clients. He quickly diagnoses the field's principal defects. He observes that in general "the profession is practiced extremely indifferently." The prospective buyer was expected to arrive at the agency with very specific ideas on their purchase: "He has to indicate the precise type of building he has in mind, the price he intends to pay, the site he prefers, almost the name of the street." Showing any hesitation or confusion led to immediate disinterest on the part of the agent. Haverkamp found such behavior inexplicable. In his eyes the undecided client was the most desirable. After all, hesitation in these affairs was natural ("You're not selling hats") and moreover this sort of client "is likely to be the most malleable." Haverkamp understands the psychology of the client as needing guidance and direction: "What led the visitor to cross your threshold was the hope of a vaguely defined 'opportunity.' Or he came to see you, as he would go to a stockbroker, because he has money to invest. He'll invest more or less depending on the circumstance, and the cleverness of your advice." Consequently, Haverkamp's approach is to be respectful and attentive, even when the client begins with comments as vague as "Well! Here we are. This morning with my wife I said we might do well to buy a property somewhere."[110] Instead of bombarding him with unsettling questions, the agent presents the buyer with different opportunities promising a good return, and is able to judge from the responses all the information needed to further tailor his suggestions.

Haverkamp's studies capture the general impressions of the field that motivated its organizational efforts. He concludes that "very often, agency directors don't know the business themselves."[111] They do a minimum of labor, contenting themselves with basic information, reducing their intermediation to merely transcribing the details brought to them by interested parties. When performed in this manner, the occupation appears superfluous. As a client remarks skeptically to Haverkamp, "The entirety of [your] job is to bring together two men who could just as easily have come to an agreement on their own."[112] Haverkamp represents another way of operating, characteristic of the best agents in the capital. Rarely in his office, he prefers scouring the streets of Paris, evaluating available lands, recording the conditions and age of a building for sale, its average annual maintenance costs, the nature of the soil under its foundations, and myriad other details that allow him to shape the choice of the investor.

The discourses of fin-de-siècle agents mirrored these imperatives closely. The directors of the Agence Léon, founded in 1893, criticized the passive method of "mechanical advertising," insisting that only active intervention could make the real estate intermediary effective. They explained that their vision of the job meant "seeing the building, visiting it from top to bottom, evaluating its size and its value, studying it from every perspective, so that we can promote all its advantages and indicate all the benefits to be gained from it."[113] The numerous duties involved in facilitating property transactions—the visits, the investigations, the correspondence, the meetings—ensured that "mere" publicity could never replace "the connections produced by the absolute confidence of parties in their representative, who knows how to make their affairs simple and pleasant."[114] The emphasis was on mastering the field through energy and perseverance. The *Moniteur de la Location* described its agency's method in 1881: "My God! It's naively simple. Instead of choosing to wait for the tenant on our curule seat, we go and look for him wherever he might be found, in the street, in the café, in the reading room, the club, etc., etc."[115] The vigor of the property agent typified the vigor demanded of commerce more broadly. The modern commercial actor was captured in Gabriel Hanotaux's 1902 career guide: "It no longer means sitting there, behind on the chair, quill on the ear, sheltered by the metal grill or the administrative wicket, waiting for the client. You have to get ahead of him, chase him if he flees, overtake him, guess his tastes, take inspiration from his ideas, surprise the secret of his muddled desires."[116]

Finding clients was indeed one of the biggest challenges facing beginner agents. Lacking the official status, professional networks, and social standing enjoyed by the notary, agents had to be extremely enterprising when it came to conjuring business opportunities. They sent sheaves of letters to property owners, vaunting the experience and respectability of their agencies, the esteem, professional capacities, and business connections of its director, and its recent successful sales (Figure 4.3).[117] Others took a more roundabout route. In 1887 Paris's director of public works received a request from an agent named Lescure who wished to obtain daily access to building permit applications. While the municipality's official publications included summaries of the owners, architects, and addresses of new buildings in the city, Lescure wanted "details on the division of apartments, the number of stories, and the size of the building," which would allow him to locate likely new clients or respond to the demands of apartment searchers.[118] (His demand was refused.) In addition to these avenues, the most important tools at the disposal of estate agents remained advertising, and, like the buyers and tenants they aimed to assist, their own explorations of the city.

At times efforts to overtake clients could slide—perhaps necessarily, and hopefully temporarily—into dishonesty. Romains depicts the daily ruses and incremental duplicities necessary to drum up business, from false advertisements used to lure in buyers to staged phone calls with famous personalities to impress potential clients.[119] Haverkamp finds such subterfuges personally mortifying (just as Charton's career guide had described) but necessary in order to achieve the appearance of a thriving, first-class establishment. He counters these unfortunate charades with a scrupulous attention to customer service, which forms the core of his business strategy. The importance of pleasing the client means that he does not shrink from involving himself even

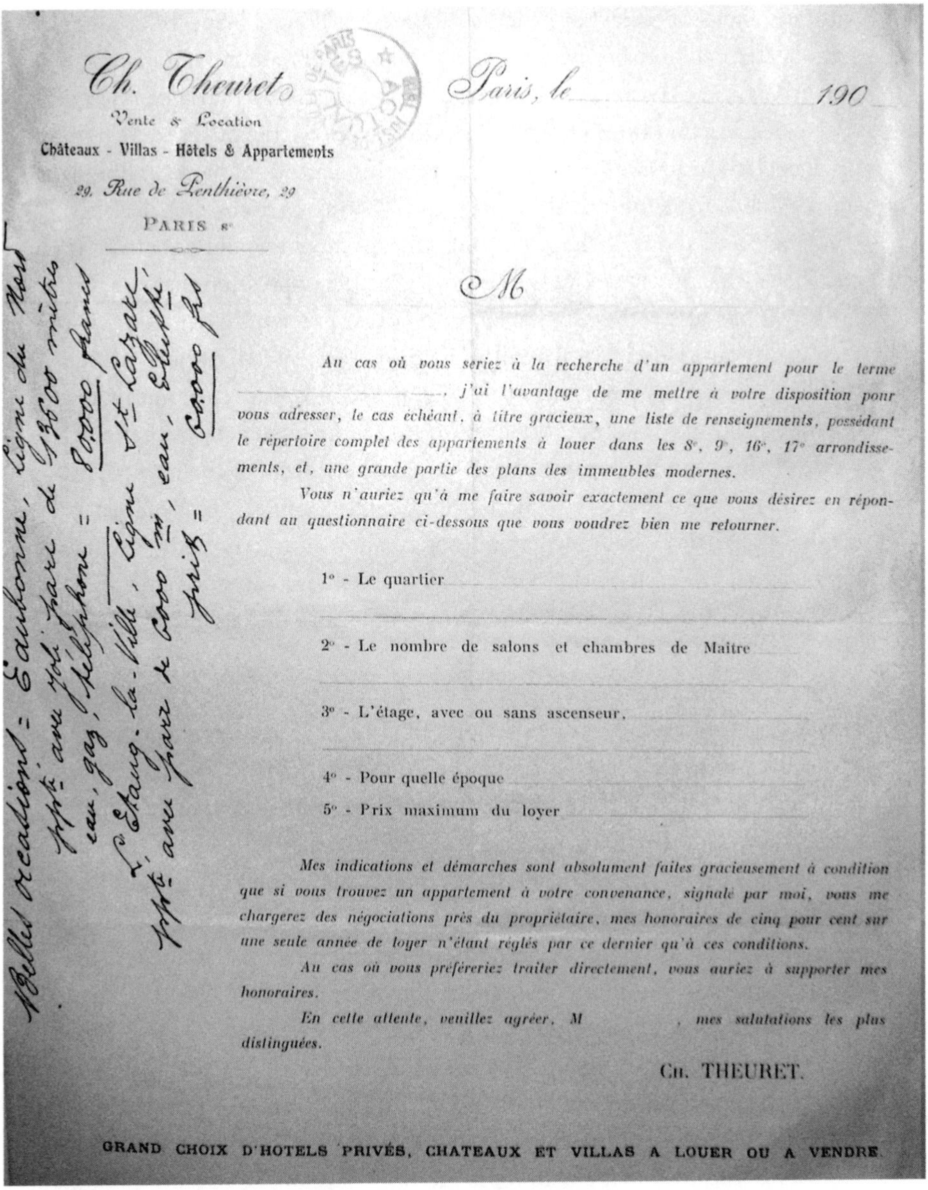

Ch. Theuret
Vente & Location
Châteaux - Villas - Hôtels & Appartements
29, Rue de Penthièvre, 29
PARIS 8e

Paris, le 190

M

Au cas où vous seriez à la recherche d'un appartement pour le terme ...., j'ai l'avantage de me mettre à votre disposition pour vous adresser, le cas échéant, à titre gracieux, une liste de renseignements, possédant le répertoire complet des appartements à louer dans les 8e, 9e, 16e, 17e arrondissements, et, une grande partie des plans des immeubles modernes.

Vous n'auriez qu'à me faire savoir exactement ce que vous désirez en répondant au questionnaire ci-dessous que vous voudrez bien me retourner.

1° - Le quartier

2° - Le nombre de salons et chambres de Maître

3° - L'étage, avec ou sans ascenseur,

4° - Pour quelle époque

5° - Prix maximum du loyer

Mes indications et démarches sont absolument faites gracieusement à condition que si vous trouvez un appartement à votre convenance, signalé par moi, vous me chargerez des négociations près du propriétaire, mes honoraires de cinq pour cent sur une seule année de loyer n'étant réglés par ce dernier qu'à ces conditions.

Au cas où vous préféreriez traiter directement, vous auriez à supporter mes honoraires.

En cette attente, veuillez agréer, M , mes salutations les plus distinguées.

CH. THEURET.

GRAND CHOIX D'HOTELS PRIVÉS, CHATEAUX ET VILLAS A LOUER OU A VENDRE

FIGURE 4.3 Estate agent solicitation letter, early twentieth century.
Source: Bibliothèque Historique de la Ville de Paris, Actualités Série 78, Logement

with the official sales held by solicitors at the Civil Tribunal. Speaking to the complicated relationship between the public and private mediators of the property market, the agent notes that most offices fail to signal such sales to clients, fearing that their public nature will encourage the buyer to filch on his agent's commission. Haverkamp rejects this fear out of hand, calling it shortsighted. Concluding his study of competing agencies, he declares: "Maxim: Be able to treat the client and inform him as I would have liked to have been when I came in [to the agency]. Give the impression that our first priority is his satisfaction, so that he has no cause to regret his troubles, that the first reward we expect from him is his esteem, and that there will be time later to discuss payment. Avoid having the prospect of a commission bearing down like a gun on the client from the first moment of the interview."[120] This mantra removed the commercial elements of the occupation as far as possible from interactions with clients. Similarly, he declined to take on properties whose owners refused to allow him to honestly divulge any vices. He understood the agency and its activities as an extension of his personal credit and reputation, and would not engage the latter for the sake of quick profit.

As a vital corollary to this emphasis on customer satisfaction, Haverkamp pursues perfection in the organization of his agency's listings. He reasons, "An agency is an information center; hence the particular importance that must be paid to filing."[121] He adopts a methodical filing system to maximize the efficacy of his distribution, dividing his offerings by type of sale (private or public), then creating further subdivisions. Public sales are grouped by region (Paris and surrounds together, provincial offers separately), then by price in increasing order; private sales, the real meat of the agency, are divided by type of building (apartment house, land, private dwelling), and then subject to a double classification, the first by arrondissement, the second by price (in turn grouped by region of the city). A general registry of all affairs completed the system, summarizing their history from the moment they came into the agency's orbit. The attention Romains pays to this procedure—he goes so far as to reproduce an image of one of Haverkamp's filing cards in the text—suggests that the work of the estate agent was primarily conceived of in terms of constituting and rationalizing information networks.

A physical site centralizing supply and demand proved a singularly persuasive, though persistently elusive, vision of the organization of the property market. In 1899 Charles Paulet and Etienne Oudin, the former an author of a commodities markets treatise and the latter a property owner, published a preliminary plan for a "Bourse Immobilière" or a Real Estate Exchange. Citing the critical place that real estate occupied in economic and everyday life, the authors sketched a plan for a central location intended "not, of course, to determine real estate prices," as central exchanges did for other goods, "but simply to encompass all acts and operations bearing some relation to real estate." An exchange would provide a center of calculation for the property and housing markets, "a meeting place, at once central, permanent, and professional . . . to which anyone interested in real estate questions would be admitted for an annual fee."[122] A modest fee of twenty francs would allow broad access, and the property sales and rental division—consisting of twenty offices, one for each district in the capital city—would give information freely to the general public. Some may have hoped that market centralization would also effect a kind of moralization; reporting on the opening of the Real Estate Exchange and Auction Room in New York City in 1885, one French commentator observed that "this establishment, directed with integrity, provided huge services and quickly attracted a clientele of serious buyers who were as dubious of illicit brokers as they were of unscrupulous sellers."[123] Yet the most immediate goal of a centralized exchange was to improve the circulation of real estate capital, allowing it to compete effectively with other forms of investment and speculation.

Situating property intermediaries as important economic agents working for the general interest of the entire nation, the real estate press threw itself into the contest for middle-class savings playing out in the last decades before the Great War. As *Le Reveil Immobilier* stated in 1893, "The fight is on between stock market gamblers and *pères de famille* who want to invest their savings in real estate."[124] These journals were champions of investment in land and apartment buildings, mobilizing a prominent investment discourse to further the image of their social utility. The safety and solidity, as well as profitability, of real estate investments were of benefit not only to individual owners, but also to the condition of French savings in general. In 1884 the editors of *Annonce Immobilière* described their role with great solemnity. "The task we are assuming is serious," they wrote. "By helping the development of property transactions," they would guide the nation's savings, "turning capital away from those stock operations that are so dangerous, in favor of true, stable speculation, which can only consider an investment to be *advantageous* if it is also absolutely *secure*."[125] As intermediaries between other professionals—architects, building entrepreneurs, notaries—as well as between property owners and property seekers, agents were erecting a marketplace where supply and demand could allocate effectively, rather than merely operating for their own profit.

As estate agents rationalized their advertising and information networks and established modern agencies, the stock market provided the dominant model for marketplace organization. In 1884 the agency of John Arthur et Tiffen presented readers of its pioneering journal, the *Grand Journal Officiel des Locations et de la Vente des Terrains et Immeubles* (The Official Journal of Rentals and Sales of Land and Buildings), with its project for a Bourse des Transactions Immobilières, or Real Estate Transactions Exchange.[126] As the agency explained, the real estate crisis of the early 1880s had its roots in completely unorganized and ineffectual information management: "All stocks, state securities, shares and bonds in corporations . . . any and all types of goods and commodities have central sites, exchanges, markets, where supply and demand meet. There is nothing similar for real estate; nothing is organized, everything is abandoned to chance, to fortunate circumstances, to random, fortuitous encounters." In response the agency proposed its own offices as an innovative "central site, a market, an exchange, concentrating supply and demand for all real estate business, sales, rentals and loans."[127] The term "bourse" was eagerly adopted by real estate agents as shorthand for the centralization, specialization, and incessant encounter of supply and demand necessary to efficient market organization. Edmond Schwob described his agency, founded in 1879, as a "building exchange," a central marketplace rendering distribution and consumption of properties an unproblematic question of choosing from a catalog. A. Chusin's Bourse des Locations Immobilières, or Rental Exchange, offered clients "a perfectly arranged site, to which access *is open for all*" in the prestigious Galerie Vivienne from 1874.[128] Meanwhile the Agence Lagrange, a serious real estate concern founded in 1876, made use of its prominent storefront near the Stock Exchange to advertise its commercial prowess and parade its pretentions to playing an analogous role as a clearinghouse for property (Figure 4.4).

Placing Haverkamp's endeavors alongside the evidence of the practices and priorities of actual agents highlights their key role as information managers dedicated to the creation of a modern, commercial marketplace. In rationalizing his "merchandise" and ordering his office so as to make the experience

FIGURE 4.4 En-tête of a client solicitation letter, Agence Lagrange, showing the Stock Exchange in the background, ca. 1900. *Source:* Archives de Paris, Collection l'Esprit (D.18 Z11)

of property shopping as pleasant, unintimidating, and efficient as possible, Haverkamp mimicked these real-life efforts of individual agencies to establish "unceasing marketplaces" for property transactions. By employing the model of the stock exchange, agents not only testified to the Bourse's status as the archetype of commercial culture, but also implied that property—buildings, land, and apartments—could and ought to be as effectively centralized as any other commodity.[129] This was a political as much as a market strategy. In important ways, the models used to comprehend and structure the real property market—the auction house for the sale of movables or a Bourse for the exchange of commodities and securities—were inadequate to the goods and exchange practices that defined it. They failed to reckon with the physical immobility of real property; unlike furniture and other personal goods that could be transported to an auction house, or stocks or commodities graded and abstracted for the purposes of centralized exchange, real estate remained intractable and *in place,* its locations irreproducible. Ultimately, perhaps, the limitations of locality could be overcome and an exchange for real property, particularly investment properties, established. (Chapter 5 will show that the advertising for apartment houses in Paris was amenable to such a move.) More resistance stemmed from the legal and political character of real property, which posed obstacles to its exchangeability and ensured that the model of the bourse would meet with opposition. When notaries resisted promoting their auction room as a property exchange, they were fighting a rearguard action against the commercialization of the real estate market, one they continued until their position within it was secured.

Regulation of the field of real estate brokerage, which had eluded both the self-appointed representatives of the occupation and government officials throughout the fin de siècle, enjoyed moderate success in the interwar period. In 1921 the Chambre Syndicale des Agents Immobiliers de France was founded, an organization that would be the capital's longest-lasting and most successful real estate agents' association, and the national budget of 1925 introduced a minimal regulatory model that required standardized bookkeeping practices from agents d'affaires.[130] The Chambre Syndicale des Agents Immobiliers continued the task of organizing the market as it organized the profession. It encouraged collaboration between its members, reminding those in attendance at its first general assembly that "the exercise of our profession requires a broad interpretation of our interests." What appeared as conflict—contests over commissions and clients—was to be transformed into alliances ensuring "that the proportion of transactions carried out by the members of our Association continually grows."[131] The Association secured its members discounted rates for special publicity columns in large circulation newspapers such as *Le Figaro* and *L'Ami du Peuple,* and by 1929 had established a real estate section in the *Journal des Débats.* Yet it did not produce its own advertising vehicle, and when the idea of a centralized exchange was raised, the Association replied by reprinting the articles of Lucien Lagrave, a real estate expert whose columns appeared in *Le Figaro* and who authored his own *Revue de la Propriété Immobilière.* Lagrave denied the utility—even the possibility—of a physically centralized property marketplace. In an article entitled "For a Real Estate Market" in *Le Figaro* in 1932, Lagrave acknowledged that "the idea of a market instantly takes the shape of something like the Stock or Commodities Exchange," but stressed that "for a Real Estate Market, nothing is more misleading than such a comparison." Instead, he defined a real estate market as "a series of measures" that would serve to coordinate, moralize, and increase the transactions and intermediaries in the field of property exchange.[132] Professional regulation, particularly, would ensure investor confidence and guarantee the regularity and reliability needed for market coherence.

Official licensing served real estate agents as a means of defining the contours of both their field and the market they proposed to manage. They took inspiration from the organizational efforts of their counterparts in America, where they believed licensing had "much improved [the field's] reputation in the eyes of both its clientele and public authorities."[133] Yet whereas the first statewide regulatory laws appeared in the United States in 1918, spreading throughout the 1920s and reaching nearly all states by the early 1950s, France's real estate agents did not gain a true professional charter and licensing until the loi Hoguet (Hoguet Law) of 1970.[134] The explanation for this difference lies in many arenas. French agents d'affaires faced opposition from the entrenched legal professions, particularly notaries, who were resistant to the promotion of an institutionalized occupation dealing with property brokerage. The Paris Chamber of Commerce reported unfavorably on estate agents' licensing efforts well into the post–World War II period, seeing it as an infringement on freedom of enterprise. They refused to grant their approval to the 1907 inquiry on the field's professional regulation, and also denied their support to the project of Deputy Jules Brunet in 1913.[135] As late as 1959 the Chamber of Commerce commented on a project of FNAIM (the Fédération Nationale des Groupements Professionnels d'Agents Immobiliers et de Mandataires en Vente de Fonds de Commerce, founded in 1946): "We cannot forget that the desire of real estate agents is the creation of a professional statute. The position of the Chamber of Commerce has always been one of hostility with regard to professional charters, which often enough end with the institution of monopolies or quasi-monopolies that are directly opposed to the principle of the freedom of commerce and industry."[136] Indeed, what is most in evidence in the failure of these regulation schemes is a deep suspicion of limitations of freedom of commerce on the part of both the broader business community and legislators. Concerns for the possible danger untested intermediaries posed to the public were insufficient to overcome an entrenched belief in the ultimate responsibility of the client or consumer operating in the marketplace. Only the crises of wartime housing situations could prompt the government to intervene in the arena of property transfer, a realm encompassing that most sacred republican right, private property.

Finally, resistance to licensing came from the very nature of the occupation itself. It was an individualist, fluid field with genuinely ill-defined boundaries. Specialization was certainly making headway. Witness the 1914 article in the *Fonds de Commerce,* the journal of the Syndicate of Intermediaries in Commercial and Industrial Property Sales (founded 1913), expressing frustration that still, "numerous tradesmen make no distinction between the agent d'affaires and the commercial property intermediary." Specialization was a route to social and economic distinction: "While the agent d'affaires is involved in a little bit of everything . . . the commercial property agent has a much more defined location and mission. He deals only in the transmission of commercial properties. This is a clear and precise status."[137] Even though the field's openness was a bar to its institutionalization, it was also a powerful point of attraction for the many individuals who approached the field with no previous experience and sought to achieve economic and personal independence through their success. A notice advertising the sale of a rental agency in the *Affiches Parisiennes* in 1911 chirped: "RENTAL AGENCY. Property sales in the Parisian suburbs. May be directed even by a woman, no special knowledge/experience required. Net profits 7000 fr a year."[138] The promotional pamphlet of one J. Francès, published after the Great War, promised to reveal "the ease, available to all people knowing how to read and write, of creating an independent situation with almost no capital, and without the support of an employer or anyone else," or indeed, without even an office, in the real estate business.[139] A similar document, published by a centralizing real estate bureau based in Nantes called the Institut Foncier, was peppered with bold declarations such as "Don't be a slave!," "It's not necessary to leave your current job," and "No capital necessary." Real estate was an open road to freedom, a future with dignity, and financial success. Advertising the Institute's thirty-lesson distance real estate training course, the pamphlet appealed to those seeking social advancement through more prestigious, intellectual labor: "Machine or Mind? Aren't you worthy of doing something better than a laborer's work?"[140] Real estate typified social mobility; it allowed for a more refined existence, dealing with weighty financial matters and circulating among the best classes of citizens.

The efforts of these associations to achieve the institutionalization of their occupation prompt us to reconsider the marketplace as an appropriate locus for the construction of self-identity in late-nineteenth-century France.[141] The commercial professionalism expounded by these associations was not a retreat from their commercial nature; it was the creation of a specific mode of practicing business that allowed for mastery of the marketplace through assertive individuality. These projects were an effort to define a community that could contest the atomizing potential of the commercial realm, but they were also laudatory epistles to modern commercial activity. Through association the marketplace was to be rendered efficient, transparent, and business affairs would increase healthily. These ideals found practical articulation in the eager adoption of the model of the stock exchange for the publicity and organizational priorities of individual agencies. Indeed, a comparison of real estate agents with their American colleagues shows similar attitudes toward both the market and the nature of the property intermediary, throwing into doubt the consistent opposition drawn between the business cultures of both countries, a reminder that such comparisons must be sensitive to the particularities of time, place, and industry. The real estate sector presents us with a field of activity prized for its independence, for the opportunities it allowed to become a self-made person. And indeed, by the end of this period, the disinclination of estate agent groups to support proposals for regulation that would impose stringent educational and experiential requirements indicates that the value of self-making in the marketplace was broadly acknowledged.

Real estate agents portrayed themselves as the only solution to the chronic inefficiencies that characterized both property markets in general and the particular networks of the French property distribution system. Agents presented their offices as sites of neutral intermediation and deployed their occupational organizations to impose forms of cooperation that would improve the reliability of market encounters, providing new frameworks for the organization of competition among autonomous individuals and institutions. There were significant limitations to their efforts, emerging from both within the field and without, which meant that a centralized market for property and housing remained an unrealized vision. Yet apart from their contributions to the specialized agent's profession-boosting discourse, efforts to achieve market rationalization were critical contributors to the marketization of housing and property, providing both the material and discursive terrain upon which property exchange could be conceptualized as a commercial endeavor. The chaotic activity of competitive estate agents, each claiming to out-perform the next, pulled the world of property distribution into the consumer culture of the late nineteenth century.

5

Marketing the Metropolis

Writing in the *Journal des Économistes* in January 1886, Abel Lemercier, a legal expert and former functionary at the mortgage registry (Conservation des Hypothèques), asserted that publicity, effectively and centrally organized, was the key to rectifying Paris's real estate crisis. Contrary to the opinions of many of his contemporaries, Lemercier located the problems of Paris's residential real estate market in its faulty distribution channels, rather than in the realm of housing production. The building industry, he admitted, had turned in a disappointing performance; its entrepreneurs "poorly informed, and in the grips of a speculative fever that nothing could ease, constructed thoughtlessly, without concern for already existing, empty buildings, without studying the aspects and needs of each neighborhood." Yet fundamentally, he continued, this building fever "would not have led to a real estate crisis, if publicity had been what it should." He suggested the industry focus on regulating rents by creating a rational system of supply and demand, which required the availability of merchandise to be perfectly transparent. Once housing consumers could be thoroughly and accurately informed on the totality of available rentals, competition would force a reasonable leveling of rents, curing the problem of vacancies and overcrowding that plagued tenants, property owners, and developers. Moreover, Lemercier was certain this undoubtedly popular service would prove lucrative to private industry: "Won't an intelligent entrepreneur take advantage of this opportunity to make a fortune with only modest outlays?"[1]

Flourishing in precisely this period, the Parisian real estate press was unanimous in its insistence that the capital city was illegible, difficult to both navigate and comprehend. Moreover, it showed a marked concern that the development sector was making the city's residential networks more chaotic rather than less so. The voluminous press of Paris's real estate agents provides a means of investigating both the commercialization of property distribution and the nature of the urban environment that real estate advertising reflected and constructed. Historians have argued persuasively for the particular role of periodicals and other forms of mass media in simultaneously narrating and ordering approaches to the modern metropolis.[2] The real estate press of metropolitan centers is a unique example of this urban writing, one that operates overtly as a guide to the city's geography while emphasizing its private rather than public spaces. It addresses visitor and local alike as an undifferentiated public of the uninitiated, proposing a method of deciphering urban space that generated a particular quotidian knowledge of the city. The Parisian property press, which was published by self-described specialized intermediaries and developed its recognizably modern form in the last decades of the nineteenth century, addressed the capital in its entirety, rarely focusing on anything but the city as a whole. Appearing independently of the traditional *termes* or quarterly moving periods (these were the eighth and fifteenth of January, April, July, and October, depending on the cost of the apartment), the press represented residential spaces as a flow of ready availabilities, constantly cycling through the market.

Real estate agents and their widely diffused press did more than merely reflect the built environment that they publicized. Publicity was as productive of Paris as a *social* space as were the speculative construction ventures it sought to advertise. Agents' activities and publications helped constitute an image of the capital's built environment that facilitated the commercialization of property and housing, creating the conditions in which buildings and apartments could be viewed and circulate as exchangeable goods. Real estate agents were not the only participants in this process. The flyers, gazettes, and posters that helped establish the contours of the city's real estate market competed with and complemented the market models of other intermediaries. They also confronted and were shaped by the traditions and practices of mobility already in place in Paris at the end of the nineteenth century. The publications of the estate agency sector were the result of constant dialogue between these models and impulses. When agents attempted to convince property owners that the *écriteau* (the "For Sale" and "For Rent" signs dappling the capital's building façades) was both outmoded and unproductive, proposing instead the services of their popular gazettes and citywide information networks, they were attempting to replace localized patterns of property distribution that were deeply ingrained and over which they never achieved dominance. Nevertheless, their innovative advertising and specialized bureaus played a significant role in integrating both urban buildings and domestic interiors in the circulatory imperatives shaping the modern metropolis. Situated in the broader context of fin-de-siècle efforts to render domestic life amenable to contemporary consumerism, the advertising press of specialized property bureaus constitutes an important and unacknowledged agent in the day-to-day acculturation of urban living.[3]

Owning and Renting in the City of Light

The question of demand and consumer needs in the housing market was particularly cogent to diagnoses of the real estate crisis of the early 1880s. The buildings constructed during the boom were erected expressly for the purposes of sale. As building entrepreneur Onésime Masselin reminded readers of the real estate journal *Le Foncier* in 1882, "a speculative real estate venture can only be settled advantageously by the *Sale of buildings*. Buildings must be SELLABLE."[4] As buildings were slapped up across the city by companies whose resources were of short duration, communicating to the rental and sales marketplace was crucial for the viability of their ventures. In 1884 an early issue of one of the city's foremost property rental and sales journals, the *Grand Journal Officiel des Locations et de la Vente des Terrains et Immeubles*, criticized the market in the following manner:

> We wrote, in our last issue, of how under the whip of *adventurers* [*lanceurs d'affaires*], construction took a wild course that pushed more than one inexperienced entrepreneur to financial collapse.
>
> One of the first and unavoidable consequences of this state of affairs is the considerable quantity of apartments available to rent in almost all neighborhoods of Paris . . . they [the builders] produced, and to employ an

> expression that captures the situation, they produced well in excess of the needs of *consumption*.[5]

Driven by profiteering speculators, a dangerously off-kilter real estate market had emerged, an arena in which supply and demand could not be relied on as regulatory mechanisms. The result, property agents argued, was that whether one sought to buy an apartment building or to rent lodgings, consumers experienced an unprecedented need for reliable guidance, objective advice, and constant assistance.

The real estate press addressed rental as well as sales, or investment, markets. Rental gazettes brokered housing to the city's tenants, while sales columns, journals, and posters marketed apartment buildings, private homes, and suburban estates as residential and investment opportunities to capitalists. Only in the early years of the twentieth century did a robust market for single-family homes destined for owner occupancy appear in the capital city region.[6] The vast number of Parisians owned no property at all. The percentage of individuals dying without wealth in the nineteenth century remained about 70 percent for Parisians, and only 50 percent for the rest of the country. Yet alongside this conglomeration of poor, the city also sheltered the nation's richest families, so that Parisians owned about a quarter of the country's wealth.[7] Regardless of whether or not they owned property in the city, nearly all Parisians lived in rented dwellings.[8] These varied from shared dormitories or small furnished rooms in the city's extensive network of boarding establishments, to apartments ranging widely in size, amenities, and cost, to private dwellings that were rented rather than purchased. In 1891 the city contained nearly 75,000 buildings dedicated to residential use, almost half of them four stories or taller, averaging approximately thirteen dwellings per building, or nearly one million apartments.[9]

The majority of this housing stock was comprised of apartments renting for less than 300 francs annually, an amount that was still unattainable for the high percentages of the population that failed to attain the minimum of one franc per day in income required to live in freedom from social assistance and want.[10] One has to travel rather far up the income ladder to find budgets that allowed for some exercise of choice in housing. A guide from 1885 addressed to families with incomes of 1,800–2,000 francs a year observed: "Wives of workers or lower-level employees, we have to know how to make do with that [amount]. Certainly it is not easy, above all in a large city, where life is difficult, food expensive, rents unaffordable. But *it is possible* . . . as long as we *desire* it, and know how to go about it."[11] Following the contemporary rule of thumb that housing expenses should not exceed one-fifth of a household's income, these families might dedicate 400 francs per year to their rent.[12] The cost of owning a building in the city, most generally an apartment building, had increased sixfold over the course of the nineteenth century, reaching in 1880 an average of 260,000 francs for buildings within the old boundaries of the city, though buildings in the zone annexed in 1860 (today's 14th through 20th arrondissements, and parts of the 12th and 13th) could still be had for 80,000 francs.[13] The city's tax evaluations cited an average price of 132,171 francs for a Parisian building in 1889.[14]

Defining demand is by no means straightforward when dealing with a good such as housing. It simultaneously responds to general, basic needs for shelter and occupies the unique, affect-laden status of "home," and is as much a matter of production (as a site of work and of social reproduction) as the site and product of consumption. As a result, the expectations and behaviors of housing consumers are not immediately reducible to demographic patterns or straightforward economic rationality. As Maurice Halbwachs observed in his 1909 analysis of Paris's property market, the population of housing consumers "obeys, in its movements, preferences, and passions, patterns of an order entirely different [from economic or demographic], more confused, less defined, and which are more difficult to predict."[15] The question of housing choice was an increasingly democratized criterion of social distinction at the end of the nineteenth century. Taste professionals promoted the domestic interior as a site of creative, fulfilling self-expression for its inhabitants, and the ability of the residential environment to communicate and help reproduce social status was widely acknowledged.[16] Even the most humble tenants, whose meager resources left no room for considerations of fashion and discernment, were advised to privilege the dictates of hygiene as they sought lodgings in the capital city.

As the home became a site for the exercise of a kind of aesthetic citizenry, the choice of an apartment was not a subject to which one could be indifferent, even if contemporary building practices and architectural discourse emphasized the standardization of modern constructions. As one apartment guide for modest families advised, "Don't rush in to choosing your lodgings; visit many, and when one particularly pleases you, visit it many times, using your imagination to place each piece of furniture and each object in the particular place you designate for them."[17] Another guide on apartment decorating also stressed the importance of careful choice, and recommended that tenants negotiate with owners for long leases, in order to carry out the upgrades and repairs that would help establish the desired domestic setting: "Once the choice of an apartment has been made, when after studying it with care one has determined exactly what remains to be done in order to decorate and improve it as one pleases—which is necessary whatever state the apartment is in—there will be changes to make, some more and some less important, either in the paint of one room or the hangings of another. It is thus absolutely necessary to ensure that one will have it for as long a period as possible."[18] Décor served to personalize homogeneous apartments, and to remedy the shortcomings that inevitably arose in living spaces that one could not craft for oneself. Indeed, it may well be that part of the French concern with furnishings as expressive vehicles of both individual and national identity originated in the common experience of renting in the nation's large cities.

The diffusion and reception of these ideals were conditioned by a number of factors, from an increasingly institutionalized concern with urban hygiene to the fledgling emergence of a mass consumer marketplace for domestic accoutrements.[19] All were linked to shifts in the capital city's labor and consumption regime, of which the rapid growth of white-collar employees in Paris between 1870 and 1911 was one of the most important aspects. The number of employees of railroads, banks, and insurance companies increased an estimated threefold between the Commune and the Great War; between 1866 and 1911, the number of white-collar employees in the capital city grew from 126,006 to 352,744.[20] A figure Balzac described as "misery in a black tailcoat," the employee allegedly suffered "from a poverty and a discomfort *sui generis*, generally more painful than that of the worker" owing to his intense and often unrealizable need for social distinction, for a style of living that would approximate the middle classes and distinguish him from the working orders below.[21] Affordable, hygienic, and tasteful—in a word, appropriate—housing was crucial to the efforts of this group to establish their status. In novelist Paul Margueritte's *Jours d'épreuve: Moeurs bourgeoises* (1886), a young bureaucrat named André is forced to find a more affordable apartment after the birth of a second child. His wife joins him on the search, which first takes them through the prestigious and newly built speculative districts of the city to which their (hopefully) mobile social status makes her aspire: "A need for luxury pushed her toward the grand buildings of damp plaster near the Trocadéro, toward the deserted avenues leading to the Arc de Triomphe and their lines of private homes far from markets and merchants. With difficulty, he fought against these desires, and led Toinette toward the popular neighborhoods, teeming with life."[22] André is secretly happy that their reduced circumstances oblige them to move to the working-class areas near the Bastille, where he can escape the pressures of appearances: "In his decent poverty, he had suffered in the house at Saint-Sulpice, where he felt the disdain of the concierges. He preferred to live here, on the third floor in a house full of life, in the middle of these poor households. Socially, it was a step backward, but who would visit to see?"[23] While André is able to avoid suffering at this social sacrifice (tellingly, his wife is not so fortunate), the importance of residential choice is clear. Moreover, this housing search, from the wealthy west end to the popular east, reflects the extreme geographical diffusion of the white-collar group, which even more than members of the working class, spread throughout the city.[24] These developments provided part of the context for the increasing utility of the real estate press's services.

If workers and employees had little choice but to lodge themselves in rented dwellings, the apparent preference of the capital's wealthy for apartment living provoked commentary from many fin-de-siècle observers. Developers concentrating on the higher end of the market established more socially homogeneous districts, fashionable neighborhoods where the presence of elegant apartments allowed one to live where one could not perhaps buy. Historian and essayist Georges d'Avenel marveled in 1897 that "there is a peculiarity among Parisians that there are more lower middle class individuals than millionaires who enjoy the use of *the entirety of a building,* as expensive rents are found exclusively in rich districts where there are hardly any constructions of less than four stories."[25] Commentators attributed this trend to sources as diverse as building height regulations and tax incentives. For instance, an anonymous author suggested in *Paris Journal* in 1911 that "after the increase in taxes on unbuilt property, little by little the number of private homes diminished, [and] rich tenants turned, infatuated, to the well-appointed apartments of luxurious buildings."[26] Most explanations for the phenomenon, however, focused on questions of taste and fashion. Summarizing the development of the city's west end, Émile Rivoalen, prolific architectural critic, recounted how the rich turned from private residences to apartments in shared buildings: "After some experience, a retreat from the alleged advantages of the private house began: service and supervision was more difficult owing to the number of stories to climb, or to descend; more servants were needed, and they lived promiscuously in the basement, far from the master's watchful eye; the kitchen, in the lower levels, emitted cooking odors that invaded the upper apartments, etc., etc. In short, it just wasn't as good as the single-floor apartment, the 'everything at hand.'"[27] Responding to demands for convenience and luxurious appearances—Rivoalen noted that "appearance is before everything"—builders constructed palatial apartment houses for which the wealthy traded the permanence of their large households so that they might instead "change coach, horse, driver, and car renter as their fancy strikes."[28] An illustrated supplement to *Le Temps* in 1893 offered advice on apartment décor and trendy purveyors of home goods, and was careful to include an advertisement for the rental services of the John Arthur et Tiffen agency, "known to most Parisians and almost all visiting foreigners," particularly those who "want to set themselves up in luxurious and comfortable surroundings," as "inventors of a special kind of press: rental advertising."[29] Fashion came to characterize both the demand for and supply of apartments, with apartment living thus deeply connected to both the emancipation of the marketplace and the trivialities of consumer culture.

The conditions of housing production in the second half of the nineteenth century were shot through with imperatives that placed particular importance on the merchandizing efforts of property intermediaries. Critics of this urbanism repeatedly drew analogies between the new buildings favored by the rich and mass-produced consumer goods. Rivoalen dismissed the banal buildings churned out in blocks for anonymous tenants as *l'architecture de fabrique*, manufactured architecture.[30] Even when he found new construction aesthetically pleasing, as he did in the developing Trocadéro quartier, Rivoalen could not get past the absurdity of the small mansions that were promoted as "individual homes for sale," as if a home could actually be something acquired on the market rather than created.[31] His preferred term for such buildings was "confectionné": trivial articles intended to be enticing for buyers. Their falsity went beyond matters of taste and corrupted the core of the constructions: "Houses manufactured for sale—and resale—can slump with impunity on their limp foundations of soft cinder block, slapped over with plaster, on cellars arched in plaster, as long as at the end of a stucco and marble stairway sprawls a chocolate-colored antechamber, with rickety stained glass made of bits of old rubbish glass thrown together in lead; and as long as the dining room, in the 16th-century style, has a monumental fireplace of wood, plaster, and pastry, a 'historied' ceiling, without, of course, leaving out the high paneling made of molded fir nailed on plaster, painted in dark tones to look like oak or feudal yew."[32] The construction processes in the capital were not only reducing the level of architectural integrity, they were also generating superficial clients and new modes of consuming urban spaces. A public trained in the purchase of goods at Parisian department stores, Rivoalen commented bitingly, "prefers to pay more in exchange for a ready-made product; instead of having a house made, this man makes himself to his new house."[33] Showy buildings and sham artistry overwhelmed and mastered the consumer, who was molded to fit the shabby goods on offer. The danger that such an apartment could seduce (and mislead) a prospective consumer was deeply disturbing in a period that drew increasingly close links between consumption, particularly domestic consumption, and national identity.[34]

The impression that the wealthy preferred apartment houses to private homes needs to be contextualized by a consideration of the number of individuals who owned property outside the city but remained tenants within its boundaries. If proprietors, particularly wealthy owners of several buildings, chose to rent rather than live in their own buildings, how far was this choice determined by the affective and/or economic anchor provided by the ownership of a "home" outside the city? Seasonal retirement to a country estate was a venerable tradition of the Parisian upper classes. Even in the seventeenth and eighteenth centuries, aristocratic residences in the city were often rented rather than owned, enabling their occupants to easily obey the demands of fashion. These urban properties were regarded as exchangeable by nature, as opposed to rural holdings, which were matters of patrimony and privilege.[35] In the eighteenth century this trend of pastoral escape was increasingly mimicked by those of the humbler classes who could afford the luxury of country property.[36] Country excursions became more popular throughout the nineteenth century, facilitated by improvements in rail and transit lines, fueling a market for country homes to buy and rent. Already in the 1820s, property owners in Belleville, a suburban village to the northeast of Paris, were drawing significant revenues from letting buildings or parts of buildings to Parisian "tourists," and advertising was beginning to consolidate land and an "experience" of nature into a commodity image of the *maison de campagne*.[37] Advertisements hawked a huge range of properties, from 3,500 to 350,000 francs, and studies of the composition of the fortunes of the middle classes in the first half of the nineteenth century demonstrate the proclivity of this class for purchasing suburban properties.[38] In 1845 more than 30 percent of owners of land in Belleville were nonresident, and living chiefly in Paris.[39] These patterns of consumption constitute the origin of a *banlieue choisie*, the suburb as a site of attraction rather than banishment, leading to the emergence of both middle- and working-class subdivisions on the periphery of the city by the end of the nineteenth century.[40] Of the 30 percent of Parisians who died with assets to bequeath at the end of the century, the middling fortunes in this group had more real estate assets located outside the city than did those in the top 10 percent, the wealthiest fraction of society, whose real estate was concentrated instead in the capital.[41]

Our most reliable figures on the propensity of Parisian residents and property holders to own real estate outside the capital city come from studies of elite groups under the Second Empire and early Third Republic. All of the twenty-two Bank of France regents whose portfolios have been reconstituted by Alain Plessis, for instance, owned property in the capital, though only eleven of them were living in any of these properties upon their death, and at least two were tenants elsewhere in Paris. Overall, the regents held only 16.5 percent of their wealth in buildings, as compared with 37 percent for the bank's 200 largest shareholders, and 57 percent of the millionaires who died in Paris in 1847. Plessis observes that many of the regents maintained country estates, but he finds it more noteworthy that several did not. By the end of the Second Empire, provincial land represented only 6 percent of the regents' fortunes, a rate much lower than that of the shareholders, for whom it represented 23 percent. The author suggests that these elites may have prefigured the tendency of wealthy families to divest themselves of provincial holdings; by the end of the century, the percentage of wealth represented by provincial properties in the fortunes of all of Paris's richest individuals had declined to only 6 percent.[42] These figures are, of course, only percentages of total estates; the relatively low value of provincial and suburban land meant that it figured for comparatively less in total portfolios than other assets.

A study by Christophe Charle of elite circles in the early Third Republic provides some complementary information. Studying 1,093 individuals who appeared in various academic almanacs, business directories, and contemporary guides to elite society, Charle traces the residential habits of three groups, defined as business elites, administrative elites, and intellectual elites.[43] His study confirms the low rate of owner-occupancy in the city during his period—54 percent of businessmen, 89 percent of bureaucrats, and 85 percent of university elites lived in rented apartments—while also providing data on the ownership of secondary residences. Business elites led in this category, with 77 percent maintaining properties outside the capital; 54.2 percent of university elites did likewise, followed by 51.2 percent of bureaucrats. Whereas businessmen generally maintained residences close to the capital, functionaries tended to own provincial lands, and university elites, when they did not live close to Paris, owned properties in the regions from which they issued.[44] Thus, many wealthy individuals who chose to live in apartments in the capital also owned property outside the city, a type of investment that not only was much more affordable than urban property but also was bound up with a series of social and cultural imperatives regarding traditions of sociability, conspicuous leisure, and personal, affective ties to one's provincial origins (in 1886, after all, only 25 percent of Parisian heads of households had been born in the department of the Seine).

In sum, while in popular depictions Paris was regularly divided into "those who rent and those who rent to others," these two groups involved considerable overlap, with owners more likely to rent lodgings than live in buildings they owned, and many tenants in the capital possessing property elsewhere. Renting in no way implied a low social status, and it was not until the end of the nineteenth century that the mobility facilitated by rental arrangements began to be problematized by reformers dedicated to the social question. Paris had long been known as a mobile city. Not only did its position as a capital of tourism and a center of seasonal labor immigration ensure a significant floating population, but permanent residents were themselves frequent movers. The demographic study by Alain Faure and Jean-Claude Farcy reveals a remarkable mobility among urban residents, averaging 4.5 moves in the twenty-year period between 1880 and 1900, with 46 percent of their studied population moving between four and eight times. Moreover, these moves, while showing strong tendencies toward localized patterns, were not uncommonly carried out on the scale of the city as a whole, particularly among the wealthier classes, whose housing changes more often involved leaving both the arrondissement and the city.[45]

Lacking more comprehensive studies, it is difficult to be certain whether these high rates of mobility represent an increase over previous patterns. Conditions facilitating greater mobility were certainly in place in the capital city at the end of the century. Paris underwent one of its most significant periods of population growth between 1872 and 1911, and until the end of this period, housing construction kept pace with population increase, meaning that for all but the humblest classes, residential choice remained plentiful. For the consumer of "bourgeois" housing—apartments with rents exceeding 500 francs annually, which represented about 22 percent of total dwellings in 1884, and 26 percent in the mid-1890s—an overabundance of housing kept rents from increasing and created the conditions for a favorable tenant's market. These middle-class tenants were, moreover, more solvent than ever. If you were lucky enough to accumulate an estate in nineteenth-century Paris, it enjoyed undeniable enhancement across the century; wealth left to successors in the capital multiplied by 9.5 from 1815 to 1911, whereas it multiplied only by 4.8 for France as a whole. Most of this growth took place at the level of middling and upper bourgeoisie.[46] Transit developments at the beginning of the century may have also loosened some constraints on housing choice. The subway or *métro* had 16 million passengers annually in 1900, 149 million in 1905, and 254 million in 1909; "clearly," historian Anthony Sutcliffe observes, "the new facilities were encouraging people to move about who otherwise would have stayed where they were."[47] Studies of residential mobility in the nearby town of Versailles for this period have determined that mobility was on the rise among all classes as the nineteenth century progressed; it is likely that this trend was similar in the capital.[48] Finally, mechanisms supporting residential mobility—a host of new agents and innovative technologies dedicated to the distribution of commercialized property—were increasingly available, advanced, and appealing at the end of the century. As we saw in Chapter 4, intermediaries for whom housing and property distribution was a livelihood were able to undertake the consolidation of professional organizations during this period, approaching the sector of housing distribution as a viable career. These specialists earned money when families moved and vacancies needed to be filled; it was in their interest to stimulate and maintain residential turnover, and they set about organizing their profession, offices, and publicity vehicles to achieve just this.

Advertising Apartments in the Early Nineteenth Century

Reports that followed the ruin of famed real estate agent John Arthur in 1884 described rental brokerages as "an industry that he imported, or perhaps even created."[49] At the time of his scandalous bankruptcy and flight to England,

Arthur was running the firm that his father had founded in 1818. Originally an agency dedicated to assisting foreign tourists who were returning to Paris in droves following the end of the Napoleonic wars, the firm would eventually become one of the city's most important rental and sales brokerages. The younger John Arthur took the reins in 1850 and developed the company fully along the lines of the spectacular urbanity fostered by the Second Empire, his huge storefront and embossed windows a notable fixture near the Place Vendôme.[50] A well-known man about town, Arthur was said to have provided the author Alphonse Daudet with the basis for the character Tom Lévis in his 1879 novel *Les rois en exil,* his agency a model "that summed up all I knew of certain ways of making money under the Empire."[51] Once Arthur fled the country, the company was auctioned off and eventually acquired by a former associate, William Tiffen, a Niçois who had joined the agency in 1873. Tiffen oversaw the increasing specialization of the firm in the domain of real estate brokerage, steered its new publication, the *Grand Journal Officiel des Locations et de la Vente des Terrains et Immeubles,* to the front of the pack of the booming real estate press, and transformed the company into a limited liability venture. All the while he stove off merciless competition from Arthur's son, who set up a rival agency in the 1880s, and then Arthur himself, who returned in the same period and embarked on a flurry of legal suits, eventually forcing his way—temporarily—back into the company.[52]

The John Arthur et Tiffen firm exemplifies many of the dominant features of the real estate sector in late-nineteenth-century Paris, notably its fiercely competitive nature (the dueling John Arthur firms stole one another's employees and repeatedly ripped down and covered each other's posters), its reliance on innovative publicity, and its imbrication in the world of Parisian tourism. Turf was precious. At one point, when the two firms had taken up locations scarcely 500 meters from one another on Rue des Capucines and Rue Castiglione, lawyers for those who had purchased John Arthur's business argued that "rental agencies are, by their nature, connected above all with foreigners," who will "naturally address themselves to agencies that are located in those places they tend to frequent, which are obviously the Boulevard des Italiens, the Place Vendôme, Rue Castiglione, Rue des Capucines." In breaking into this privileged zone, the younger John Arthur was engaged in unfair competition.[53] Yet while the company frequently touted its services as novel and readily claimed credit for inventing property brokerage as Parisian residents and visitors knew it, many elements of the specialized real estate press that multiplied in the fin-de-siècle had antecedents in earlier—and indigenous—forms of property advertising.

Property sales and rental notices featured prominently in the widely disseminated *affiches* or *petites annonces,* gazettes that circulated throughout the country from the eighteenth century onward.[54] In Paris the *Affiches Parisiennes et Départementales* (1818) and the *Journal Général d'Affiches,* known as the *Petites Affiches* (in existence in various forms since the seventeenth century) were important venues for sales advertisements throughout the nineteenth century, though they had only small rental sections. Specialized real estate publications made their appearance in the capital city around the time of the July Monarchy. Sporting titles such as *L'Indicateur Perpétuel* (1828), *Le Moniteur Général des Locations et des Ventes* (1834), *Gazette des Locations* (1841), and *Le Plan. Journal Spécial pour Locations ou Ventes Immobilières* (1843), these gazettes promoted a more orderly process of property seeking, promising to save time and improve profits. Invoking the virtues of "this era of enlightenment and civilization," the *Gazette des Locations* boasted that "today, rental opportunities are left to chance; from now on, they shall be the fruit of our labor and the activities of our agents."[55]

These gazettes were addressed to two key demographics: intermediaries engaged in the market (landlords, notaries, solicitors, architects, and agents d'affaires), and the mass of Parisian residents, foreign and local, deemed to be in need of a residence or property investment. They charged for advertisements and were often available to readers for free. *Le Vendeur,* for instance, a weekly commercial property sales journal that appeared in 1838 and 1839, grandiosely promised advertisers that "sufficient copies of the Journal will be printed to ensure that it is read in all public administrations, reading rooms, cafés, omnibus offices, hotels, by all merchants, in all the cities and regions of France."[56] Access to listings was open to all and sundry who frequented the Right Bank sites around which most journals located their bureaus and placed their catalogs (the *Moniteur Général des Locations* did note two "branches" on the Left Bank, on Rue Dauphine and the Place Odéon). Yet most of these publications were rather unreliable as guides, undergoing repeated changes in the format, length, content, and the frequency with which they appeared. At times they might emphasize apartment rentals, at others private sales, and still other times industrial or commercial leases. There is little espousing of the specialized capacities of property agents that will appear in later real estate publications. These variations reflected the wide range of activities to which estate agencies were often dedicated, as well as the ephemeral nature of many such business ventures.

The overall trend in these publications across the nineteenth century was toward specialization and rationalization. Aspirations to efficiency notwithstanding, publications in the earlier decades of the century presented their offers and demands in an incoherent manner. All types of properties—rural, urban, single-family houses for rent or purchase, apartments, and commercial spaces—were commonly intermingled. Lists of available rentals were predictable in their content (typically, they provided the street address, floor, the number of rooms in a unit) but not in their organization. Only rarely was either a spatial or price-oriented organization followed. In short, hunting for properties in these journals remained disordered and time consuming. These presentation methods reflected a view of Parisian space as holistic and undifferentiated; even in those instances where classification separated sales from rentals, apartments from buildings, or residential from commercial spaces, readers encountered availabilities from across the city, in no particular order. While putatively engaged in a mission to clarify the urban environment by improving awareness of property availabilities, the actual form and content of these publications worked against either market or urban segmentation.

More self-consciously and recognizably systematic publications emerged at midcentury. This was not merely the result of competitive practices within the industry converging around a "better" model of provisioning. It was also closely linked to the transformations in urban space particular to the city of Paris, namely, the impact of the 1848 revolutions and Haussmann's massive renovations. The revolutions of 1848 are often considered events that forced a radical reconceptualization of the relationship between urban community and the urban environment. The patterns of street fighting, starkly divided between east and west, revealed a geography of class separation with ominous consequences for the body politic.[57] The kind of urban guidance provided by the real estate press had a new role to play in this context of revolutionary dislocation. As an antidote to disordered and discomfiting rounds from apartment to apartment—and as an alternative to exploration of the recently riotous spaces of the city—the *Journal des Locataires et des Acquéreurs*, for example, proposed its services as an auxiliary that "takes you from your home straight to your desired goal."[58] The gazette debuted in 1849 (it was renamed *Les Grandes Affiches* in 1850) and approached space marketing as a science: "Listings proceed in the order of districts and neighborhoods. For rentals, descriptions are given in descending order of price." The goal of this organization was to simplify and streamline apartment hunting, "as it will be sufficient to throw a quick look at the neighborhood where one would like to live, and then search the price column"; those seeking lodgings required only "a single glance" to locate twenty or thirty apartments matching their needs and desires.[59]

Focusing easily on particular, predetermined areas, and doing so from the comfort of one's residence, correlated well with anxieties of urban dispossession. It contrasted sharply with the street-front advertisement that seduced wandering passersby, as depicted in the 1840 urban tableau *Les Français peints par eux-mêmes:* "From every side the big black letters of provocative signs gleam like the blazing eyes of courtesans. You're under their spell; there is seduction at each step, in every form, at every door. . . . Large, handsome apartment . . . Apartment newly decorated. . . . Small apartment. . . . Even when you don't have a particular desire to leave your current housing . . . you enter without hesitation."[60] Walking the city, waiting for a *coup de coeur* to jump into your path, might have struck some Parisians as a less than ideal way of approaching the housing search in the aftermath of urban insurgency. Rental advertising at midcentury reflected and catered to the worries of a momentarily disoriented Parisian bourgeoisie. In its promotion of specialized services—*Les Grandes Affiches* was published by an Office Général des Locations et des Ventes, which "dedicated a *special* office to sales, to which *special* agents are allocated"—the press suggested that the urban setting was no longer one that could be reliably navigated on one's own.[61] Yet if real estate, particularly rental, publications exploited such sentiments, it would be going too far to say that they faithfully mirrored and reproduced a general experience of alienation. The real estate press facilitated rather than replaced individual urban explorations, integrating itself into existing patterns of housing acquisition that were pedestrian, localized, and personal.

A bureau operating at the end of the Second Empire provides an example of how advertising capitalized on the existing networks through which housing was located. In 1867 an estate agency called the Administration des Répertoires proposed to expand its system of centralized housing registries by placing copies in public venues in each of Paris's twenty arrondissements, where they were available to be consulted free of charge by interested parties (Figure 5.1). The registers not only provided individuals with information

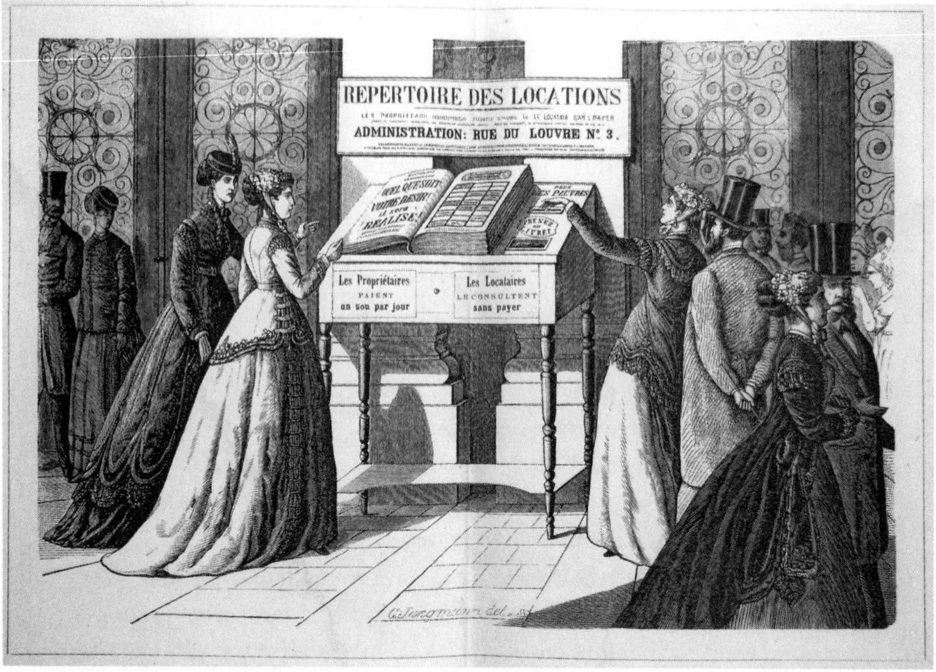

FIGURE 5.1 "The Rental Directory," drawn from life (Town hall of the 2nd arrondissement), 1868. *Source:* Archives de Paris V.D6 733 no.4

about housing in their immediate vicinity, but also advertised properties for rent from across the entire city; the twenty registers, it was emphasized, were exactly the same. The presumed consumers of this publicity were individuals who desired access to accurate information on a citywide scale. In conjunction with the agency's offices, the registers acted as "a center accessible to all, where all needs can meet and hence find satisfaction."[62] This system gained the particular support of Prefect Haussmann, who viewed it as an "ingenious enterprise."[63] By placing registries throughout the city, the Administration des Répertoires sought to combine the localized traditions of apartment seeking with the diffusion of availabilities compiled in a gazette.

The Administration des Répertoires envisioned itself as a harmonizer of supply and demand. The register in the engraving announces to its well-heeled readers, "Whatever you desire! It will be realized!," casting housing as another fashionable consumer good satisfying whims and fancies. By facilitating the informed exercise of consumer choice, the agency promised to increase the volume of market activity. This was the first time the notion of desire featured in rental advertising, and it is noteworthy that it occurred alongside a representation of largely female consumers, as well as in the context of a broader argument for the need to increase transactions in the market. The role of the real estate press—and agency—was beginning to be conceived of in new terms. Its goal was not simply to inform and facilitate, but to guide and ultimately amplify market activity. The Administration des Répertoires had its sights on what it approximated as 15,000 tenants every quarterly term who desired to move but found their desires frustrated, resulting in empty, unproductive apartments.[64] Tenants ended up forced "to remain where they are because they can't find better. And yet this better exists, and they'll find it once they're given the means."[65] These were the stories of property that agents deployed to consolidate the city's spaces and residents into a market amenable to their intervention.

Sales and Rental Advertising in the Early Third Republic

If 1848 is understood as a break in the relationship between the urban environment and the types of communities it supported, a break perpetuated by the alienating renovations of the Second Empire, there is somewhat less consensus on the impact on urban culture of the immense upheavals in the capital city in 1870–1871. Guided by the work of Henri Lefebvre, a spatialized interpretation of the origins and course of the Commune—from the reclaiming of a right to the city by those driven to its periphery, to the revolutionary use of space during the conflict itself—is now well established.[66] But the fate of the spatial politics and practices of the Commune is less clear. Did new solidarities and identities die on the barricades, along with thousands of Communards? Certainly some works on Paris's distinctive urban culture during the Second Empire have suggested that the potential for lasting collective identities was dead before the Versaillais entered Paris, the victim of Haussmann's inauthentic *ville décor* and the depoliticizing tendencies of consumer society.[67] Yet more recent studies of the crowd in the fin de siècle show that the urban masses of the early Third Republic, far from behaving as alienated individuals, found new sources of collective meaning in the modern urban experience itself.[68] These identities were less tied to older divisions of class and space; they were linked instead to public sites of consumption and leisure, and emphasized inclusion rather than division.

Yet were the public spaces and collectivities of the city truly as unproblematic as this work implies? If the need to reclaim Paris for the bourgeoisie was, arguably, at the heart of Haussmann's efforts to reconstruct the capital in the wake of the bloody and unsettling events of 1848, the trauma of the Commune was an episode of urban upheaval that was just as dramatic, and, in matter of fact, bloodier. The creation of vast residential districts of bourgeois apartments in the speculative booms of both the 1880s and the immediate prewar period reasserted a form of control of the urban environment by the middle and upper classes, while also representing a retreat from engagement with various elements of that public realm. For instance, author and critic Alphonse de Calonne observed in 1895 that the most sought after and expensive buildings in the capital were those that eliminated ground floor commerce, thus achieving a firm delineation between domestic and public spaces.[69] Literary scholar Sharon Marcus has argued that Haussmannian Paris underwent a distinct "interiorization" as the value of hermetically sealed interiors began to become paramount in literary and architectural discourse.[70] Without following her line of argument in its totality—privacy had certainly been a powerful cultural trope and social need well before an extroverted public life became idolized in the discourse of modernity—it can safely be argued that interior urban spaces became increasingly construed as comforting and necessary retreats from the hazards of city life.

The real estate advertising press of the early Third Republic provides a unique source through which to address these divergent positions. Exploring the qualities of this press that were distinct to the period helps determine the approaches to and appropriations of space it both enabled and reflected. Exploiting the heightened perception that Paris was an unfathomable urban space, agents broadcast their efficiency and superior knowledge as key selling points of their services. Yet, contrary to what might be assumed, these agents were not professed apostles of domesticity. The words "chez soi" or "home" (an Anglicization appearing in French in the nineteenth century) are strikingly rare in these texts.[71] Certainly, with their stress on discretion, particularly in the realm of sales, agents sought to maintain the integrity of interiors and protect the privacy of clients. At the same time, however, they worked to facilitate mobility and circulation, rationalizing the city and mobilizing its residents in a constant search for "a new residence, a little more comfortable and at a better price."[72] Freedom of movement, to whatever part of the city, whenever one desired, was the goal, and one they argued that only the neutral mediation of the real estate agent could achieve.

The publication of real estate listings of all kinds increased dramatically from the 1880s onward.[73] While exact numbers are difficult to calculate, owing to inconsistencies between press bibliographies and directories as well as the chronically ephemeral nature of many of the real estate sector's publications, the numbers provided by the *Annuaire de la Presse Française* for 1884 and 1908 register an increase from twelve to twenty-six publications in Paris. These figures underreport the actual number of rental bulletins that were circulating in the city, but nevertheless provide an indication of a steady increase in volume. Some long-established estate agencies began publishing rental gazettes at this point. In 1884 the John Arthur et Tiffen firm introduced its *Grand Journal Officiel,* quickly to become one of the city's most innovative and longest-lasting real estate publications. Similarly, the Agence Largier, founded in 1859, introduced its lavish *Journal Illustré des Ventes et Locations* at the turn of the century.[74] In choosing this moment, these agencies were latching onto a broader trend in the French press of allocating more space to reportage on the real estate market and rental opportunities. Even though official and private sales of properties had always featured to some degree in the advertising sections of large-circulation daily newspapers, these papers began including rental listings among their commercial notices only after 1871. *Le Figaro* began posting small rental notices in their rear-page advertising section in 1874; by 1885 they had a designated section exclusively for apartment and house rentals in the capital. In the 1880s *Le Gaulois* began running rental ads, including a small "sales and rentals" category throughout this period. *La Presse* consolidated its sporadic rental notices into a weekly section in 1897, following a reduction of its advertising rates for apartment and property notices.[75] Similarly, *L'Illustration* added a rental supplement to its popular weekly journal in the 1890s.[76]

Part of this increase is attributable to the new conditions of housing production and management generated by the speculative boom of the 1870s and 1880s. This particular market situation was critical for constituting building management as a service and tenants as a consumer group.[77] Property construction and financing firms found themselves managing large groups of newly built apartment houses; by the mid-1890s the Compagnie Foncière de France was managing nearly 170 apartment buildings, the Rente Foncière 147, the Société Foncière Lyonnaise 235.[78] Insurance companies such as the Compagnie d'Assurances Vie "La France," "La Générale," and "La Foncière" were also acquiring significant property portfolios in the fin de siècle.[79] Much of this housing, particularly the more expensive, bourgeois apartments constructed in the 1880s, suffered high vacancy rates for nearly two decades. Not only did marketing become an important element in generating returns on corporate investments, but the buildings themselves were also understood as competing for a *clientèle locataire* (rental clientele). The dictates of the competitive housing market also permeated the rhetoric of professionalized property owners. A speaker at the 1900 International Congress of Built Property attended to the productive economic role of property owners in the following fashion: "A property owner who wants to rent must not only carry out repairs, but also update his facilities in accordance with contemporary tastes and needs. He has to take heed of the desires of his tenants and give in to the laws of competition."[80]

Estate agents certainly found it in their interests to accentuate and exploit this understanding of the housing market. The *Moniteur de la Location,* a journal founded by the Agence Lagrange in 1879, assimilated housing to any other kind of merchandise that needed publicity in order to sell. As merchants exploited advertising "to stimulate business and draw buyers into their stores," so "intelligent and far-seeing landlords must, like merchants, ensure their apartments and shops against vacancies, which become more burdensome the longer they drag on."[81] Similarly, witness the appeal to property owners who did not wish to see their investments sit idle, published in one of the early issues of the *Grand Journal Officiel:* "Tenants go to the most skilled, to those who know how to attract them by clever advertising, and they're right to do so. As apartments have become commercial goods, they ought to be offered like merchandise. It's by advertising, by making *a commodity* [*l'article*], by publicizing the advantages of an apartment, that one apartment gets rented over another."[82] In a market filled with new, undifferentiated merchandise, often in recently developed parts of the city, the real estate press had a key role to play in capturing and fixing the attention of tenants on particular sites. The *Grand Journal Officiel* was particularly clear about this point, asserting in 1884, "Paris has undergone such an expansion in recent years that a guide has become necessary to direct the searches of those seeking to house themselves comfortably and agreeably." It was up to the particular services of the real estate intermediary to help populate newly constructed regions: "The firm of John Arthur will continue, as it has always done, to publicize the new neighborhoods; it's thanks to the experience of their well-chosen rental services personnel that the districts of the Champs-Elysées, Etoile, and the Plaine Monceau were populated."[83] The real estate press, in other words, acted as a harmonizer of the marketplace, building the social spaces of the capital as it intervened to connect owners and tenants.

This emphasis on merchandizing found expression in both the publicity of the real estate sector and the material spaces of the agencies themselves. The offices of real estate agencies complemented their journals as sites of persuasive display for housing as merchandise. In contrast to the somber offices of the notary, agents integrated their bureaus into the extroverted urbanism of the capital city. The Agence Largier carefully selected and boasted of its monumental location on the Boulevard Malesherbes—a wealthy commercial thoroughfare in a district heavily reconstructed during the Second Empire—while the *Indicateur Dufayel* included a grand image of the real estate department established at the Dufayel Department Store in 1903 in its biweekly publication (Figure 5.2). The Agence Lagrange and the agency of Cadé, Lewidof, et Chaumier both deployed their impressive storefronts in the heart of Paris's business districts as shorthand for the capacity, experience, and reputation of their services (Figure 5.3). When agencies included maps in their publicity, the effect was to place real estate brokerage, and the services of a particular firm, at the heart of mapping and navigating the capital (Figure 5.4). These efforts reflected and reinforced the more assertive and influential place of estate agents in the Parisian property market.

Advertising materials depicted agencies as monumental elements of the urban landscape, surrounded by the vibrancy and luxury of the boulevards, implying mastery of the urban spaces of which they constituted a vital part. The *Journal de l'Union des Propriétaires* offered in 1896 to subject the very geography of the city to standardization, announcing that their journal would be accompanied by maps of the city "established by a new patented method," which, by reducing street names to numbers, would permit "even the least knowledgeable to instantly grasp the topographical orientation of a street, a house for rent, or a lot for sale."[84] These efforts at rationalizing urban space were required, this press argued, by the nature of Paris itself. In 1880 the *Moniteur de la Location* cited a letter from a grateful reader that praised their gazette as invaluable to a city such as Paris. The same article announced that the *Moniteur* would be appearing in special display boxes including a map

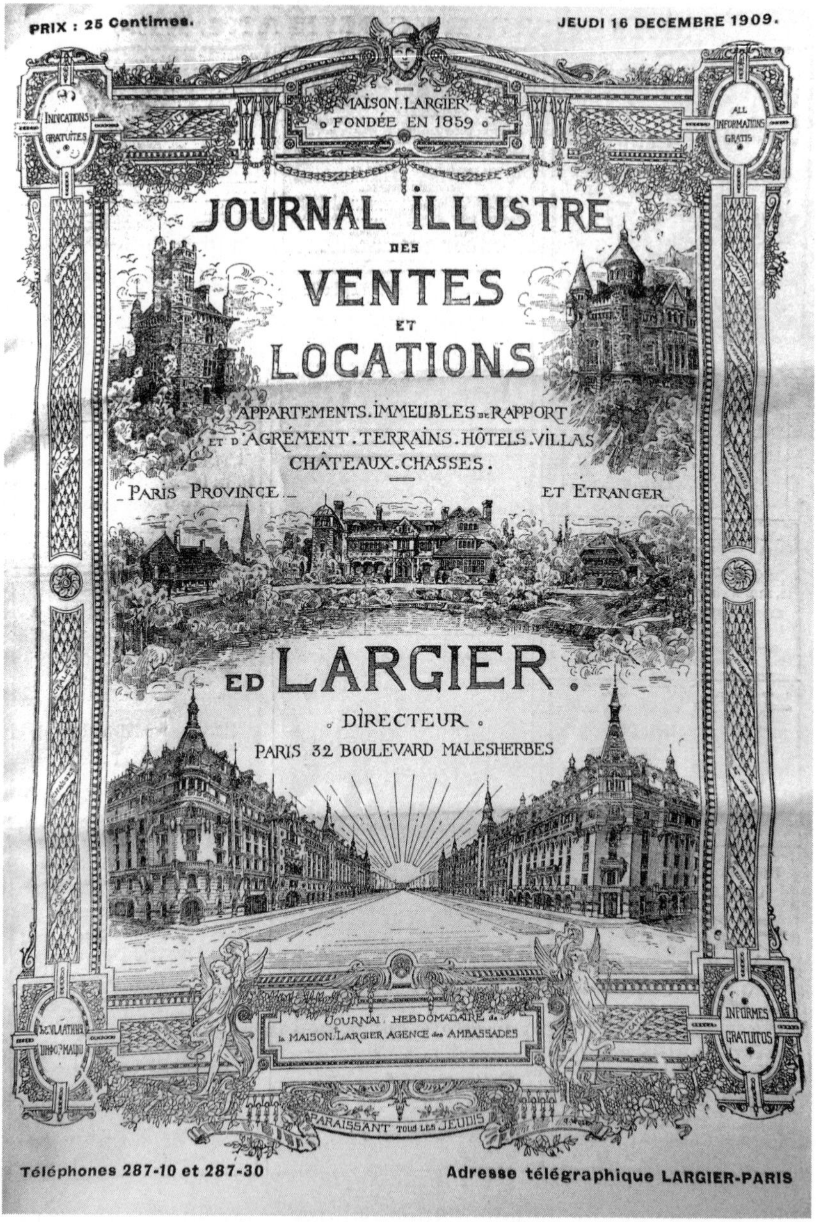

FIGURE 5.2 Front cover of the weekly rental and sales gazette of the Agence Largier, 1909. *Source:* Bibliothèque Historique de la Ville de Paris

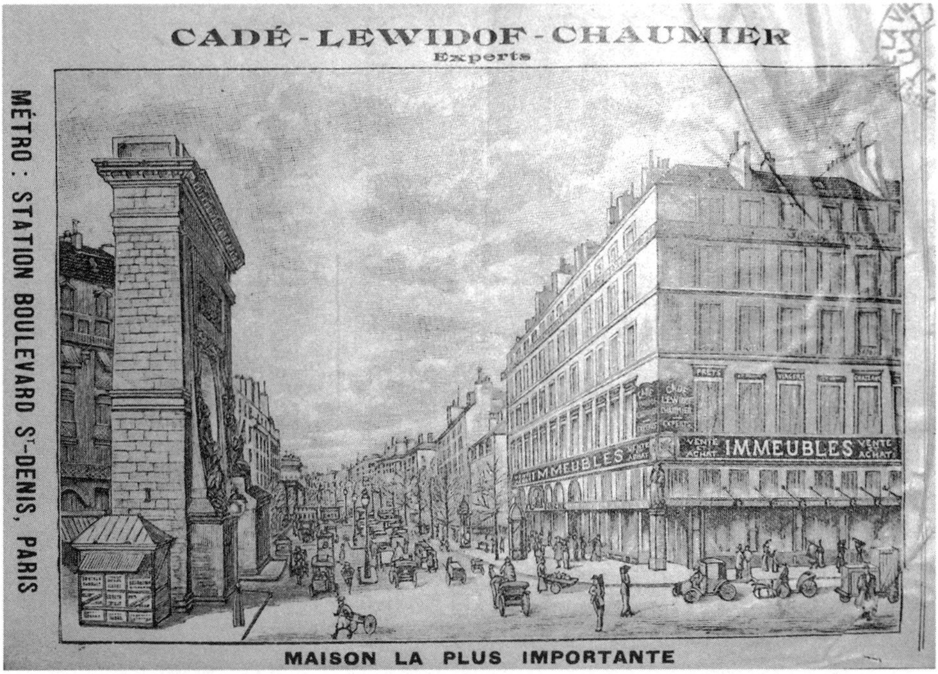

FIGURE 5.3 Bureau of the property brokerage Cadé, Lewidof, et Chaumier, 19 Boulevard Saint-Denis, ca. 1914. From publicity pamphlet. *Source:* Bibliothèque Historique de la Ville de Paris, Actualités Série 78, Logement

of the city and, importantly, a complete list of new street names, in order to make best use of the directory.[85] What's more, the introduction of gazettes that specifically targeted the lower classes implied that no one class bore a privileged relationship to the space of the city, and that all housing consumers could benefit from the specialist eye of the estate agency.

Real estate gazettes referred frequently to their role as centralizers and lauded their "scientific" methods. The *Moniteur de la Location* highlighted the straightforwardness of their presentation, which allowed apartment seekers "from a simple skimming" to "grasp all the rentals available in all of Paris's neighborhoods in a detailed fashion. Thanks to the simple and methodical organization we've adopted, the reader can find the district in which he'd like to live and the price he'd like to pay, at a single glance."[86] Such rapid and analytical evaluations of the marketplace prevented useless expenditures of time and money. The weekly publicity journal *Annonce Immobilière,* founded in 1884, declared rigor and order its guiding mantra, thereby

FIGURE 5.4 Advertisement for the commercial and residential property brokerage Petitjean, featuring a map of the Paris subway system. Early twentieth century. *Source:* Bibliothèque Historique de la Ville de Paris, Actualités Série 78, Logement

overcoming the failures of the past: "One of the greatest inconveniences of the advertising tried thus far was the absolute absence of method, the total lack of organization; an ad for a five-story apartment building in Paris knocked up against twenty lines dedicated to a farm in the Beauce. You needed the patience of a monk to find yourself in all that mess."[87] The arrangement of their rental gazettes reflected this emphasis on organization. It became very rare for rental notices to appear without any organizing principle; they were nearly always arranged by price or arrondissement, and often by both. While real estate journals addressed the urban spaces of Paris as a totality, generally including all arrondissements in their listings (though, to be sure, all did not include an equal number of listings), this structure allowed a reader to pick and choose the parts of the city to which he or she would dedicate their time. It reflected the increasing relevance of the arrondissement as a framework for reading urban space, as well as the increasing sociospatial homogeneity that these districts represented. In mirroring the city's social geography, these gazettes facilitated its reproduction.

The standardization to which rental listings were subject contrasted sharply with the persistent disorder of columns listing apartment buildings for sale. These notices did, at times, appear in order of arrondissement, or else in descending/ascending price order, with the latter format being more common. Frequently, however, they appeared in randomly assembled lists in sales journals. One could count on being informed of the price and the revenue of the buildings—these figures helped establish the return on one's capital—but the types of information included beyond these basic points were few.[88] Ads offered only the briskest specificities on a building; a reader might learn that it was "modern," "handsome," or "in good condition," with a façade in pierre de taille or brick, but little more. As for a building's location, a street might be offered, or simply a neighborhood, which could be designated by official arrondissements or quartiers, or by more pedestrian references to monuments, parks, or public buildings. In the name of protecting both the privacy of the seller—for whom such affairs were often matters of family patrimony—and the commissions of the agents, exact addresses were rarely provided.

The real estate press reflected the division between ownership and occupancy that characterized Paris's residential patterns. For apartments, spaces where one was to actually live, location was paramount. This was particularly true for more modest tenants, for whom living arrangements remained more tightly bound with the requirements of their work.[89] The *Indicateur Général des Locations,* founded by the Agence Lagrange in 1897, was aimed at the rental range of 2,000 francs and below (and featured mainly apartments below 500 francs) and organized its suburban apartment advertisement along tramway and rail lines, emphasizing the importance of public transit to this demographic. For apartment building sales, however, the main priority was financial return, and location was a matter of less pressing concern.

Envisioning Real Estate: New Representational Strategies for Residential Space

Residential advertising was transformed in the fin de siècle by the introduction of images and other graphic elements to the promotion of both sales and rentals. The interior floor plan became the particular icon of the rental market.

As agents declared themselves privileged decoders of an increasingly complex urban setting, their journals began fashioning a transparent city, penetrating apartment house façades and laying bare the built form of domestic living. Having appeared on rare occasions in the past, by the 1880s the floor plan was a consistent feature in a number of Paris's most substantial real estate gazettes. Graphic elements increased in all kinds of advertising during this period. Printing and lithography advances made the integration of image and text easier and less costly, at the same time as publicity practitioners were advancing claims to professional expertise and technical proficiency based on a scientific model of perception that granted increased agency to the visual in human thought processes.[90] As France took on the challenges and opportunities of mass visual communication, typified in the emerging mass culture of the capital city, real estate advertising integrated the consumption of housing merchandise into the new empire of images that constituted Belle Époque commercial culture.

Floor plans were initially included in gazettes as a series of grouped images, assembled separately on the front pages of a journal. The *Indicateur Illustré des Appartements à Louer* began publication in 1880 and included several pages of floor plans placed in advance of their rental listings, a pattern that the *Grand Journal Officiel* also adopted when it was introduced in 1884 (Figure 5.5). Assembled at the beginning of the journal, floor plans caught a viewer's attention by their graphic, sensory impact. The *Grand Journal Officiel* declared in 1884 that "consulting them, everyone can, at *first* glance, gain an exact account of [an apartment's] location and interior layout."[91] Sometimes more than a glance was needed. The plans included in the *Indicateur Illustré* denoted individual rooms by letter designations rather than labels, meaning that a reader had to compose some of the layout of the apartment on their own by referencing an adjacent legend (Figure 5.6). Whether through instant visual impact or somewhat more concentrated engagement, floor plans could pique curiosity, encouraging the reader to turn to the rental section in order to find a particular listing and survey comparable units. They acted like the storefront window of the agency, presenting desirable affairs and encouraging the consumer to step inside, where more choice was offered.

Floor plans did not remain limited to front pages for long, however. Within a few years the *Grand Journal Officiel* complemented the vibrant, concentrated assemblage of front-section images with floor diagrams peppered throughout the entire gazette, a format followed by other early-twentieth-

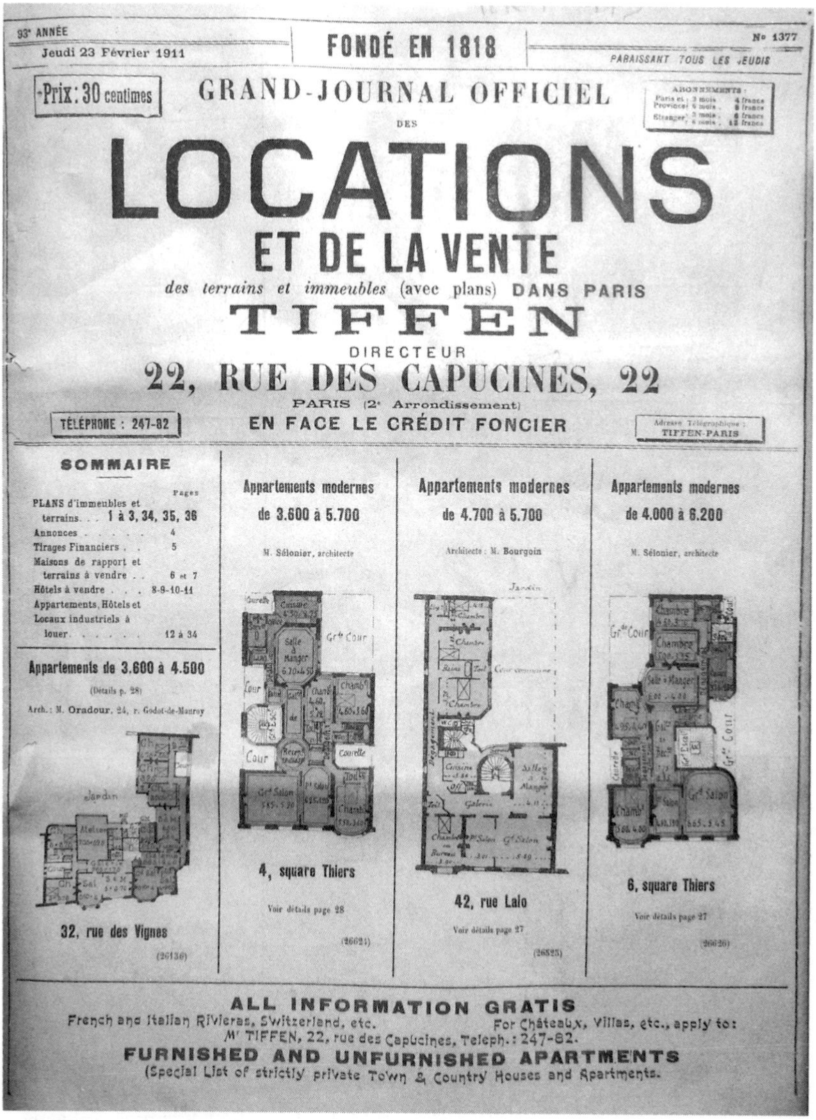

93e ANNÉE
Jeudi 23 Février 1911

FONDÉ EN 1818

No 1377

PARAISSANT TOUS LES JEUDIS

Prix : 30 centimes

GRAND-JOURNAL OFFICIEL DES

ABONNEMENTS :
Paris et Province : 3 mois . 4 francs ; 6 mois . 8 francs
Étranger : 3 mois . 6 francs ; 6 mois . 12 francs

LOCATIONS
ET DE LA VENTE

des terrains et immeubles (avec plans) DANS PARIS

TIFFEN

DIRECTEUR

22, RUE DES CAPUCINES, 22

PARIS (2e Arrondissement)

EN FACE LE CRÉDIT FONCIER

TÉLÉPHONE : 247-82

Adresse Télégraphique : TIFFEN-PARIS

SOMMAIRE

	Pages
PLANS d'immeubles et terrains . . .	1 à 3, 34, 35, 36
Annonces	4
Tirages Financiers . .	5
Maisons de rapport et terrains à vendre . .	6 et 7
Hôtels à vendre . . .	8-9-10-11
Appartements, Hôtels et Locaux industriels à louer	12 à 34

Appartements de 3.600 à 4.500
(Détails p. 28)
Arch. : M. Oradour, 24, r. Godot-de-Mauroy
32, rue des Vignes
(26136)

Appartements modernes de 3.600 à 5.700
M. Sélonier, architecte
4, square Thiers
Voir détails page 28
(26624)

Appartements modernes de 4.700 à 5.700
Architecte : M. Bourgoin
42, rue Lalo
Voir détails page 27
(26523)

Appartements modernes de 4.000 à 6.200
M. Sélonier, architecte
6, square Thiers
Voir détails page 27
(26626)

ALL INFORMATION GRATIS
French and Italian Rivieras, Switzerland, etc. For Châteaux, Villas, etc., apply to:
Mr TIFFEN, 22, rue des Capucines, Teleph. : 247-82.
FURNISHED AND UNFURNISHED APARTMENTS
(Special List of strictly private Town & Country Houses and Apartments.

FIGURE 5.5 Step inside: Cover of a 1911 issue of the *Grand Journal Officiel des Locations et de la Vente des Terrains et Immeubles,* published by the real estate agency John Arthur et Tiffen. The format of the journal remained largely unchanged from 1884 through the interwar period. *Source:* Bibliothèque Historique de la Ville de Paris

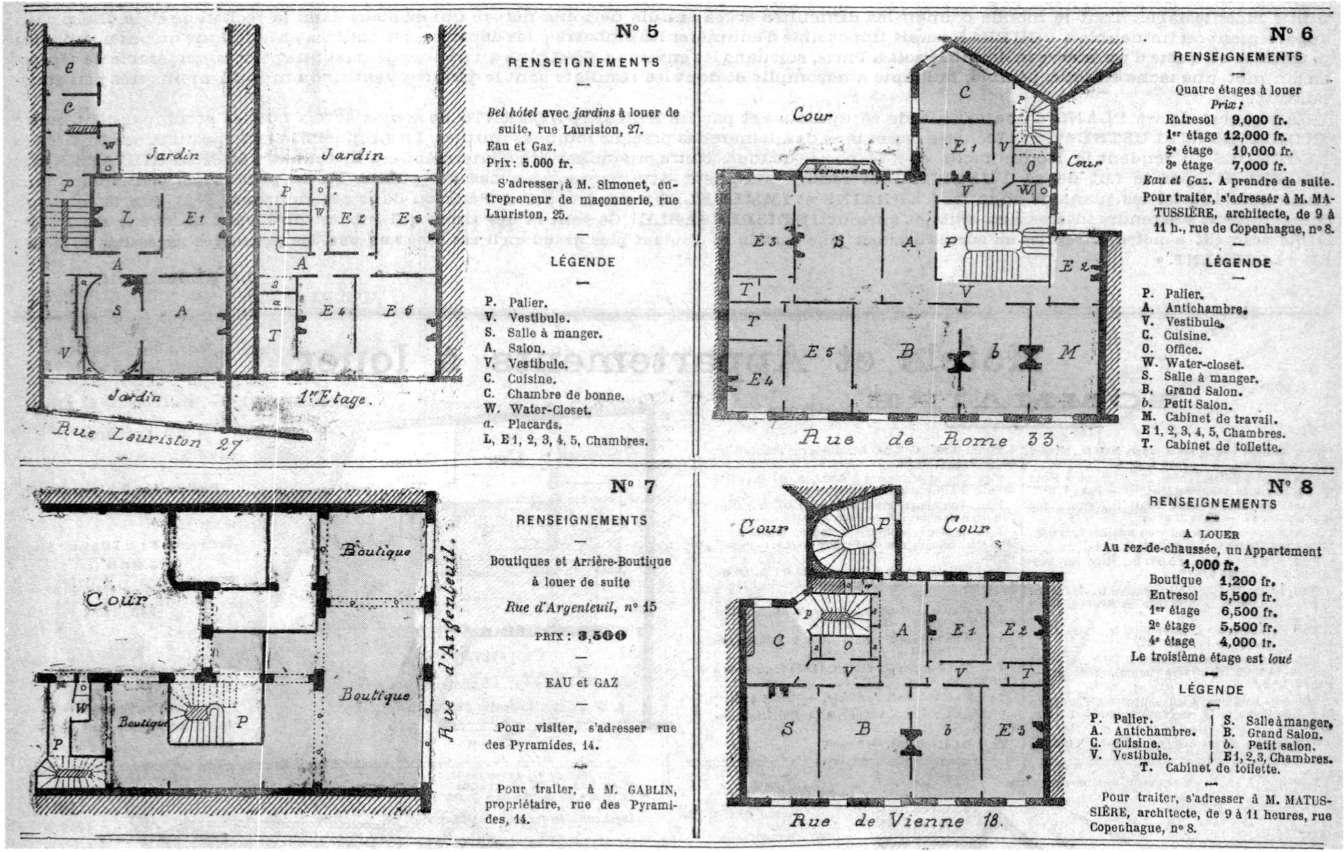

FIGURE 5.6 Advertisement from the *Indicateur Illustré des Appartements à Louer* using a legend to accompany floor plans, August 10, 1880. *Source:* Bibliothèque Nationale de France

century publications. Intermediaries also began to use floor plans in other forms of publicity, such as flyers and person-to-person mailings.[92] Occasionally advertisements appeared that employed floor plans to help potential buyers visualize the properties that could be constructed on a particular piece of land, a kind of staging that helped the empty geometry of a lot appear as an inhabited—and revenue-generating—place. This sort of selling on plans would become much more common in the interwar period, but it was nevertheless starting to find a place in the real estate publicity of the beginning of the century.

How did the public receive and read these schematics, which, after all, are a particular form of professional iconography? By and large, estate agent journals constituted an initiation for many consumers in deciphering this kind of spatial representation. Unless one was connected to the building or furniture trades in this period, there were few sources from which practice in reading plans could be acquired. Many professional journals published architectural plans in both their weekly issues and special volumes; *La Construction Moderne, La Réforme du Bâtiment, La Semaine des Constructeurs,* and the *Revue Général de l'Architecture et des Travaux Publics* were among the most prominent of such publications. Architects also published large volumes that gathered together prominent examples of Parisian apartment building architecture, but like professional journals, these were not intended for unspecialized readers.[93] The relative novelty of these depictions in fact explains some of their persuasive capacity. They permitted a kind of licit spectatorship over privatized spaces, and created a visual register from which to imagine new lifestyle possibilities. Plans deployed in rental journals were much simplified from actual architectural plans, or even those reproduced in folio publications. Representing only the main walls and partitions of an apartment, promotional plans emphasized movement and space within units. Elements necessary to understanding the use of an apartment—such as the location of windows, fireplaces, and rectangles indicating beds—helped the reader navigate the plan, as did the use of color blocking, which differentiated between apartments. Blocked off in pink and blue (or green and yellow), apartments were neatly packaged as self-contained, legible units, a convention that reflected the decline in flexible room arrangements, while also training readers in the standardized housing packages of new apartment buildings.

Floor plans necessarily engaged the viewer in a bird's-eye perspective on the dwelling. Neither the cross sections common to architectural practice, which open a building laterally in order to show room height and interior features, nor the interior room views common to furnishing and décor manuals, were ever employed. In the *Grand Journal Officiel,* at least, the dominance of the floor plan as the sole graphic advertising tool emerged gradually but definitively. In its early years the journal occasionally included renderings of building façades, or images that showed large portions of surrounding streetscape (Figure 5.7). Although these never entirely disappeared from the pages of the journal, they became uncommon by the mid-1890s. The eye of the real estate gazette focused definitively on the individual apartment unit in two-dimensional format. If the layout of the building required that portions of other units be included in the schematic, these were either effaced with crosshatching or depicted as empty white space. Still, the advertised apartments were not delocalized interiors. Floor plans nearly always included labels for a unit's surrounding streets, as well as descriptions of spaces upon which the apartment took views, such as courtyards, terraces, parks, or even the Seine. The interior—designated for the first time in terms of meters of floor space—remained linked to and defined by its locality.

Thus, by 1900 consumers of the Parisian rental press were participating in an entirely new regime of property representation. Floor plans that allowed a reader to consume interior spaces from a distance served to collapse the geographic spaces of the city and enhance the imaginative elements of the house-seeking process. These tools were part of the estate agent's broader goals of making urban space easier to decipher, rationalizing housing consumption, and minimizing the time spent in physical exploration of the city. While more traditional (textual) forms of rental advertising continued to dominate the information networks of estate agents, the deployment of these kinds of images suggests the ways in which the city's private spaces remained open to the public spaces of the city. These images render more complex the process of "interiorization" discerned by Sharon Marcus. The diffusion of floor plans signals the increasing importance of domestic interiors in the search for dwellings, yet these interiors remained readily available to be incorporated into the intense visuality and extroversion that constituted a defining element of the experience of the modern metropolis.

The particular vision of metropolitan domesticity at work in rental advertising becomes clearer when compared to advertising for owner-occupied housing, particularly for country homes and properties on suburban estates. Advertising of rural properties differed markedly from both urban sales and

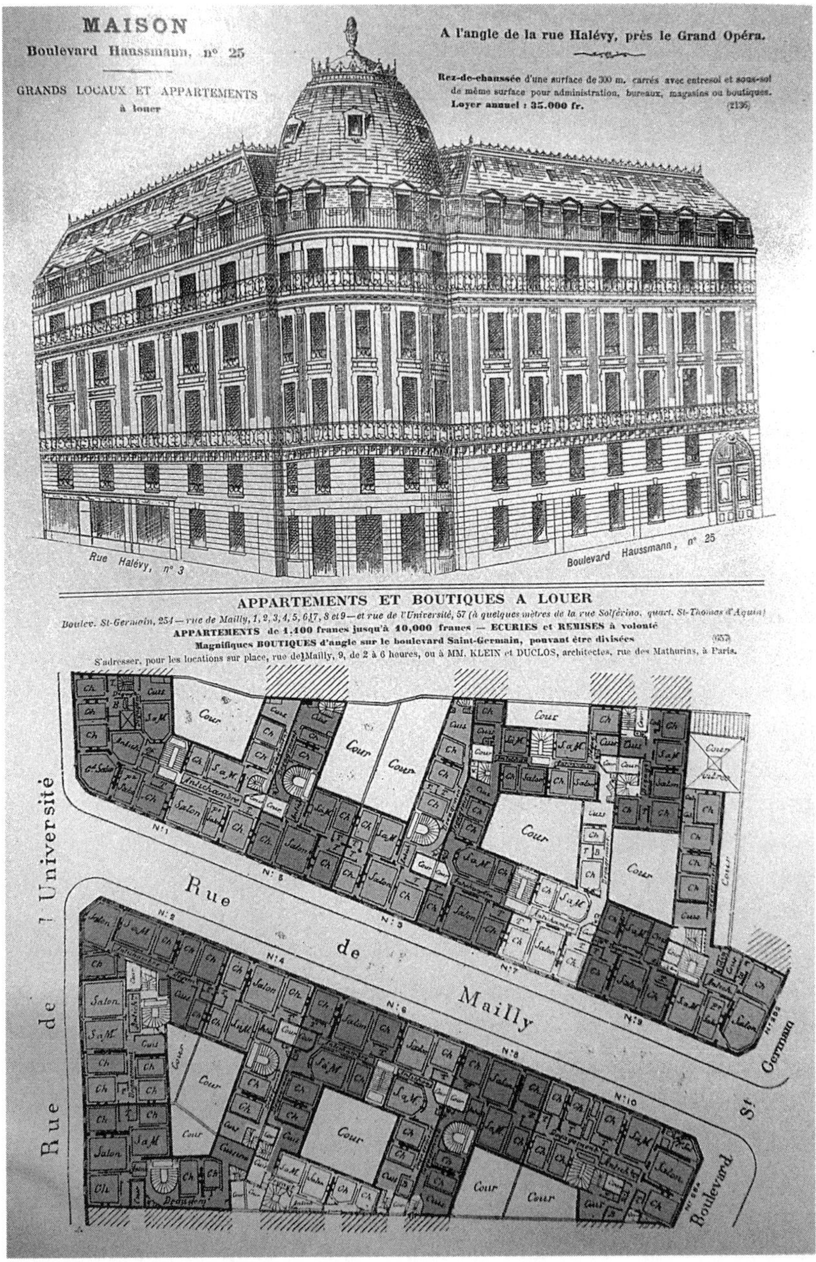

FIGURE 5.7 The speculative housing package: Image from the *Grand Journal Officiel des Locations et de la Vente des Terrains et Immeubles,* September 10, 1885. *Source:* Archives Nationales du Monde du Travail, 65 AQ I 1163

rentals. Whereas investment opportunities in Parisian real estate or the availability of a particular apartment were tersely presented, advertisements for properties outside the capital composed narratives that struck an emotional note. They gave mini-tours of the inside and outside of a property, emphasizing the pastoral setting, the view, the benefits of privacy and of local attractions. Provincial sales were the first sections in real estate gazettes to include photographs as selling tools, allowing potential buyers to take in the appearance of a property and its surroundings. *Le Reveil Immobilier* announced its new method of "real estate advertising with images" in 1893, reasoning that "an image always grabs the attention of the reader, even more so when the general aspect is pleasant and it is easy to immediately appreciate the beauty of the site and the advantages of the location."[94] These methods were informed by an approach to the rural based on the consumption of surface appearances or the picturesque. Rural properties were inscribed within a discourse of diversion, with publicity emphasizing easy access to fishing and hunting and the satisfactions of gardens. In short, advertisements for rural properties engaged in a narration of property ownership that focused on lifestyle. In contradistinction to the dominant pattern of urban ownership, rural properties were about occupation and affective, rather than financial, investment.

The greatest commercial devices of this lifestyle marketing were the real estate sales posters that joined the ranks of the increasingly glamorous poster advertising designed by renowned artists of the Belle Époque. Although posters had long been a distinctive presence in the public spaces of the capital city—Mercier dedicated long passages of his *Tableau de Paris* to those of pre-Revolutionary Paris—poster publicity evolved to become a distinctive artistic form that permeated and, in a large measure, defined Paris's distinct urban modernity.[95] As Sarah Howard writes, "The city's so-called 'spectacular culture' was held together by the twin pillars of advertising and retailing. Belle Époque advertising had provided the symbol systems essential to the construction of a consumer society."[96] Advertising for the sales of properties in the middle-class suburban subdivisions whose development was accelerating in the Paris region from the 1880s joined wholeheartedly in the burst of artistic fervor that found a particular outlet in marketing posters.[97] Emphasizing an indulgent immersion in nature made possible by an easy commute to Paris, these advertisements promoted a rural proprietorship based on self-expression and independence, at once escapist and, in the words of historian Nicholas Green, "integral to the living-out of metropolitan culture."[98] Explicit associations with entertainment and easy lifestyles were common. One poster for a development in Colombes noted the public gardens; another for the same locality featured a prominent depiction of a jockey and the nearby racetrack. A poster for the Franceville subdivision in Montfermeil (east of Paris) was dominated by a well-off family in an automobile and a vista of the luxurious countryside, and did not forget to include an insert of a local bicycle track (Figure 5.8). More than investments or places of residence, suburban properties were experiences; these experiences, moreover, were intimately bound up with the trappings of consumer society: automobiles, mass sporting culture, fashion, and tourism. Promotional strategies were overtly gendered, simultaneously evoking the feminized realm of consumer desire as well as that of the domestic hearth. Indeed, as Figure 5.9 shows, the verdant imagery of lush country retreats could be replaced entirely with body of a woman clothed in the latest fashion, standing in for taste, discernment, pleasure, and possession. Throughout, the bourgeois male, driving his family in the countryside, balanced suburban frivolities with an endorsement of commendable investment, both emotional and financial, in his family's well-being.

These advertisements for suburban homes mobilized the subjective elements of space, its emotional connotations, as part of a merchandising strategy. In contrast, urban rental journals marketed residential rather than domestic space; the units on offer were sheared down to their essentials, envelopes waiting to be filled with the personal effects and affections that would constitute a meaningful *foyer.* When ads for apartments took on a grand scale that flaunted the amenities of a particular site, the emphasis was on buildings as full-service providers and marvels of physical comfort, rather than as sites of emotional fulfillment (Figure 5.10). In both form and content, rental advertising emphasized rationalized space, mobility, and exchangeability; its patterns encouraged comparative reading, weighing multiple factors in order to maximize utility (however that utility was defined). Rural sales, on the other hand, were to a large degree impossible to compare among themselves. Properties were extremely differentiated, with views and features singular to a site. Moreover, advertising posters often did not include the sorts of information that would make such comparisons possible, serving rather to entice viewers by stimulating long-cherished desires and new aspirations for easy living.

FIGURE 5.8 Consuming the countryside: Marketing poster for Franceville, Montfermeil, ca. 1900. *Source:* Personal collection, Jean Marc Levet, used with permission

The division between marketing practices for rural sales and urban rentals raises intriguing questions with regard to the particular understanding of "home" at play in urban housing. Historians such as Michèle Perrot have argued that habitation was little other than a material matter for the working classes of Paris in the nineteenth century; concerns regarding its quality were slow to surface, and workers remained far more concerned with their experience of and rights to the city's public spaces until after the First World War.[99]

FIGURE 5.9 Publicity poster for a development in Fontenay aux Roses, ca. 1896, noting an elegant lifestyle, proximity to Paris, and flexible payment options. *Source:* Personal collection, Jean-Marc Levet, used with permission

FIGURE 5.10 1909 advertisement for new apartments in Paris's 16th arrondissement, *Grand Journal Officiel des Locations et de la Vente des Terrains et Immeubles,* presenting the new street and modern amenities as selling features. *Source:* Bibliothèque Historique de la Ville de Paris

Building on Lefebvre's theories concerning the importance of proprietary understanding of public space, she argues that the mobility of the working classes, combined with their use of the city's public spaces and services, could not only prove a pleasurable means of experiencing the city, but also worked to generate a sense of metropolitan identity. The press examined in this chapter, largely aimed at a middle-class readership, suggests that urban mobility could serve a similar purpose among the better-off classes in the city. While it was in property agents' interest to depict the apartment search as drudgery best left to the expertise of a specialist, their gazettes in fact provided a means for individuals to diversify and pursue their own housing searches. Rationalized publications facilitated comparative searching, selective inquiry, and, through the inclusion of floor plans, a kind of visual affirmation that better housing—bigger, more tasteful, more affordable, more fashionable, "whatever you desire"—was waiting to be unveiled. While they persisted in claiming to save their clients precious time, agents in fact worked to *increase* the amount of time a Parisian resident spent dreaming of new housing.

The mobility imposed by urban apartments subjected all Parisians to a geographically diverse experience of the capital. An article in the luxury women's journal *Femina* in 1910 recounts: "Parisians by origin or Parisians by chance, almost no one owns a family home. Our *foyers* are dispersed to the four winds by fantasy, fashion, or necessity. We live in a provisional, temporary manner, without memories and almost without future projects and plans." Changing circumstances meant changing housing: "Every stage of our life is marked by a move. When fortune favors us, instead of adding a wing or a floor to the house of our ancestors, we say: 'I am . . . going to move to another apartment.'"[100] As an antidote to this residential instability, the taste professionals of the end of the century glorified the opportunities for individual expression and creative investment in interior décor, situating "home" in the personalized environment that one established through furnishings and art within the standardized form of the late-nineteenth-century apartment. Yet as often as not this mobility did not need to be "solved"; it provided instead opportunities for the kinds of expression and self-representation that were so important to turn-of-the-century homemakers and their advisors. A contribution to *Femina* in the immediate postwar period wrote of "Le Home": "There are two sorts of home: one you create for yourself, and one you inherit; one that lasts four or five years at the most, and one that's already at least a hundred years old; one that you'll see die and one that you didn't even see born. I know, Madame, that only the first type is of interest to you, that it's your deepest pleasure and source of greatest pride that you've created your own home, according to your tastes and desires, having discovered the furnishings one by one at antique dealers, having chosen the wall hangings and the trinkets, and being able to change everything and throw it all over."[101]

While the author was critical of this "modern" tendency toward constant re-creation of one's home, these remarks captured the possible pleasures of a frequent rewriting of one's environment. Importantly, the ability of a household, under the particular guidance of the mother or wife, to establish a home seemed in no way impoverished by the lack of property ownership. Writing of her experiences changing apartments in Paris in the period leading up to the Great War, the author Colette described her slow realization that apartments allowed a flexible expression of identity and choice: "Gradually, once I came to Paris, the idea of changing house—which initially horrified me—came to be linked to the idea of free choice, of whims, a dream of ease: 'Really, I could, if I wanted, live in Paris in a store, a converted chapel, or a tiny house near the Bois?' "[102] While the marketing of suburban properties differed markedly in emotional valence from that of apartment rentals, it should not therefore be concluded that apartments were experienced as a form of dispossession. As the observers who commented upon the broad perception of the popularity of apartment living among the upper classes noted, these dwellings came with a multitude of deeply valued benefits to their occupants, not least of which was the ability for residence to change along with the needs and desires of its inhabitants.

The real estate press of the early Third Republic provides important clues as to how the changing spaces of the city may have been understood and used by its inhabitants. While the *flâneur* has provided a privileged perspective on mobility in the modern urban setting, this chapter's focus on the search for housing opens that perspective to reveal the purposeful pedestrianism that continued to provide the foundation for much daily experience of the metropolis.[103] In place of the aimless wandering of the man in the crowd, our urban dwellers are intent, armed with guides that take the straightforward dissection of the built environment as their raison d'être, and that are used to plan excursions with designated routes and goals. Although these guides encouraged a new way of looking at urban space, they were also fundamentally about inhabiting that space, about dwelling rather than passing through, about seeing a multitude of homes in the spaces of transience. Early accounts of apartment hunting emphasized the ability of this search to transcend the public/private divide that governed the social space of the modern city. In 1831 an account in *Paris, ou le Livre des Cent-et-un* stressed that until, like the author, one has "an Englishman who has asked you to find him housing," most of the city will remain a mystery: "until then, with the exception of public spaces and the houses of a few friends, you know only the outside skin of cities." The author proceeded to devour the city and its secrets, taking up the position of "an inquisitor penetrating everywhere."[104] Later writers also used the apartment hunt as an excuse to investigate apartment interiors; in 1907, for example, art critic Gabriel Mourey, "observing all around him so many people who amused themselves by 'looking for an apartment,'" took advantage of this "almost universal craze" to enter apartments and offer his reflections on contemporary decoration and architecture to readers of *Le Figaro*.[105] Apartment hunting was a means by which the boundaries of public and private were traversed throughout the century. Yet the difference between these two accounts is also significant. In the first the writer uses a foreign visitor, uninitiated to the city, as an excuse for wide-ranging and indiscriminate searching; in the second the author participates in what he sees as a "decadent" universal obsession for apartment hunting, associated with residents rather than newcomers, and with trends rather than necessity. The entire urban citizenry is encapsulated in the ebb and flow of apartment hunting and residential relocation.

The fin-de-siècle real estate press was concerned with eliminating the elements of this search that could constitute a frustrating chore and infusing it instead with the ease, satisfaction, and even pleasure that constituted the best elements of modern consumerism. This press provided one set of tools with which to navigate and experience the city, but it jockeyed for influence among other methods of exploration available to Parisian residents. All manner of intermediaries proposed methods and offered services for deciphering the residential availabilities of the capital city, from architects and former notaries, to property owners and estate agents, to private individuals and fly-by-night entrepreneurs. And while they emphasized the physical toll of the apartment search that they sought to relieve—"After all," the Syndicat Professionnel des Hommes d'Affaires reminded readers in 1910, "it's hardly pleasant to go from concierge to concierge asking: What floor is the apartment on? How many rooms does it have? . . . and an infinite number of similar questions"—estate agency publications did not replace the physical exploration of the city with the representational spaces provided in their gazettes.[106] (As Figure 5.11 shows, they could work together quite well.) One advice manual for everyday living penned in 1887 stressed the material engagement with the city that apartment seeking involved: "After determining the area in which social relations and daily occupations oblige you to be located, undertake your search, investigations, and discussions with concierges boldly; don't hesitate to take the painful climb from story to story anywhere where the price and type of housing seems to be suitable!"[107] Even here the need for improved information networks in the housing search was acknowledged, and the author suggested that property owners install permanent signs on the front of their buildings giving detailed explanations of available properties. An estate agent named Henry Rozès proposed similar signage in 1889, writing to the city's director of works to request permission to install permanent publicity boards in each arrondissement, affixed to the sides of private buildings, which would feature complete lists of all available rentals. Rozès was certain that the director would recognize the immense utility of such publicity if he considered that "the modest employee, the worker, and people whose position requires that they frequently change their dwelling cannot waste their time wandering neighborhoods and asking at each concierge (who only permit visits at certain times), climbing from floor to floor, generally resulting only in exhaustion and a poor choice because it was made in haste."[108] The local nature of the housing hunt, as well as the immovable nature of the goods constituting the market, continued to weigh heavily in the methods of estate agents.

As technologies that simultaneously collapse urban space and facilitate its exploration, this press captures the tensions between circulation and rootedness, between public and private, and between use and exchange value, that lie at the heart of the modern urban experience. The process of commercialization that the housing market was undergoing in the early Third Republic brings to the fore the role of consumption in shaping the urban landscape, as well as a new range of actors who contributed to the normalization of the transience of modern urban spatial relations. The obstacles that these efforts encountered as they sought to interpose themselves in existing information

FIGURE 5.11 Interiors visible from the street: Floorplan for an apartment rental hangs on a building on the avenue de la République, ca. 1908. *Source:* Personal collection, Jean-Pierre Rigouard, used with permission

networks, networks that were deeply personalized, embodied, and spatialized, point to the limits of the historiographic model that considers Parisians in the second half, and particularly last third, of the nineteenth century as alienated inhabitants of their city. While impersonal networks of property intermediation attempted to establish themselves as privileged agents of urban navigation in this period, asserting as justification the increasingly confounding and anonymous nature of the city, established patterns of housing acquisition proved both accommodating and resilient. As its growing volume and increasingly rationalized form attests, the rental press was able to gain purchase in the culture and practices of house seeking in Paris at the turn of the century by providing the tools for an increasingly masterful exploration of the expanding and densifying urban fabric.

6

Districts of the Future

A POLICE COMMISSIONER reporting on housing conditions in the 11th arrondissement in 1882 observed that recent and sudden increases in the area's rents "weigh heavily on workers and the petty bourgeoisie, the employees." To explain the particularity of the phenomenon, he focused on one building in particular, an apartment house on Boulevard Voltaire. An apartment on the fifth floor that had cost 1,500 francs only two years before was now renting for 1,700 francs. The building was owned by a corporation called Nouveaux Quartiers de Paris, which had paid a high price for it and thus "had costs that it had to recoup."[1] The increase in rents was the predictable consequence of this mode of acquisition and management. The commissioner was pointing to one of the most important consequences of the building boom of the 1880s: the emergence of property development and investment corporations as significant participants in the Parisian housing market. While the majority of property in the city remained in the hands of private individuals, the vast districts and housing portfolios assembled by corporate bodies between 1880 and 1914 made a significant impact on both the city's built environment and the priorities and routines of housing administration and consumption. The properties and management practices of the city's

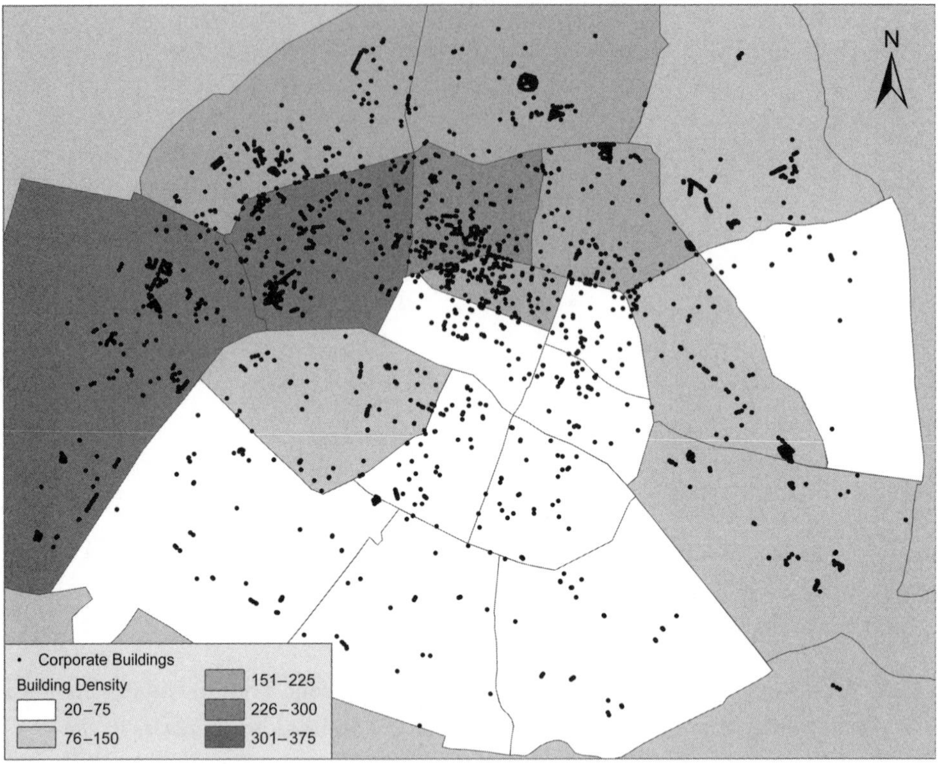

MAP 6.1 Map of the 2,543 buildings owned by insurance and real estate companies in Paris in 1910. Many points indicate more than one building. Map © 2015 by Alexia Yates.

corporate real estate interests ensured that the social experience of the urban landscape was increasingly shaped by financial imperatives.

Corporate ownership was a citywide phenomenon. Banks, insurance companies, and investment institutions lavished their attentions on the highly commercialized central districts and the west-end residential areas they labeled "districts of the future," but no area of the city entirely escaped their interest (Map 6.1). In the 8th arrondissement, 13 percent of property belonged to corporations or institutions *(personnes morales)* already in 1901.[2] In 1910, entries for insurance companies in the *Annuaire des propriétaires* indicated that La Nationale owned apartment buildings on forty-one streets in Paris, La France owned buildings on forty-five, La Générale had properties on sixty. The eight separate pages of entries dedicated to corporate owners reveal that the Compagnie Foncière de France et d'Algérie (CFF) owned buildings on

46 streets, the Foncière Lyonnaise owned buildings on 41, and the Société des Immeubles de France owned 260 buildings on an impressive 141 Parisian streets. By 1932 the number of pages dedicated to corporate owners in the *Annuaire* had grown from ten to forty-five.[3]

The portfolios and management procedures of these firms initiated housing consumers to a new form of ownership, one characterized by the organization of management on a large, often citywide scale and the dominance of a pure profit-and-loss model of service provision. Some companies, such as the Rente Foncière (founded 1879), were management enterprises dedicated to generating long-term returns from a portfolio of apartment houses. In the 1890s the Rente Foncière owned and managed a total of 200 buildings containing more than 7,200 apartments.[4] Others, like the CFF, assembled their real property assets as a by-product of other activities. Founded in 1881 as a lending institution, the CFF saw its mandate radically transform as the building boom in which it had been an important participant came to a halt; within a decade it had acquired 167 apartment houses. There were differences in how each firm approached its management tasks, but both emphasized rational administration and profit maximization for the benefit of shareholders. The Rente Foncière reminded investors in 1881 that their share certificates entitled them to "a revenue that increases in the same measure as the rents in our buildings go up," and administrators for the CFF assured its shareholders (numbering nearly 7,400 in 1882) that "as part of the transformation your Company is undergoing, its top priority is obtaining the highest possible returns from its real estate portfolio."[5] Drawing attention to the priorities of the Rente Foncière and the CFF as they embarked on their century-long task of administering Parisian apartment houses is not to imply that there was a necessary gulf dividing "traditional" owners from "modern" business organizations—though this was undoubtedly true in many cases. Rather, examining the management practices of large corporate entities allows us to capture changes that affected all property owners to varying degrees in this period, while also reflecting on the particular strategies and impact of large-scale ownership on the residential spaces of the city.

The rapid transformation of the CFF, in particular, provides an illuminating example of the ways real property moved through different modes of mobilization under the development regime of the early Third Republic. Its annual reports are replete with appraisals of the Parisian housing market, justifications for particular construction ventures, and explanations for its successes and failures. Their evaluations ultimately relied on specific understandings of Parisian growth and the residential practices of its inhabitants. Certainly they must be read with an eye to their nature as exercises in self-preservation; company administrators in the 1880s and 1890s were overseeing a dismal business situation that required all their powers of persuasion in shareholder assemblies. Nevertheless, annual reports articulated a narrative of the firm's behavior that strove to be comprehensible, acceptable, and believable to investors. Perhaps nowhere else is the impact of corporate structures and market imperatives on the production, distribution, and consumption of the city's built fabric so much in evidence.

The specific ways in which changing scales of property production influenced the use value of urban real estate can be further clarified with a close-grained, biographical analysis of the buildings these large investment bodies constructed and managed. We can penetrate these buildings by treading in the footsteps of the municipal tax evaluators who regularly traveled through the courtyards, up the stairwells, down the corridors, and into the dwellings of Paris's apartment houses. In 1852, 1862, 1876, and 1900, administrators for the city's direct taxation bureau *(Contributions Directes)* undertook assessments of the city's built properties, gathering data to establish the basis for cadastral revenues and taxation levels.[6] In their notebooks *(calepins),* they privileged written descriptions over visual plans; graphical representations were included only rarely, and ranged widely in detail and accuracy (as demonstrated by Figures 6.1 and 6.2).[7] Instead the evaluator described his path through the building, proceeding by the route he walked. Taking the principal stairwell first, the inspector alighted at each landing and described the apartments in the order in which he encountered them. He proceeded likewise inside the apartments, listing each room as it was encountered on a trip around the unit, indicating the room's purpose and whether it was located on the courtyard, air well, or main street.

The purpose of this inspection was to account for all the exterior windows and doors that opened from the apartment, for which the building was taxed. It also helped establish a typology for the building so that it could be compared to others of similar distributions and in similar condition. Along with this description, the evaluator recorded tenants' names, occasionally their occupations, and their rents. The latter was particularly important for businesspeople, whose professional tax (the *patente*) was based on the value of their business premises, though all individuals in apartments costing more

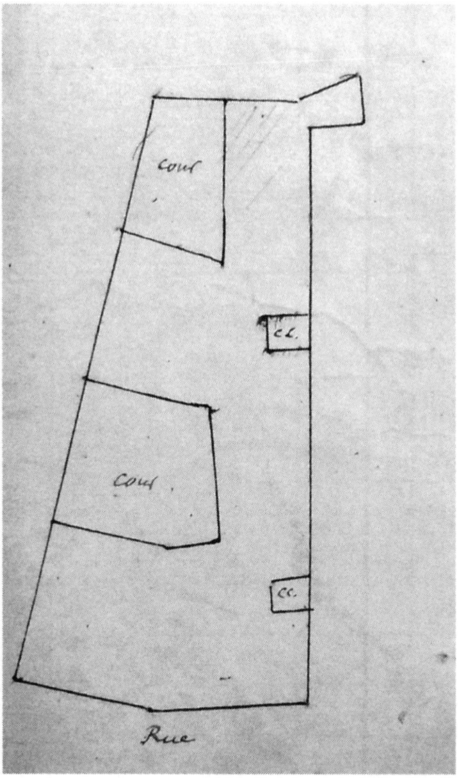

FIGURE 6.1 Sketch from an 1876 *calepin,* Rue de Panama. *Source:* Archives de Paris, D.1 P4 840

than 500 francs in annual rent were subject to a tax (the *contribution mobilière*) based on their rent. Once he completed his journey up the main stairwell, the evaluator returned to the ground floor and then traveled up alternate stairwells as needed, taking the service stair to the top-floor maids' rooms, for example, or climbing a secondary stairwell to examine the apartments in the building's courtyard wing. He passed through the courtyard to buildings at the rear of the lot, which were explored in the same manner. In this fashion, an inspector could visit eight to ten buildings a day.[8]

These tax assessments offer a pedestrian exploration of the interiors of residential buildings, providing a narration of these spaces that grows up from the ground level, unfolding as one passes through stairwells and doorways. Rather than adopting an omnipresent, aerial eye that unveiled a total space in the manner of an architectural plan, these official sources were structured

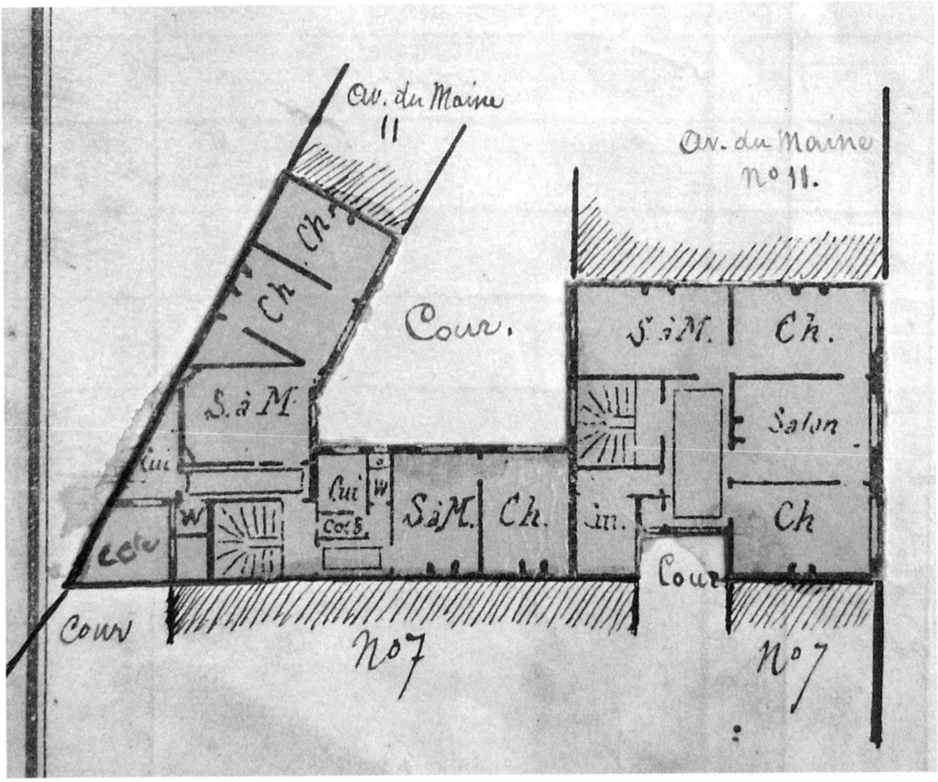

FIGURE 6.2 Rare detailed sketch from an 1876 *calepin,* Rue d'Alençon. *Source:* Archives de Paris, D.1 P4 8

by the tangible possibilities of navigating an individual building—apartments that were contiguous but accessed from different stairways do not appear side-by-side in evaluations, for instance. Thus, municipal evaluators reproduced part of the lived experience of an apartment building, their examinations constrained and channeled by its structure, their travels following its residents' routes. Yet they also transcended these quotidian pathways, exploring the totality of a structure likely only ever partially experienced by any of its inhabitants. In the bureaucratic practices of tax reportage, the pedestrian perspective on space enjoyed methodological dominance.

As might be guessed from such methods, the faithfulness of these records varies widely. Streets were not canvassed consistently, and it is certain that not all tenants who passed through an apartment were recorded.[9] Assessed rent levels were frequently contested by both property owners and tenants, so recorded rents cannot always be taken as accurate accounts of amounts owed on an apartment. The vagaries of recording practices also means that rents are sometimes difficult to attribute to a specific year or tenant, entries are frequently crossed out and overwritten, and coverage varies widely between streets—even between sides of the same street. Despite such difficulties, these records reveal vital information on the human structure of the lots and buildings manipulated by developers, investors, and owners, and remain crucial for discerning the nature of social space in nineteenth-century Parisian apartment houses.

Little is known about the social life of the thousands of apartment buildings that were added to Paris's built landscape in the late 1800s.[10] As the products of speculative building, they were long presumed unworthy of serious study by contemporary architects. Historians have largely perpetuated this disregard, venturing only rarely into the allegedly standardized landscape of market-produced domestic architecture. And yet these buildings constituted an "entrepreneurial vernacular" that shaped the material conditions of daily life for the majority of Paris's residents.[11] As Onésime Masselin reported in 1880, in classic booster style, "aside from a few private homes and a small number of buildings constructed for certain owners obsessed with real estate investment, the future belongs to speculative companies."[12] The work of architectural historians Monique Eleb and Anne Debarre is an important exception to the lack of interest in these structures.[13] Their studies on apartment house architecture argue that these buildings sought to respond to the perceived desires of a marketplace of diverse consumers, incubating norms and expectations regarding modern urban living. The previous chapters have illuminated the agents whose activities of production and distribution generalized the speculative building model at the end of the nineteenth century. Here, we venture into the everyday life of these spaces in order to discern the practices that constitute and constrain the commercialization and financialization of the urban environment.

Assembling Portfolios and Managing Properties: The Compagnie Foncière de France

The CFF began its career as a mortgage institution in 1881 amid much fanfare. Something of a late arrival to the boom, it was hailed as a stabilizing influence on an increasingly troubled sector. *La Réforme du Bâtiment* praised the firm's coordination with existing companies such as the Société Foncière Lyonnaise, and others welcomed its ability to "act forcefully on the capital's property market, imposing moderation and calm and preventing regrettable exaggerations."[14] Founded in coordination with the Crédit Foncier and the Sous-Comptoir des Entrepreneurs, the building industry's two most important lending institutions, the CFF used shareholder capital and favorable loans from the Crédit Foncier to acquire land in prime development areas, mobilizing it through the system of purchase options and transfers of mortgage priority that have been discussed in previous chapters. Building entrepreneurs looking to undertake new constructions could rent land from the CFF with the option to buy, usually on a three-year term. The CFF relinquished its position as privileged creditor, allowing the tenant to borrow on the rented land in order to commence their operations. The operation was successful when, by the end of the lease, the developer found a buyer for the building and the land, and could use the money from the sale to pay the CFF, with some left over as profit.

As the firm's administrative council explained in stock market lingo, "the company buys land on the spot market [*au comptant*] and sells it on a forward contract [*à terme*]; the difference in prices constitutes its profit."[15] The system was intended to prevent long-term immobilization of the company's capital, fostering development and quick turnover. Within its first months of existence, the CFF acquired and rented out over 22 million francs' worth of Parisian land, thereby helping to build 233 apartment houses containing 319 shops and 3,096 apartments.[16] Yet doubts quickly followed this rapid expansion. Reporting to its shareholders on its first year of operations, the company's administrative council announced that it thought it best to restrain this activity in favor of its secondary field of operation: mortgage lending in second position after the Crédit Foncier.[17] Curtailing its land acquisitions, the CFF's administrators explained that "it seemed useful to refrain from further overexciting the spirit of enterprise, which appears to have developed too rapidly and too vigorously."[18] The company also abandoned its ambitions for development activities in Algeria, dropping the territory from its title in 1883.

This appeal to moderation arrived too late to prevent the firm from engaging its capital in doomed ventures. Though it resisted the need to do so for as long as possible, the CFF found itself obliged to begin acquiring buildings erected on its lands once the three-year rental engagements of its builders started coming due in 1884. Buildings were acquired at auction, generally for less than their projected or actual value, and placed on the company's account books at their *prix de revient,* a figure arrived at by combining the price of the land and the amount of the loans guaranteed by the company for the particular operation.[19] This accounting method avoided the lower valuation of the firm's assets that would have resulted from the traditional mode of determining property value, which was to capitalize a building's revenue at 5 percent. Low rental revenues threatened the firm not only with depressed returns but also with an inability to deliver a shareholder dividend and a critically damaging devaluation of its assets. As the Crédit Lyonnais (the nation's and the world's largest bank at the turn of the century) reported of the CFF in 1892–1893, if its rental revenues were used to evaluate its properties on the basis of the customary 5 percent return, the company's assets would be valued not at 57,096,800 francs, the figure that appeared in its annual reports, but at 36,460,000 francs, a value insufficient to cover the loans the company had contracted with the Crédit Foncier. The Crédit Lyonnais concluded that four-fifths of the CFF's capital should be considered compromised.[20] The company's share value fell persistently in the 1880s and 1890s, and it was unable to issue any dividend at all for many years during this difficult period. These financial circumstances placed incredible upward pressure on rental returns, as well as considerable downward pressure on maintenance expenditures.

The CFF initially viewed its new position as property manager as a passing predicament. It summed up its approach as *"acquire, rent, pay off, and sell."*[21] Administrators were confident that its housing stock was superior to that generally on offer, and reminded shareholders that "people prefer new buildings, better organized and more comfortable than older ones, and this shift is occurring in all neighborhoods. . . . Those like us who can wait for the right moment are guaranteed to find the opportunity to sell the buildings they've acquired and fully developed, perhaps sooner than one might imagine."[22] They congratulated themselves for their foresight in monitoring the types of constructions the company was funding, hiring experts who "carefully verified the builders' plans, modifying them when necessary, and always ensuring that the apartments would be simple, well appointed, and relatively affordable."[23] (Masselin noted that the CFF was one of the only financing firms to engage in such close oversight.)[24] Intent on distancing itself from the widespread criticism of new buildings, "palaces where the smallest attic room costs 10,000 francs," the company boasted of its solidly middle-class housing stock, further testimony to its expertise and farsightedness (Table 6.1).[25]

Table 6.1 Rental units owned by the CFF, 1891

Annual rent	Number of units
9,001 francs or more	17
9,000–6,001 francs	24
6,000–3,001 francs	107
3,000–2,001 francs	75
2,000–1,001 francs	339
1,000–601 francs	667
600 francs or less	3087
	Total 4,316

Total number of buildings: 167.
Percentage of apartments renting for less than 1,000 francs/year: 81 percent.
Source: Archives Nationales du Monde du Travail, 65 AQ I 102, Compagnie Foncière de France, Rapport du Conseil d'Administration, Rapport des Commissaires et Extrait du Procès-verbal, Exercice 1891, 10–11.

The majority of the firm's units were indeed residences for the middle and lower middle classes. The forty-nine buildings that entered its portfolio in 1883–1884 were 313 square meters on average, valued at 200,000 to 300,000 francs each. These figures placed them squarely in the range of second-class apartment buildings in architect César Daly's typology of residential constructions (in between the buildings for the rich and those for the poor).[26] Claims to serve the needs of modest Parisians were, however, certainly exaggerated. When a staggering 40 percent of the firm's apartments were sitting empty in 1885, the majority—879 of 1,308 vacant units—fell in the lowest rental bracket, a situation explained by the fact that the company's cheaper apartments either were small, top-floor units unsuitable for families, or were located in working-class neighborhoods where their rents far exceeded the average housing budgets of nearby tenants.[27]

Moreover, the CFF's administrators evidenced frustration and even discomfort with the firm's lower-class tenants, attributing to them many of their early difficulties with vacancies and high repair costs. The company reported that it had to contend not only with the well-known "ease with which tenants of small units—the largest group present in our buildings—transport their belongings from one place to another," but also with the disappointing quality of its early tenants, "who move as soon as the rents are adjusted to a more normal level, tempted by cheap apartments in new and empty buildings."[28] The CFF soon began separating larger apartments from medium-sized lodgings and single rooms in its reports to shareholders, demonstrating where the true responsibility for its financial underperformance lay and justifying the vigilance with which it monitored its tenants. In defense of "the good standing and honorability of your buildings," the Council explained, the firm's managers didn't hesitate to "reject or terminate any lease which doesn't provide satisfactory guarantees from every perspective."[29] Likewise, the Rente Foncière was cautious with the populations of its cheaper buildings, described as "careless, nomadic, and often insolvent"; the company let these apartments only when "certain guarantees" could be supplied.[30] While communications between tenants and corporate managers have not survived, the nature of this enforcement can be gleaned from other sources. Tax assessments show that rents for modest apartments in corporate buildings were aggressively negotiated, with increments of 10 and 20 francs being won and lost as tenants changed over. Tolerance for delayed payments was slim; registers from Justices of the Peace, the local officials responsible for the eviction process, show that the CFF and other corporate owners had frequent recourse to legal procedures for removing delinquent tenants, in some cases for as little as 20 francs in late rent.[31] The resulting turnover was partially to blame for the company's high vacancy rates, which dropped from a third to a quarter throughout the 1880s but remained far in excess of the city's average of 4.3 percent.[32]

By the time the number of buildings in its portfolio had stabilized in 1891, the CFF owned 167 apartment buildings in more than half of the city's districts (Appendix; Map 6.2). As the council summarized, it owned buildings "in populous neighborhoods, such as Faubourg du Temple, Boulevard Montparnasse, Rue des Martyrs; in wealthy or commercial districts, such as Rue du Mail and Vieille-du-Temple, Rue de Provence, Rue de Varenne; and in the districts of the future, such as Avenue Victor Hugo and Rue des Belles Feuilles."[33] In each area the company was certain that its constructions were suited to the "needs of the neighborhood"—in other words, that their design and rent levels were in harmony with those of their locales.[34] As the company's reporting evolved, it sorted these properties into groups of roughly comparable assets, held together by their location and the nature of their rentals. These classifications were readings of the city's socioeconomic landscape that performed crucial work in determining the styles of management most suited to "the needs" of particular areas.

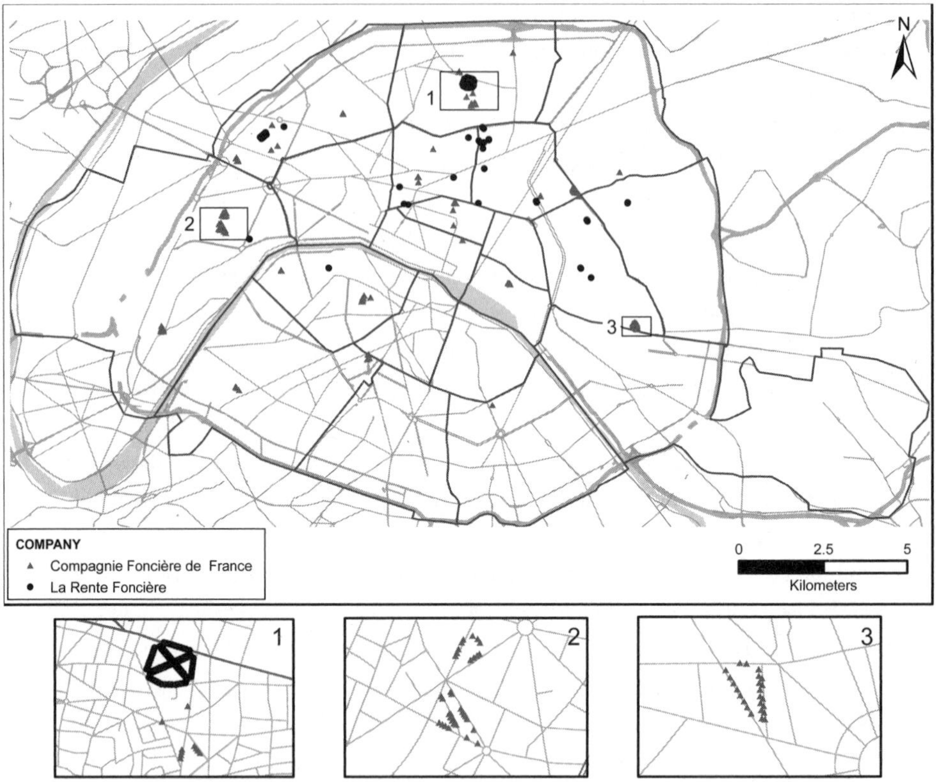

MAP 6.2 Map showing the locations of the properties of the Compagnie Foncière de France and the Rente Foncière, 1910. Courtesy of the Center for Geographic Analysis, Harvard University. Used with permission.

The new categories captured the social geography of the city as it was reproduced by the firm's holdings. The first group included buildings in the 1st, 2nd, 8th, and 9th arrondissements, forming a tight territory on the Right Bank. It boasted both the highest number of expensive rental units and the smallest number of cheap rentals of the firm's four groups. Only 302 of the 541 units available in these arrondissements were described as lodgings (units without designated salons, often sharing toilet facilities), and the number of units costing less than 600 francs numbered only 315 (58 percent of the group's units). The 7th, 13th, and 15th arrondissements formed the second group, a more geographically disparate assemblage linked by their common location on the Left Bank. Nearly as small as the first, this group had the lowest proportion of commercial rentals and was the most socially polarized; 76 percent of its units were available for 600 francs or less, but significant numbers were available at much higher rents (55 apartments rented for 3,000 to 9,000 francs).

The third category was the largest, made up of the firm's holdings in the 10th, 11th, and 18th arrondissements. These districts were home to the largest proportion of cheap rentals (89 percent of units rented for less than 600 francs annually). Geographically, the third category mixed peripheral and central districts; the 10th and 11th arrondissements were both part of the historic, pre-1860 area of the city, and the 18th arrondissement had been a suburban region before this date. Yet the 11th arrondissement was often counted with the peripheral districts, thanks to its new numbering and working-class character, and as for the company's possessions in the 10th, these were located on the extreme northern border of the district, separated by only half a boulevard from the 19th. This category is thus best described as working-class peripheral. The company's fourth group was comprised of the 16th and 17th arrondissements, also peripheral neighborhoods but with a very different socioeconomic makeup. Home to 1,708 of the company's units, this category was almost as large as the previous group and had similar rent distributions: in both cases, nearly all the firm's units cost less than 2,000 francs. Yet apartments outnumbered dwellings in this group (meaning the units were more substantial), commercial rentals were less significant, and a greater proportion of its residential units rented for over 600 francs.

With this classification method, the CFF's annual reports presented accounts on the standing of urban neighborhoods rather than evaluations of individual properties or streets. In contrast, when the Rente Foncière restructured its reporting format in 1896, the four categories of properties it created were ranked from most to least profitable, descending from the lucrative Hotel Scribe and the Grand Hôtel (ventures acquired from the liquidation of the Compagnie Immobilière) to those buildings that, "owing either to the nature of their clientele or to their location, are in a completely unfavorable situation."[35] These included eighty-eight apartment buildings the company owned in the 18th (those Fouquiau had constructed just a few years before), several in the 10th, and an especially disappointing group on Rue Moret in the 11th arrondissement. Just above them were the mediocre buildings near the Gare du Nord, whose tiny courtyards and dark apartments contributed to high vacancies and correspondingly high maintenance costs.

As these examples indicate, these recording methods generated two different representations of urban real estate. The Rente Foncière populated its portfolio categories with addresses and descriptions of specific buildings, accounting for successful rental rates and difficult conditions with factors particular to each building's situation. The CFF, on the other hand, presented its buildings as incidental by-products of their geographical location. A shareholder saw how well a region and various rent categories were performing, rather than being informed on the productivity or maintenance expenditures applicable to specific buildings. These differences emerged partly from the firms' different ownership patterns; the CFF tended to own large groups of buildings clustered on neighboring streets, while the Rente Foncière owned individual buildings and small groups (the Montmartre conglomeration was an important exception). But they also sprang from the divergence in the long-term goals of the two entities. The Rente Foncière was dedicated from the outset to generating profit through owning and managing Parisian rental housing. It considered each building as a unit whose revenue-generating potential could be maximized through policies addressing its specific challenges and opportunities. The CFF, on the other hand, began as and remained, at heart, a mortgage provider. Its core concern, even after it was forced to drastically rework its business model, remained land values and the propensity for properties in a region to generate returns. The firm reported on maintenance costs, but only in the aggregate, communicating little information on the status of individual houses or streets. As the discussion below shows, these categorizations could have important consequences for management priorities.

The Privately Produced City

A traveler alighting in mid-1882 from an omnibus at Place d'Eylau in the 16th arrondissement, soon to be renamed Place Victor Hugo, would have been flooded by the dust and noise arising from dozens of nearby construction sites. The transformations under way were striking, even for those with only a passing familiarity with the area. In place of the low buildings, gardens, workshops, and small houses that had characterized this part of Paris until very recently, six-story apartment buildings were climbing rapidly in all directions.[36] "For Rent" signs hung in some windows, even though buildings were not yet completed, and tenants occupying apartments whose plaster was scarcely dry entered and exited via unfinished sidewalks.[37] Our pedestrian's business lies further into the chaos of scaffolds and heaps of cut stone along the newly named Avenue Victor Hugo. To the right and left, new streets are

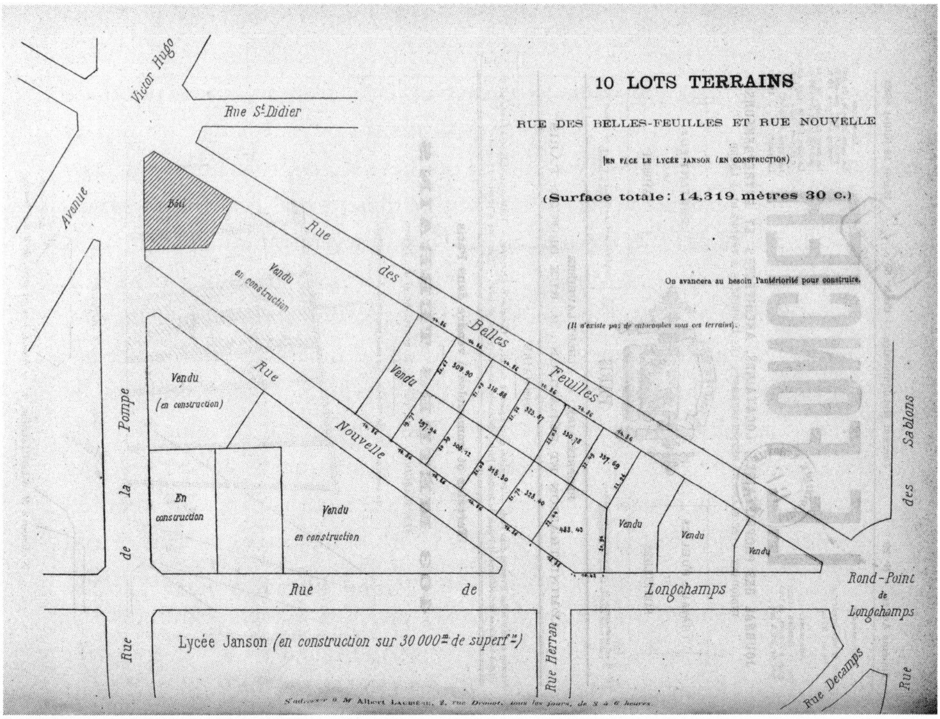

FIGURE 6.3 Advertisement for building land owned by the CFF on Rue de Longchamp, Rue des Belles Feuilles, and Rue de la Pompe. *Le Foncier,* July 18, 1882. *Source:* Bibliothèque Nationale de France

being opened up, piercing empty lots in order to provide frontages for residential buildings. To the north of the avenue, the SA des Immeubles de l'Avenue Victor Hugo has made a residential block by creating Rue de l'Amiral Courbet between the avenue and Rue de la Pompe. On the other side of the intersection, to the south of the avenue, a handful of speculators are in the midst of developing nearly 18,000 square meters of land between Rue de Longchamp, Rue de la Pompe, and Rue des Belles Feuilles (Figure 6.3). A new, still unnamed street already divides this triangle of land, offering space for the façades of nearly twenty apartment houses. Less than a year ago the cornerstone had been laid for the largest *lycée* in the city, the Lycée Janson de Sailly, under construction on 33,000 square meters of land bordering this development. Drawn by the advertisements in *Le Foncier,* a real estate journal that has been brokering these lots for nearly a year, our pedestrian has come to see what opportunities remain in the area, thoroughly awash in speculative construction.

The buildings already erected on the street (soon to be christened Rue Gustave Courbet), as well as their neighbors on Rue des Belles Feuilles, were only slightly distinguishable from each other or from hundreds of others springing up across the city. Part of this consistency is explained by the fact that several of the architects building on these streets were simultaneously overseeing construction elsewhere with different real estate companies. Georges Brière de l'Isle, for example, had begun several buildings in this area as well as three on Rue Mozart elsewhere in the 16th arrondissement, and two in the 17th as part of the Société de Construction du Boulevard Pereire. An architect named Migevant was building both here and in the 11th arrondissement, where he was part of another development being brokered by *Le Foncier*, while Joseph Jeannot was putting up several buildings on Rue Réaumur in the 2nd arrondissement at the same time as he was erecting eleven apartment buildings here on Rue Gustave Courbet. The CFF financed the architect François Dauby to build on both Boulevard de la Villette and Cité Vaneau (though in this case the class of the buildings under construction could not have been more different), and E. Soty operated under the aegis of the firm on both Boulevard Pereire and Rue d'Uzès.[38] Everywhere the buildings were constructed as high as street widths and municipal regulations allowed; everywhere, space was cunningly arranged so as to provide a seemingly varied array of slight alterations on a housing package that was rapidly becoming standardized.

In the area just traveled by our pedestrian, dozens of apartment houses were erected between 1882 and 1887. Those uncompleted or unsold when the market began to collapse in the early 1880s were taken over by creditors such as the CFF. A few were successfully sold off to interested investors; indeed, the majority of the CFF's sales in the 1880s and 1890s were from the streets in this area, whose upper-middle-class buildings and location in the promising west end of the city found favor among buyers looking for stable returns and low maintenance. As fashionable districts went, the Porte Dauphine area had certainly not yet "arrived." It had to await the monumental buildings undertaken by insurance firms and other investment companies at the turn of the century in order to begin its full-scale transformation into the new home of the city's elite.[39] In the meantime, the buildings on offer provided an array of middle-class lodgings and commercial rentals belying the uniformity of their façades, while market conditions were such that a multiplicity of perhaps unforeseen uses were tolerated and encouraged by their proprietors.

The buildings that sprouted from the CFF's rented land in the developing neighborhoods in the west and northwest of the city helped set the patterns of a new residential landscape. In the 17th arrondissement, the company's four apartment buildings on Boulevard Pereire, as well as their building at the intersection of Rue Saussure and Rue Salneuve, were among the most substantial in their vicinities when finished. In both cases their neighbors were low buildings with few tenants, modest private residences, undeveloped land, and industrial operations. The same company that erected apartment houses on Boulevard Pereire—the SA des Terrains et Constructions de la Porte Maillot—built similar structures on the nearby Rue du Débarcadère, introducing a spur to construction on a street that had been developing very slowly, despite having been originally opened during the July Monarchy.[40] Within a few years the builders financed by the CFF would plant dozens of tightly sown, sky-high apartment buildings in this formerly loosely ordered space.

Yet the firm also favored operations in the capital's older districts, critiquing the "creation of new neighborhoods" as it sought to rein in its land-leasing operations early in its existence.[41] After the 16th arrondissement, where the firm's possessions numbered approximately fifty-four buildings by the mid-1890s, the company owned its largest numbers of buildings in the 10th and 11th arrondissements, some of the highest density areas of the city.[42] In these established neighborhoods many of the CFF's buildings exceeded their neighbors in size, amenities, and cost. On Rue de Montreuil in Faubourg Saint-Antoine, the firm's two apartment buildings at nos. 68 and 70 were the largest on that part of the street, and would remain so for some time. They supplied water and gas on all floors and offered apartments for 400 to 600 francs annually. In contrast, the two-story boardinghouses across the street rented their single rooms for 100 francs (Figure 6.4).[43]

The firm's building projects involved more than new apartment houses. They required the establishment of public services such as extended water and sewer lines, paved streets, sidewalks, and lighting. Developers financed by the CFF built at least a dozen entirely new streets in the capital city.[44] The impact of these infrastructural expansions was more visible in newly developing regions, where the firm's apartment houses might for a time provide the only stretch of completed sidewalk or the only streetlights in an area.[45] By building entire streets and blocks rapidly, the ventures financed by the CFF aimed to eliminate the worst aspects of new development, which could lead to lone buildings floating amid unbuilt lots. Large-scale corporate

FIGURE 6.4 The new buildings constructed on Rue Chevreul (receding to the right) and Rue des Boulets stand in contrast to the lower, older constructions (left) among which they were implanted. *Source:* www.parisavant.com, used with permission

developments could introduce services to a street in only a few months, where the efforts of individual property owners often failed to result in significant improvements over decades.[46] Lightning-fast construction also meant occasionally shoddy workmanship. On Rue Saint-Philippe du Roule, opened in 1882, substandard sewerage works and inadequate paving and sidewalks required upgrading and replacing as soon as 1886.[47] As a rule, however, the formal processes of road opening to which corporate builders submitted, the economies of scale made possible by the coordinated development of many lots at once, as well as the pressures of building for resale meant that these projects generally upheld municipal regulations on street improvements. The result was the introduction of new and improved services to many urban areas—for those who could afford to live in them.

The CFF's entrepreneurs did not conjure districts out of whole cloth. The imperatives of loan structures, the prospects of municipal works, the operations of competing developers, building norms and regulations, as well as preexisting development plans and existing territory all shaped the landscape from which speculators worked to carve their fortunes. The firm's involvement in the city's western regions was dictated by the availability of land and the clustering of construction activity, reflecting a common belief in the district's increasing popularity among the upper classes. Thanks to the activities of other firms in the area, the CFF could anticipate continued and rapid development in the northwest. Slightly to the east of the firm's lands on Boulevard Pereire, for instance, the Rente Foncière was in the process of acquiring several newly erected apartment buildings; continuing east, the apartment houses of the Société Pereire were fully established, and that company was continuing to sell building lots to developers with the obligation to build within six months of acquisition.[48] A similar intensity of corporate development characterized the environs of the firm's numerous undertakings in the 16th arrondissement, where it competed and collaborated with insurance and property investment companies investing heavily in the development of the region. In both areas, public works and improvements—such as the construction of the Lycée Janson in the 16th, the connection of Avenue Niel with Avenue des Ternes (1889), or the extension of Rue de Longchamp to Place d'Iéna, abutting the sites of the 1878 and 1889 World's Fairs—also influenced development decisions and property sales.[49]

The apartment houses that entered the firm's portfolio offered little that was innovative or refreshing in architectural terms. They typified the critiques

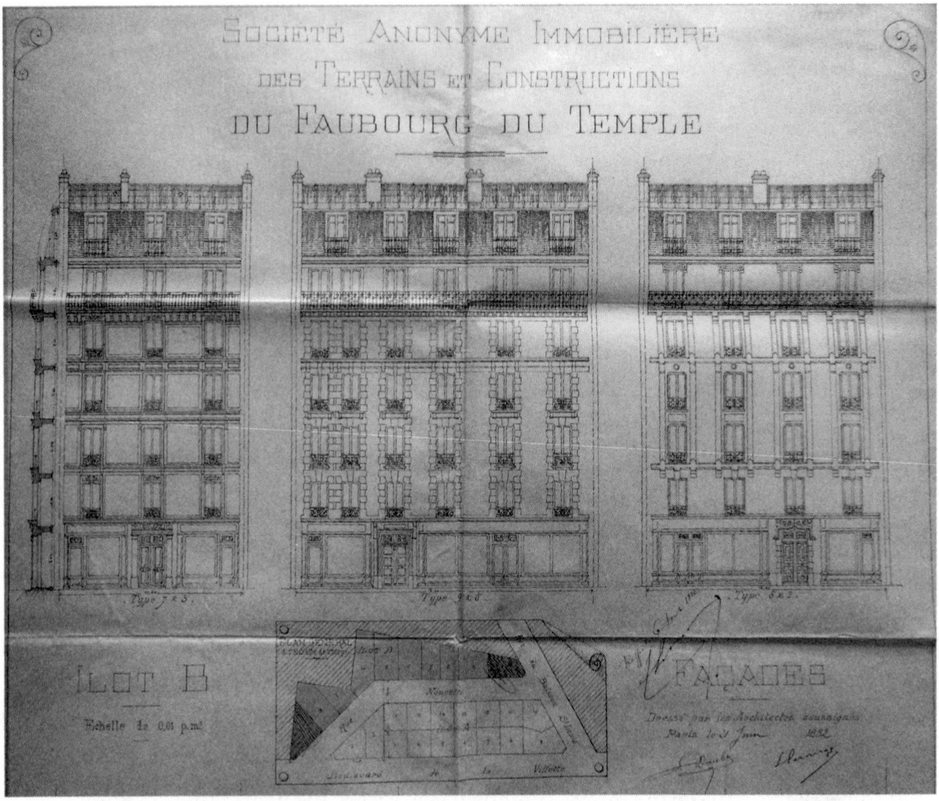

FIGURE 6.5 AND 6.6 Plans for the apartment houses erected by the SA Immobilière des Terrains et Constructions du Faubourg du Temple on Rue Civiale (10th arrondissement), showing three of the five façade "types" adopted on the street, and the repetition of floor plans. *Source:* Archives de Paris VO11 3921

leveled at "mass producers of buildings" whose predictable patterns accorded with contemporaries' lowest opinions of the apartment house: a structure intended for anonymous inhabitants and consequently devoid of "any marked originality in appearance," forced to adopt "an unassertive character, corresponding to—and satisfying, as far as possible—the general tastes and needs shared by the great mass of the population."[50] Speculative architects replicated façades and reproduced floor plans within their developments (Figures 6.5 and 6.6). The firm's buildings were nearly always erected with a basement, a main floor and *entresol,* or mezzanine level, surmounted by either four or five full floors and an additional top floor arranged as attic rooms.[51] The buildings were all *double en profondeur,* meaning that they had

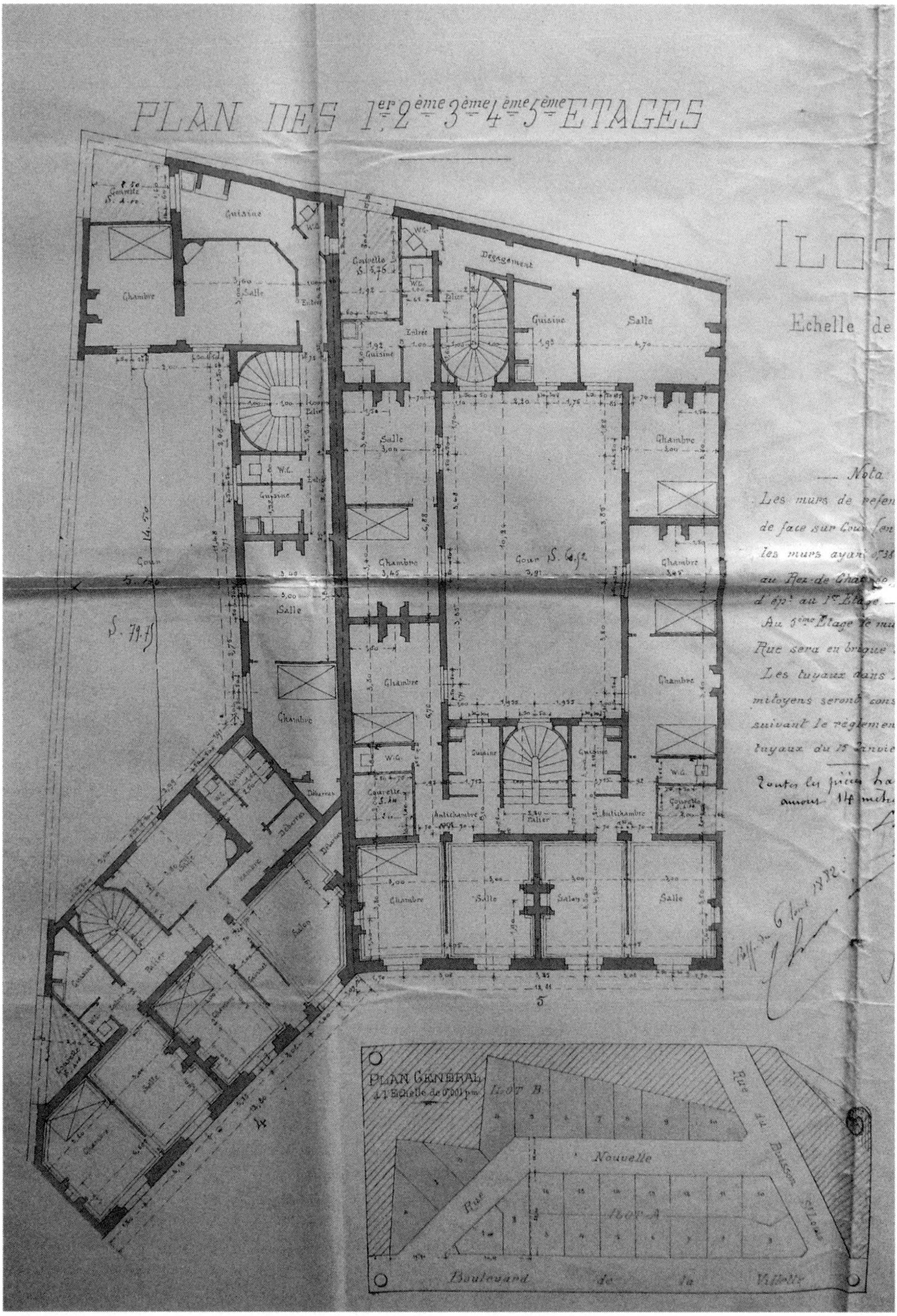
PLAN DES 1er 2ème 3ème 4ème 5ème ETAGES
ILOT
Echelle de
Nota
Les murs de refen
de face sur Cour
les murs ayant
au Rez-de Chaussée
d'ép. au 1er Etage
Au 5ème Etage le mur
Rue sera en brique
Les tuyaux dans
mitoyens seront cons
suivant le règlemen
tuyaux du 15 Janvie
Cuisine
Chambre
Salle
Entrée
Dégagement
Cour
Antichambre
Palier
Salon
PLAN GÉNÉRAL
Nouvelle
Rue
ILOT B
ILOT A
Boulevard de la Villette

a width of at least two rooms between the front and rear of the construction, and they often included one or two wings extending along a central courtyard. Apartment layouts repeated on all floors, with occasional deviations between the entresol and first floor, and a different division of space on the attic floors. Though builders constructed to maximum heights, they seem to have been sufficiently aware of criticism of overbuilt lots to avoid reducing their courtyards to absolute legal minimums. Moreover, the construction of entire blocks by a single company allowed developers to coordinate the courtyard spaces between individual lots and achieve more harmonious and pleasant arrangements of open spaces, a practice deployed for both more expensive housing on Avenue Victor Hugo (16th arrondissement) and more modest apartments on Rue Civiale (10th).[52]

Building materials were also quite consistent; most buildings, even in less wealthy districts, had façades in cut stone, though some constructions comprised of cheaper apartments employed a mixture of brick and rough-hewn stone. What variety there was shifted predictably with neighborhood: cut stone with façade-length balconies for the graceful buildings of Cité Vaneau, located on a private street in the prestigious 7th arrondissement; mixed stone with intermittent window balconies for Rue Chevreul in the working-class 11th. In more mixed and rapidly developing neighourhoods, such as the Porte Dauphine quartier in the 16th arrondissement, significant variations in façade materials could occur on the same street. Here, brick was juxtaposed with cut-stone frontages, the legacy of multiple developers and reflecting the status of this new district as a mixed middle-class area (Figure 6.7).

More variety was evident in the apartment houses' internal arrangements. The number of apartments per floor, the presence of primary and secondary stairwells, the existence of servants' accommodations on the top floor—these distinctions were powerfully culturally coded and weighed significantly in both the understanding and the use of a building's space. The company owned many buildings that were organized into only one apartment per floor, an arrangement characterizing César Daly's highest class of apartment house. The apartment houses of Rue Saint-Philippe du Roule in the wealthy and fashionable 8th arrondissement, for instance, were divided by floor into single apartments that followed traditional rental patterns, with the first floor above the entresol earning the highest rents, and subsequent floors declining in cost while following identical room distribution. On the opposite end of the scale, such as in the working-class north of the city, the company's buildings on

Rue du Mont-Cenis were divided into four apartments per floor, all renting for less than 400 francs annually. Similar buildings were found on Rue du Trésor, in the dense city center, as well as Rue de Longchamp in the 16th. This last street was also home to the company's most subdivided building, a *hôtel garni* or furnished boardinghouse with seven rental rooms per floor. This intense division of space was not the norm, however. The majority of the buildings owned by the company had two or three apartments per floor; those with two sometimes aligned apartments to share exposure on the courtyard and the street equally, at other times one apartment enjoyed the street view while the other was relegated entirely to the less-esteemed courtyard view. When a third apartment was included, this was generally located on the courtyard.

As the tax assessor's itinerary made clear, stairwells were markers and determinants of a building's social space. Several of the CFF's buildings included the separate service stairwells deemed so necessary to the privacy and status of the (tenant) family.[53] The majority, however, accommodated servants on their top floors without providing for separate access to apartments; even the relatively well-off tenants whose apartments took up entire floors at no. 102 Rue de Longchamp, for example, had to share their main stairwell with the residents of the nine fifth-floor maids' rooms. Buildings with cheaper apartments removed service accommodations altogether (falling into Daly's third—and lowest—class of apartment building), dedicating their top floors not to maids' rooms but to smaller lodgings available for rent at 200 francs or less.[54] In between the extremes of expensive, fashionable housing and modest lodgings, the arrangements of residence and service space in the CFF's buildings were rather unpredictable. Some highly subdivided and cheaper buildings included service stairs while nearby buildings housing better-off tenants did not, perhaps reflecting uncertainty about the place of domestic help in the homes of the lower middle class.[55]

Stairwells served to create alternate circulatory networks not only for servants but also for different classes of tenant. The typical lot layout of many apartment houses in Paris featured a street-front building, one or more wings extending to the rear, and a building at the back of the lot, with multiple stairwells servicing different parts of the structure. Because apartments on courtyards were cheaper than those facing the street, these secondary stairwells served to isolate the humbler tenants of an apartment house. On occasion such stairwells combined access to cheaper apartments with access to

FIGURE 6.7 Brick and cut-stone façades share streetscape on Rue des Belles Feuilles (16th arrondissement). *Source:* Photo by author

the quarters of servants working in the more expensive units; this was the case with houses on both Boulevard Pereire and Avenue Victor Hugo, where tenants of cheaper and smaller apartments were required to use the service stair to access their dwellings. Commentators concerned by the problem of declining social mixing within the city often endorsed these spatial segregations, as they were thought to facilitate cohabitation of the classes without imposing a troublesome and embarrassing cross-class familiarity on upper-class tenants.[56] In practice the social distance between those separated by such stairwells was rarely so large as to constitute "cross-class" cohabitation. Speculators may have deployed these arrangements in order to broaden the rental base for their products, but a truly heterogeneous clientele was hardly a selling point for a new apartment building.

As was evident from their recording practices, the investment patterns of the CFF tended to reinforce the territorialization of social class already long under way in the capital city. Building to suit the "needs of the neighborhood" meant that elite apartment houses were erected in the 7th and 8th arrondissements, expansive buildings suitable for expensive corporate and commercial rentals were built in the 2nd and 9th arrondissements, and extremely subdivided buildings were the norm in the 18th. In Cité Vaneau, a street opened on the site of a former aristocratic *hôtel* in the 7th, the CFF maintained an elite private street in the heart of an elegant residential district by establishing one of the city's first property owner associations in accordance with the law of December 22, 1888.[57] Here and in the ritzy Faubourg-du-Roule neighborhood, the CFF's rents were above the average of even these pricey areas. In the city's less expensive regions, the company's buildings clearly also contributed to the growing gentrification of the city. The rents for its buildings in Faubourg Saint-Antoine were far in excess of the average for that district (one of the cheapest in the city) in both 1890 and 1900. For example, on Rue Chevreul a three-room apartment with a kitchen cost around 450 francs, while single top-floor rooms could be had for 150 francs, and larger apartments with salons and additional rooms could cost as much as 850 francs—this in a neighborhood whose annual rent levels averaged 266.54 francs in 1889.

Yet between the extremes of the most and least expensive neighborhoods, the impact of the firm's constructions on the *embourgeoisement* of Paris was more mixed. Its most numerous buildings were found in developing neighborhoods where diversity intended to broaden the revenue-generating net was the rule. On Rue d'Alençon in the 15th arrondissement and Rue de l'Amiral Courbet in the 16th, apartment houses built by the SA des Immeubles du Boulevard Montparnasse and the SA des Immeubles de l'Avenue Victor Hugo shifted from one-apartment-per-floor layouts to more subdivided buildings, resulting in a range of apartment types and rent levels. These were also areas in which the CFF's buildings offered housing at rates that either just met or were well below the neighborhood's average. In 1890 the corporate-owned buildings of Rue de Longchamp offered the cheapest housing on that street (for comparable apartments), while on Rue des Belles Feuilles rents in the company's buildings were below even the average for those of the city as a whole (which stood at 570.85 francs). The average rent in the Porte Dauphine quartier increased from 1,255.92 francs to 1,911.67 francs between 1890 and 1900, far outpacing the rent increases in most of the firm's properties. As new construction financed by insurance companies and other corporate institutions gathered speed in the 1890s and prewar period, the buildings of the CFF maintained some of the most affordable housing in the area. And although its buildings in the 11th arrondissement were expensive for their neighborhood, they maintained spaces for the commerce and industry traditional to the area, incorporating workshops and storage facilities along with commercial spaces, ensuring a mixture of sites of production and social reproduction.[58]

The CFF's buildings were about as far from individualized creations as a building industry not yet in the grips of prefabrication could make them. Yet they were not quite the homogeneous mass that dismissive observers perceived them to be. Variations in the façades were subtle but many; the lengths of balconies and the patterns of their ironwork, decorative motifs around doors and under balconies, the stonework of window facings, and a varied application of stone on the façade all served to distinguish a building from its immediate neighbor, providing the small but important distinctions by which a tenant (and prospective buyer) might judge and choose a building. Most buildings contained two apartments of different sizes on each floor, and buildings on the same street housed apartments that varied in sizes and attributions. The inclusion or absence of a salon, the addition of an extra room, a layout that wrapped east or west around a courtyard, a view on the street or avenue, a kitchen that communicated with the apartment directly or through an office—these were the differences that builders incorporated into their spaces (and advertised in rental notices) in order to maximize their use of lot space and to diversify the appeal of their products for tenants with multiple desires and needs. Importantly, as tenants sought to make homes and managers worked to promote profitability, the uses to which these structures were put could escape the intentions of the builders and owners who cast these housing packages across the city.

Use and Exchange Value in Speculative Buildings

The tenants who moved into CFF and Rente Foncière buildings were responding to an aggressive distribution system established by corporate property owners and managers. Initially some were undoubtedly tempted by the rental concessions that nearly all corporate owners of buildings in the city's west end were forced to adopt in the face of high vacancies and continued construction throughout the 1880s.[59] Elsewhere, perhaps other promotional activities caught their attention. Principal tenants—individuals who leased a building and then sublet apartments at a rate sufficient to make an income from the property—were scattered throughout corporate buildings and needed to attract renters in order to meet their obligations.[60] Corporate owners found these arrangements extremely desirable, as they secured income while relieving them of many maintenance and even tax responsibilities.[61] But the small margins gleaned by both owners and principal tenants meant that renters paid dearly for the spaces on offer and could expect little flexibility in their leases. In the CFF's buildings in the 11th arrondissement, an individual named Durand rented various houses for sums ranging from 5,610 francs to 10,390 francs per year and stood to make approximately 1,000 francs per building, whereas the CFF would receive a return of 3.2 to 4.9 percent. Both profits were modest, and depended on the small three-room apartments Durand managed being fully rented at an exaggerated cost.[62] The result was that rents in the company's "working-class" housing were less flexible than those in similarly priced housing located elsewhere in the city.

A bevy of other agents was on hand to entice precious tenants. Where the CFF did not succeed in recruiting principal tenants, it installed property managers, rental agents, and rental bureaus to manage the distribution and maintenance of its apartments. For its buildings on Avenue Victor Hugo, Rue de la Pompe, and Rue de l'Amiral Courbet, the company had a manager in the entresol apartment of no. 108 Avenue Victor Hugo, as well as a rental office on the same floor at no. 104.[63] An individual named Monsieur Roquier as well as one Monsieur Landrin managed buildings in the nearby Belles-Feuilles development, lodged in apartments on Rue Gustave Courbet and Rue de Longchamp.[64] The twenty-six apartment buildings of Rue Civiale and Boulevard de la Villette had a rental bureau run by Monsieur Saint-Jean at no. 5 Boulevard de la Villette. Similarly the large commercial buildings of Rue d'Uzès housed a main floor rental office at no. 21, and one of the first-floor apartments of no. 16 Rue du Débarcadère was dedicated to a management bureau.[65] The eight apartment buildings of Rue du Trésor, built on land belonging to the CFF but not owned outright by the company, were overseen by a manager named Brunet who lived "offsite" at 84 Rue La Condamine. The Rente Foncière had a similar coterie of agents and managers, interested directly in the returns of their respective buildings by the commissions the company introduced in 1897.[66]

The Rente Foncière dedicated particular attention to establishing an appealing brand for its housing.[67] Its administrators were committed to "developing more amicable relations with the public," "drawing upon the services of rental agencies, as well as broader advertising" in order to move their units.[68] The prospective tenants who visited any of the Rente Foncière's rental offices found employees who "not only quickly supply visitors with a list of apartments responding to their ideas, but will also furnish them with floor plans of these apartments." In sum, the company's advertising boasted, whether they can afford to spend 10,000 francs or only 300 francs, new tenants could choose from over 200 buildings and "will congratulate themselves for having as a landlord a company whose overriding concern is to be pleasant to its tenants and to assure them the deference and respect they are due on the part of its personnel, particularly from its concierges."[69] This promotional machine helps explain successes like the firm's new building on Rue de Magdebourg (16th), which was fully let before the company completed construction in 1912.[70]

Customer service was a key corporate survival strategy. The Rente Foncière's experience in the 8th arrondissement, where it calculated that housing had been produced for 5,658 people whereas the population of the area in fact *dropped* by 4,767, made it acutely aware of the crippling overabundance of high-end rentals. The "formidable competition" between buildings required that steps be taken "to adjust rentals to the tastes of their first tenants and determine their choice."[71] The company adopted an aggressive renovation policy, upgrading apartments as soon as tenants departed in order to avoid having visitors tour tired-looking or damaged units. In 1897 more than a thousand apartments throughout its portfolio were renovated, and in 1898 the buildings on Rue de la Michodière, Boulevard de La Tour-Maubourg, and Rue Le Peletier—all from the company's highest and most profitable category of buildings—received elevators. In 1900 twenty buildings in the quartier Marbeuf had their acoustics refitted, in addition to significant renovations to stairwells, courtyards, and entranceways. The administrators explained that in this market segment, "the strong desire we have to control our expenditures must be moderated by the importance of doing nothing to compromise the upkeep of our buildings and by the necessity of giving legitimate satisfaction to the demands of our tenants." Otherwise "we will see them desert our buildings; their requirements steadily increase as new buildings appear, offering them improvements in comfort that our buildings cannot."[72]

Corporate owners' understanding of the market kept them responsive to the housing needs of better-off tenants. Poorly faring buildings classified in the Rente Foncière's more problematic third and fourth categories waited longer for improvements. In 1910 several buildings on Boulevard Pereire received new bathrooms and electric lighting throughout, and four were fitted with elevators; in 1912 seven of the firm's buildings in the 10th arrondissement received similar upgrades. These buildings were third-category apartment houses; the firm's reports make no mention of improvements for those in the fourth category other than those required by law (such as mandatory connections to public sewers in the early twentieth century, which the firm delayed for as long as legally possible) or those that reduced costs (such as more economical water counters and gas lighting fixtures). That the better-off classes were perceived to have the capacity to absorb and even embrace rent increases in exchange for housing improvements meant that they were the tenants most fiercely courted and their spaces were the most conscientiously attended to.

The need for continued and increasing returns and the ongoing burden of persistent vacancies meant that corporate owners were willing to consider a range of strategies to reduce unproductive spaces in their buildings. Struggling to fill their commercial rentals, of which "too great a number" had been installed "in buildings on streets where traffic is minimal," the CFF began converting them to ground-floor residential rentals in 1890.[73] Because these apartments commanded rents far lower than commercial leases, the council took this decision with great reluctance and abandoned the policy as soon as conditions improved.[74] The market situation forced similar repurposing in the firm's buildings in the 11th arrondissement. The buildings on Rue Chevreul and Rue des Boulets were located in a historically artisanal area. They shared courtyard space with the buildings of the neighboring Rue des Immeubles Industriels, a project constructed in the early 1870s by architect Émile Leménil that mixed residential and industrial space for artisan tenants. In 1892 the firm took these nearby buildings as a model and introduced motor power to the ground floor commercial rentals of Rue Chevreul, hoping to draw local workers and artisans to their units.[75] The company was willing to reconfigure the arrangements of residential and industrial spaces in their buildings, adjusting lower-middle-class buildings to working-class neighborhood usages, in order to defend its bottom line.

Whether these impulses meant that tenants truly had reason to be pleased for having chosen a corporate building is difficult to determine. The CFF's buildings at nos. 102–108 Avenue Victor Hugo housed a slice of the middle-class Parisians in whose (presumed) image the districts of the future were being remade. An array of liberal professionals—architects, doctors, and dentists—as well as military men, a comptroller for the Ministry of Finances, a teacher, a midwife, and a translator for the court of appeals called these buildings their home in the 1880s and 1890s. They also housed several merchants with nearby shops, a few business representatives, several custom tailors and dressmakers, and independent commercial actors like a publicity agent and a real estate agent. Some must have found the services and spaces of the CFF to their liking. Residents of the expensive street-front apartments in no. 108 Avenue Victor Hugo (renting at 1,400 to 1,800 francs between 1885 and 1908) stayed in their apartments for an average of seven years, a significant period of time for those with the means to seek more satisfactory accommodations elsewhere. In the adjacent buildings, tenants were more mobile but frequently moved within or between the CFFs buildings, downgrading to save money or moving to more impressive or comfortable units when they became available. In no. 102, Dame Stevenson rented a second-floor apartment in 1889, and reduced her rent from 970 to 700 francs by moving to a ground-floor unit in 1895. M. Aubey, a publicity agent whose business was located in the distant 2nd arrondissement, rented the second-floor apartment in 1890 after having lived on the third floor since 1885. Meanwhile, on the third floor an individual named Coche rented the cheaper apartment from 1885, before moving to the more expensive unit on the same floor in 1898. Evidently these individuals found living in a corporate building sufficiently rewarding to maintain the arrangement. Interestingly, these particular buildings seemed to have found special favor among independent female tenants. The proportion of female leaseholders recorded in tax surveys ranged from 24.6 percent of tenants at no. 110 (a building the CFF sold in 1890) to 33 percent at no. 106. In contrast, none of the company's buildings on Rue des Boulets registered more than 13 percent female tenancy for the period under consideration.

The portfolio-wide management procedures of corporate bodies might be expected to have generated inflexible dynamics between owner and tenant. The president of the 1884 Parliamentary Commission on the industrial situation in Paris remarked, "Workers have told us that they are dissatisfied that they no longer have any dealings with property owners, but interact only with managers, with rental agents, who are arrogant and tend not to consider their [the tenants'] social position, the needs of their families, who don't show the concern and solicitude for a tenant's situation that they ought."[76] As they enjoyed resources considerably more substantial than those of individual owners, however, corporations were also in a position to extend concessions to tenants. In 1888, for example, the Union Immobilière des Capitalistes, des Constructeurs et des Propriétaires Fonciers (a development company founded in 1877 by architect Émile Leménil) reported to its shareholders that 1,142 francs of the previous year's loss in revenues reflected "individual concessions granted to certain tenants who found themselves in temporary difficulty, and to whom your Council thought it appropriate to extend a sign of our concern."[77] In a similar vein, in 1879 the SA Compagnie du Parc de Bercy, a firm that had developed a large dock and warehouse enterprise on the Seine in the suburban village of Charenton, held meetings with representatives of the more than 800 individuals who had come to call the development home, soliciting their contributions on the future direction of the development.[78] Productive communication between corporate owners and inhabitants was clearly possible. Both these firms were, however, much smaller than the corporate entities with which we have been concerned.[79]

Apart from early concessions on rents and toleration for some adaptive uses of the spaces in their buildings, there are few indications that the CFF engaged in any give-and-take with its tenants. As its vacancies declined, the company exerted consistent upward pressure on rents. It began raising them as early as 1888, starting with 150 apartments whose leases were up for renewal or that were leased term-to-term in the 16th arrondissement and reversing concessions elsewhere.[80] To return to the buildings on Avenue Victor Hugo, those with the highest percentage increases in rent revenues (nos. 102 and 106) were also those with the largest turnover in leaseholders (42 and 46, respectively) in the two and a half decades of 1885–1910. Many of the apartments available in these buildings remained under the average rent for the neighborhood in 1890 (1,255.92 francs), so an increase in rent may have meant that tenants were priced out of the district entirely. The pattern of rent increases continued unabated in the early twentieth century, when middle-class vacancies were declining across the capital city. In 1899 gross income from rents increased by more than 30,000 francs over the previous year; in 1900 the increase was 77,000 francs; in 1905 rents improved by 47,025 francs; 1906, by 49,633 francs; and so on, until gross revenues from buildings had increased from 2,476,957 francs in 1899 to 3,021,731 francs in 1913.

Tenants responded creatively to these pressures. One of the more remarkable phenomena to emerge from a study of the records for the properties of the CFF is the prominence of boarding and subletting within its buildings. Paris boasted an extensive network of temporary housing. This system of *garnis*, or furnished rentals, ranged from group dormitories and windowless rooms just large enough for a bed to the luxurious suites of the city's grand hotels; in between was an array of boardinghouses and apartments, reputable and otherwise.[81] The most overcrowded and unhygienic were the lot of poor migrants and urban unfortunates, while the more comfortable were the province of better-off travelers and tourists. This housing was indispensable to the management of Paris's huge immigrant and floating population; in 1882 nearly 10 percent of Paris's residents were housed in furnished rentals.[82] Renting out parts of a living space, however, particularly letting a room or even just a bed in an apartment, was less common in Paris than it was in cities such as Berlin and Vienna, where it was a familiar and important part of working-class housing provision. The practices of CFF tenants amounted to a middle-class boarding and subletting regime, a phenomenon that deeply complicates our understanding of domestic realities in the fin de siècle. Even for renters, an apartment building could serve a financial strategy, its entrepreneurial vernacular sheltering vernacular entrepreneurialism.

Individuals who rented out parts of their own domiciles were subject to be taxed as professional housing providers, depending on factors like the number and types of spaces that were let, the services included with the rent payment, and whether lessors sublet on a regular basis.[83] Hence, fiscal surveys include notations on the renting out of rooms or furnished apartments by principal leaseholders. The class of tax to which they were subject indicated the scale of rental activity: those in the sixth class let more than one furnished room or an entire apartment, while those in the eighth rented out only a room.[84]

On occasion the evaluators' notations include information on the specific rooms that were let, as well as their cost, along with other indications that shed some light on the nature of the transaction and the use of the apartment. For example, an individual named Besson was recorded in 1892 as taking over the leases of both first-floor apartments in no. 12 Rue du Débarcadère, replacing the former management bureau of the CFF with a "pension bourgeoise" in which two individuals were "housed and fed."[85] In 1893 at no. 27 on Rue des Belles Feuilles, Demoiselle Borel, a resident of one of the fourth-floor apartments, was described as a "renter of furnished rooms," providing two furnished rooms and a kitchen to two tenants.[86] At no. 29 in 1887, the "very old" widow Thiery let a furnished room in her courtyard-facing first-floor apartment to "a servant sent by her daughter on Rue Gustave Courbet, 32, who runs an employment agency."[87] Nearby, on Rue de la Pompe, Dame Phulpin took advantage of the "extra" space in her apartment on the entresol of no. 150 to rent out the corner salon—the room with the most windows in the apartment—as a furnished room between 1885 and 1888.[88] Even such short descriptions can help establish an image of domestic life in the apartment. For instance, in 1899 on the courtyard-facing entresol apartment of no. 140 Rue de la Pompe, Demoiselle Trille was listed as a lessor of a furnished apartment, while the notation further specified that she rented three furnished rooms. As her apartment consisted of a salon, a dining room, and one additional room, along with a kitchen and toilet facilities, it seems that the salon and dining room were converted to bedrooms, and the entirety of the apartment's living spaces rented out.[89]

The smallest apartment that recorded a rented room in the CFF's holdings was on Rue des Belles Feuilles at no. 39, where one Dumorat gained authorization to rent out a furnished room in 1893. His apartment on the ground floor of the building was comprised merely of a dining room, a kitchen, a bedroom and a windowless room or "cabinet."[90] Nearly as small, at no. 3 Rue Chevreul in 1896, Dame Oelhuter hosted a roomer in her three-room apartment on the second floor.[91] This unit did not have a designated salon or dining room, just a kitchen and three *pieces à feu,* and toilet facilities were on the landing, shared with other tenants. The rent at both apartments was 450 francs, among the cheapest of those sheltering lodgers. More commonly, tenants who sublet portions of their apartments between 1882 and 1900 were paying rents above 500 francs; most cost 700 to 900 francs, though two second-floor apartments that rented rooms at nos. 14 and 16 on Rue du Débarcadère cost 1,100 francs each. A lodger's financial contribution to the household was substantial. On Avenue Victor Hugo, one room rented for 200 francs in an apartment costing 900 francs, another for 230 francs in one costing 850 francs.[92] These figures alone confirm the middle-class character of room-letting in the French capital at the end of the nineteenth century.

As fiscal records record only the primary leaseholder, mentioning spouses and children only occasionally, it is difficult to discern whether adding a roomer to an apartment meant crowding a family into a smaller space, or whether the practice took advantage of extra, underused, or unused rooms. Many of the individuals listed as *loueurs*—as many as three-quarters of those in the CFF's buildings—were women, either widows, *demoiselles,* or *dames,* indicating that they lived without a male head of household. While this does not preclude the presence of children, it may indicate that a significant portion of lessors were women living alone. For women facing social constraints on their economic pursuits, subletting was one somewhat respectable manner in which to make or increase an income. Perhaps it also fulfilled desires for companionship or occupation among the steadily growing percentages of older single women—whether widowed or never married—present in Paris and other French cities at the end of the nineteenth century.[93] Whatever the reason, it was an avenue by which women engaged—perhaps reluctantly, perhaps enthusiastically—in the commercializing real estate market.

The residential spaces of an apartment building could fluctuate easily between "normal" and "hotel" space—or between use and exchange value. Tenants could become hosts when it suited them, letting rooms opportunistically. Paris hosted two World's Fairs in the fin de siècle, one in 1889 and the other in 1900, both held in areas close to the buildings the CFF owned in the city's west end. In addition to the general increase in Paris's population in the last decades of the century, the influx of visitors to these events may have encouraged many tenants to rent out portions of their apartments.[94] A Monsieur Mancillon, for example, rented out rooms in his third-floor, courtyard-facing apartment at no. 23 Rue des Belles Feuilles for less than a year between 1900 and 1901. Tenants could live in a building for some time before deciding to begin renting out rooms, as in the case of Monsieur Dumorat, who lived in his apartment at no. 39 Rue des Belles Feuilles for two years before seeking status as a *loueur* in 1893. By the same token, a tenant who rented out rooms could enter and leave a building quickly; in 1893 Demoiselle Borel housed two tenants in her fourth-floor apartment in no. 27 Rue des Belles Feuilles, but was a tenant in the building for only one year.[95]

In other cases, subletting took on a habitual, even professional, character. At nos. 15 and 17 Rue des Belles Feuilles, in buildings owned by the Crédit Foncier et Agricole d'Algérie, a tenant named Villard rented contiguous first-floor apartments in the two buildings between 1895 and 1899, opening a communication between them and renting out furnished rooms in both.[96] Subletting could be linked to a tenant's profession. A decorator named Guillon, whose business was located on the chic Boulevard Malesherbes, kept a furnished apartment at no. 7 Rue de l'Amiral Courbet between 1894 and 1896 for the purposes of subletting.[97] This was a common practice among these taste professionals, who used furnished apartments as showrooms for their wares and skills. Similarly, the midwife Préant was listed as renting a furnished room in her apartment in no. 41 Rue des Belles Feuilles in 1888; midwives often dedicated such rooms to their patients for periods leading up to and following births.[98] On Avenue Victor Hugo, Dame Baguet, a grocer who had her store and dwelling at no. 104 between 1885 and 1888, maintained and rented out a furnished apartment on the entresol of neighboring no. 102 during the same period. Her dual role as shopkeeper and landlady fit easily within the established Parisian tradition of main-floor commercial renters operating as subletters for both apartments and entire buildings.[99]

In some instances whole buildings were given over to subletting. At no. 102 Avenue Victor Hugo, a woman named Berthe Verdin rented an apartment on the entresol in 1894 and commenced acquiring the leases for other units in the building as they were vacated by their tenants. By 1899 she was the principal tenant for both apartments on the second floor, as well as the third, and also let one apartment on the first. Verdin had honed her craft nearby at no. 1 Rue de l'Amiral Courbet, where from 1885 she had rented two apartments as a *maîtresse de pension,* providing furnished rentals as well as giving lessons for female students.[100] This operation may have given her the practice and confidence required to expand her activities, and no. 102 Avenue Victor Hugo became an established hotel known as The Verdin (today, the Hôtel Alexander). Number 86 Rue de Longchamp, at the corner of Rue des Belles Feuilles, also became a building dedicated to furnished rentals, though here the transformation was not so piecemeal. The building was divided into single-room rentals from the outset, eight per floor, and their rentals were divvied up between the ground-floor tenants: Decaudin, a wine seller who offered consumption on the premises; Mademoiselle Bricaud, a dairy woman; and Lubin Chainet, listed as a *loueur de chambres meublées.*[101] They let rooms at 150 to 200 francs, some of the cheapest accommodation in the neighborhood. Today this building is the Hôtel Métropolitain. Elsewhere in the west end the company rented its building at 10 Rue Saint-Philippe du Roule to a firm that converted it to the Hôtel Bradford. All located in the west end of the city, steps from the Champs-Elysées, these hotels rented furnished rooms and apartments to visitors attracted to the prestige and diversions of these increasingly fashionable shopping and administrative districts.[102]

Although lodging was present across the rental spectrum and geographic range of the CFFs portfolio, it had a definite spatial organization. As far as it was declared to municipal authorities, lodging was largely limited to the middle-class apartments of the new districts of the city. The twenty-four apartment buildings the company owned in the 11th arrondissement show only three instances of individuals renting out rooms. Similarly, not a single registered room-letter appeared among the tenants of those eighty-eight buildings the Rente Foncière owned on Rue Eugène Sue and Rue Simart in the 18th arrondissement.[103] It is probable that lodging was underreported in working-class areas, where taxes were a particular burden on family income; tax records are also less detailed for these regions. Yet, given that the rents and sizes of many apartments in both these areas were comparable to some of the apartments that hosted lodgers in the 16th arrondissement, the difference remains striking. Lodgers and lodging houses were reported among CFF properties on nearly every street in the 16th and 17th arrondissements for which tax surveys survive. The concentration of lodging on Rue des Belles Feuilles in the 16th and Rue du Débarcadère in the 17th is particularly pronounced. Nearly every building the company owned on Rue des Belles Feuilles—and those on the same street owned by other corporate entities—contained several tenants who also rented furnished rooms and apartments. The CFF's buildings on Rue du Débarcadère each housed multiple tenants who became hosts off and on during the last decades of the century. The surrounding buildings that were not the property of the CFF showed similarly intense patterns of lodging activity, and many lodging houses were established on this street in the interwar period.[104] These patterns confirm those discerned in a recent study of furnished housing, which emphasizes the tendency of lodging in the capital to be spatially concentrated.[105]

While these sources cannot answer questions on the utility of boarding for those who offered it, it may be that steadily increasing housing costs in these buildings—most registered subletters begin appearing in the 1890s as the CFF was raising rents—and the examples of neighbors combined to encourage its generalization. It is indisputable that the CFF knew of (and perhaps encouraged) its tenants' proclivities for subletting. Standard leases of the time required the authorization of the property owner for these activities, and even though such injunctions could naturally do little to stop informal lodging ventures, the tendency to register with tax officials suggests that many individuals undertook their activities openly. Moreover, the presence of CFF employees within these buildings makes it difficult to credit that the comings and goings of boarders went consistently unnoticed. Despite its omnipresence in the city, furnished housing—particularly that for the working classes—was broadly perceived as disreputable and undesirable. Housing created by affordable housing groups explicitly prohibited subletting, as did subsequent laws on affordable housing, which dictated that individual homes be inhabited by no more than one family.[106] Furnished housing among the middle classes was also not exempt from suspicion. Private owners or tenants who sublet furnished rooms were subject to inspection by the police, and though these regulations seem to have been rather loosely applied, they nevertheless placed furnished rentals under a separate regime of control, heightening their associations with dubious individuals and behaviors. The availability of furnished rooms or apartments required that an owner publicly mark the house with a yellow sign (unfurnished rentals were advertised with a white sign), and courts recognized that such a sign could infringe on the enjoyment of their apartment by those tenants "who had entered the house while it was *louée bourgeoisement* ['normal,' unfurnished residential rental]," as the addition of furnished rentals "leads necessarily to a more frequent turnover of tenants, to more visitors, more noise, less security."[107]

Nevertheless the CFF easily accommodated the practice. If the concerns of the corporation regarding the protection of its portfolio and reputation are to be believed, then perhaps reservations regarding lodging were exaggerated—by-products of a moralizing discourse on the destructive promiscuity of shared dwellings—or simply inapplicable to the middle-class phenomenon at work in these buildings. From the types of spaces that were rented and their cost, it is clear that neither subletters nor their lodgers were among the most destitute of the city's residents. Subletting, boarding, and the attendant branding of the area helped tenants meet their rent obligations and could assist the firm with its constant efforts to locate new tenants. The hotels at no. 102 Avenue Victor Hugo, no. 86 Rue de Longchamp, and no. 10 Saint-Philippe du Roule catered to a range of individuals, diversifying the firm's rental network. Finally, the presence of subletters devolved some management tasks (and maintenance costs) to hosts.

What all this shows is that the residential landscape overseen by the CFF was thoroughly commercialized. Corporate owners facilitated the adaptation of domestic space for revenue-generating purposes, with the result that private space was mobilized for productive ends at a number of levels. This layering of property intermediaries complemented investment firms' proclivity for dissociating management and ownership, ensuring that the districts of the future were monuments to the business of housing.

The financial operations of the CFF resulted in the addition of hundreds of new apartment buildings to the built landscape of early Third Republic Paris. East and west, Left Bank and Right, speculators supported by the company produced buildings that contained increasingly standardized housing packages. They added road improvements, installed public amenities, and constructed entire streets, choosing their sites on the basis of a web of public and private development activity that helped define districts of "potential." In most respects the architectural forms that the firm spread across the city contributed to the already existing territorialization of social class—no truly wealthy or working-class housing appeared in localities where developers determined that it did not "belong." Yet many developments also resulted in a mixed landscape reflective of neighborhoods in the making. Attention to the evolution of these buildings once completed reveals the varied uses that animated them as social spaces. Importantly, the market situation in which these buildings came to life as revenue-generating investments reveals the key role of building management in defining the conditions of possibility for the social uses of particular spaces.

The buildings produced under the aegis of the CFF represent only the best-documented portion of the new buildings produced by property development and management companies in this period. Firms such as the Rente Foncière, the Crédit Agricole et Foncier d'Algérie, the Foncière Lyonnaise, and the Société des Immeubles de France, to name only a few of the largest concerns to emerge from the 1880s building boom, erected and managed thousands of apartment buildings in Paris. From the overflowing portfolios of insurance companies such as La Foncière to the modest holdings of working-class capitalization ventures such as La Fourmi Immobilière, these enterprises introduced the phenomenon of large-scale, corporate property ownership and management to the French capital.[108] The network of intermediaries installed by corporate owners to oversee the management of their properties included new actors on the property scene, such as real estate agents and the staff of management offices, as well as traditional actors such as *locataires principaux*. These practices accentuated the professionalization of residential property management, a trend that was increasingly pronounced as specialized intermediaries became more thoroughly embedded in the rental economy and as property owner organizations such as the Chambre des Propriétés elaborated a role for the urban property owner based on expert service in housing provisioning and wealth management.

Corporate ownership on a citywide scale represented the fullest expression of contemporary trends toward the commercialization of property. The management policies of corporate owners were determined by the requirements of profit maximization that stemmed from both the form of their businesses and the financing mechanisms that had underwritten the initial production and acquisition of their buildings. As joint stock ventures whose financial standing was based on the valuation of their assets and their capacity to generate dividends for their investors, these companies pursued profit maximization to the exclusion of other concerns. In the process they developed a discourse and approach to management that constructed property and apartment brokerage as a service aimed at a mass market of housing consumers.

This discussion of some key elements of the lived history of these spaces as they evolved as commercial objects has given us a case study of how the imperatives of rationality, efficiency, and standardization at work in corporate property development are influenced and transformed by existing social spaces and unforeseen market conditions. Studying the use value of a commercial object whose biography is thought to be exhausted by its exchange value opens a window on the domestic worlds of particular urban settings; it also demonstrates the importance of locality and historical contingency as the financial market began to play a more important role in the production and distribution of urban space. Some of the adaptations these buildings experienced worked to accommodate new spaces to the existing needs of a neighborhood, while others—such as the little-known prominence of middle-class boarding and subletting—highlight how the needs that a neighborhood imposes upon residents can be transformed under the influence of new financial organizations. The emergence of these types of adaptations is precisely why a history of built space and its relationship to the urban environment cannot stop with the production of an apartment building, or even an entire district of apartment buildings, but must also consider the intentional and inadvertent social spaces produced by these structures.

Epilogue

Illicit Speculation and Impossible Markets

In an article published in the interwar monthly *Revue de la Propriété Immobilière et de la Construction,* property expert Lucien Lagrave offered readers a chronology of the market evolution of real estate. From the mid-nineteenth century, he contended, "a habitation no longer seemed a simple material device for housing, but rather—and increasingly so—it was seen as a source of revenue. Houses were no longer built for any purpose other than generating a return." The "immeuble de rapport," or "revenue building" (also known as apartment houses), became the definitive article of the real estate market. Lagrave suggested that this phenomenon altered the entire urban experience, changing cities from simple agglomerative entities to units with a common economic purpose. Moreover, he isolated a second stage, which occurred in the period roughly preceding the Great War, whereby urban properties became a form of capital "whose importance as a component of the economy would grow in direct relation with the volume of trade . . . regardless of whether this was intentional, or even understood, buildings were linked directly to consumption." He concluded succinctly: "In a word, the building was commercialized."[1]

Commercialization referred to a number of interrelated phenomena that Lagrave did not begin to detail. The agents, laws, economic conjunctures, and political impulses that worked to transform the life of real estate as a commercial object in the nineteenth century were, after all, numerous and difficult to recover. As he explained, this long evolution "had the great fault of occurring too naturally; it garnered no attention and remained unnoticed."[2] Insofar as Lagrave was correct, this appearance of natural evolution was itself part of the process of real estate's commercialization, a process that was neither automatic nor inevitable but whose ordinary unfolding it was often in the interests of proponents to promote. Yet it had not truly passed unremarked. From journalists who complained of corporate overproduction to police commissioners who correctly diagnosed the impact of shareholder-owners on rent levels; from mortgage reformers who struggled to loosen property's value from its landed roots to elected representatives who toiled to reconcile urban development with urban citizenship; from real estate agents who artfully arranged and advertised their wares to speculators who traded in mortgage transfers and purchase options—whether mission or anathema, the new commerce in real estate was an unmistakable force in the nation's political economy. The commercialization that so interested him was also, as Lagrave was writing, far from hegemonic. The dream of a centralized market for real estate—which he himself dismissed as an impossibility—repeatedly eluded its most fervent acolytes, while the persistence of legal doctrines such as *rescision pour lésion d'outre-moitié*—a provision allowing a seller of real property to seek damages or an invalidation of the sale if they suffered a prejudice in excess of half its value—maintained the assumption that real property had an intrinsic and identifiable value that existed independently of the marketplace. Furthermore, continued opposition to renovating the state's cadastre and property registration system revealed further ways that property remained a problematic good. If, as historian Alain Pottage has documented in the English case, the triumph of title registration marked "a transition from contractual property to property proper," the conditions necessary to move French property from a regime in which it was "irremediably uncertain" to one in which it was a "presupposition" had not yet occurred.[3]

Nevertheless, the war brought important changes to the market situation of real estate that no doubt contributed to the seeming inevitability of the commercialization Lagrave described. The conditions imposed on the housing—and by extension, the real property—market in the unprecedented circumstances of the Great War played an important role in further cementing the commercial status of housing merchandise. The rent moratoriums that accompanied wartime mobilization—temporary at first, then instituted more permanently in 1916—were initially measures of social provision and public order, but were quickly inscribed within a discourse of consumer rights by mobilized tenants' groups and their representatives.[4] Rent moratoria also established numerous rent and property categories that significantly complicated the housing market while slowing investment in real property. From this period onward, freedom of contract between owners and tenants was replaced by a special regime governing housing relations. Paradoxically, as residential space was removed from free-market conditions, it was also increasingly clearly defined as merchandise (owner-tenant relations in France today, for instance, are governed by regulations and bodies charged with consumer protection). Moreover, opposition to the special regime coalesced around its "other," a free market in housing, elevated to a universal good and widely demanded by property owner associations and building entrepreneurs, particularly those who did not benefit from the public housing construction that took off in the interwar period.

One measure that formed part of the special rental regime is of particular importance. Fears of brutal rent increases likely to accompany peacetime and the end or moderation of the special rental regime saw legislators introduce a law creating the infraction of illicit speculation in rents in 1919. This law attempted to apply the principles of earlier legislation controlling wartime speculation on a variety of merchandise to urban housing, and to hold accountable any individuals deemed to be exaggerating rent levels beyond the "natural" limits determined by supply and demand.[5] The legitimacy of expanding such legislation to housing was doubtful. Legally speaking, because renting was a civil rather than commercial act, several of the elements necessary to constitute illicit speculation in the commercial realm either didn't exist or were difficult to quantify when it came to housing. One legal observer summarized: "The truth is that there is no marketplace for rents, there is no Exchange that centralizes supply, there's nothing that makes the play of supply and demand transparent. Different markets form from neighborhood to neighborhood, and different prices apply according to the needs of each client; the laws of supply and demand have a very small influence."[6] In seeking to regulate the market for housing, then, legislators found themselves engaged in *creating* one, or at least establishing one whose conditions were amenable to public intervention. Recognizing the central role of information networks in the functioning of this market, the 1919 law included stipulations requiring that property owners and managers post notices of their available apartments on their buildings. This was one means by which authors of the legislation sought to prevent the "hoarding" of merchandise with which speculation had long been legally linked.[7]

Organized tenants' groups in the immediate postwar period were particularly concerned about the ability of property owners, in concert with estate agents, to dissemble the existence of available lodgings and manipulate the prices of their merchandise. Accusations of conspiracies in the housing market were abundant. In May 1919 a Parisian representative in the Chamber of Deputies wrote, "There are no more 'For Rent' signs; it seems the Association of Property Owners has recommended that its members take in all their signs, in order to increase the price of rents." What is more, he continued, "it is fruitless to walk the streets in search of lodgings; you are obliged to undergo humiliating treatment at the hands of expensive and cynical intermediaries who have generated a new industry in collusion with property owners and concierges."[8] In a letter in early 1919 to the minister of justice, Paris's prefect of police agreed that some owners were not posting their apartments when they became available, though he put this down not to an effort to inflate market prices, but rather to their fear of taking tenants who would be difficult to evict under the conditions of new legislation.[9]

Estate agents suffered the same fate as many other commercial intermediaries during the Great War, accused of exploiting circumstances to manipulate markets at the expense of consumers. Tenants' advocate Maurice Maurin wrote in 1919 of "the scandalous and immoral collaboration between building managers and apartment rental agencies," whom he accused of angling to maintain artificially high rents.[10] A newspaper article chronicling the search for housing in the capital expressed amazement that despite the complete absence of "For Rent" signs, moving trucks blocked the streets. When the author asked a friend in the moving industry to explain this, he was informed that apartments were plentiful: "The clever ones who want housing—and whose wallets are flush enough—go through certain agencies and get what they want."[11] According to critics of the profession, the conditions of the postwar housing market had put estate agents in a position to exert dominance over distribution networks. The public's desperation for housing helped reinforce this dynamic as individuals paid huge commissions for decent apartments and gladly offered "inscription fees" in exchange for the hope of being offered one of the apartments advertised by agencies in their alluring window displays.[12]

Facing what they understood as an increasing monopolization of information by estate agents that threatened to replace democratic and locally based signage networks with "publicity columns and shady rental bureaus," housing activists called for the establishment of municipal rental offices.[13] All property owners would be obliged to announce their vacancies immediately to these offices, located in each district of the city. In language that could easily have been that of a self-promoting real estate agent, Maurin described how the process of finding housing would be rendered more efficient: "No need to search through neighborhoods and streets, to climb story after story, to deal with the insolence of concierges and suffer their repugnant extortion. You want to live in a specific district, neighborhood, a given region? It's easy, you go to the town hall, you consult a table or a special register, and you see immediately whether you can find something suitable in terms of price, size, floor, etc."[14] Henri Sellier, housing reformer, urbanist, and member of the General Council of the Seine, proposed similar bureaus, confessing his astonishment that the housing market of the capital city did not already possess such an invaluable mechanism. While rationality had entered every other aspect of modern life, he remarked, "the inhabitant of the immense agglomeration that is Greater Paris has no means at his disposal other than those of the Middle Ages when it comes to finding housing." The absence of a centralized rental bureau was so irrational as to be nearly unthinkable, bringing to mind "a modern city in which the inhabitants have no means of illumination other than candles."[15]

Real estate agents were well accustomed to the general disregard for their occupation and the slights or even accusations it could generate. But the politics of the postwar housing market were more challenging than any they had previously confronted. Several leading representatives of the field sought defense by founding the Chambre Syndicale des Agents Immobiliers de France (Association of Real Estate Agents of France).[16] Presided over by Edmond Largier, an established real estate agent in Paris and a future deputy, its initial membership of 63 agents was drawn principally from the capital city, but quickly expanded across the country. By 1923 it boasted 120 members, by 1925 there were 250, and by 1928 membership reached more than 500 agencies across France. The first issue of the Association's journal in 1921 pointed out how often "ignorant individuals have accused our occupation of being one of the causes of the present housing crisis, because they think that it is in our interest to drive prices up."[17] But hostility and resentment were only some of the group's challenges. The Association was formed in particular response to legislative propositions made by Parisian deputy Arthur Levasseur (Socialist) that sought to centralize housing distribution in large cities. In the context of proposals for new legislation governing rental agreements, Levasseur called for mandatory housing registries that would become the sole information network for apartment and house rentals. He explicitly aimed to replace rental agencies, stressing that pursuant to this legislation, "no rental contract could be established outside the offices of this bureau."[18]

The organizers of the Association of Real Estate Agents were outraged by this campaign for "the suppression *pure and simple of rental agents and building managers!*"[19] Denying any complicity with efforts to manipulate the housing market, the Association defended the agent as a simple indicator in the market, a publicity node that informed buyers and sellers without exerting any influence over prices.[20] It noted that "in order to adapt to circumstances" agents had abandoned the time-honored practice of receiving their rental commissions from property owners, and instead received them from tenants, a move that was intended to position them as representatives of tenants rather than owners (but which could do little to defend them from charges of exploiting desperate home-seekers).[21] The closest Levasseur's proposals came to realization was in 1926, with the passage of a new law governing urban housing rentals. Articles 25 and 26 of the law of April 1, 1926, reiterated the obligation for owners and managers to publicly post vacancies on the front of their buildings, as well as the requirement that vacant lodgings be declared at the city hall, or, in cities where they existed, at municipal housing offices.[22] Moreover, it prohibited any form of private advertising for those apartments whose availability was not also publicly posted and declared. Without obliging proprietors to treat solely through municipal conduits, the law sought to maintain sufficient transparency to prevent the unfair monopolization of housing information by privileged intermediaries. It seems, however, that enforcement of these regulations was virtually nonexistent.[23] While the principle of a monitored and centralized market was reinforced, in practice consumers were left to navigate the city and its housing on their own.

A lack of political will along with the protests of property owners and real estate agents contributed to this failure. Yet the effort also epitomized the contradictions of previous attempts to establish centralized markets for the brokerage of property and housing. The quandaries public officials faced in imagining—let alone structuring—"the" market for housing in the nation's capital city sprang from the material qualities of the goods on offer, ingrained practices of housing provisioning, and legal frameworks that defied the assimilation of civil and commercial affairs. Their endeavors provide a further example of the historically specific agents and institutions involved in the elaboration of the norms and practices of urban real estate markets, belying the inevitability of this market's power to shape the landscape and conditions of everyday life. Bringing land, buildings, and apartments to market was not a straightforward or uncontested matter. Approaching the Parisian real estate market as a social product has allowed us to recover the processes of marketization—and the failed paths in that process—that are responsible for its establishment and maintenance.

This book has examined the commercialization of the housing and property markets in fin-de-siècle Paris from the perspective of the production, distribution, and consumption of residential space, giving particular attention to the built spaces and networks of mediation that constituted the form and experience of the urban landscape. From perfected credit networks to new business forms, from increasingly assertive commercial intermediaries to new advertising practices, from corporate management firms to professionalized property owners, this period saw the introduction and consolidation of a range of new actors and imperatives that worked to redefine the conditions of distribution and consumption of residential space in the capital city. These changes were elements of a broader transformation in the understanding of the place of urban property and property-holding in the nation's political economy. As the century drew to a close, the rise of participation in the stock market served to particularize the nature and status of property investment while also leading to innovations that sought to accommodate real property to the desires for liquidity and circulation generated by movable assets. Shares in property management firms aimed to democratize ownership by improving its affordability and transferability; along with the wide net cast by the bonds issued by the Crédit Foncier based on the value of that institution's mortgage loans, these instruments familiarized an increasingly broad demographic with the revenue-generating potential of real estate, while also contributing to the persuasiveness of the stock market—*the* market par excellence—as a model for the organization of the property market.

While thus helping to make the productive capacity of real assets ever more prominent in the portfolios of individual savers, the increased mobilization of real estate capital heightened its status as an object of exchange—and as an object suited to Exchanges.

Consequently, the meaning of property ownership in the economic imaginary, its status as an activity of production or consumption, was increasingly conflicted. Urban property owners organized, led by the Parisian Chambre des Propriétés, articulating a business model of proprietorship that aimed to define a collective economic interest—which granted them the power to claim status as a professional association—and to align that interest with the common good of the country as a whole by emphasizing their contributions to the collective productive endeavor. In principle (if not, finally, in practice), organized property owners embraced demands that they contribute to public works on the basis of their privileged ability to benefit from betterment values, and mobilized to pass legislation that provided the means for their individual activities to coordinate in collective projects on behalf of the public interest. Ultimately this legislation found application in the maintenance and management of private roadways, physical and juridical spaces that manifested the difficulty of associating private proprietorship with collective municipal stewardship.

Examining the built landscapes that resulted from the new priorities shaping the market for real property in the fin de siècle reveals how these priorities shaped the conditions of everyday life. Although the forms of production that characterized the construction of new housing in the Third Republic sprang from a reorganized market that privileged a property's exchange value over its use value, this same market birthed buyers, managers, and consumers who placed use value—whether their own or someone else's—squarely at the core of their market behaviors. Speculatively produced and corporately owned buildings supplied housing packages and management practices that sought to commercialize the experience of selecting and dwelling in new apartments by emphasizing consumer choice, satisfaction, and the virtues of professional intermediation. That housing consumers were no longer housing producers—a status most Parisian inhabitants lost centuries before—did not amount to an alienated experience of the urban landscape. Moreover, as the study of corporate housing reveals, their spaces remained adaptable to the needs of users and neighborhoods, even as they imposed more homogeneous façades and living arrangements on the built fabric of the city.

The history the Parisian real estate market excavates the ambiguous place of liberal capitalism in Third Republic France. Certainly the self-restricting tendencies often popularly associated with the French experience of capitalism were much in evidence. The property market remained populated and managed in part by traditional monopolistic bodies, namely, notaries and solicitors, who benefited from state-endorsed positions and resisted the commercializing imperatives of specializing agents d'affaires. Municipal administrators who argued in liberal market terms against public intervention in the property market at the height of the 1880s building bust were also deeply suspicious of the role of speculative enterprise and amalgamated capital in urban development, and state representatives inquiring into the status of industry in the capital city were perturbed by the possible ramifications of a free market in labor on Paris's political and social vitality. Finally, organized property owners evidenced strident opposition to the introduction of mechanisms such as the livre foncier that tended toward facilitating the mobilization of real estate capital, or rendering buildings "an object of frequent purchase and sale."[24] Contesting the demoralization of land that would allegedly result from its increased exchangeability, these self-appointed representatives of the property-owning class articulated the political and economic values traditionally associated with land ownership. These values were also evident in declared motivations and goals of the housing reform movement, which privileged property owning—and would eventually succeed in securing state intervention for its support—for its ability to root the working classes, transforming this group from transient, wasteful, and discontented workers to invested (and investing) laborers contributing to the national good.

While these concerns and others were vital to constituting the particular networks and form of the real estate market, French citizens in the early Third Republic easily accommodated and facilitated the revenue-producing potential of urban property. The opportunities provided by flexible business forms and easy credit led hordes of speculative developers to descend upon the unbuilt areas of the capital city, emboldened by the spectacle of endless gain emanating from the stock market and eager to make their fortunes from property trafficking in the nation's largest marketplace. These builders undertook constructions in accordance with a model of urban growth that privileged unending expansion and the democratization of consumer needs with regard to improved housing. They showed no hesitation at taking on multiple levels of debt in order to bring their visions to fruition, engaging in public credit arrangements that called on associates, known and unknown, to pool their resources and attempt monumental levels of production. In the case of Paul Fouquiau and Albert Laubière, eventual bankruptcies slowed but did not halt their enterprises. In 1893, legislation eased the juridical confusion regarding the status of limited liability joint-stock companies dealing with civil affairs—such as companies dedicated to the construction, management, and resale of residential properties—classifying all sociétés anonymes henceforth as commercial ventures.[25] Organized estate agents sought to establish commercially based identities that staked their honor and reputation on their ability to navigate and improve market relations. When they agitated to institute these identities in the form of occupational monopolies, the doctrine of the freedom of enterprise repeatedly blocked their efforts.

Consumers of Paris's speculatively built apartment houses, as well as investors in property development and management companies, were also active participants in the commercialization of the capital city's residential space. The long history of mobile (rental) housing arrangements in urban centers heightened an appreciation of the exchangeability of built space. Whether as rooms to let in an apartment or as shares in a property management firm, residential space was available to generate revenues for a widening demographic. More than demonstrating how the spaces of residence (consumption) and business (production) were imbricated in the fin-de-siècle metropolis, an appreciation of the attitudes of average Parisians toward the uses of urban property reveals the ways in which the everyday experience of commercialized property articulated with and contributed to the market culture of the end of the nineteenth century. This culture was based not only on a new appreciation for the role of consumption in the body politic and the national economy, but also on a recognition of the legitimacy of the productivity of capital and the unique capacities of the French for savings and investment.

This returns us to the particular perspective on transformations in economic practice and culture that is afforded by the study of real property markets. Nothing better reveals the contestation, ambiguity, and deep uncertainties that characterize the process of market-making than the long debate surrounding the commercial status of property and the economic role of property holding. At the end of the nineteenth century, a period marking a crucial shift in capitalist development, businessmen, legal experts, farmers, rural reformers, politicians, and property owner associations were preoccupied by the problem of legally defining the modes by which real estate could circulate. The progressive integration of real property into circuits defined by commercial law not only amounted to a certain commercialization of the civil realm, but also forced a redefinition of the very idea of the market. Just as real property could not be centralized in an exchange, the market itself—as it was understood in juridical terms—could no longer be contained to physical sites of transactions.[26] It became instead an abstract sphere of possible exchanges, in which all individuals were potential consumers.

France's legal structure provides a particularly useful perspective on the contested process of transforming real property into a commercial good. Secure in the civil realm, real property provided the immovable base for the dynamic transits of commercial movables; once real property is unmoored, even if only partially, it becomes amenable to the types of operations that eventually plunged the world into an economic crisis at the beginning of the twenty-first century.[27] As attendees at France's property owner conferences recognized more than a century ago, this mobilization inevitably privileges financial intermediaries at the expense of modest landowners; assembled in Paris in 1900, delegates noted presciently that "the trade in these property securities won't occur in the village square, between people in clogs, but in the city, at the Stock Exchange. *(Applause).*"[28] Indeed, the enthusiasm for providing the poor with marketable property titles in today's global south is but the latest interpretation of long-standing dreams of unlocking and circulating the property values of embedded territories for the benefit of financial capital.[29] Paris's example in the late nineteenth century, a local chapter in an ongoing, international history of marketizing real estate, helps illuminate the ways that territory, politics, and individual agents determine the course of this process, a process that is anything but inevitable and that profoundly shapes the daily experience of the urban environment.

Appendix

Notes

Acknowledgments

Index

APPENDIX

Apartment buildings belonging to the Compagnie Foncière de France, 1898

Source: ANMT 65 AQ I 102: Compagnie Foncière de France, Assemblée Générale Ordinaire des Actionnaires du 23 avril 1898, Rapport du Conseil d'Administration, Rapport des Commissaires et Extrait du Procès-verbal, Exercice 1897, 65–67

1st arrondissement:
1 building, Rue Montmartre, 32, and Rue Etienne Marcel, 39

2nd arrondissement:
1 building, Rue du Mail, 24
4 buildings, intersection of Rue d'Uzès (nos. 15, 17, 19, and 21) and Rue Montmartre

4th arrondissement:
Land of Rue du Trésor and buildings nos. 3–10 of the same street

7th arrondissement:
10 buildings, Cité Vaneau 3, 5, 7, 9, 10, 11, 12, 14, and Rue de Varenne, 63 and 63bis
2 buildings, Avenue de La Bourdonnais, 19, 21

8th arrondissement:

5 buildings, Rue du Faubourg-Saint-Honoré, 131; Rue Saint-Philippe du Roule, 4, 6, 8, 10

9th arrondissement:

3 buildings, Rue de Provence 60, and Rue de la Victoire, 65 and 67
1 building, 26 Rue de Navarin
Land of Rue Alfred Stevens, nos. 1–10

10th arrondissement:

25 buildings, Boulevard de la Villette, 9, 11, 15, 17, 19, 21, 23, 25; Rue Civiale, 1, 2, 5–17, 19; and Rue du Buisson Saint-Louis, 32
1 building, 137 Rue du Faubourg du Temple
2 buildings, Rue Marie-et-Louise, 13, 15

11th arrondissement:

24 buildings, Rue de Montreuil, 68 and 70; Rue des Boulets, 4, 6, 8, 10, 12, 14, 16, and 18; Rue Chevreul, 1, 3, 4, 5, 6, 7, 8, 9, 10, 11, 13, 14, 15, and 16

13th arrondissement:

1 building, Rue de la Reine-Blanche, 24

15th arrondissement:

5 buildings, Avenue du Maine, 11, and Rue d'Alençon, 4, 6, 7, and 9
4 buildings, Avenue Vaugirard nouveau, 7, 9, 11, and 19 (Rue Lecourbe, 292)

16th arrondissement:

12 buildings, Avenue Victor Hugo, 102, 104, 106, 108; Rue de la Pompe, 140, 142, 144, 146, 148; and Rue de l'Amiral-Courbet, 3, 5, 7
25 buildings, forming the Belles Feuilles group, beside the Lycée Janson in Passy, Rue des Belles Feuilles, 9, 19, 21, 23, 25, 27, 39, and 41; Rue de Longchamp, 86, 94, 102, 104, 106, 108; and Rue Gustave Courbet, 3, 5, 7, 8, 9, 10, 12, 14, 16, 28, and 30
17 buildings, forming the former Villa Caprice group, Rue Poussin, 2, 4, 6; Rue Pierre-Guérin, 19, 19bis, 21, 23bis, and 25, Rue Bosio, 1, 3, 4, 5, 6, 7, 9, 11, and 13

17th arrondissement:

8 buildings, forming the Porte-Maillot group, Rue du Débarcadère 14, 16, 18, 18bis, Boulevard Pereire, 259, 261, 263, and 263bis

2 buildings, with a hall, Rue Salneuve, 29, and Rue Saussure, 69
1 building, Rue Fourcroy, 2 and intersection of Avenue Niel

18th arrondissement:
10 buildings, forming the former Château-Rouge group, Rue Clignancourt, 46, 48, 50, 52, and 52bis; Rue Custine, 7, 9, 11, 13, and 13bis
2 buildings, Rue du Mont-Cenis, 85, 87

Total: 167

Notes

Introduction

1. Maurice Block and Henri de Pontich referred to the compulsory purchase order on behalf of Paris's Archbishopric as "a serious exemption to the principles of public utility informing the powers of expropriation": *Administration de la ville de Paris et du département de la Seine* (Paris: Guillaumin, 1884), 265.

2. Archives de la Préfecture de Police de Paris (hereafter APP) E/B 35 (Dossier d'arrondissements généralités, 18e arrondissement): "Les travaux de Paris: Le quartier neuf de Montmartre," *Ville de Paris,* September 22, 1881.

3. APP E/B 35: "Les travaux de Paris: Un nouveau quartier à La Chapelle," *Ville de Paris,* June 10, 1883.

4. Archives Nationales (hereafter AN) AJ/52/365 (Dossiers des élèves, École des Beaux-Arts).

5. Paul Planat, "La maison de Victor Hugo," *La Construction Moderne,* July 2, 1887, 449.

6. AN F12 5148 (Dossiers de la Légion d'honneur). Fouquiau appears to have received the Legion of Honor as part of what became known as the "Scandal of Decorations," in which the son-in-law of President Jules Grévy was found to have sold the prestigious awards to business associates.

7. See his entry in Michel Fleury, Anne Dugast, and Isabelle Parizet, *Dictionnaire par noms d'architectes des constructions élevées à Paris au XIXe et XXe siècles*

(Paris: Service des Travaux Historiques de la Ville de Paris, 1990–1996), vol. 1, which indicates that he undertook constructions in all but the 1st, 5th, and 6th arrondissements. Fouquiau's career is treated in part in Gérard Jacquemet, "Spéculation et spéculateurs dans l'immobilier parisien à la fin du XIXe siècle," *Cahiers d'Histoire* 31, no. 3 (1976): 273–306.

8. APP B/A 451: Crédit de France; APP B/A 463: Banque de la Chaussée d'Antin; "Cour d'Appel de Paris, 1re Chambre, 15 février 1887," *Revue des Sociétés*, 5 (1887): 186–190.

9. *Bulletin Municipal Officiel de la Ville de Paris*, December 29, 1887, 3089–3092.

10. Anon., *Le Crédit Foncier en 1887: Sous-Comptoir des entrepreneurs; Compagnie Foncière de France; Rente Foncière; Ses erreurs, ses fautes, ses périls* (Paris: Imprimerie Lucotte et Cadoux, 1887), 24; *Tribunal de commerce de la Seine: Audience du jeudi 20 juin 1895; Les administrateurs de la Rente Foncière contre MM. Naslin, Ponceau et Gaillochet* (n.p., n.d.).

11. Archives Nationales du Monde du Travail (hereafter ANMT) 2003 040 616: Note pour Messieurs les Administrateurs de la Société du Quartier Marbeuf, de la Rente Foncière, n.d. (1883).

12. Conseil Municipal de Paris, *Rapport, présenté par M. Alfred Lamouroux, au nom de la 1re Commission, sur la valeur locative actuelle des propriétés bâties de la ville de Paris, en exécution de la loi du 8 août 1885* (Paris: 1888), 25.

13. F. V., "Causerie foncière," *Grand Journal Officiel des Locations*, October 1–15, 1884, 19.

14. Onésime Masselin, *Formulaire d'actes et notice sur la législation et l'utilité des sociétés anonymes immobilières par actions* (Paris: Ducher et Cie, 1880), 8.

15. On Haussmannization, see David H. Pinkney, *Napoleon III and the Rebuilding of Paris* (Princeton, NJ: Princeton University Press, 1959); Louis Girard, *La politique des travaux publics du Second Empire* (Paris: Colin, 1952); Jeanne Gaillard, *Paris, la ville, 1852–1870* (Paris: H. Champion, 1977); and more recently, David H. Jordan, *Transforming Paris: The Life and Labors of Baron Haussmann* (New York: Free Press, 1995), and Jean des Cars and Pierre Pinon, eds., *Paris-Haussmann: "Le pari d'Haussmann"* (Paris: Pavillon d'Arsenal, 1991). More recent examinations have shifted focus to the period preceding the famous prefect's tenure. See Nicholas Papyanis, *Planning Paris before Haussmann* (Baltimore: Johns Hopkins University Press, 2004); Karen Bowie, ed., *La modernité avant Haussmann: Formes de l'espace urbaine à Paris, 1801–53* (Paris: Recherches, 2001).

16. William C. Baer, "Is Speculative Building Underappreciated in Urban History?," *Urban History* 34, no. 2 (2007): 296–316. For an examination of the political economy of Parisian building in an earlier period, see Allan Potofsky, *Constructing Paris in the Age of Revolution* (New York: Palgrave Macmillan, 2009).

17. The importance of private enterprise to Parisian development is suggested in the conclusion of David Van Zanten, *Building Paris: Architectural Institutions and*

the Transformation of the French Capital, 1830–1870 (Cambridge: Cambridge University Press, 1994), 281–282; see also Ralph Kingston, "Capitalism in the Streets: Paris Shopkeepers, *Passages Couverts,* and the Production of the Early-Nineteenth-Century City," *Radical History* 114 (Fall 2012): 39–65. Recent work in French on the development of Paris has indeed given more focus to the work of private developers, following pioneering articles by Jeanne Pronteau, "Construction et aménagement des nouveaux quartiers de Paris (1820–26)," *Histoire des Entreprises* 2 (November 1958): 8–31, and Jacquemet, "Spéculation et spéculateurs." See in particular: Pierre Pinon, *Paris: Biographie d'une capital* (Paris: Hazan, 1999); Annie Térade, "La formation du quartier de l'Europe à Paris: Lotissement et haussmannisation (1820–1870)" (PhD diss., University of Paris 8, 2001); Amina Sellali-Boukhalfa, "Sous la ville, jadis la campagne: Une mosaïque de lotissements privés à l'origine de l'urbanisation de Belleville et de Charonne (1820–1902)" (PhD diss., University of Paris 8, 2002). The phrase "capital of modernity" is from David Harvey, *Paris, Capital of Modernity* (New York: Routledge, 2003).

18. Vanessa Schwartz, *Spectacular Realities: Early Mass Culture in Fin-de-Siècle Paris* (Berkeley: University of California Press, 1998); Lisa Tiersten, *Marianne in the Market: Envisioning Consumer Society in Fin-de-Siècle France* (Berkeley: University of California Press, 2001); Leora Auslander, *Taste and Power: Furnishing Modern France* (Berkeley: University of California Press, 1996); Rosalind Williams, *Dream Worlds: Mass Consumption in Late-Nineteenth-Century France* (Berkeley: University of California Press, 1982).

19. David Landes established this perspective in English; see his articles "French Entrepreneurship and Industrial Growth in the Nineteenth Century," *Journal of Economic History* 9, no. 1 (May 1949): 45–61; "L'esprit d'entreprise en France," *Nouvelle Revue de l'Économie Contemporaine,* no. 48 (1953): 4–11; "French Business and the Businessman: A Social and Cultural Analysis," in *Modern France: Problems of the Third and Fourth Republics,* ed. Edward Mead Earle (New York: Russell and Russell, 1964), 336–352; "Religion and Enterprise: The Case of the French Textile Industry," in *Enterprise and Entrepreneurs in Nineteenth-Century France,* ed. Edward C. Carter, H. Robert Forster, and Joseph N. Moody (Baltimore: Johns Hopkins University Press, 1976), 41–86. Landes responds to historians who have set him up as a straw man generalizing about the nature of French entrepreneurialism in "New-Model Entrepreneurship in France and Problems of Historical Explanation," *Explorations in Entrepreneurial History* ser. 2, vol. 1, no. 1 (Fall 1963): 56–75.

20. For a review of the historiographic swings and the political stakes of the theorization of France's economic development, see François Crouzet, "The Historiography of French Economic Growth in the Nineteenth Century," *Economic History Review* 56, no. 2 (2003): 215–242. See Jean-Pierre Hirsch, *Les deux rêves du commerce: Entreprise et institution dans la région lilloise, 1780–1860* (Paris: Éditions de l'EHESS, 1991); Louis Bergeron and Patrice Bourdelais, eds., *La France n'est-elle pas douée pour*

l'industrie? (Paris: Belin, 1998); Victoria Thompson, *The Virtuous Marketplace: Women and Men, Money and Politics in Paris, 1830–70* (Baltimore: Johns Hopkins University Press, 2000); Steven Kaplan and Philippe Minard, eds., *La France, malade du corporatisme? XVIIIe–XXe siècles* (Paris: Belin, 2004); Jeff Horn, *The Path Not Taken: French Industrialization in the Age of Revolution, 1750–1830* (Cambridge, MA: MIT Press, 2006); Michael S. Smith, *The Emergence of Modern Business Enterprise in France, 1800–1930* (Cambridge, MA: Harvard University Press, 2006); David Todd, *L'identité économique de la France: Libre-échange et protectionnisme, 1814–1851* (Paris: B. Grasset, 2008); Hervé Joly, *Diriger une grande entreprise au XXe siècle: L'élite industrielle française* (Tours: Presses Universitaires François Rabelais, 2013).

21. The most significant legislative reforms of the period were the 1894 "Siegfried Law," which gave permission for the establishment of departmental offices for low-income housing (*habitations à bon marché*) (the 1906 loi Strauss made these offices mandatory, and the 1912 loi Bonnevay made them public institutions), and the 1908 loi Ribot, which pioneered public subsidies—by way of private corporations and organizations—for low-income housing construction. Hygienic legislation passed in 1902 and 1912 was also instrumental in extending public authority over private property. For housing reform in nineteenth-century France, see Roger H. Guerrand, *Les origines du logement social en France* (Paris: Éditions Ouvrières, 1967); Ann-Louise Shapiro, *Housing the Poor of Paris, 1850–1902* (Madison: University of Wisconsin Press, 1985); Susanna Magri, *Les laboratoires de la réforme de l'habitation populaire en France: De la Société française des habitations à bon marché à la section d'hygiène urbaine et rurale du Musée social, 1889–1909* (Paris: Ministère de l'Équipement, du Logement, des Transports et du Tourisme, 1995); Marie-Jeanne Dumont, *Le logement social à Paris, 1850–1930: Les habitations à bon marché* (Liège: Mardaga, 1991).

22. On the question of responsibility, see the discussion of the Société d'Economie Politique, "Des sociétés commerciales et en particulier des sociétés anonymes et des sociétés à responsabilité limitée," *Journal des Économistes*, no. 37 (March 1863): 526–539. Charles E. Freedeman, *Joint-Stock Enterprise in France, 1807–1867: From Privileged Company to Modern Corporation* (Chapel Hill: University of North Carolina Press, 1979); Freedeman, *The Triumph of Corporate Capitalism in France, 1867–1914* (Rochester, NY: University of Rochester Press, 1993).

23. Jacquemet, "Spéculation et spéculateurs." Company statutes using the phrase "Le tout dans un but de spéculation" were frequent. See, for example, ANMT 65 AQ I 69 (Constructions Rationnelles, 1882), 65 AQ I 142 (SA Terrains et Constructions de la Place d'Italie, 1882), 65 AQ I 93 (SA Immobilière des Terrains et Constructions du Faubourg du Temple, 1881).

24. Michel Lescure, *Les banques, l'état, et le marché immobilier en France à l'époque contemporaine, 1820–1940* (Paris: Éditions de l'EHESS, 1982).

25. Bibliothèque Historique de la Ville de Paris (hereafter BHVP), Actualités Série 78: Logement, undated circular.

26. Throughout this study, the term *homme* or *agent d'affaires* will be translated as "estate agent" in order to differentiate it from the more general English term "businessman," with the important proviso that these agents managed many aspects of an individual's estate, their business, property, and investment concerns, not simply real property. Alternatively, it will be left in the original French. Anne Boigeol and Yves Dezalay, "De l'agent d'affaires au barreau: Les conseils juridiques et la construction d'un espace professionnel," *Genèses* 27, no.1 (1997): 49–68.

27. Albert Amiaud, *Études sur le notariat français: Réformes et améliorations que cette institution réclame* (Paris: L. Larose, 1879). On notaries and their particular role in mortgage markets, see Philip T. Hoffman, Gilles Postel-Vinay, and Jean-Laurent Rosenthal, *Priceless Markets: The Political Economy of Credit in Paris, 1660–1870* (Chicago: University of Chicago Press, 2001).

28. "Causerie foncière," 19.

29. Chambre des députés, "Procès-verbaux de la commission chargée de faire une enquête sur la situation des ouvriers de l'industrie et de l'agriculture en France et de présenter un premier rapport sur la crise industrielle à Paris," *Annales de la Chambre des Députés, Documents Parlementaires,* 12 (Paris, 1884): 1619.

30. Émile Rivoalen, "À travers Paris: Première promenade," *Revue Générale de l'Architecture et des Travaux Publics* 39 (1882): 34.

31. Jule Romains, *Les hommes de bonne volonté* (Paris: Flammarion, 1932), 4:28.

32. Bernard Bodinier and Eric Teyssier, *L'événement le plus important de la Révolution: La vente des biens nationaux (1789–1867) en France et dans les territoires annexés* (Paris: Éditions du CTHS, 2000). On the relation of housing merchandise and urban space in the eighteenth century, see Natacha Coquéry, *L'hôtel aristocratique: Le marché du luxe à Paris au XVIIIe siècle* (Paris: Publications de la Sorbonne, 1998). On medieval and early modern property markets, see Laurent Feller and Chris Wickham, eds., *Le marché de la terre au Moyen Âge* (Rome: École Française de Rome, 2005); Dan Smail, "Accommodating Plague in Medieval Marseille," *Continuity and Change* 11, no. 1 (May 1996): 11–41; Gérard Béaur, *Le marché foncier à la veille de la Révolution: Les mouvements de propriété beaucerons dans les régions de Maintenon et de Janville de 1761 à 1790* (Paris: Éditions de l'EHESS, 1984). Regarding other areas in Europe, see Jean-François Chauvard, *La circulation des biens à Venise: Stratégies patrimoniales et marché immobilier, 1600–1750* (Rome: École Française de Rome, 2005).

33. Bas J. P. van Bavel and Peter Hoppenbrouwers, eds., *Landholding and Land Transfer in the North Sea Area (Late Middle Ages—19th Century)* (Turnhout, Belgium: Brepols, 2005), 13.

34. Arjun Appadurai, "Introduction: Commodities and the Politics of Value," in *The Social Life of Things: Commodities in Cultural Perspective,* ed. Arjun Appadurai (Cambridge: Cambridge University Press, 1986), 3–63, quotation at p. 13; Igor Kopytoff, "The Cultural Biography of Things: Commoditization as Process," in Appadurai, *The Social Life of Things,* 64–92.

35. C. M. Hann, "Introduction: The Embeddedness of Property," in *Property Relations: Renewing the Anthropological Tradition,* ed. C. M. Hann (Cambridge: Cambridge University Press, 1998), 1–47. The notion of embeddedness stems from Karl Polanyi's now famous analysis of market society in *The Great Transformation* (New York, 1944). For its many afterlives, see "Polanyi Symposium: A Conversation on Embeddedness," *Socio-Economic Review* 2 (2004): 109–135, and Jens Beckert, "The Great Transformation of Embeddedness: Karl Polanyi and the New Economic Sociology," in *Market and Society: The Great Transformation Today,* ed. Chris Hann and Keith Hart (Cambridge: Cambridge University Press, 2009), 38–55.

36. Koray Çaliskan and Michel Callon, "Economization, Part 1: Shifting Attention from the Economy towards the Processes of Economization," *Economy and Society* 38, no. 3 (2009): 369–398; Çaliskan and Callon "Economization, Part 2: A Research Programme for the Study of Markets," *Economy and Society* 39, no. 1 (2010): 1–32.

37. Polanyi, *The Great Transformation,* esp. chap. 6; Karl Marx, *Capital,* vol. 3 (New York: Vintage Books, 1977 [1894]), esp. pt. 6.

38. David Harvey, *Limits to Capital* (Oxford: Blackwell, 1982).

39. Rebecca Spang, *Stuff and Money in the Time of the French Revolution* (Cambridge, MA: Harvard University Press, 2015). Another famous project for reforming the nation's land was the *cadastre perpétuel* of François Noël (Gracchus) Babeuf; it proposed a reformed system of land registration, property taxation, and topographical surveying that would (literally) prepare the ground for an egalitarian, communist republic: F. N. Babeuf and J. P. Audiffred, *Cadastre perpétuel* (Paris: Chez les auteurs et Garnery et Volland, 1789).

40. See, in particular, the projects of Martin-Philippe Mengin, which were instrumental in the new mortgage code, and those of Jacques-Annibal Ferrières, which were the basis for André-Daniel Laffon-Ladébat and Dupont de Nemours's ill-fated Banque Territoriale, founded 1799. Martin-Philippe Mengin, *Ce qu'est réellement et politiquement une cédule* (n.p, n.d.); Martin-Philippe Mengin, *Nouveau plan d'hypothèque* (Paris: Imprimerie des Amis Réunis, n.d. [1790]); Martin-Philippe Mengin, *Plan de Banque nationale immobilière, dédié à la nation* (Paris: Chez La Villette, 1790); Jacques-Annibal Ferrières, *Plan d'un nouveau genre de banque nationale et territorial, présenté à l'assemblée nationale* (Paris: l'Imprimerie de Monsieur, 1789); Jacques-Annibal Ferrières, *Plan de la Banque Territoriale inventée par citoyen Ferrières* (Paris: Imprimerie de la Rue Lepelletier, n.d. [an VII]); André-Daniel Laffon de Ladebat, *Observations sur le crédit territorial* (Paris: Imprimerie de la Banque Territoriale, floréal an X [May 1802]).

41. This phrase occurs throughout discussions of the need for reformed systems of land mobilization. See Louis Wolowski, "De la division du sol," *Revue des Deux Mondes,* July 1, 1857, 640–667, 645; Léon Michel, ed., *Ministère du commerce, de l'industrie, et des colonies, Direction générale de l'exploitation: Congrès international*

pour l'étude de la transmission de la propriété foncière; Tenu à Paris du 8 au 14 août 1889; Procès-verbaux sommaires (Paris: Imprimerie National, 1889), 6.

42. The depopulation of the countryside was a matter of tremendous concern to contemporary politicians. The plunging value of rural lands—which decreased by a third from 1880 to 1900—helped shift the country toward protectionism, notably with the Méline tariff of 1892. Pierre Caziot, *La valeur de la terre en France* (Paris: J.-B. Baillière et Fils, 1914), 8; Edmond Michel, *Études statistiques économiques, sociales, financières et agricoles,* vol. 3: *La propriété* (Paris: Berger-Levrault et Cie, 1908), 101–103. In land reform, however, progress was nearly nonexistent. The cadastral commission convened by Parliament in 1891, for instance, undertook studies on the reform of the nation's cadastre for nearly fifteen years, with no result from its efforts other than providing background for legislation passed in 1930 and 1955.

43. "Déposition de M. André Cochut, directeur du Mont-de-piété de Paris: Séance du 29 mars 1884," in "Procès-verbaux de la commission," 316–317.

44. Onésime Masselin, "Des effets du krach de la bourse sur les placements immobiliers," *Le Foncier,* January 31, 1882, 1. In this period the term *entrepreneur* referred to employers in the building trades. In this work, I use the term "building entrepreneur" (or "speculator" or "developer" as appropriate) to refer to these individuals and firms, and employ the term "entrepreneur" in its more broadly accepted general usage. See Robert Carvais, "La force du droit: Contribution à la définition de l'entrepreneur parisien du bâtiment au XVIIIe siècle," *Histoire, Economie et Société* 14, no. 2 (1995): 163–189.

45. "Causerie foncière," *Grand Journal Officiel des Locations et de la Vente des Terrains et Immeubles,* September 16–30, 1884, 15.

46. Hubert Bonin asserts that returns from movable assets amounted to three-quarters those of real estate in individual estates in 1878, equaled them in 1904, and surpassed them by 1914 (*L'argent en France depuis 1880: Banquiers, financiers, épargnants dans la vie économique et politique* [Paris: Masson, 1989], 135). The timeline given by Pierre-Cyrille Hautcoeur is slightly different. He finds parity between returns from movable and immovable assets in individual estates in the 1880s, but notes that this figure holds only when "movable" income is expanded to include more than stocks and bonds (the category includes furnishings, jewelry, merchandise, and other goods). In terms of stocks and bonds versus real property, parity is reached around 1915. See Pierre-Cyrille Hautcoeur, ed., *Le marché financier français au XIXe siècle,* vol. 1: *Récit* (Paris: Publications de la Sorbonne, 2007), chaps. 9 and 14.

47. Paul Leroy-Beaulieu, *L'art de placer et gérer sa fortune* (Paris: Ch. Delagrave, 1906), chaps. 1–4.

48. Alexis Bailleux de Marisy, "Les nouvelles sociétés foncières: Moeurs financières de la France, IV," *Revue des Deux Mondes,* November 15, 1881, 432–452, 444.

49. Ibid., 434.

50. "Conférences de la Société Centrale des Architectes: Séance du 24 Avril," *Semaine des Constructeurs,* May 10, 1884, 533–534.

51. Much as the proliferation of department stores appeared to challenge the place of Paris's small shopkeepers in the urban political economy: Philip Nord, *Paris Shopkeepers and the Politics of Resentment* (Princeton, NJ: Princeton University Press, 1986).

52. Both Harvey and urban theorist Henri Lefebvre have demonstrated the utility of deploying this dynamic as a window on urbanization. Henri Lefebvre, *Urban Revolution,* trans. Robert Bononno (Minneapolis: University of Minnesota Press, 2003), 9, 159–160. Among David Harvey's works, see *The Urbanization of Capital* (Baltimore: Johns Hopkins University Press, 1985) and *Consciousness and the Urban Experience* (Baltimore: Johns Hopkins University Press, 1985). See also Neil Brenner, "Between Fixity and Motion: Accumulation, Territorial Organization, and the Historical Geography of Spatial Scales," *Environment and Planning D: Society and Space* 16 (1998): 459–481.

53. David Scobey has traced the emergence of a commercialized market for real estate in New York City during the same period, and Desmond Fitz-Gibbon has illuminated similar developments in nineteenth-century Britain. David M. Scobey, *Empire City: The Making and Meaning of the New York City Landscape* (Philadelphia: Temple University Press, 2002); Desmond Fitz-Gibbon, "Assembling the Property Market in Imperial Britain, 1750–1925" (PhD diss., University of California at Berkeley, 2011).

54. Léon Salefranque, "Les mutations à titre onéreux en France: Mouvement de ces transmissions d'après les comptes de finances, 1826–1898," in *Congrès international de la propriété foncière: Documents, rapports, comptes rendus, mémoires et notes* (Paris: Imprimerie Paul Dupont, 1901), 211–241.

55. The failure of the Compagnie Immobilière, a large property speculation company founded and headed by the financiers Isaac and Émile Pereire, was generally attributed to their ventures in land outside the capital, particularly in Marseille. See *Extrait du Paris-Journal: Affaire de la Société immobilière; plaidoirie de Me Nicolet, suivie des conclusions de l'Avocat Général Dupré Lassalle et de l'Arrêt de la Cour Impériale du 22 avril 1870* (Paris: Bureaux du Paris-Journal, 1870).

56. Bernard Rouleau, *Paris, histoire d'un espace* (Paris: Éditions du Seuil, 1997), 379; Pierre Lavedan, *Histoire de l'urbanisme à Paris,* 2nd ed. (Paris: Hachette, 1993), 500.

57. Walter Benjamin, "Paris, Capital of the Nineteenth Century," in *Reflections: Essays, Aphorisms, Autobiographical Writings,* trans. Edmund Jephcott (New York: Schocken Books, 1986); Harvey, *Paris, Capital of Modernity;* Patrice Higonnet, *Paris: Capital of the World* (Cambridge: Harvard University Press, 2002).

58. Schwartz, *Spectacular Realities;* Hazel Hahn, *Scenes of Parisian Modernity: Culture and Consumption in the Nineteenth Century* (New York: Palgrave Macmillan,

2009); Michael Miller, *The Bon Marché: Bourgeois Culture and the Department Store, 1869–1920* (Princeton, NJ: Princeton University Press, 1981). The phrase "extroverted urbanism" is from Gaillard, *Paris, la ville, 1852–1870*. The reverberations of this urbanism were felt in the period's defining artistic movements: T. J. Clark, *The Painting of Modern Life: Paris in the Art of Manet and His Followers* (Princeton, NJ: Princeton University Press, 1984).

59. Classic studies of the Parisian crowd include Robert Nye, *The Origins of Crowd Psychology: Gustave Le Bon and the Crisis of Mass Democracy in the Third Republic* (London: Sage, 1975), and Susanna Barrows, *Distorting Mirrors: Visions of the Crowd in Late-Nineteenth-Century France* (New Haven: Yale University Press, 1981). On the *badaud* as a counterpoint to the flâneur and the anonymous crowd, see Gregory Shaya, "The *Flâneur*, the *Badaud*, and the Making of a Mass Public in France, circa 1860–1910," *American Historical Review* 109 (February 2004): 41–77. On the flâneur in the Parisian context, see Priscilla Parkhurst Ferguson, *Paris as Revolution: Writing the Nineteenth-Century City* (Berkeley: University of California Press, 1994).

60. Denise Z. Davidson, "Making Society 'Legible': People-Watching in Paris after the Revolution," *French Historical Studies* 28, no. 2 (Spring 2005): 265–296; Victoria Thompson, "Telling Spatial Stories: Urban Space and Bourgeois Identity in Early-Nineteenth-Century Paris," *Journal of Modern History* 75, no. 3 (September 2003): 523–556.

61. Sharon Marcus, "Haussmannization as Anti-modernity: The Apartment House in Parisian Urban Discourse, 1850–1880," *Journal of Urban History* 27, no. 6 (September 2001): 723–745. See also Marcus, *Apartment Stories: City and Home in Nineteenth-Century Paris and London* (Berkeley: University of California Press, 1999).

62. Lizabeth Cohen, "Is There an Urban History of Consumption?," *Journal of Urban History* 29, no. 2 (2003): 87–106. Elizabeth Blackmar's *Manhattan for Rent, 1785–1850* (Ithaca, NY: Cornell University Press, 1985) is an exemplary social history of a land market that insists particularly on integrating the role of housing users into our understanding of metropolitan development.

63. Claire Hancock, "*Capitale du plaisir:* The Remaking of Imperial Paris," in *Imperial Cities: Landscape, Display and Identity*, ed. Felix Driver and David Gilbert (New York: St. Martin's Press, 1999), 64–77.

64. Miles Ogborn, *Spaces of Modernity: London's Geographies, 1680–1780* (New York: Guilford Press, 1998).

65. Jean-François Cabestan, *La conquête du plain-pied: L'immeuble à Paris au XVIIIe siècle* (Paris: Picard, 2004); Anthony Sutcliffe, *Paris: An Architectural History* (New Haven, CT: Yale University Press, 1993), 65–66.

66. Conseil Municipal de Paris, *Rapport présenté par M. Alfred Lamouroux*, 21.

67. Préfecture de la Seine, *Résultats statistiques du dénombrement de 1891 pour la ville de Paris et le département de la Seine* (Paris: G. Masson, 1894). Census numbers differ from those of the city's tax assessments, which give 81,291 as the number

of residential buildings in 1890, and 804,011 as the number of dwellings in the city in the same year. The Census explains this discrepancy with reference to different measurement techniques, and the tendency for the tax assessors to omit professional rental establishments (particularly the numerous furnished hotels) from the total figure for dwellings.

68. Historian Adeline Daumard calculates that the 14,000 owners of Parisian property possessed an average of two buildings per person at midcentury, while Marc Choko's study of ownership patterns in the fin de siècle confirm that this level of diffusion was maintained, with the approximately 46,699 individual owners of Parisian properties in possession of an average of 1.6 buildings apiece in 1897. See Adeline Daumard, *Maisons de Paris et propriétaires parisiens au XIXe siècle (1809–1880)* (Paris: Éditions Cujas, 1965), 235; Marc Choko, "Investment or Family Home? Housing Ownership in Paris at the Turn of the Twentieth Century," *Journal of Urban History* 23, no. 5 (July 1997): 531–568.

69. P[aul] Planat, "Actualités," *La Construction Moderne,* April 13, 1901, 326.

70. Christian Topalov, *Le logement en France: Histoire d'une marchandise impossible* (Paris: Presses de la Fondation Nationale des Sciences Politiques, 1987), 117.

71. In absolute numbers, the increase in cheaper lodgings far exceeded that of the more expensive. Between 1890 and 1900, 30,000 units costing less than 300 francs were constructed, while the increase in apartments costing between 2,500 and 3,000 francs, for example, was about 1,400, and fewer than 100 apartments were constructed that cost between 15,000 and 20,000 francs. See Préfecture de la Seine, Direction des Finances, Service des Contributions Directes, *Les propriétés bâties de la ville de Paris en 1889 et en 1890* (Paris: Imprimerie Nationale, 1890); Préfecture de la Seine, Direction Municipale des Travaux du Cadastre de Paris, Commission des Contributions Directes, *Le livre foncier de Paris (Valeur locative des propriétés bâties en 1900)* (Paris: Imprimerie Chaix, 1900–1902).

72. Émile Rivoalen, "À travers Paris: Deuxième promenade," *Revue Générale de l'Architecture et des Travaux Publics* 39 (1882): 77.

73. Émile Rivoalen, "Menus propos: La féerie immobilière," *La Semaine des Constructeurs,* August 21, 1886, 86. On the rise of taste professionals and the national stakes of consumption, see Leora Auslander, "'National Taste'? Citizenship Law, State Form, and Everyday Aesthetics in Modern France and Germany, 1920–1940," in *The Politics of Consumption: Material Culture and Citizenship in Europe and America,* ed. Martin Daunton and Matthew Hilton (Oxford: Berg, 2001), 109–128.

74. "Cours et courettes," *La Construction Moderne,* April 1, 1899, 319.

75. Georges d'Avenel, "La maison parisienne," in *Mécanisme de la vie moderne,* 2nd ed. (Paris: Colin, 1903), 3:10; Jean-Claude Farcy and Alain Faure, *La mobilité d'une génération de français: Recherche sur les migrations et les déménagements vers et dans Paris à la fin du XIXe siècle* (Paris: Institut National d'Études Démographiques, 2003).

76. Tiersten, *Marianne in the Market,* chap. 5; Auslander, *Taste and Power,* pt. 3; Deborah Silverman, *Art Nouveau in Fin-de-Siècle France: Politics, Psychology, and Style* (Berkeley: University of California Press, 1989), 75–106.

77. BHVP Actualités Série 78, Logement: Émile Cheysson, "La maison et la famille," *L'Idéal du Foyer: Revue Littéraire, Artistique, Économique et Sociale de la Famille,* March 1, 1903, 38.

78. Marcel Daly, "L'influence de l'architecte sur le goût public," *La Semaine des Constructeurs,* October 6, 1888, 169–170. Emphasis in the original.

79. Ernest L'Épine, *Lettres à une honnête femme sur les événements contemporains/Quatrelles* (Paris: Calmann Lévy, 1885), 126.

80. "Promenades à travers Paris: Maisons et locataires," *Revue Générale de l'Architecture et des Travaux Publics* 39 (1882): 259.

81. "Districts of the Future" was one of the categories applied by the Compagnie Foncière de France to a portion of its portfolio, corresponding to the new, west-end districts in which many of their properties were located (the 16th and 17th arrondissements).

82. For exceptional (in both senses of the word) works treating the speculative apartment building in France, see Monique Eleb and Anne Debarre, *L'invention de l'habitation moderne: Paris, 1880–1914* (Paris: Hazan, and Archives d'Architecture Moderne, 1995); Monique Eleb-Vidal and Anne Debarre-Blanchard, *Architecture de la vie privée: Maisons et mentalités, XVIIe–XIXe siècles* (Brussels: Archives d'Architecture Moderne, 1989).

1. The Business of the City

1. Roger Alexandre, *La musée de la conversation: Répertoire de citations françaises,* 3rd ed. (Paris: Librairie Émile Bouillon, 1897), 45. Nadaud's actual phrasing was "Vous le savez, à Paris, lorsque le bâtiment va, tout profite de son activité."

2. The census of 1891 indicated that approximately 95,000 Parisians were employed in the building industry, with dependents totaling 170,000. It was the third largest sector in the city, following small retailers and the garment industry. Préfecture de la Seine, Service de la Statistique Municipale, *Résultats statistiques du dénombrement de 1891 pour la ville de Paris* (Paris: Imprimerie Municipale, G. Masson, 1891), 154–157.

3. Casey Harison, *The Stonemasons of Creuse in Nineteenth-Century Paris* (Newark: University of Delaware Press, 2008).

4. Pierre Caziot, *La valeur de la terre en France* (Paris: J.-B. Baillière et Fils, 1914), 8; Edmond Michel, *Études statistiques économiques, sociales, financières et agricoles,* vol. 3: *La propriété* (Paris: Berger-Levrault et Cie, 1908), 101–103; Alfred de Foville, *Études économiques et statistiques sur la propriété foncière: Le morcellement* (Paris: Guillaumin, 1885).

5. Louis Lazare, "Les grands travaux de Paris, l'industrie du bâtiment," *Le Courrier Municipal,* May 1, 1873, 2.

6. Carl Abbott, *Boosters and Businessmen: Popular Economic Thought and Urban Growth in the Antebellum Middle West* (Westport, CT: Greenwood Press, 1981); Harvey L. Molotch and John R. Logan, *Urban Fortunes: The Political Economy of Place* (Berkeley: University of California Press, 1987).

7. Susanna Magri and Christian Topalov, "De la cité-jardin à la ville rationalisée: Un tournant du projet réformateur (1905–1925) dans quatre pays," *Revue Française de Sociologie* 28, no. 3 (1987): 417–451; Jean-Pierre Gaudin, *L'avenir en plan: Technique et politique dans la prévision urbaine, 1900–1930* (Seyssel: Éditions du Champ Vallon, 1985); Viviane Claude and Pierre-Yves Saunier, "L'urbanisme au début du siècle: De la réforme urbaine à la compétence technique," *Vingtième Siècle*, no. 64 (1999): 25–40.

8. Marcel Poëte, *Introduction à l'urbanisme: L'évolution des villes, la leçon de l'antiquité* (Paris: Boivin et Cie, 1929), 2, 99, 110; Donatella Calabi, *Marcel Poëte et le Paris des années vingt: Aux origines de* L'Histoire des Villes (Paris: L'Harmattan, 1998); Charissa N. Terranova, "Marcel Poëte's Bergsonian Urbanism: Vitalism, Time, and the City," *Journal of Urban History* 34, no. 6 (September 2008): 919–943.

9. Marcel Poëte, *Introduction à l'urbanisme* (Paris: Sens et Tonka, 2000), 93–95.

10. Marcel Roncayolo, "Mythe et représentation de la ville à partir du 18e siècle," *Encyclopaedia Universalis,* suppl., issue 2 (1980): 1502–1506; Allan Potofsky, "The Construction of Paris and the Crises of the Ancien Régime: The Police and the People of the Parisian Building Sites, 1750–1789," *French Historical Studies* 27, no. 1 (2004): 39–48; Léon Cahen, "Recherches sur l'agglomération parisienne au XVIIIe siècle," *Vie Urbaine* (1922): 131–145.

11. Frédéric Moret, "Définir la ville par ses marges: La Construction des fortifications de Paris," *Histoire Urbaine* 24 (April 2009): 97–118.

12. Cited in Claude Grison, *L'évolution du marché du logement dans l'agglomération parisienne du milieu du XIXème siècle à nos jours* (thesis, University of Paris Law School, 1956), 65.

13. Peter M. Wolf, *Eugène Hénard and the Beginning of Urbanism in Paris, 1900–1914* (The Hague: International Federation for Housing and Planning, Centre de Recherche d'Urbanisme, 1968). Hénard was head of the Musée Social's commission for Parisian development plans, and died shortly before he was to assume the presidency of the French Association of Architect-Urbanists (Société Française des Architectes Urbanistes) in 1913.

14. The royal declarations fixing the limits of the capital and its faubourgs had been in place since 1724. On visitors to the city, see Vincent Milliot, "La surveillance des migrants et des lieux d'accueil à Paris du XVIe siècle aux années 1830," in *La ville promise: Mobilité et accueil à Paris (fin XVIIe–début XIXe siècle),* ed. Daniel Roche (Paris: Fayard, 2000), 21–76. For contemporary jurisprudence, see Émile Agnel, *Code-manuel des propriétaires et locataires de maisons: Hôteliers, aubergistes et logeurs* (Paris: Mansut, 1845), 442.

15. Natalie Montel, "Chronique d'une mort annoncée: L'annexion par Paris de sa banlieue en 1860," *Recherches Contemporaines, Université Paris X* 6 (2000–2001): 217–254.

16. Marie Charvet, *Les fortifications de Paris: De l'hygiénisme à l'urbanisme, 1880–1919* (Rennes: Presses Universitaires de Rennes, 2005).

17. Long-running efforts to eliminate the city's customs taxes (the *octroi,* which constituted the chief source of income for most French cities) typify this effort. See William B. Cohen, *Urban Government and the Rise of the French City* (New York: St. Martin's Press, 1998), esp. chap. 2. On the importance of circulation in understanding and engineering the urban experience before Haussmann, see Nicholas Papayanis, *Planning Paris before Haussmann* (Baltimore: Johns Hopkins University Press, 2004); Karen Bowie, *La modernité avant Haussmann: Formes de l'espace urbain à Paris, 1801–1853* (Paris: Recherches, 2001); Lloyd Jenkins, "Utopianism and Urban Change in Perreymond's Plans for the Rebuilding of Paris," *Journal of Historical Geography* 32 (2006): 336–351; and François Laisney, *Règle et règlemen: La question du règlement dans l'évolution de l'urbanisme parisien, 1600–1902* (Paris: IPRAUS, 1989). For Haussmannization as an effort to adjust the city to the needs of circulation, see Françoise Choay, "Pensées sur la ville, arts de la ville," in *Histoire de la France urbaine,* vol. 4: *La ville de l'âge industriel: Le cycle haussmannien,* ed. Maurice Agulhon, rev. ed. (Paris: Éditions du Seuil, 1998 [1983]), 170–284. David Harvey has shown how circulation meant movement not only of people and things, but of capital and its reproduction through the built environment. See Harvey, *Paris: Capital of Modernity* (New York: Routledge, 2003), and Harvey, *Consciousness and the Urban Experience* (Baltimore: Johns Hopkins University Press, 1985).

18. Yvan Combeau, *Paris et les élections municipales sous la Troisième République: La scène capital dans la vie politique française* (Paris: L'Harmattan, 1998); Stephen Sawyer, "Définir un intérêt particulier parisien: Les élections et l'administration municipale de Paris au milieu du XIXe siècle," *Annales: Histoire, Sciences Sociales* 64, no. 2 (March–April 2009): 407–433.

19. Roger V. Gould, *Insurgent Identities: Class, Community, and Protest in Paris from 1848 to the Commune* (Chicago: University of Chicago Press, 1995).

20. Taxile Delord, *Histoire illustrée du Second Empire* (Paris: Librairie Germer Baillière et Cie, 1880–1883), 5:27.

21. Claire Hancock, "*Capitale du plaisir:* The Remaking of Imperial Paris," in *Imperial Cities: Landscape, Display and Identity,* ed. Felix Driver and David Gilbert (New York: St. Martin's Press, 1999), 64–77; Jean-Marc Lesur, *Les hôtels de Paris: De l'auberge au palace, XIXe–XXe siècles* (Neuchâtel: Alphil, 2005), 63–80, for the creation of American-style hotels built by Émile and Isaac Pereire, the Hôtel du Louvre (1855) and the Grand Hôtel de la Paix (1862).

22. Comments of Councilors Jacques Songeon and Ernest Rousselle, Commission spéciale de l'emprunt, *Bulletin Municipal Officiel* (hereafter *BMO*), May 8, 1883, 687.

23. Figures from 1878; see Maurice Block and Henri de Pontich, *Administration de la ville de Paris et du département de la Seine* (Paris: Guillaumin, 1884), 52.

24. See details of the city's 1883 budget in ibid., 122–124, 219–220; for the attributions of the Parisian municipal council, see 83–84. On Paris's municipal council, see Nobuhito Nagai, *Les conseillers municipaux de Paris sous la Troisième République, 1871–1914* (Paris: Publications de la Sorbonne, 2002); Combeau, *Paris et les élections municipales;* and for a later period, Philippe Nivet, *Le conseil municipal de Paris de 1944 à* 1977 (Paris: Publications de la Sorbonne, 1994).

25. Jean-Pierre Hirsch, *Les deux rêves du commerce: Entreprise et institution dans la région lilloise, 1780–1860* (Paris: Éditions de l'EHESS, 1991). In pursuing the links between property management and city government, I have been influenced by Hendrik Hartog, *Public Property and Private Power: The Corporation of the City of New York in American Law, 1730–1870* (Chapel Hill: University of North Carolina Press, 1983).

26. "Le Quartier Marbeuf," *La Réforme du Bâtiment,* February 13, 1881; "Les derniers actes du ci-devant conseil municipal," *Économiste Français,* January 15, 1881, 65–66.

27. "La propriété foncière: De l'expropriation," *Le Figaro,* April 12, 1882.

28. Rapport, présenté par M. Ernest Hamel, au nom de la 3e Commission, sur le relèvement du quartier Marbeuf, annexe au procès-verbal de la séance du 14 décembre 1880, 6.

29. Jules Ferry, *Les comptes fantastiques d'Haussmann* (Paris: Armand le Chevalier, 1868), 11.

30. Contre-projet présenté par MM. Songeon et Vauthier, aux conclusions du rapport de M. Ernest Hamel, relatif au projet de relèvement du quartier Marbeuf, annexe au proces-verbal de la séance du 21 décembre 1880, 1; emphasis in the original.

31. On Blondel's company, see Archives Nationales du Monde du Travail (hereafter ANMT), 65 AQ I 175: Société du Quartier Marbeuf. See also records within the archives of the Crédit Foncier: ANMT 2003 040 616; 2003 040 618; 2003 040 619; 2003 040 620; 2003 040 623; 2003 040 640. Blondel's company was formed under the auspices of the Société des Immeubles de Paris (ANMT 65 AQ I 227), itself a creation of the Banque d'Escompte de Paris. For the development process, see Archives de Paris (hereafter AP) VO NC 1449, 1450, 1455, 1457–1462.

32. Jean-Louis Harouel, "L'expropriation dans l'histoire du droit français," in *L'expropriation: Recueils de la Société Jean Bodin pour l'histoire comparative des institutions,* no. 67 (Brussels: De Boeck University, 2000), pt. 2, 39–77; Luigi Lacchè, "Expropriation pour cause d'utilité publique en France au XIXe siècle: Origines et développement d'un modèle juridique," in *L'expropriation: Recueils de la Société Jean Bodin,* 79–103; Yvon Leblicq, "De l'expropriation pour cause d'utilité publique: Expropriation par zones en Belgique et en France au XIXe siècle," in *L'expropriation: Recueils de la Société Jean Bodin,* 105–162.

33. AP D.5 K3 13: Procès-verbaux des séances du Conseil Municipal, Séance du 24 mars 1881, Projet de relèvement et d'assainissement du Quartier Marbeuf, Résultats d'Enquête; "Le Quartier Marbeuf," *La Réforme du Bâtiment,* December 26, 1880.

34. On Blondel, see David Van Zanten, *Building Paris: Architectural Institutions and the Transformation of the French Capital, 1830–1870* (Cambridge: Cambridge University Press, 1994), 185–187. Blondel also submitted unsuccessful proposals to complete portions of Rue Réaumur (Rapport présenté par M. Mesureur, au nom de la 3e commission, sur une proposition de M. Blondel, tendant à l'ouverture de la rue Réaumur, annexe au procès-verbal de la séance du 9 mai 1883) and Rue Étienne Marcel (*BMO,* January 1, 1883, 71). He bid successfully on the construction of the Bourse de Commerce under conditions similar to those of the Quartier Marbeuf (see council discussions, *BMO,* July 18, 1884, 1349; March 24, 1885, 639–646; April 12/13, 1885, 748–750). He faced penalties for fraudulent bankruptcy in 1895, leaving at least 25 million francs in debt: "La faillite d'un entrepreneur," *Reveil Immobilier,* August 13, 1895.

35. In a few cases, such as the completion of Boulevard Haussmann, the Baron's projects were an active issue into the 1920s.

36. Louis Lazare, "Les grands travaux de Paris, l'industrie du bâtiment," *Le Courrier Municipal,* May 1, 1873, 5.

37. Combeau, *Paris et les élections municipales,* chap. 2; and Anthony Sutcliffe, *The Autumn of Central Paris: The Defeat of Town Planning, 1850–1970* (London: Edward Arnold, 1970), chap. 3. Haussmann's projects cost as much as 2 billion francs, most of which was financed by loans; Georges Gallais-Hamonno, "La création d'un marché obligatoire moderne: Les emprunts de la Ville de Paris au XIXe siècle," in *Le marché financier français au XIXe siècle,* vol. 2: *Aspects quantitatifs des acteurs et des instruments à la Bourse de Paris,* ed. Georges Gallais-Hamonno (Paris: Publications de la Sorbonne, 2007), 293. In 1871 Prefect Léon Say put the city's outstanding debt (long and short term) at 1.63 billion francs; Gaston Cadoux, *Les finances de la ville de Paris, 1798–1900* (Paris: Berger-Levrault et Cie, 1900), 104–108. In 1900 Cadoux placed Paris's debt at nearly three times that of London, its nearest competitor (*Les Finances,* 698–699).

38. "Les derniers actes du ci-devant conseil municipal," *Économiste Français,* January 15, 1881, 65–66.

39. Say's stance is discussed in E[ugène] Delahaye, "La guerre aux travaux de Paris," *La Réforme du Bâtiment,* November 3, 1872, 169. Say had discovered and been one of the principal opponents of Haussmann's financing schemes in the 1860s: Léon Say, *Observations sur le système financier de M. le Préfet de la Seine* (Paris: Guillaumin 1865); Say, *Examen critique de la situation financière de la ville de Paris* (Paris: Dentu, 1866).

40. J[ules] D[elahaye], "La Place du Château-d'Eau," *La Réforme du Bâtiment,* February 11, 1872, 22.

41. Bibliothèque Historique de la Ville de Paris, Actualités Série 47, Urbanisme: "V[e] arrondissement, Quartier du Faubourg Saint-Denis, la rue Neuve de Strasbourg," *Gazette Municipale,* August 1, 1852, 840.

42. J. D., "Commerce d'expropriations," *La Réforme du Bâtiment,* June 6, 1875, 89. Expropriation agents published guides priming potential clients, such as A. E. Lambert's *Manuel pratique des jurés et des expropriés pour cause d'utilité publique* (Orléans: Imprimerie Ch. Constant, 1882). Émile Zola's novel of Parisian real estate speculation, *La curée* (1871), includes the character of Larsonneau, an expropriation agent. See also "La propriété foncière: De l'expropriation," *Le Figaro,* April 12, 1882.

43. Rapport par M. Marius Martin, au nom des 1re, 3e et 7e commissions, sur la création d'une Bourse de commerce et le dégagement des Halles centrales, 2 mars 1885, 18; Rapport par M. Adrien Oudin, au nom des 3e et 1re commissions sur le projet de cahier des charges relatif à la mise en adjudication restreinte de l'achèvement du boulevard Haussmann, 28 décembre 1912, 13.

44. J. D., "Commerce d'expropriations," *La Réforme du Bâtiment,* June 6, 1875, 89. Cantagrel was a Fourierist in his youth and a radical democrat in both the municipal council and (later) the national legislature.

45. *BMO,* March 24, 1885, 640.

46. "Le Quartier Marbeuf," *La Réforme du Bâtiment,* February 13, 1881.

47. Lefèvre's report reprinted in "Travaux de Paris," *La Réforme du Bâtiment,* May 14, 1876, 78.

48. "Travaux de voirie: Vote de l'emprunt," *La Réforme du Bâtiment,* May 21, 1876, 81.

49. AP D.5 K3 21: Séance du 5 août 1885, Suite de la Discussion du Rapport de M. Cernesson tendant à la Création de ressources extraordinaires en vue de l'exécution de grands travaux, 253. The phrase originated with Louis XV's mistress, Mme de Pompadour.

50. AP D.5 K3 21 (1885, 2e semestre): Création de ressources extraordinaires pour l'exécution de grands travaux, 196.

51. AP D.5 K3 21 (1885, 2e semestre): Création de ressources extraordinaires pour l'exécution de grands travaux, 201.

52. AP D.5 K3 21: Séance du 3 août 1885, Suite de la Discussion du projet de création de ressources spéciales pour exécution de grands travaux.

53. AP D.5 K3 14: Séance du 5 mai 1882, Révision de la Série des prix de la Ville, 628. On the longer history of municipal price series, see Alain Cottereau, "Droit et bon droit: Un droit des ouvriers instauré, puis évincé par le droit du travail (France, XIXᵉ siècle)," *Annales: Histoire, Sciences Sociales,* 57th year, no. 6 (2002): 1521–1557.

54. On the evolution of customary and "normal" costs and salaries in public accounting, see Alfred de Tarde, *L'idée du juste prix* (doctoral thesis, University of Paris Law School) (Sarlat: Michelet, 1906), 278–285.

55. Hélène Lemesle, "Réglementer l'achat public en France (XVIIIᵉ–XIXᵉ siècle)," *Genèses* 80 (September 2010): 8–26.

56. Morel, *Prix de base et de règlement des travaux de bâtiments, conformes à ceux adoptés par le Conseil des bâtiments civils* (Paris: Imprimerie de Cosse et G. Laguionie, 1839), published annually through 1856. Préfecture de la Seine, Ville de Paris, *Prix de règlement applicables aux travaux de bâtiment exécutés en 1857* (Paris: Cosse et Marchal, 1857).

57. AP VO NC 3193, Extrait du procès-verbal du Conseil des Travaux d'Architecture de la Préfecture de la Seine, Séance du 8 août 1871.

58. "Rapport de M. Gavrel sur l'établissement de la Série des prix de la Ville de Paris: Extrait du procès-verbal de la séance du 15 janvier 1872," in *Monographies municipales: Les conditions du travail dans les chantiers communaux,* ed. Lucien Lambeau (Paris: Imprimerie Municipale, 1896), 4.

59. AP VO NC 3193, Requête Série de la Ville, 1872.

60. On implications for wage increases, see AP VO NC 69, Commission de la révision de la Série des prix de la Ville de Paris, 8e sous-commission (peinture, tenture et enduisage).

61. "Mémoire de M. le Préfet de la Seine au Conseil Municipal relatif aux mesures à prendre au sujet de la Série des prix de la Ville de Paris (29 décembre 1879)," in *Monographies municipales: Les Conditions du travail,* 55; and "Rapport de M. Alphand, Directeur des Travaux, relatif à la Série des Prix de la Ville (18 décembre 1879)," in *Monographies municipales: Les Conditions du travail,* 63.

62. AP D.5 K3 14: Séance du 5 mai 1882, Révision de la Série des prix de la Ville, 631–632.

63. AP D.5 K3 14: Séance du 5 mai 1882, Révision de la Série des prix de la Ville, 628–629.

64. AP D.5 K3 14: Séance du 5 mai 1882, Révision de la Série des prix de la Ville, 633.

65. A decree promulgated by Minister of Commerce Alexandre Millerand on August 10, 1899, allowed cities to set "normal and current wages" on public projects.

66. "Associations ouvrières," *La Semaine des Constructeurs,* February 4, 1882; "Nouvelles concernant l'entreprise et le bâtiment: Les associations ouvrières et les adjudications," *La Semaine des Constructeurs,* April 22, 1882.

67. Lenard Berlanstein, *Big Business and Industrial Conflict in Nineteenth-Century France: A Social History of the Parisian Gas Company* (Berkeley: University of California Press, 1991), chaps. 1 and 2.

68. Peter Soppelsa, "The Fragility of Modernity: Infrastructure and Everyday Life in Paris, 1870–1914" (PhD diss., University of Michigan, 2009), 227–238.

69. Daniel Rodgers, *Atlantic Crossings: Social Politics in a Progressive Age* (Cambridge: Harvard University Press, 1998), chap. 4. See also Pierre-Yves Saunier and Shane Ewen, eds., *Another Global City: Historical Explorations into the Transnational Municipal Moment* (New York: Palgrave Macmillan, 2008).

70. Untitled article, *Le Temps,* July 12, 1888. Arguments in favor of municipal ownership can be found in the articles of the *Annales de la Régie Directe,* published in Geneva from 1908 to 1924, and in volumes of committed municipal socialists such as former municipal councilor and deputy Adrien Veber, *Le socialisme municipal* (Paris: Giard et Brière, 1908).

71. On domain, see Cadoux, *Finances de la Ville de Paris,* 305–313; and see Pontich and Block, *Administration de la Ville de Paris,* 517–527 for domain, and 393–409, 429–445, 459–482 for utilities.

72. Law of April 5, 1884, art. 72. See Léon Morgand, *La loi municipale: Commentaire de la loi du 5 avril 1884 sur l'organisation et les attributions des conseils municipaux* (Paris: Berger-Levrault, 1884–1885), 1:34, 381–382.

73. Pierre Rosanvallon, *The Demands of Liberty: Civil Society in France since the Revolution,* trans. Arthur Goldhammer (Cambridge, MA: Harvard University Press, 2007), 221–225.

74. It was unsuccessful even when granted authority by specific ordinances, such as the Royal Ordinance of September 3, 1843, permitting recovery of betterment values for the construction of Rue Rambuteau. See Adolphe Alphand, ed., *Recueil des lois, ordonnances, décrets et règlements relatifs aux alignements, à l'expropriation pour cause d'utilité publique, spécialement dans les voies de Paris* (Paris: Imprimerie Nouvelle, 1886), 146–147.

75. Jean-Pierre Gaudin, "L'intervention de la puissance publique dans la création et la circulation des valeurs attachés aux usages du sol (de 1840 à 1940)," in *Ville, espace et valeurs: Un séminaire du plan urbain,* ed. Jean-Loup Gourdon, Evelyne Perrin, and Alain Tanius (Paris: Harmattan, 1995), 327–343.

76. Léon Salefranque, "Les mutations à titre onéreux en France: Mouvement de ces transmissions d'après les comptes de finances, 1826–1898," in *Congrès international de la propriété foncière, Documents, rapports, comptes rendus, mémoires et notes* (Paris: Imprimerie Paul Dupont, 1901), 211–241.

77. AP VO NC 182: États statistiques des maisons construites dans Paris (d'après les permissions de voirie délivrées), 1875–1885.

78. On Paris's "drift" to the northwest, see *Mémoire sur le déplacement de la population dans Paris et sur les moyens d'y remédier* (Paris: Imprimerie de L. Bouchard-Huzard, 1840). The consequences of this phenomenon on urban politics are explored in Philip G. Nord, *Paris Shopkeepers and the Politics of Resentment* (Princeton, NJ: Princeton University Press, 1986).

79. Archives de la Préfecture de Police de Paris (hereafter APP) BA 486: Rapport, Commissariat de Police des Quartiers de la Santé et du Petit-Montrouge, 19 juin 1882.

80. APP BA 501: Rapport sur la situation industrielle et commerciale, 5 avril 1879.

81. The inquiry's reports and depositions were published: Chambre des députés, "Procès-verbaux de la commission chargée de faire une enquête sur la situation des

ouvriers de l'industrie et de l'agriculture en France et de présenter un premier rapport sur la crise industrielle à Paris," *Annales de la Chambre des Députés, Documents Parlementaires,* 12 (Paris, 1884).

82. "La crise du bâtiment," *Le Temps,* January 23, 1884.

83. ANMT 2001 026 0649, Crédit Foncier, Assemblée Générale des Actionnaires, 27 avril 1878.

84. Jean-Pierre Allinne, *Banquiers et bâtisseurs: Un siècle de Crédit Foncier, 1852–1940* (Paris: Éditions du CNRS, 1984); Aline Raimbault and Henri Heugas-Darraspen, eds., *Crédit Foncier de France: Itinéraire d'une institution* (Paris: Éditions du Regard, 1994); Michel Lescure, *Les banques, l'état, et le marché immobilier en France à l'époque contemporaine, 1820–1940* (Paris: Éditions de l'École des Hautes Études en Sciences Sociales, 1982), pt. 2.

85. Alexis Bailleux de Marisy, "Les nouvelles sociétés foncières: Moeurs financières de la France, IV," *Revue des Deux Mondes,* November 15, 1881, 432–452, quotation at pp. 440–441.

86. Anon, *Le Crédit Foncier en 1887: Sous-comptoir des entrepreneurs; Compagnie Foncière de France; Rente Foncière; Ses erreurs, ses fautes, ses périls* (Paris: Imprimerie Lucotte et Cadoux, 1887), 12.

87. Jeanne Gaillard, *Paris, la ville: 1852–1870* (Paris: H. Champion, 1977); Marcel Roncayolo, "La production de la ville," in *Histoire de la France urbaine,* vol. 4: *La ville de l'âge industriel, le cycle haussmannien,* 81–167; Harvey, *Paris, Capital of Modernity.*

88. For an example of the iterative public-private development process in an earlier period, see Annie Térade, "L'élaboration du plan d'un 'nouveau quartier' sous la Restauration: Aménagement urbain et spéculation privée," in *Villes françaises au XIXe siècle: Aménagement, extension et embellissement,* ed. Michèle Lambert-Bresson and Annie Térade (Paris: Éditions Recherches/Ipraus, 2002), 93–107.

89. AP VO NC 332: Préfecture de la Seine, Direction des Travaux de Paris (2e Division, 1er Bureau)—Note pour M. l'Ingénieur en chef de la 2e Division: Voies nouvelles à ouvrir entre les rues Marcadet et Ordener. Proposition de la SA immobilière de Montmartre (30 mars 1881). See Pierre Pinon, *Paris, biographie d'une capitale* (Paris: Hazan, 1999), 211, for a discussion of *engagements.* For a brief examination of this development project, see Serge Santelli, "Les lotissements post-haussmanniens des quartiers nord de Paris: De l'immeuble bourgeois au logement à bon marché," in *Paris-Haussmann: Le pari d'Haussmann,* ed. Jean des Cars and Pierre Pinon (Paris: Éditions du Pavillon d'Arsenal, 1991), 297–303.

90. The October 1881 report was discussed by the municipal council the following spring: AP V.1 D.1* Procès-verbaux des délibérations du Conseil Municipal, séance du 5 avril 1882. Fouquiau penned a new *engagement* with the city on May 1, 1882, in light of this deliberation.

91. AP VO11 3464, rue Simart.

92. Ibid. For the process of street construction when initiated by the city, see de Pontich and Block, *Administration de la ville de Paris,* 54–55.

93. AP VO11 3463, rue Simart, Enquête à la Mairie du 18e arrondissement, Procès-verbal, E. Lefort, 15 novembre 1883.

94. AP VO NC 34, Procès-verbaux de la commission consultative de voirie, 1871–1882; Laisney, *Règle et règlement,* 28–36.

95. On the Lebaudys, see Nathalie Montel, "Mutations spatiales, stratégies professionnelles et solidarités familiales à Paris au XIXe siècle: Le rôle des raffineurs de sucre villettois dans la formation d'un espace industriel," *Histoire Urbaine* 4 (2001–2002): 47–65. The long history of Fouquiau's Montmartre development is documented in AP VO NC 332, which contains correspondence between owners and the city, engineer reports, and development plans. On Rue Simart, see the decrees of June 8, 1858, and May 23, 1863, in Ville de Paris, *Recueil des lettres patentes, ordonnances royales, décrets et arrêtés préfectoraux concernant les voies publiques* (Paris: Imprimerie Nouvelle, 1886).

96. AP VO NC 332: Rapport de l'ingénieur ordinaire (Direction des Travaux de Paris, Service de la Voie Publique, 8e section) (24 mars 1879).

97. AP VO NC 332: Note pour la Direction des Travaux (2e Division, 1er Bureau), de la Direction des Affaires Municipales (1ère division, 1ère bureau). Terrain communal rue Ramey, Echange avec M. Fouquiau (9 décembre 1881).

98. AP VO NC 332: Note pour Monsieur le Président de la 3e Commission, de la Direction des Travaux de Paris (31 janvier 1882).

99. AP VO NC 332: Rapport de l'Ingénieur en chef (Direction des Travaux de Paris, Service de la Voie Publique, 2e Division). Sté immobilière de Montmartre, Echange avec Soulte, rue Simart prolongée et rue X (d'accès aux Écoles) (21 octobre 1881); Note pour la Direction des Travaux (2e Division, 1er Bureau), de la Direction des Affaires Municipales (1ère division, 1ère bureau). Terrain communal rue Ramey, Echange avec M. Fouquiau (9 décembre 1881).

100. Monique Eleb, *L'apprentissage du 'chez-soi': La Groupe des Maisons Ouvrières, Paris, avenue Daumesnil, 1908* (Marseille: Éditions Parenthèses, 1994); Monique Eleb and Anne Debarre, *L'invention de l'habitation moderne: Paris, 1880–1914* (Paris: Hazan, and Archives d'Architecture Moderne, 1995).

101. Roger H. Guerrand, *Les origines du logement social en France* (Paris: Éditions Ouvrières, 1967); Ann-Louise Shapiro, *Housing the Poor of Paris, 1850–1902* (Madison: University of Wisconsin Press, 1985); Marie-Jeanne Dumont, *Le logement social à Paris, 1850–1930: Les habitations à bon marché* (Liège: Mardaga, 1991); Susanna Magri, *Les laboratoires de la réforme de l'habitation populaire en France: De la Société française des habitations à bon marché à la section d'hygiène urbaine et rurale du Musée social, 1889–1909* (Paris: Ministère de l'Équipement, du Logement, des Transports et du Tourisme, 1995); Janet Horne, *A Social Laboratory for Modern France: The Musée Social and the Rise of the Welfare State* (Durham, NC: Duke University Press, 2002).

102. Paul Leroy-Beaulieu, "La construction des maisons de luxe et des maisons à bon marché à Paris: 2e article," *Économiste Français,* April 22, 1882, 469–471; "Société d'économie politique: Réunion du 5 mars 1884," *Journal des Économistes,* March 1884, 442–454.

103. Archives du Crédit Agricole SA, DEEF 19377/2: Rapport présenté au nom du Conseil d'Administration par M. le Baron Haussmann, président (Assemblée générale du 14 Avril 1883), 11.

104. Alain Faure and Claire Lévy-Vroelant, *Une chambre en ville: Hôtels meublés et garnis à Paris, 1860–1990* (Paris: Créaphis, 2007), 31, 36.

105. In July 1883 the Municipal Council's Commission on Affordable Housing declared that they were dealing with approximately 350 separate proposals; AP D.5 K3 17, p. 235. See also Shapiro, *Housing the Poor of Paris,* chap. 5.

106. APP BA 486, Enquêtes sur les loyers, 1871–1891: Réunion, Salle Gruber, 15 bd St-Denis, 27 mars 1882.

107. APP BA 486, Enquêtes sur les loyers, 1871–1891: Pétition, "La Question des loyers," signé V. Gelez, employé.

108. APP BA 486: Projet de logements à bon marché: Imprimé adressé au Conseil Municipal, signé par des associations ouvrières (ca. March 29, 1884). See also APP BA 486: Projet de logements à bon marché, Note signé 'Brice,' 3 mai 1884.

109. Gérard Jacquemet, "Spéculation et spéculateurs dans l'immobilier parisien à la fin du XIXe siècle," *Cahiers d'Histoire* 31, no. 3 (1976): 273–306.

110. *La Réforme du Bâtiment,* April 13, 1884, 54.

111. "Rapport no. 136 de 1883 présenté par M. Amouroux, au nom de la Commission spéciale, sur diverses propositions relatives à la construction des logements à bon marché: Annexes au rapport de M. Amouroux; Proposition de M. A. Olivier," in *Monographies municipales: Les logements à bon marché,* ed. Lucien Lambeau (Paris: Imprimerie Municipale, 1897), 769. Difficulties quickly arose between Fouquiau and his collaborator, architect A. Olivier. After the failure of the project, Olivier sought to gain municipal support for a more modest proposal, but could not win the confidence of the workers' associations, who "believe they are right to see M. Olivier as a schemer who wants to use them in order to become their representative and make a nice situation for himself, maybe become a municipal councilor, maybe another such position." See APP BA 486: Projet de logements à bon marché, Note signé 'Brice,' 3 mai 1884.

112. "Rapport présenté par M. Gamard, conseiller municipal, au nom de la 3e Sous-commission des logements à bon marché, relativement au projet de convention à intervenir entre l'État et le Crédit Foncier (31 mars 1883)," in *Monographies municipales: Les logements à bon marché,* 370–384.

113. "Suite de la discussion du rapport de M. Amoureux relatif au projet de convention avec le Crédit Foncier pour la création de logements à bon marché: Extrait du procès-verbal de la séance du 20 juin 1883," in *Monographies municipales: Les logements à bon marché,* 593.

114. "Extrait du procès-verbal de la séance du 15 février 1884, Suite de la discussion du rapport de M. Amouroux relatif à la création de logements à bon marché," in *Monographies municipales: Les logements à bon marché,* 841–879, 874.

115. "Suite de la discussion du rapport de M. Amoureux relatif au projet de convention avec le Crédit Foncier . . . 20 juin 1883," in *Monographies municipales: Les logements à bon marché,* 595.

116. "Extrait du procès-verbal de la séance du 20 février 1884: Fin de la discussion relative au projet de construction des logements à bon marché," in *Monographies municipales: Les logements à bon marché,* 921.

117. "Société d'économie politique: Réunion du 5 mars 1884," *Journal des Économistes,* no. 3 (March 1884): 442–454.

118. "Sous-comptoir des Entrepreneurs, Déposition de M. Robinot, Directeur," in "Procès-verbaux de la commission," 62, 63.

119. "Chambre syndicale des maçons de la Seine et Sté égalitaire des maçons du 14e arrondissement, Séance du 14 mars 1884," in "Procès-verbaux de la commission," 223.

120. APP BA 446: Société Anonyme des Constructions de la Seine, Note pour M. le Contrôleur Générale. Les services Extérieurs. Paris, le 29 août 1883.

121. Cottereau, "Droit et bon droit."

122. "Déposition du sénateur Corbon, Séance du 4 mars 1884," in "Procès-verbaux de la commission," 97.

123. "Déposition de M. André Lyonnais, Séance du 5 mars 1884," in "Procès-verbaux de la commission," 105.

124. "Déposition écrite de Dr. Paul Dubuisson, inspecteur départemental du travail des enfants: Séance du 26 mars 1884," in "Procès-verbaux de la commission," 296.

125. "Proposition de la Caisse centrale du travail et de l'épargne, relative au prolongement de la rue Réaumur," *BMO,* November 14, 1882, 710. This company was one of a number of ventures by the banker Armand Donon that came under police investigation in the 1880s; see APP BA 455.

126. "Agrandissement de la Banque de France," *BMO,* June 26, 1883, 1050.

127. Paul Leroy-Beaulieu, *Essai sur la répartition des richesses et sur la tendance à une moindre inégalité des conditions* (Paris: Guillaumin et Cie, 1881), 188.

128. Nadine Vivier, *Propriété collective et identité communale: Les biens communaux en France, 1750–1914* (Paris: Publications de la Sorbonne, 1998).

129. AP VO11 3128, Rue de la Roquette.

130. Archives Nationales, Minutier Central des Notaires, ET/XIII/1029—Me Segond, Bail et Promesse de Vente par MM. Laubière, Fouquiau, et Bal à M. Blanchon, 6 mars 1883.

131. For a history of the use of these leasing arrangements, see Hélène Lemesle, *Vautours, singes et cloportes: Ledru-Rollin, ses locataires et ses concierges au XIXe siècle* (Paris: Association du Développement de l'Histoire Économique, 2003). On developers' preference for them, see Onésime Masselin, *Formulaire d'actes et notice sur la*

législation et l'utilité des sociétés anonymes immobilières par actions (Paris: Ducher, 1880), 14.

132. "Les terrains de la rue de la Roquette," *La Réforme du Bâtiment,* February 25, 1883, 30.

133. Ibid.

134. "L'assistance publique: Question de M. Manier sur l'adjudication récente de terrains appartenant à cette administration," in *Monographies municipales: Les logements à bon marché,* 49.

135. Maxime Maucorps, "Revue foncière: Le lotissement des terrains," *La Semaine des Constructeurs,* March 31, 1883, 477.

136. AP D.5 K3 16: Séance du 31 janvier 1883, 52.

137. AP D.5 K3 14: Séance du 21 juin 1882, Avis favorable à la mise en adjudication par lots, avec faculté de réunion, d'un terrain sis rue de la Roquette et rue Saint-Maur, 955.

138. Maucorps, "Revue foncière," 478. The city council had in fact approved the sale of these lands in July 1882, on the condition of their subdivision before sale.

139. AP D.5 K3 14 (1882, 1er semestre), 916. The request was repeated in January 1883, adding the suggestion that the map be displayed in each of the arrondissement town halls, "so that the population of Paris can know what buildings it owns" (AP D.5 K3 16, Séance du 31 janvier 1883, 51).

140. AP D.5 K3 15, Séance du 8 décembre 1882, 819; AP D.5 K3 15, Séance du 28 juillet 1882, Mis en adjudication de terrains en bordure du parc du Champ-de-Mars, 229.

141. AP D.5 K3 14, Séance du 7 avril 1881, Proposition, 595–693; "Réponse de M. Manier au rapport de M. Villard sur les logements à bon marché: Extrait du procès-verbal de la séance du 16 mai 1883," in *Monographies municipales: Les logements à bon marché,* 464–476.

142. AP D.5 K3 19, Séance du 15 décembre 1884, Proposition de M. Vaillant pour soumettre aux impôts des terrains non-bâtis et des logements vacants, 1481–1486. See also the tax suggestions of Councilor Georges Martin, "Commission des logements à bon marché (nommée par le Conseil Municipal): Procès-verbal de la séance du lundi 12 novembre 1883," in *Monographies municipales: Les logements à bon marché,* 659.

143. AP D.5 K3 22, Séance du 19 mars 1886, Propositions de M. Vaillant concernant la vente des terrains communaux, 350.

144. APP BA 486, Enquêtes sur les loyers, 1871–1891: La Question Paris: A Monsieur Jules Ferry, Ministre de l'instruction publique, président du Conseil. Paris, le 10 avril 1883.

145. Rapport présenté par M. Cernesson, au nom de la Commission de l'Emprunt sur les propositions de création de ressources extraordinaires en vue de l'exécution de grands travaux (Annexe au procès-verbal de la séance du 22 juillet 1885), 35–36.

146. AP D.5 K3 22, Séance du 7 avril 1886: Fixation du Tableau d'Emploi de l'emprunt de 250 millions, 604.

147. AP D.5 K3 24, Séance du 28 mars 1887: Exécution des opérations de voirie votées par le Conseil et approuvées par la loi du 19 juillet 1886, 628–629.

148. "Débats parlementaires, 1er mars 1884," in "Procès-verbaux de la commission," 583. Louis Lazare,"Les grands travaux de Paris, l'industrie du bâtiment," *Le Courrier Municipal,* May 1, 1873, 2.

149. "Syndicat des ouvriers peintres en bâtiment, Séance du 20 février 1884," in "Procès-verbaux de la commission," 43.

150. "Fédération des ouvriers peintres en bâtiments des 8e, 9e, 17e et 18e arrondissements de Paris et quartiers limitrophes, Séance du 13 mars 1884," in "Procès-verbaux de la commission," 197.

151. APP EB 33: Affiche, Election Municipale du 1er juillet 1883, Quartier de la Muette, Comité de l'Union républicaine du XVIe arrondissement. M. A. Branicki, candidat.

2. Seeing Like a Speculator

1. Maurice Halbwachs, *Les expropriations et les prix des terrains à Paris (1860–1900)* (Paris: Publications de la Société Nouvelle de Librairie et d'Édition, 1909), 169.

2. Halbwachs, *Les expropriations,* 381–382. On Halbwachs's theory of urban development, see Christian Topalov, "Maurice Halbwachs et les villes: Les expropriations et le prix des terrains à Paris (1909)," in *La ville des sciences sociales,* ed. Bernard Lepetit and Christian Topalov (Paris: Belin, 2001), 12–40; Bernard Lepetit, "L'appropriation de l'espace urbain: La formation de la valeur dans la ville moderne (XVIe-XIXe siècles)," *Histoire, Économie, et Société* 13, no. 3 (1994): 551–559; Michel Amiot, *Contre l'état, les sociologues: Eléments pour une histoire de la sociologie urbaine en France (1900–1980)* (Paris: Éditions de l'EHESS, 1986), chap. 1; Alain Faure, "Spéculation et société: Les grands travaux à Paris au XIXe siècle," *Histoire, Economie, et Société* 23 no. 3 (2004): 433–448.

3. Archives de la Préfecture de Police de Paris (hereafter APP) BA 486: Rapport, Commissariat de Police du Quartier de la Roquette, 22 juin 1882; Abel Lemercier, "De la crise locative et immobilière à Paris: Moyen d'y remédier," *Journal des Économistes* (January 1886): 85; Auguste Fougerousse, "La crise immobilière," *Économiste Français,* March 17, 1883, 318.

4. Christian Topalov, *Les promoteurs immobiliers: Contribution à l'analyse de la production capitaliste du logement en France* (Paris: Mouton, 1974).

5. William C. Baer, "Is Speculative Building Underappreciated in Urban History?," *Urban History* 34, no. 2 (2007): 296–316.

6. Christian Topalov, *Le logement en France: Histoire d'une marchandise impossible* (Paris: Presses de la Fondation Nationale des Sciences Politiques, 1987).

7. Daily and weekly real estate columns were introduced in national papers as follows: 1881, "La propriété foncière" in *Le Figaro*; 1885, "Chronique immobilière" in *Le Gaulois* and "Revue foncière" in *Le Matin*; 1886, "Revue foncière" in *Gil-Blas*; 1891, "Bulletin foncier" in *Le Temps*; 1893, "Chronique foncière" in *Le XIX*[e] *siècle*; 1897, "Chronique immobilière" in *La Presse*. In 1888, the *Journal Officiel de la République Française* began carrying a "Statistique immobilière." All of the above appeared with varying frequency, and titles changed over time.

8. See the magisterial study by Georges le vicomte d'Avenel, *Histoire économique de la propriété, des salaires, des denrées et de tous les prix en général, depuis l'an 1200 jusqu'en l'an 1800* (Paris: Imprimerie Nationale, 1894–1898).

9. For a look at this question in the contemporary context, see Susan J. Smith, Moira Munro, and Hazel Christie, "Performing (Housing) Markets," *Urban Studies* 43, no. 1 (January 2006): 81–98.

10. David Harvey, *The Limits to Capital* (Oxford: Blackwell, 1982), esp. chaps. 11–13. Manu Goswami makes the point of distinguishing capital's homogenizing spatial thrust and its historical appearance in *Producing India: From Colonial Economy to National Space* (Chicago: University of Chicago Press, 2004), 36–37.

11. James C. Scott, *Seeing Like a State: How Certain Schemes to Improve the Human Condition Have Failed* (New Haven: Yale University Press, 1998). I have been influenced in this approach by Mariana Valverde, "Seeing Like a City: The Dialectic of Modern and Premodern Ways of Seeing in Urban Governance," *Law & Society Review* 45, no. 2 (June 2011): 277–312.

12. Daniel Miller, "Turning Callon the Right Way Up," *Economy and Society* 31, no. 2 (May 2002): 218–233; Koray Çaliskan and Michel Callon, "Economization, Part 1: Shifting Attention from the Economy towards the Processes of Economization," *Economy and Society* 38, no. 3 (2009): 369–398; Çaliskan and Callon, "Economization, part 2: A Research Programme for the Study of Markets," *Economy and Society* 39, no. 1 (2010): 1–32.

13. "La propriété foncière," *Le Figaro*, May 30, 1883. On the expansion of the field, see Denyse Rodriguez Tomé, "L'organisation des architectes sous la IIIe République," *Le Mouvement Social*, no. 214 (January–March 2006): 55–76.

14. Édouard Charton, "Architecte," in *Guide pour le choix d'un état, ou Dictionnaire des professions* (Paris: Veuve Lenormant, 1842), 20–32.

15. Archives Nationales du Monde du Travail (hereafter ANMT) 65 AQ I 235: SA Paris Nouveau, Statuts, 1881.

16. "Déposition de M. Fernoux, architecte. Séance du 5 mars 1884," in "Procès-verbaux de la commission chargée de faire une enquête sur la situation des ouvriers de l'industrie et de l'agriculture en France et de présenter un premier rapport sur la crise industrielle à Paris," *Annales de la Chambre des députés: Documents parlementaires*, 12 (Paris, 1884): 110.

17. The professional contest between architects and engineers is better known than that between architects and building entrepreneurs, despite the importance of the latter. See Hélène Lipstadt, *Architecture et ingénieur dans la presse* (Paris: CORDA-IERAU, 1980); Marc Saboya, *Presse et architecture au XIXe siècle: César Daly et la* Revue générale de l'architecture et des travaux publics (Paris: Picard, 1991); Annie Jacques, ed., *La carrière de l'architecte au XIXe siècle* (Paris: Musées Nationaux, 1986).

18. "La patente des architectes," *Le Plan: Journal Spécial pour Locations ou Ventes,* March 16, 1844. On the law of April 25, 1844, see the entry for "Architecte" (art. 14) in D. Dalloz, *Répertoire méthodique et alphabétique de législation, de doctrine et de jurisprudence* (Paris: Bureau de la Jurisprudence Générale, 1847), 5:200.

19. "De la responsabilité des architectes: Première conférence nationale de la Société centrale des architectes," *Revue Générale de l'Architecture et des Travaux Publics* 30 (1873): 169–173.

20. "L'architecture au jour le jour," *La Semaine des Constructeurs,* October 15, 1892, 182.

21. Émile Rivoalen, "Décor intérieur des habitations," *La Semaine des Constructeurs,* January 3, 1885, 318.

22. Émile Rivoalen, "À travers Paris: Première promenade," *Revue Générale de l'Architecture et des Travaux Publics,* 4th series, vol. 9 (1882): 27, emphasis in the original.

23. On vocation in the nineteenth-century social imaginary, see Kathleen Kete, "Stendhal and the Trials of Ambition in Post-revolutionary France," *French Historical Studies* 28, no. 3 (Summer 2005): 467–495.

24. V. Ruprich-Robert in the *Forum Artistique,* reprinted as "Causerie: Le diplôme," *La Construction Moderne,* December 18, 1886, 109–110.

25. Charton, *Guide pour le choix d'un état,* 266–267.

26. Ibid., 267.

27. Ibid., 268.

28. Édouard Charton, *Dictionnaire des professions, ou Guide pour le choix d'un état,* 3rd ed. (Paris: Librairie Hachette et Cie, 1880), 214.

29. Ibid.

30. "Fédération des ouvriers peintres en bâtiments des 8e, 9e, 17e et 18e arrondissements de Paris et quartiers limitrophes: Déposition de MM. Bret-Morel, Valdin et Wachter, Séance du 13 mars 1884," in "Procès-verbaux de la commission," 197.

31. Michel Lescure, *Les banques, l'état, et le marché immobilier en France à l'époque contemporaine, 1820–1940* (Paris: École des Hautes Études en Sciences Sociales, 1982), 320.

32. Onésime Masselin, "Des effets du krach de la Bourse sur les opérations immobilières (suite)," *Le Foncier,* March 14, 1882, 1.

33. Onésime Masselin, *Formulaire d'actes et notice sur la législation et l'utilité des sociétés anonymes immobilières par actions* (Paris: Ducher, 1880), 11.

34. Baer, "Is Speculative Building Underappreciated in Urban History?"; H. J. Dyos, "The Speculative Builders and Developers of Victorian London," *Victorian Studies* 11 (Summer 1968): 641–690; J. W. R. Whitehand, "The Makers of British Towns: Architects, Builders, and Property Owners, c. 1850–1939," *Journal of Historical Geography* 18, no. 4 (1992): 417–438; Richard Rodger, "Speculative Builders and the Structure of the Scottish Building Industry, 1860–1914," *Business History* 21, no. 2 (1979): 226–246; Donna Rilling, *Making Houses, Crafting Capitalism: Builders in Philadelphia, 1790–1850* (Philadelphia: University of Pennsylvania Press, 2001). In geography, Richard Harris has argued forcefully for further studies on the networks and commodity chains of the home-building industry: Richard Harris and Michael Buzzelli, "Cities as the Industrial Districts of Housebuilding," *International Journal of Urban and Regional Research* 30, no. 4 (December 2006): 894–917.

35. Masselin, *Formulaire d'actes et notices,* 84. Figures for the city as a whole give an average sales price of 132,171 francs per building in 1889; see Préfecture de la Seine, Direction des Finances, Service des Contributions Directes, *Les propriétés bâties de la ville de Paris en 1889 et en 1890* (Paris: Imprimerie Nationale, 1890), 47.

36. Préfecture de la Seine, *Annuaire statistique de la Ville de Paris,* vol. 3: *Année 1882* (Paris: Imprimerie Municipale, 1884), 365; *Annuaire statistique,* vol. 5: *Année 1884* (1886), 346–347. The 18th arrondissement continued in its leading position throughout this period; the Crédit Foncier reported in 1908 that nearly 9 percent (3,332 out of a total 37,387) of its loans in Paris since its founding in 1852 through 1906 were issued on properties in the 18th arrondissement, the single largest concentration in the city. In terms of cash value, however, over that same period the company dedicated a whopping 25 percent of its funds to two arrondissements, the 8th and 9th (Préfecture de la Seine, *Annuaire statistique de la Ville de Paris,* vol. 27: *Année 1906* [Paris: Masson et Cie, 1908], 221).

37. The 1891 census for the city of Paris shows most architectural practitioners were over forty (1,158 out of 1,947 *patrons* and 1,244 out of 1,499 *employés*). Préfecture de la Seine, Service de la Statistique Municipale, *Résultats statistiques du dénombrement de 1891 pour la ville de Paris et le département de la Seine* (Paris: G. Masson, 1894), 174.

38. ANMT 65 AQ I 228: SA des Nouveaux Quartiers de Paris, Statuts, 1881.

39. Ordinance of January 4, 1843, article 12. Philip T. Hoffman, Gilles Postel-Vinay, and Jean-Laurent Rosenthal, *Priceless Markets: The Political Economy of Credit in Paris, 1660–1870* (Chicago: University of Chicago Press, 2001), chap. 10.

40. *Journal des sociétés civiles et commerciales: Liste des sociétés* (1880–1882).

41. Maître Segond, for instance, oversaw the constitution of Fouquiau's SA Immobilière de la Rue de Monceau (June 10, 1881), the SA Immobilière de la Rue des Martyrs (January 13, 1882), and the Société Foncière Parisienne (SA, August 12, 1881), though at least this last was jointly signed by Latapie de Gerval.

42. The journal was initially directed by Lucien de la Saigne before fusing with another journal, *Le Foncier,* in 1879 and being transferred to Laubière.

43. Article from *Le Temps,* January 23, 1884, reprinted as "Chronique: La crise du bâtiment," *La Semaine des Constructeurs,* February 9, 1884, 374.

44. Masselin, *Formulaire d'actes et notice,* 8, my emphasis.

45. Frederick Lavington, *The Trade Cycle: An Account of the Causes Producing Rhythmical Changes in the Activity of Business* (London, 1922), cited by Lucien Flaus, "Les fluctuations de la construction des habitations urbaines," *Journal de la Société de Statistique de Paris* 90 (1949): 185–211, 205.

46. L. de la Saigne, "En avant!," *Le Foncier,* December 30, 1879.

47. Archives Nationales, Minutier Central des Notaires, ET/XIII/1029—Me Segond, Statuts de la Foncière Parisienne.

48. "Bulletin," *Indicateur Général des Terrains et Immeubles à Vendre,* October 18, 1879.

49. "Les constructions nouvelles à Paris," *Le Foncier,* June 14, 1881, 1–2.

50. ANMT 65 AQ I 227: SA des Immeubles de Paris, Rapport du Conseil d'Administration, Assemblée Générale du 29 mars 1881, 5.

51. Onésime Masselin, "De la spéculation immobilière," *Le Foncier,* September 5, 1882, 1.

52. Paul Leroy-Beaulieu, "La construction des maisons de luxe et des maisons à bon marché à Paris (1er article)," *L'Économiste Français,* April 15, 1882, 437–439.

53. Paul Leroy Beaulieu, "La situation de la propriété immobilière à Paris (2e article)," *L'Économiste Français,* August 23, 1884, 221–223.

54. On the invention of the notion of "filtering" in the housing market in the U.S. context, see Richard Harris, "The Rise of Filtering Down: The American Housing Market Transformed, 1915–1929," *Social Science History* 37, no. 4 (2013): 515–549.

55. "Déposition de M. Fernoux, architecte: Séance du 5 mars 1884," in "Procès-verbaux de la commission," 112.

56. "Chronique," *Journal des Économistes,* no. 8 (August 1882): 307–312.

57. Adeline Daumard, *Maisons de Paris et propriétaires parisiens au XIXe siècle (1809–1880)* (Paris: Éditions Cujas, 1965).

58. Leroy-Beaulieu, "La construction des maisons," 439.

59. ANMT 65 AQ I 69: SA Constructions Rationnelles. Procès-verbaux de l'Assemblée Générale du 4 avril 1906, 3.

60. See the annual reports of the Compagnie Foncière de France (ANMT 65 AQ I 102), as well as the property transaction records for the streets concerned: Archives de Paris (hereafter AP) D.1 P4 900, rue de la Pompe, 1876; AP D.1 P4 1199, avenue Victor Hugo, 1876; AP D.1 P4 1054, rue Saint-Philippe du Roule, 1876, 1900.

61. Fougerousse, "La crise immobilière," 319.

62. "Les terrains de la rue de la Roquette," *La Réforme du Bâtiment,* February 25, 1883, 30.

63. "Déposition de M. André Cochut, directeur du Mont-de-piété de Paris: Séance du 29 mars 1884," in "Procès-verbaux de la commission," 317.

64. Halbwachs, *Les expropriations,* 238–240.

65. "Bulletin des propriétaires et locataires: Comment on fait un bon placement immobilier," *Le Foncier,* November 18, 1879, 3–4.

66. M. Blottas, *Manuel d'évaluation des propriétés immobilières* (Paris: Victor Dalmont, 1856), 6.

67. André Haussmann, *Paris immobilier: Notions sur les placements en immeubles dans les zones parisiennes* (Paris: Amyot, 1863), 12. Parts of this work appeared in installments in the *Revue Municipale* in 1860–1861.

68. Haussmann, *Paris immobilier,* 66.

69. Préfecture de la Seine, Direction Municipale des travaux du Cadastre de Paris, Commission des Contributions Directes, *Le livre foncier de Paris (Valeur locative des propriétés bâties en 1900)* (Paris: Imprimerie Chaix, 1900–1902), 6.

70. Gaston Duon, *Évolution de la valeur vénale des immeubles parisiens: Communication faite à la Sté de statistique de Paris, 17 novembre 1943* (Nancy: Berger-Levrault, 1943); Nicolas Lyon-Caen, "Un prix sans aménité: L'indemnisation des propriétaires parisiens à la fin de l'Ancien Régime," *Histoire et Mesure,* 28, no. 1 (2013): 75–106. In England this was the "years purchase": William C. Baer, "The Institution of Residential Investment in Seventeenth-Century London," *Business History Review* 76 (Autumn 2002): 515–551.

71. Crédit Foncier loan assessments; see ANMT 2001 026 2743–2952 (Dossiers de prêts individuels, 1853–1920). In the Paris Archives, expropriation assessments are located throughout their collections; see, e.g., expropriations for the Bourse de Commerce, VO NC 284–289. Methods of valuing real estate are explained in manuals such as Jean-Baptiste Josseau, *Traité du Crédit foncier, ou Explication théorique et pratique de la législation relative au Crédit foncier* (Paris: Cosse, 1853), 400–403; E. Lambert, *Manuel pratique des jurés et des expropriés pour cause d'utilité publique* (Orléans: Imprimerie Ch. Constant, 1882), 13–24; Georges Roux, *L'habitation: 'Ma maison', généralités et conseils* (Paris: Librairie Armand Colin, 1912), 134–137, 140–144.

72. Augustin Charles Guichard, *Guide des experts, ou Instructions et formules sur les expertises et estimations, dans les cas de réduction de prix, ou de rescision des contrats de ventes d'immeubles* (Paris: Dépôt des Loix, n.d. [1798]); Paul Anglès, *De la lésion en droit romain et en droit français* (doctoral thesis, Lyon Law School) (Lyon: Imprimerie Schneider frères, 1878). See also Judith A. Miller, "Des contrats sous tension: Rétablir la propriété après la Terreur," *Annales Historiques de la Révolution Française,* no. 352 (April–June 2008): 241–262.

73. On the particular challenges Parisian space posed to early tax officials, see Florence Bourillon, "De continuité et de rupture: L'élaboration de l'évaluation fiscale urbaine au tournant des XVIIIe–XIXe siècles, l'exemple de Paris," in *La mesure cadastrale: Estimer la valeur du foncier,* ed. Florence Bourillon and Nadine Vivier (Rennes: Presses universitaires de Rennes, 2012), 137–149.

74. AP D.2 P4 49: Commission des contributions directes de la Ville de Paris, *Evaluation des propriétés bâties de la Ville de Paris effectuée en 1888 et 1899: Procès-verbal des opérations* (Paris, 1890), 4–5.

75. AP D.5 K3 22: Procès-verbaux des séances du Conseil Municipal séances du 22, 24 et 29 mars 1886, Projet de Modification de la Procédure actuelle en matière d'expropriation.

76. Haussmann, *Paris immobilier,* 76, 83. That evaluation could not function without subjective judgment would be a long-standing concern of those charged with assessing real property value. Nearly eighty years later, Edmond Michel, a former official with the Crédit Foncier, used similar terms to explain that the science of estimates ultimately depended on an expert's intuition, refined through long experience in grappling with the nuance and variability of property values: Edmond Michel, O'Brien de Burgue, and G. Nicolas, *Evaluations immobilières (Propriétés bâties)* (Paris: n.p., 1942).

77. Johann Heinrich von Thünen, *Von Thünen's 'Isolated State': An English Edition,* trans. Carla Wartenberg (Oxford: Pergamon, 1966 [1826]).

78. *Mémoire sur le déplacement de la population dans Paris et sur les moyens d'y remédier, présenté, par les trois arrondissements de la rive gauche de la Seine (10e, 11e et 12e), à la commission établie près le ministère de l'intérieur; M. E. de Chabrol-Chaméane, rapporteur* (Paris: Imprimerie de L. Bouchard-Huzard, 1840). On the east–west division of the city, see Maurice Agulhon, "Paris: A Traversal from East to West," in *Rethinking France: Les Lieux de Mémoire,* ed. Pierre Nora (Chicago: University of Chicago Press, 2001), 3:523–554. Victoria Thompson provides examples of how narratives of social mobility include movement from east to west: Victoria Thompson, "Telling Spatial Stories: Urban Space and Bourgeois Identity in Early-Nineteenth-Century Paris," *Journal of Modern History* 75, no. 3 (September 2003): 523–556.

79. Elaine Lewinnek, "Mapping Chicago, Imagining Metropolises: Reconsidering the Zonal Model of Urban Growth," *Journal of Urban History* 36, no. 2 (March 2010): 197–220.

80. John Merriman, *The Margins of City Life: Explorations in the French Urban Frontier, 1815–1851* (New York: Oxford University Press, 1991); Tyler Stovall, *The Rise of the Paris Red Belt* (Berkeley: University of California Press, 1990); Annie Fourcaut, *La banlieue en morceaux: La crise des lotissements défectueux en France dans l'entre-deux-guerres* (Grâne, France: Créaphis, 2000). The pattern, of course, contrasted sharply with that Burgess was seeking to model in Chicago.

81. Préfecture de la Seine, Direction des Affaires Municipales, Service de la Statistique Municipale, *Annuaire statistique de la ville de Paris* (Paris: G. Masson, 1880ff).

82. Préfecture de la Seine, *Les propriétés bâties de la ville de Paris en 1889 et en 1890*; Préfecture de la Seine, *Le livre foncier de Paris . . . 1900*; Préfecture de la Seine, Commission des Contributions Directes, *Le livre foncier de 1911* (Paris: Imprimerie

Chaix, 1911). The earliest publication did not include figures of property values, only rental revenues.

83. P[aul] Planat, "Statistique," *La Semaine des Constructeurs,* March 22, 1884, 445–448.

84. On Vauthier's map, see Antoine Picon and Jean-Paul Robert, *Le dessus des cartes: Un atlas parisien* (Paris: Pavillon de l'Arsenal, 1999), 209.

85. "Programme du journal," *Le Foncier,* November 18, 1879, 2.

86. "Les affaires de construction," *La Réforme du Bâtiment,* January 7, 1883, 1.

87. "Revue foncière," *Le Matin,* April 20, 1885.

88. "La maison à Paris," *La Construction Moderne,* March 14, 1903, 282–283.

89. "Bulletin des propriétaires et locataires: Comment on fait un bon placement immobilier," *Indicateur Général des Terrains et Immeubles à Vendre,* November 18, 1879, 4.

90. Maxime Maucorps, *Annuaire de la propriété foncière de Paris,* 4 vols. (Paris, 1867–1870). In the 1870s and 1880s, Maucorps penned analyses of the state of the Parisian property market that ran, with slight variation, in large industry weeklies such as *La Construction Moderne* and *Semaine des Constructeurs,* as well as a variety of other gazettes, such as *Moniteur de la Propriété Mobilière, Immobilière, Commerciale et Financière,* and the *Indicateur Général des Terrains et Immeubles à Vendre.*

91. In addition to those works discussed above, see Louchard, *Sages précautions contre des spéculations ruineuses ou l'Art d'acquérir sans crainte d'être trompé une maison d'habitation ou un terrain propre à bâtir* (Paris: Librairie Scientifique-Industrielle de L. Mathais, 1850), and A. Gauthier, *Code des placements fonciers, acquisitions d'immeubles, prêts hypothécaires* (Paris: Paul Dupont, 1865).

92. Haussmann, *Paris immobilier,* 77, 283, emphasis in the original.

93. *Le guide foncier: Cours de la propriété foncière de 1866 à 1885* (Paris: n.p., n.d. [1886]), subsequently updated as the *Indicateur de la propriété foncière et des voies de Paris* (1887) and the *Indicateur des voies de Paris et du cours de la propriété foncière* (1888).

94. Maublanc et Fils, *L'aide-mémoire foncier de l'architecte et du propriétaire* (Paris: Au Bureau de la Revue des Terrains de Paris et de la Banlieue, 1893).

95. Maxime Petibon, *Indicateur du bâtiment et de la propriété foncière dans Paris et le département de la Seine* (Paris: La Parisienne, 1887); Petibon, *Manuel officiel des affaires immobilières et foncières de la ville de Paris* (Paris: n.p., 1899).

96. Petibon, *Indicateur du bâtiment,* 1887, 11.

97. Petibon, *Indicateur du bâtiment,* 1888, 253–254.

98. The interwar property evaluation guide published by architects Bourdilliat et A. Drouet in 1934 followed the same pattern of reproducing property transactions, adding coefficients to translate land values to the new franc. See their *Recueil des ventes foncières de terrains nus dans la région parisienne réalisées de 1885 à 1933 au Palais de justice et à la Chambre des notaires de Paris* (Paris: Librairie de la Construction Moderne, 1934).

99. Haussmann, *Paris immobilier,* 301. In his analysis of the late-twentieth-century U.S. housing market, economist Robert Shiller has suggested the importance of the availability of such information as preconditions for destructive bouts of "irrational exuberance." Robert J. Shiller, *Irrational Exuberance* (Princeton, NJ: Princeton University Press, 2005), 25–27.

100. *Bulletin Municipal Officiel de la Ville de Paris* (hereafter *BMO*), December 25, 1887, 3021. Hervieux seems to have been referring to Madame Roch-Sautier, who purchased the former John Arthur Company after the fraudulent bankruptcy of its eponymous owner in 1884. By this period, however, the company was directed by a former associate of John Arthur's, William Tiffen; the role of Mme. Roch-Sautier is unclear, though Hervieux's comment seems to imply her active collaboration in the management of the firm.

101. *BMO,* December 25, 1887, 3021.

102. Halbwachs, *Les expropriations,* 18.

103. Onésime Masselin, "Des effets du krach de la Bourse sur les opérations immobilières (suite)," *Le Foncier,* April 4, 1882, 1, emphasis in the original.

104. "Union amicale des maîtres compagnons et appareilleurs, Séance du 15 mars 1884," in "Procès-verbaux de la commission," 218.

105. "Causerie foncière," *Grand Journal Officiel des Locations et de la Vente des Terrains et Immeubles,* September 16–30, 1884, 15.

106. Émile Rivoalen, "Promenades à travers Paris: Maisons et Locataires," *Revue Générale de l'Architecture et des Travaux Publics* 4e série, vol. 9 (1882), 258–260, emphasis in the original.

107. "Sous-comptoir des entrepreneurs, déposition de M. Robinot, directeur: Séance du 23 février 1884," in "Procès-verbaux de la commission," 62.

3. The Problem of Property

1. Archives de Paris (hereafter AP) VO NC 238: Compte rendu historique, moral et financier de 1870 à 1899.

2. Pierre Pinon, "L'archéologie des lotissements: quelques exemples parisiens," in *Paris, formes urbaines et architectures,* ed. Pierre Pinon, Annie Térade, and Michèle Lambert-Bresson (Paris: Éditions Recherches/IPRAUS, 1998), 15–28.

3. Louis Lazare, "Plantations parisiennes," *Le Courrier Municipal,* June 15, 1873, 6.

4. Vanessa Schwartz and Phil Ethington, eds., "Special Issue: Urban Icons," *Urban History* 33, no. 1 (2006).

5. Bibliothèque Historique de la Ville de Paris (hereafter BHVP) Actualités, Série 47, Urbanisme: Louis Lazare, [no title] *Revue Municipale,* March 1, 1856, 1656.

6. See the statements of Councilor Cantagrel, "Conseil Municipal de Paris: Séance du samedi 19 juillet 1873," *La Réforme du Bâtiment,* July 27, 1873, 118.

7. See Hélène Michel, *La cause des propriétaires: État et propriété en France, fin XIX*e*–XX*e *siècle* (Paris: Belin, 2006), for an excellent study of the emergence of property owners as a lobbying body in France.

8. Paul Gilles, *La question des loyers et la guerre: Droits et obligations des locataires et des propriétaires d'après la loi, les décrets de 1914, et les précédents de 1870–1871* (Paris: Librairie des Publications Officielles Georges Roustan, 1914), pt. 2.

9. Eric Fournier, *Paris en ruines: Du Paris haussmannien au Paris communard* (Paris: Imago, 2008); Alisa Luxenberg, "Creating *Désastres:* Andrieu's Photographs of Urban Ruins in the Paris of 1871," *Art Bulletin* 80, no. 1 (March 1998): 113–137; Jeanne M. Przyblyski, "Moving Pictures: Photography, Narrative, and the Paris Commune of 1871," in *Cinema and the Invention of Modern Life,* ed. Leo Charney and Vanessa Schwartz (Berkeley: University of California Press, 1995), 253–278.

10. This organization changed its name several times, becoming in turn the Chambre Syndicale des Propriétés Immobilières du XIe arrondissement de la Ville de Paris et des Arrondissements Circonvoisins, the Chambre Syndicale des Propriétés Immobilières de la Ville de Paris, and finally the Chambre Nationale des Propriétaires. The Chamber's journal continues to be published today as the *Revue de l'Habitat Français.*

11. See, for instance, Christiane Beroujon, "La Chambre syndicale des propriétaires immobiliers de la ville de Lyon," *Bulletin: Centre Pierre Léon d'Histoire Économique et Sociale,* no. 3 (1988): 5–37.

12. Adeline Daumard, *Maisons de Paris et propriétaires parisiens au XIX*e *siècle (1809–1880)* (Paris: Éditions Cujas, 1965). Daumard's data is the most extensive for the period, but it is based on the self-identification of property sellers in official publications *(Petites Affiches).* It does not take into account the possibility that individuals may have found it increasingly desirable or appropriate to declare themselves "propriétaires," without reference to their other (or former) occupational pursuits, nor whether such labels were adopted simply for publication purposes.

13. "Discours de Dr Paul Beauregard, président du Congrès international de la propriété bâtie, 28 mai 1900," in *Premier congrès international de la propriété bâtie: Exposition Universelle Internationale de 1900, à Paris* (Paris: Société des Publications Scientifiques et Industrielles, 1901), 4.

14. Hubert Bonin, *L'argent en France depuis 1880: Banquiers, financiers, épargnants dans la vie économique et politique* (Paris: Masson, 1989), chap. 5; Pierre-Cyrille Hautcoeur, ed., *Le marché financier français au XIX*e *siècle,* vol. 1: *Récit* (Paris: Publications de la Sorbonne, 2007).

15. A[uguste] Fougerousse, "Correspondance, les logements à bon marché," *Économiste Français,* May 13, 1882, 577.

16. Archives Nationales du Monde du Travail (hereafter ANMT) 65 AQ I 227, SA des Immeubles de Paris, Rapport à l'Assemblée générale 1881, 4. Gilles Postel-Vinay,

La terre et l'argent: L'agriculture et le crédit en France du XVIIIe *au début du XX*[e] *siècle* (Paris: Albin Michel, 1998).

17. Keith Tribe, *Land, Labour, and Economic Discourse* (London: Routledge and Kegan Paul, 1978); Marthe Torre-Schaub, *Essai sur la construction juridique de la catégorie de marché* (Paris: Librairie Générale de Droit et de Jurisprudence, 2002), 28–29, 44–48; Roger Bernard, "De la commercialité des opérations immobilières au point de vue économique" (doctoral thesis, University of Paris Law School) (Paris: Éditions de "La Vie Universitaire," 1922); Georges Dreyfus, "De l'exclusion des opérations immobilières du domaine du droit commercial" (doctoral thesis, University of Paris Law School) (Paris: Librairie Nouvelle de Droit et de Jurisprudence, 1905).

18. The alignement was the state's primary mode of improving and enlarging roads from Henri IV's Edict of December 1607. See Bernard Gauthiez and Olivier Zeller, "Le dédommagement des reculements: Un instrument de la politique d'aménagement urbain à Lyon aux XVIIe et XVIIIe siècles," *Histoire et Mesure* 28, no. 1 (2013): 45–74. Citywide plans of alignments were ordered from 1765 but not undertaken until after the Revolution. Maurice Block notes that as late as 1869 prefects had to be reminded to execute these plans; see his *Dictionnaire de l'administration française* (Paris: Berger-Levrault, 1877–1885), 2:1816.

19. Ferdinand Sanlaville, *Des voies privées* (Paris: Berger-Levrault et Cie, 1899), 28. Following the Revolution, this legislation was confirmed in article 52 of the law of September 16, 1807.

20. Block, *Dictionnaire de l'administration française,* 1816.

21. AP VO NC 77: Préfecture du département de la Seine, *Instruction concernant la voirie urbaine* (Paris: Imprimerie centrale des chemins de fer, A. Chaix et Cie, 1874), 3–4.

22. The Decree of July 27, 1859, and the Decree of June 18, 1872, which reinforced it, were the first regulatory measures to introduce a maximum height limit to interior constructions; the latter was also the first to address courtyard sizes. See A. de Royou, *Traité pratique de la voirie à Paris,* 2nd ed. (Paris: Librairie Générale de l'Architecture et des Travaux Publics, 1884), and Louis Bonnier, *Les règlements de voirie: Conférences faites dans l'hémicycle de l'École nationale des beaux-arts (22 et 29 octobre 1902)* (Paris: Libraire Générale de l'Architecture et des Arts Décoratifs, 1903). Legislation passed in 1884 was much more comprehensive.

23. Article 6 of the Decree of July 23, 1884.

24. AP VO NC 182: Note à M. le Directeur de la Voie publique et des Promenades, de M. Alphand, Directeur des Travaux de Paris, 20 juillet 1888, emphasis in the original.

25. *Réglementation des constructions dans Paris: Examen du projet de décret sur la hauteur, le mode de construction et la salubrité intérieure des bâtiments; Observations présentées par MM. les architectes à M. le préfet de la Seine et au Conseil mu-*

nicipal de Paris (Paris: Librairie Générale de l'Architecture et des Travaux Publics, Ducher et Cie, 1882), 19, emphasis in the original.

26. An 1888 ruling of France's appeals court, the Cour de Cassation, raised the prefect's ire by judging that roads "opened by property owners on their own lands" were exempt from the domain of the decree of March 26, 1852, adding that "no decree exists which formally obliges builders to seek authorization to build on a private street." The ruling was challenged; the Ministry of Justice upheld the decision in 1890. AP VO NC 182: Notes à M. le Préfet, de M. Bouffet, pour le Ministre de l'Intérieur, Direction des Travaux de Paris, 6 mars 1889 and 6 janvier 1890.

27. AP VO NC 182: Note à M. le Préfet, de M. Bouffet, pour le Ministre de l'Intérieur, Direction des Travaux de Paris, 6 mars 1889.

28. "Ville de Paris. Rues et Places. Voie Privée. Autorisation de bâtir. Délai de 20 jours expiré," (July 20, 1906), *Recueil des Arrêts du Conseil d'État*, ser. 2, vol. 76 (1906): 650.

29. AP VO NC 238: Note sur les travaux de Paris pendant le XIXe siècle, 1800–1900.

30. AP VO NC 238: Compte rendu historique, moral et financier de 1870 à 1899, Notes de préparation.

31. Arrêté du Préfet de Police, 21 mars 1888. Reprinted in Sanlaville, *Des voies privées*.

32. AP VO11 3372, rue Saint-Philippe du Roule: Avis de l'Ingénieur en chef, 25 avril 1882.

33. It should not be forgotten that the passages of the city's working-class districts were sites of production and social reproduction vital to Paris's economy and urban culture: Joëlle Lenoir and Maurizio Gribaudi, "Les passages ouverts: La modernité oubliée de Paris capitale," *Histoire urbaine* no. 36 (March 2013): 73–104.

34. Louis Lazare, *Les quartiers de l'est de Paris et les communes suburbaines* (Paris: Bureau de la Bibliothèque Municipale, 1870); and *Les quartiers pauvres de Paris: Le XXe arrondissement* (Paris: Bureau de la Bibliothèque Municipale, 1870).

35. Louis Lazare, "Salubrité publique," *Le Courrier Municipal*, July 15, 1874, 9, emphases in the original.

36. Lazare, "Plantations parisiennes," 6, emphasis in the original.

37. Lazare, "Salubrité publique," 9.

38. AP VO11 3565, rue du Faubourg du Temple.

39. A. Carpentier and G. Frèrejouan du Saint, *Répertoire général alphabétique du droit français* (Paris: Recueil Sirey, 1902), 29:662.

40. AP VO11 3730, rue d'Uzès: Rapport de l'Ingénieur ordinaire, Direction des Travaux de Paris, 28 août 1872.

41. Paul Strauss, "Le règlement sanitaire," *Revue Municipale*, December 29, 1900, 2634.

42. Fernand Forgeron, *Guide administratif du constructeur à Paris* (Nemours: Ch. Massin et Cie, 1934); Jean Gilles-Lagrange, *L'assainissement des voies privées urbaines: La loi du 22 juillet 1912* (Toulouse: Imprimerie Toulousaine, 1914). The uncertainty surrounding privately opened streets would not be fully resolved until the interwar period; see Annie Fourcaut, *La banlieue en morceaux* (Paris: Créaphis, 2000).

43. The Prefecture of the Seine had to issue new regulations on heights on private roads in both 1904 and 1909 in response to decisions made in favor of property owners by the Conseil d'État. Préfecture de la Seine, Direction de l'extension de Paris, *Arrêté du 22 juin 1904, portant règlement sanitaire de la Ville de Paris, modifié par arrêtés des 10 novembre 1909 et 29 juillet 1913* (Paris: Imprimerie Chaix, 1919).

44. Paolo Grossi, *An Alternative to Private Property: Collective Property in the Juridical Consciousness of the Nineteenth Century,* trans. Lydia G. Cochrane (Chicago: University of Chicago Press, 1981 [1977]); Jean-Pierre Hirsch, "L'impossible propriété collective," in *La France, malade du corporatisme? XVIIIe–XXe siècles,* ed. Steven Kaplan and Philippe Minard (Paris: Belin, 2004), 171–194; Nadine Vivier, *Propriété collective et identité communale: Les biens communaux en France, 1750–1914* (Paris: Publications de la Sorbonne, 1998).

45. E[ugène] Delahaye, "La guerre aux travaux de Paris," *La Réforme du Bâtiment,* November 3, 1872, 169.

46. Jules Léveillé's 1872 report on behalf of the 7th Commission to the Conseil Général de la Seine, reprinted J[ules] D[elahaye], "Les travaux de Paris et les syndicats," *La Réforme du Bâtiment,* November 3, 1872, 173.

47. Léon Cochegrus, "Associations syndicales par arrondissement," *Bulletin de la Chambre Syndicale des Propriétés Immobilières du XIe arrondissement* (hereafter, *Bulletin de la Chambre des Propriétés*), no. 18 (February/March 1875): 4.

48. Léon Cochegrus, "A nos adhérents: Déclarations rétrospectives et complémentaires," *Bulletin de la Chambre des Propriétés,* no. 12 (April 1874): 2.

49. Léon Cochegrus, "Réitératif appel à la propriété," *Bulletin de la Chambre des Propriétés,* no. 27 (July 1876): 4.

50. "Rapport de l'Assemblée générale du 15 mai 1876," *Bulletin de la Chambre des Propriétés,* no. 26 (June 1876): 4.

51. A. Avézard, "A nos lecteurs," *Bulletin de la Chambre des Propriétés,* no. 1 (October 1872): 2.

52. "Statuts," *Bulletin de la Chambre des Propriétés,* no. 1 (October 1872): 6.

53. Beginning with Rue Neuve-des-Martyrs (today, Rue Manuel), further streets were developed on lands belonging to Poncet and the Société des Nu-propriétaires, known at the time as rues neuves Bossuet and Fénélon (today, Cité Charles Godon and Rue Milton). Information relative to this development can be found in the papers of one of its earliest proprietors, Jean-Baptiste Pochet, at the Bibliothèque Historique de la Ville de Paris. See BHVP Papiers Pochet, Ms2413: Propriétés, rue Jean-Jacques Rousseau, rue des Martyrs, Franconville.

54. BHVP Papiers Pochet, Ms2413: Règlement pour le passage des Martyrs, arrêté suivant acte reçu par M. Mayre, notaire à Paris, le 11 avril 1845.

55. BHVP Papiers Pochet, Ms2413: Note pour MM. Patoueille, le Bant et Ledreux, commissaires-surveillants du nouveau quartier des Martyrs, Appelants, contre MM. Leperdriel et Pochet-Desroches, intimés, 30 novembre 1854.

56. Amina Sellali-Boukhalfa, "Sous la ville, jadis la campagne: Une mosaïque de lotissements privés à l'origine de l'urbanisation de Belleville et de Charonne, 1820–1902" (PhD diss., University of Paris 8, 2002).

57. This law was passed on June 21, 1865. Its legal precedents stretched back to the edicts on draining marshland issued under Henri IV in 1599 and 1604.

58. "Les syndicats pour l'exécution des travaux de Paris," *La Réforme du Bâtiment,* November 10, 1872, 177.

59. This principle applied even in the absence of an official association of owners. See, for instance, the favorable reception of the development proposal from "reasonable property owners" on Avenue Niel: AP D.5 K3 20, 1885, p. 264. Some associations formed spontaneously and stepped forward to support proposed works in their area; see, for example, "Syndicats de propriétaires: L'avenue d'Antin et la rue Legendre," *La Réforme du Bâtiment,* January 4, 1874, 1.

60. "Les syndicats pour l'exécution des travaux de Paris," 177.

61. L. Delanney, *Les associations syndicales* (Paris: Chamerot et Renouard, 1891). On the complexity of representing intermediary interests in French political culture, see Pierre Rosanvallon, *Le modèle politique français: La société civile contre le jacobinisme de 1789 à nos jours* (Paris: Éditions du Seuil, 2004).

62. Observations of M. Clément, cited in Georges Michel, "La nouvelle législation sur les syndicats urbains," *Économiste Français,* December 1, 1888, 665.

63. This issue came to the fore in the debates leading to the passage of the law in 1888. The first *projet de loi,* presented in 1877, had maintained the "intérêt collectif" of the 1865 law. See AP Archives de la Chambre de Commerce et d'Industrie de Paris, 2ETP/1/8/21 1: Rapport fait au nom de la commission chargée d'examiner la proposition de loi, adoptée par la Chambre des députés, ayant pour objet de modifier la loi du 21 juin 1865 sur les associations syndicales.

64. Guyot would also become minister of public works in the late 1880s, as well as editor of the *Journal des Économistes.* For his connection with Ménier, see his biographical note in Adolphe Robert, Edgar Bourloton, and Gaston Cougny, eds., *Dictionnaire des parlementaires français de 1789 à 1889* (Paris: Bourloton, 1889–1891).

65. "Les travaux de Paris par l'impôt sur le capital," *La Réforme du Bâtiment,* September 28, 1873, 154. See also Émile-Justin Ménier, *Les travaux de Paris par l'impôt sur le capital* (Paris: Plon, 1873).

66. On the significance of the 1807 legislation, see Marcel Roncayolo, "Le droit et son application: Propriété, intérêt publique, urbanisme après la Révolution; Les

avatars de la législation impériale," in *Lectures de villes: Formes et temps*, rev. ed. (Marseille: Éditions Parenthèses, 2002), 317–330.

67. Georges Ripert, "Étude sur les plus-values indirectes résultant de l'exécution des travaux publics" (doctoral thesis, University of Aix-Marseille Law School) (Paris: Rousseau, 1904).

68. Jurist and commissioner at the Conseil d'État Octave Le Vavasseur de Précourt, cited in Ripert, "Étude sur les plus-values indirectes," 61–62.

69. Adrien Veber, "Les plus-values immobilières: La loi du 16 septembre 1807," *Revue Municipale*, August 12, 1899, 1487–1492. For a summary of projects to collect portions of this wealth by governments across the globe at the end of the nineteenth century, see Georges Vogt, *L'imposition des plus-values immobilières* (Alger: Imprimerie Gojosso, 1914); Jean-Pierre Gaudin, *L'avenir en plan: Technique et politique dans la prévision urbaine, 1900–1930* (Seyssel, France: Éditions du Champ Vallon, 1985); Robert Andelson, ed., *Land-Value Taxation Around the World* (Malden, MA: Blackwell, 2000); Matthew Cragoe and Paul Readman, eds., *The Land Question in Britain, 1750–1950* (New York: Palgrave Macmillan, 2010).

70. James Mill, *Elements of Political Economy*, 3rd ed. (London: Baldwin, Cradock, and Joy, 1826), chap. 4, sec. 5: "Taxes on Rent"; John Stuart Mill, *Principles of Political Economy, with Some of Their Applications to Social Philosophy* (London: J. W. Parker, 1848), bk. 5, chap. 2: "Of the General Principles of Taxation"; Henry George, *Progress and Poverty*, rev. ed. (London: W. Reeves, 1884); Paul Leroy-Beaulieu, *Essai sur la répartition des richesses*, 3rd ed. (Paris: Guillaumin et Cie, 1888), chap. 7, "De la propriété urbaine."

71. Maurice Halbwachs, *La politique foncière des municipalités* (*Les Cahiers du Socialiste*, no. 3) (Paris: Librairie du Parti Socialiste, 1908), 3–4; Léon Walras, "Théorie mathématique du prix des terres et de leur rachat par l'état," in *Théorie mathématique de la richesse sociale* (Lausanne: Corbaz et Cie, 1883), 177–253; Charles Gide, "De quelques nouvelles doctrines sur la propriété foncière," *Journal des Économistes*, May 15, 1883, 169–199. See also Émile de Laveleye, "La propriété terrienne et le paupérisme," *Revue Scientifique de la France et de l'Étranger* (1880): 708–710; Luigi Einaudi, "La municipalisation du sol dans les grandes villes," *Devenir Social* (January/February 1898): 1–42; and the discussion of the Société d'Économie Politique, "L'impôt sur la plus-value des immeubles," *Journal des Économistes* (December 1910): 482–487.

72. AP D.5 K3 16: Procès-verbaux des séances du Conseil Municipal, 16 May 1886, Réponse de M. Manier à un Rapport de M. Villard, 710–715.

73. Grossi, *An Alternative to Private Property*. For studies of the property question in Algeria, see Maurice Pouyanne, *La propriété foncière en Algérie* (Alger: Adolphe Jourdan, 1900); Rodolphe Dareste, *De la propriété en Algérie* (Paris: Challamel, 1864). Among secondary works, see Didier Guignard, "Les inventeurs de la tradition 'melk' et 'arch' en Algérie," in *Les acteurs des transformations foncières autour de la Méditerranée au XIXe siècle*, ed. Vanessa Guéno et Didier Guignard

(Paris: Editions Karthala, 2013), 49–93; Alain Sainte-Marie, "Législation foncière et société rurale: L'application de la loi du 26 juillet 1873 dans les douars de l'Algérois," *Études Rurales,* no. 57 (January–March 1975): 61–87.

74. Cited by Walras, "Théorie mathématique du prix des terres," 178.

75. Highlighting the urban nature of this phenomenon, Halbwachs's discussion of the appropriation of land-value increases focused on the "rente foncière urbaine" rather than on a general "unearned increment."

76. Paul Leroy-Beaulieu, *Traité théorique et pratique de l'économie,* 3rd ed. (Paris: Guillaumin, 1900), 1:691–692.

77. Paul Leroy-Beaulieu, *Essai sur la répartition des richesses et sur la tendance à une moindre inégalité des conditions* (Paris: Guillaumin, 1881), 183.

78. Leroy-Beaulieu, *Essai sur la répartition des richesses,* 186, 206. This shift was characteristic of a broader transformation in economic thought, away from a labor theory of value in favor of a market-driven, supply-and-demand model of value. See the entry "Valeur" by political economist Hippolyte Passy in Charles Coquelin and Guillaumin, eds., *Dictionnaire de l'économie politique* (Paris: Guillaumin et Cie, 1873), 2:806–815.

79. Halbwachs, *La politique foncière des municipalités,* 6.

80. Léon Cochegrus, "Associations syndicales par arrondissement," *Bulletin de la Chambre des Propriétés,* no. 18 (February/March 1875): 3.

81. Léon Cochegrus, "L'émancipation de la propriété en France: Demande d'extension de la loi du 21 juin 1865," *Bulletin de la Chambre des Propriétés,* no. 27 (July 1876): 1–3.

82. "Associations syndicales," *La Réforme du Bâtiment,* February 4, 1877, 18.

83. "Proposition de loi ayant pour objet d'étendre à certains travaux des villes les dispositions de la loi du 21 juin 1865, sur les associations syndicales, présentée par MM. Charles Floquet et Martin Nadaud, députés; Séance du 1er mars 1877, Annexe no. 798," *Journal Officiel de la République Française* (March/April 1877): 1955–1957.

84. Léon Cochegrus, "Représentation de la Chambre syndicale devant la Commission spéciale des députés chargée de l'examen de la loi du 21 juin 1865," *Bulletin de la Chambre des Propriétés,* no. 48 (December 1878/January 1879): 2, 3.

85. For previous unsuccessful efforts in the legislature, see "Associations syndicales dans les villes," *La Réforme du Bâtiment,* June 22, 1879, 98; "Chambre des députés: Dépôt d'une proposition de loi ayant pour objet d'étendre à certains travaux des villes les dispositions de la loi sur les associations syndicales; Déclaration d'urgence," *Journal Officiel* (November 26, 1885), 93–94. Senate debates leading to the 1888 law are summarized in Georges Gain, "Étude sur les associations syndicales (suite)," *Annales du Régime des Eaux* 3, no. 1 (1889): 65–98.

86. AP D.5 K3 24: Séance du 28 mars 1887, Exécution des opérations de voirie votées par le Conseil et approuvées par la loi du 19 juillet 1886, Renvoi à la 3e Commission de diverses propositions, 634–635.

87. AP D.5 K3 17: Séance du 27 décembre 1888, Communication de M. Yves Guyot au sujet de la loi récente qui modifie la législation sur les associations syndicales, 1108.

88. See Ministère des Travaux Publics, *Recueil des lois, ordonnances, décrets, règlements et circulaires concernant les différents services du Ministère des travaux publics (ancien Recueil Potiquet)* (Paris: Jousset, 1894), 89–103. Associations appeared earlier in the suburbs of the city, taking advantage of the diversity of rural roads in order to benefit from the law of June 21, 1865. Associations formed under the law of December 22, 1888, appear to have been slightly more numerous in the suburbs, but they did not form significantly earlier than in Paris.

89. The formation of these associations required the publication of the act of association in the *Recueil des Actes Administratifs, Bulletin Officiel d'Information de la Préfecture de Paris et de la Préfecture de Police.* These are found in the "Partie Municipale" for the city of Paris.

90. They concerned Rue de Pondichéry (15th arrondissement, 1900), Rue Jean-Vaury (14th, 1910), Boulevard Chauvelot (15th, 1910), Cité Traeger (18th, 1910), Rue de la Grotte (15th, 1912), Passage Charles-Bertheau and Impasses Elisabeth, Myrtile, et Valentin (13th, 1912), Rue de Lyannes (20th, 1912), and Rue Philibert-Lucot (13th, 1913).

91. The observation is attributed to Senator Paul Strauss from a series of 1911 debates on hygienic legislation applying to private streets. See Gilles-Lagrange, *L'assainissement des voies privées urbaines,* 39.

92. At the turn of the century, the majority of private streets were located in the city's poorest neighborhoods. In 1898, out of 1,432 private streets, 163 were located in the 20th arrondissement; 159 in the 11th; 137 in the 15th; 133 in the 18th; and 131 in the 19th. See AP VO NC 238: Compte rendu historique, moral et financier de 1870 à 1899, Notes de préparation.

93. "Arrêté préfectoral 1er mars 1913: Nomination d'un porteur de contraintes pour le recouvrement des taxes de l'Association syndicale des propriétaires de la rue Jean-Vaury;" "Arrêté préfectoral 19 février 1914: Désignation d'un porteur de contraintes pour le recouvrement des taxes de l'Association syndicale des propriétaires du bd Chauvelot," *Recueil des Actes Administratifs,* 1913, 1914.

94. Georges Liet-Veaux, *Les associations syndicales de propriétaires* (Paris: Sirey, 1947), 4–5.

95. Michel, *La cause des propriétaires.*

96. "Notre bulletin," *Journal des Propriétaires et des Locataires: Organe Officiel de la Chambre Syndicale des Propriétaires d'Amiens,* December 15, 1891, 2.

97. Gabriel-Victor-Jules Demontzey, "Études sur le développement parallèle de la propriété mobilière et de la propriété immobilière en droit français" (doctoral thesis, University of Strasbourg Law School) (Strasbourg: Imprimerie Huder, 1854), 2.

98. "Défendons-nous!," *Journal des Propriétaires et des Locataires: Organe Officiel de la Chambre Syndicale des Propriétaires d'Amiens,* March 15, 1892, 26–28. See

also Boucher d'Argis, "La Ligue pour la propriété et la liberté," in the issue of February 15, 1892, 19.

99. Émile Agnel, *Code-manuel des propriétaires et locataires de maisons, hôteliers, aubergistes et logeurs* (Paris: Cosse et Marchal, 1874).

100. F. V., "Causerie foncière," *Grand Journal Officiel des Locations et de la Vente des Terrains et Immeubles,* October 1–15, 1884, 19.

101. "Défendons-nous!"

102. Alessandro Stanziani, ed., *Dictionnaire historique de l'économie-droit, XVIIIe–XXe siècles* (Paris: Maison des Sciences de l'Homme, 2007).

103. Torre-Schwab, *Essai sur la construction juridique,* 38.

104. Jean-Yves Grenier, "Valeur fondamentale et spéculation dans l'économie politique et le droit (fin XVIIe–XIXe siècles)," in *Le capitalisme au futur antérieur: Crédit et spéculation en France, fin XVIIIe–début XXe siècles,* ed. Nadine Levratto and Alessandro Stanziani (Brussels: Bruyland, 2011), 19–67.

105. Alexandre Weill, *Qu'est-ce que le propriétaire d'une maison à Paris, suite de Paris inhabitable* (Paris: Dentu, 1860), 6, emphasis in the original.

106. Daumard, *Maisons de Paris,* esp. chap. 6.

107. Information on property transfers from the *sommier foncier* (Archives de l'Enregistrement) at the Archives de Paris: DQ18 1466, DQ18 1473, DQ18 1433, and DQ18 3128.

108. Information from the *Annuaire des propriétaires,* 1910 ed.

109. Bonin, *L'argent en France depuis 1880,* 241; Hautcoeur, *Le marché financier,* chaps. 9 and 14; Alex Preda, "The Rise of the Popular Investor: Financial Knowledge and Investing in England and France, 1840–1880," *Sociological Quarterly* 42, no. 2 (2001): 205–232.

110. A[lexis] Bailleux de Marisy, "Le prêt à l'intérêt," *Revue des Deux Mondes,* February 15, 1878, 940; Alfred Neymarck, *Le morcellement des valeurs mobilières: Les salaires, la part du capital et du travail* (Paris: Bureaux de la Revue Politique et Parlementaire, 1896).

111. Paul Leroy-Beaulieu, *L'art de placer et gérer sa fortune* (Paris: Ch. Delagrave, 1906), chap. 2; Alfred Neymarck, *Que doit-on faire de son argent?* (Paris: Marchal et Godde, 1913).

112. Onésime Masselin, "Des effets du krach de la bourse sur les placements immobiliers," *Le Foncier,* January 31, 1882.

113. Cited in Anne-Marie Patault, *Introduction historique au droit des biens* (Paris: Presses Universitaires de France, 1989), 211.

114. R. Défrétière, *Essai sur la condition des marchands de biens: Les données actuelles du problème de la commercialité des opérations immobilières* (Paris: Presses Universitaires de France, 1923).

115. For a review, see Émile Ollivier, "Acheter un immeuble avec intention de le revendre, c'est faire un acte de commerce," *Revue Pratique de Droit Français* 1

(February 15–August 1, 1856): 241–259; Eugène Garsonnet, "Les opérations qui se font sur les immeubles sont-elles des actes de commerce?," *Revue Critique de Législation et de Jurisprudence* 35 (1869): 325–361; Édouard Fuzier-Herman, ed., *Répertoire général alphabétique du droit français* (Paris: Société du Recueil Général des Lois et des Arrêts et du Journal du Palais, 1886), 1:554–563.

116. Cited in Défrétière, *Essai sur la condition des marchands de biens,* 22.

117. Arrêt du 14 février 1868, Cour de Paris, *Dalloz* 1868, pt. 2, 208–210.

118. Arrêt du 18 avril 1882, Chambre civile, *Dalloz* 1883, pt. 1, 64. Raymond-Théodore Troplong, *Commentaire du contrat de société en matière civile et commerciale* (Bruxelles: Meline, Cans et Cie, 1843), 134.

119. André Jacquemont, "La spéculation sur les immeubles et ses mécomptes," in *Premier congrès international de la propriété bâtie,* 201.

120. Jacquemont, "La spéculation," 204, emphasis in the original.

121. Torre-Schwab, *Essai sur la construction juridique,* 46.

122. Dreyfus, "De l'exclusion des opérations immobilières," 50–57; Alfred Jauffret, "L'extension du droit commercial à des activités traditionnellement civiles," in *Études offertes à Pierre Kayser,* vol. 2 (Aix-en-Provence: Presses Universitaires d'Aix-Marseille, 1979), 59–100; Paul Didier, "La terre et le droit commercial," in *Études de droit commercial, à la mémoire de Henry Carbillac* (Paris: Librairies techniques, 1968), 153–166; Joseph Frossard, "L'immeuble et le droit commercial," *Revue Trimestrielle de Droit Commercial* 19 (1966): 535–554.

123. Henri Mouret, *Sociétés anonymes à participation ouvrière et actions de travail* (Paris: Librairie Générale de Droit et de Jurisprudence, 1919).

124. "Comment placer son argent," *Circulaire Financière Bi-Mensuelle de la Société Immobilière, Commerciale et Civil,* January 15, 1911, 2.

125. ANMT 2001 026 650, Crédit Foncier, Rapports annuels.

126. ANMT 65 AQ I 100: La Fourmi Immobilière, SA. Compte rendu de l'Assemblée générale du 3 mars 1911, 13.

127. BHVP Actualités Série 78, Logement: Client solicitation letter "La Mobilisation Foncière, J.-B. Boisselot," August 25, 1906.

128. "Causerie immobilière," *Bulletin de la Chambre des Propriétés* (December 1, 1906): 539, emphasis in the original.

129. Sylvie Devigne, "La commission extraparlementaire du cadastre de 1891 à 1905: Le projet de transformation du cadastre français en cadastre juridique," in *De l'estime au cadastre en Europe: Les systèmes cadastraux au XIXe et XXe siècles,* ed. Florence Bourillon, Pierre Clergeot, and Nadine Vivier (Paris: Comité pour l'histoire économique et financière de la France, 2008), 217–231.

130. Charles Brouilhet, "La propriété bâtie et la question du livre foncier," in *Congrès de la propriété bâtie de France* (Lyon: Imprimerie du Salut Public, 1894), 3.

131. Georges Deloison, "Les livres fonciers," in *Congrès de la propriété bâtie de France,* 24, 25, emphasis in the original.

132. See the roundtable "Société d'économie politique, réunion du 5 mars 1887: Le système des exclusions de saisie en faveur du foyer domestique, connu aux États-Unis sous le nom d'*homestead* serait-il applicable en France et est-il conforme aux lois économiques?," *Journal des Économistes* (March 1887): 431–443. On the United States, see Clare Priest, "Creating an American Property Law: Alienability and Its Limits in American History," *Harvard Law Review* 120, no. 2 (December 2006): 385–459.

133. Hervé Bastien, "Le bien de famille insaisissable: Politique et législation de la petite propriété sous la IIIe République," *Études Rurales,* nos. 110–112 (1988): 377–389.

134. "Jeudi 31 mai: La propriété bâtie et le crédit hypothécaire dans les différents états; Rapport de M. Hernance, docteur en droit," in *Premier congrès international de la propriété bâtie,* 175.

135. Ibid., 176.

136. Timothy Mitchell, "The Properties of Markets," in *Do Economists Make Markets? On the Performativity of Economics,* ed. Donald MacKenzie, Fabian Muniesa, and Lucia Siu (Princeton, NJ: Princeton University Press, 2007), 244–275.

137. "Consultation de M. Waldeck-Rousseau sur la légalité des Chambres syndicales de propriétaires d'immeubles urbains," *Journal des Propriétaires et des Locataires: Organe Officiel de la Chambre Syndicale des Propriétaires d'Amiens,* September 15, 1892, 76.

138. The possession of land through its occupation and exploitation was continually supported by jurisprudence and legislation, as opposed to "property," defined by ownership by title without (necessary) use. See Donald R. Kelley and Bonnie G. Smith, "What Was Property? Legal Dimensions of the Social Question in France (1789–1848)," *Proceedings of the American Philosophical Society* 128, no. 3 (1984): 200–230; and Bastien, "Le bien de famille insaisissable."

139. "Congrès national de la propriété bâtie à Bordeaux," *Recueil de Jurisprudence Immobilière et de Législation du Bâtiment* (July 1905): 334, 335.

140. Indeed, it is at the turn of the century that the Chambre des Propriétés begins publishing its quarterly apartment rental bulletin *Le Trimestriel Location,* thus engaging in distributive activities similar to that of the burgeoning field of real estate brokerage.

141. "L'habitation et la santé publique à Paris," *Le Temps,* January 10, 1912. Quotes attributed to M. G. Mesureur, director of public assistance.

142. Yankel Fijalkow, *La construction des îlots insalubres: Paris, 1850–1945* (Paris: L'Harmattan, 1998).

143. Henri Talamon, *Le classement des voies privées* (Nice: Léo Barma, 1911), 6, 8.

4. The Unceasing Marketplace

1. See "Agences d'affaires" in *Annuaire Didot-Bottin,* 1880.

2. Michael S. Smith, *The Emergence of Modern Business Enterprise in France, 1800–1930* (Cambridge, MA: Harvard University Press, 2006), pt. 1, chap. 3.

3. Félix Desmier, *Des agents d'affaires et spécialement des intermédiaires en fonds de commerce* (Paris: Rousseau et Cie, 1916), 7–8, 3. See also Louis Cirou, *De la gérance d'immeubles* (Paris: A. Pedone, 1899).

4. These included groups such as the Chambre Syndicale des Agences de Vente et de Location de Propriété (ca. 1905) (Syndicate of Property Sales and Rental Agencies) and the Chambre Syndicale des Intermédiaires et des Mandataires en Vente de Fonds de Commerce et Industries (1913) (Syndicate of Intermediaries in Commercial and Industrial Property Sales).

5. Maxime Petibon, *Manuel officiel des affaires immobilières et foncières de la Ville de Paris* (Paris: Propriété de la Foncière Immobilière Parisienne, 1899–1903); Ministère du Commerce, *Résultats statistiques du recensement des industries et professions [Dénombrement général de la population du 29 mars 1896]* (Paris: Imprimerie Nationale, 1899), vol. 1. Figures from the *Annuaire Didot-Bottin* were compiled by sampling the commercial listings at five-year intervals from 1870 to 1930, with the additional inclusion of volumes from 1855, 1862, and 1866.

6. Arthur D. Austin, "Real Estate Boards and Multiple Listing Systems as Restraints of Trade," *Columbia Law Review* 70, no. 8 (December 1970): 1325–1364.

7. On these "commercial professionals" in the United States, see Jeffrey Hornstein, *A Nation of Realtors®: A Cultural History of the Twentieth-Century American Middle Class* (Durham, NC: Duke University Press, 2005).

8. Gabriel Hanotaux, *Du choix d'une carrière* (Paris: Flammarion, 1902), 107–108, 112–113.

9. Henry Becque, *Les corbeaux: Pièce en quatre actes, représentée pour la première fois, à la Comédie-française, le 14 septembre 1882* (Paris: Comédie-Française, 1984), act 2, scene 8.

10. Ibid.

11. In some versions, he is referred to as "Duhamel."

12. Ibid., act 3, scene 4.

13. Honoré de Balzac, *Code des gens honnêtes ou l'art de ne pas être dupe des fripons* (Levallois Perret: Manya, 1990 [1825]).

14. Patricia O'Brien, "White-Collar Crime in Late-Nineteenth-Century France," *Proceedings of the Western Society for French History* 9 (1981): 328–336.

15. The weight of succession matters in notary affairs in the nineteenth century is explored by Jean-Paul Poisson, "Introduction à une analyse de contenu du 'Journal des Notaires' (Années 1829, 1909, 1969)," in his *Notaires et société: Travaux d'histoire et de sociologie notariales* (Paris: Economica, 1985), 1:49–71.

16. Jean-Paul Poisson, "Un lieu de mémoire, l'Étude du notaire," in his *Études notariales* (Paris: Economica, 1996), 5–30.

17. The law of March 23, 1855, on the publicity of mortgage and land-sale records reasserted provisions in the law of 11 brumaire an VII (November 1, 1798) regarding the transcriptions of land transactions that had been, in the interim, omitted from

the Civil Code. It should be noted that property purchasers often carried out transcriptions on their own behalf, with some legal commentators suggesting that a notary required a specific extension of his mandate to undertake this task. Moreover, although it was a subject of debate, contracts known as "sous seing privé," or those not authenticated by a notary, could also be transcribed at the Conservateur des Hypothèques, thus entirely bypassing the need for the intervention of a notary. See Troplong, *Privilèges et hypothèques: Commentaire de la loi du 23 mars 1855 sur la transcription en matière hypothécaire* (Paris: Charles Hingray, 1856), esp. 155–157; and M. Flandin, *De la transcription en matière hypothécaire, ou explication de la loi du 23 mars 1855 et des dispositions du Code Napoléon relatives à la transcription des donations et des substitutions,* 2 vols. (Paris: Imprimerie et librairie générale de jurisprudence, Cosse et Marchal, 1861). As Troplong notes, the 1855 legislation in no way sought to establish a monopoly of notaries with regard to property sales, maintaining, on the contrary, the sanctity of private contract: "[This legislation] does not destroy the excellent and truly philosophical principle by which land is transferred between contracting parties solely on the basis of their consent" (*Privilèges et hypothèques,* 12).

18. See Poisson, "Histoire et statistiques notariales: Une étude parisienne en 1826," in *Notaires et société,* 1:457–464; and "L'étude de l'évolution économique au XIXe et XXe siècle par celle de l'activité notariale (premières données statistiques sur un Office parisien)," in *Notaires et société,* 1:465–479.

19. "Décret no. 55-22 du 4 janvier 1955 portant réforme de la publicité foncière," *Journal Officiel de la République Française* (hereafter *JO*), January 7, 1955, 346–357.

20. Ernest Vallier, *Les avoués au XXe siècle* (Paris: L. Larose et L. Tenin, 1908), 21.

21. *Annuaire statistique de la Ville de Paris* (Paris: Imprimerie Municipale, 1880–1914).

22. Philip T. Hoffman, Gilles Postel-Vinay, and Jean-Laurent Rosenthal, "No Exit: Notarial Bankruptcies and the Evolution of Financial Intermediation in Nineteenth-Century Paris," in *Finance, Intermediaries, and Economic Development,* ed. Stanley L. Engerman, Philip T. Hoffman, Jean-Laurent Rosenthal, and Kenneth L. Sokoloff (Cambridge: Cambridge University Press, 2003), 75–108.

23. Article 12 of the ordinance of January 4, 1843, barred notaries from stock speculation, commercial operations, banking or brokerage activities, as well as from participating in the administration of financial, commercial, or industrial enterprises, engaging in building speculation, or taking personal interests in affairs for which they acted as legal advisors. Legislation of January 30, 1890, obliged notaries to turn over any funds held in deposit on behalf of their clients for a period of longer than six months to the Caisse des Dépôts et Consignations, a state-run deposit bank. J.-Joseph Pagès, *Le monopole des notaires et les avantages de la vénalité des études* (Toulouse: Imprimerie Ouvrière, 1907), 94.

24. Philip T. Hoffman, Gilles Postel-Vinay, and Jean-Laurent Rosenthal, *Priceless Markets: The Political Economy of Credit in Paris, 1660–1870* (Chicago: University of Chicago Press, 2001), esp. chaps. 10 and 11.

25. Ernest de Chabrol-Chaméane, *Dictionnaire de législation usuelle, contenant les notions du droit civil, commercial, criminel et administratif* (Paris: n.p., 1835), 1:164–165; Timothy Richard Brown, "The Language of Public Service and Private Interest in France: The Vexed Case of the Paris Auctioneers, 1750–1848" (PhD diss., Stanford University, 2000), chap. 1.

26. Desmond Fitz-Gibbon, "Assembling the Property Market in Imperial Britain, c. 1750–1925" (PhD diss., University of California, Berkeley, 2011); David Scobey, *Empire City: The Making and Meaning of the New York City Landscape* (Philadelphia: Temple University Press, 2002), chap. 3. In 1880 Lyon adopted the use of a central auction room on Paris's model: *Chambre d'adjudications des notaires de Lyon, règlement* (Lyon: Imprimerie Mougin-Rusand, 1885).

27. Anon., *Mémoire sur la question de savoir si les notaires ont le droit exclusif de procéder, par enchères et adjudication, aux ventes volontaires, en actes publics ou non, de biens immeubles* (signed Évit) (Brussels: n.p., 1846); Anon., *Développements des principes sur la forme légale des ventes volontaires d'immeubles: Faisant suite aux observations des notaires de Paris, sur le même sujet* (Paris: Imprimerie de Clousier, n.d.); Albert André, *Traité pratique des ventes d'immeubles amiables, judiciaires, et administratives* (Paris: Marchal et Billard, 1894), 1:269–271.

28. Chambre des Avoués de Première Instance de la Seine, *Ventes judiciaires de biens immeubles: Loi du 22 juin 1841; mai 1894* (Paris: A. Maulde, 1894), 35–40.

29. Bibliothèque de la Chambre des Notaires (hereafter BCN), Circulaires, May 4, 1848.

30. Albert Amiaud, *Le tarif général et raisonné des notaires: Étude sur les principes et le mode de rémunération des actes notariés* (Paris: Marchal, Billard et Cie, 1875), 729.

31. Donald MacKenzie, Fabian Muniesa, and Lucia Siu, eds., *Do Economists Make Markets? On the Performativity of Economics* (Princeton, NJ: Princeton University Press, 2007).

32. Maïr Baron, *Du rôle du notaire dans la vente immobilière par adjudication purement volontaire* (doctoral thesis, University of Paris Law School) (Paris: Imprimerie Henri Jouve, 1909), 19–22.

33. Marie-France Garcia-Parpet, "The Social Construction of a Perfect Market," in MacKenzie, Muniesa, and Siu, *Do Economists Make Markets?*, 20–53.

34. BCN, Circulaires, January 30, 1846.

35. *Dictionnaire du notariat,* 4th ed. (Paris: Journal des notaires et des avocats, 1856–1887), 3:61–62; M. Rivière, ed., *Pandectes françaises: Nouveau répertoire de doctrine, de législation et de jurisprudence* (Paris: Chevalier-Marescq et Cie, 1888), 3:154–

155; Émile Paultre, "Adjudication," *Collection des observations pratiques publiées par la Revue du Notariat* (Paris: Bureau de la Revue, 1869), 1:10–17.

36. A. de Coston, *De l'office du juge en matière de ventes judiciaires d'immeubles* (Paris: Marchal et Billard, 1891), 131–132.

37. BCN, Circulaires, June 7, 1821; November 23, 1855.

38. According to Adeline Daumard's calculations, they represented less than half of total sales (from 21 percent to 47 percent) for her sample (every five years from 1855 to 1880). See Adeline Daumard, *Maisons de Paris et propriétaires parisiens au XIXe siècle (1809–1880)* (Paris: Editions Cujas, 1965), 6, 54–55.

39. "Chronique foncière," *Le XIXe Siècle,* May 23, 1893.

40. BCN, Circulaires, March 20, 1841, and June 30, 1847.

41. BCN, Circulaires, March 11, 1882. Notaries did not, for instance, establish journals of record that matched the *Estates Gazette,* published in England from 1858, or the *Real Estate Record and Builders' Guide,* published in New York City from 1868.

42. "Chronique immobilière," *Le Matin,* November 13, 1893.

43. Ibid., July 11, 1892.

44. Édouard Fuzier-Herman, Adrien Carpentier, and Georges-Marie-René Frèrejouan du Saint, *Répertoire général alphabétique du droit français* (Paris: Libraire de la Société du Recueil Général des Lois et des Arrêts et du Journal du Palais, 1904), 33:925; Lucien Recullet, *Le secret professionnel des notaires* (Paris: Journal des Notaires et des Avocats, 1905), 259. See also Ezra N. Suleiman, *Private Power and Centralization in France: The* Notaires *and the State* (Princeton NJ: Princeton University Press, 1987), 77.

45. Amiaud, *Le tarif général et raisonné des notaires,* 723.

46. "Le notariat," *La Spéculation devant les Tribunaux: Recueil de jurisprudence financière,* November 28, 1881, 482, 483.

47. BCN, Circulaires, October 23, 1919.

48. "Notre programme," *Le Mandataire du Notariat,* January 1, 1874, 1; "Administration du Mandataire du Notariat," *Le Mandataire du Notariat,* January 1, 1874, 7.

49. Bernard Cohen-Hadad calculated an average cost of nearly 415,000 francs for a notary's office under the July Monarchy: "Comptes rendus: Notaires et notariat parisiens sous la monarchie de juillet, 1830–1847," in Jean-Paul Poisson, *Essais de Notarialogie* (Paris: Economica, 2002).

50. "Administration du Mandataire du Notariat."

51. Compagnie des Hommes d'Affaires du Département de la Seine, Statuts, 19 novembre 1876, article 27.

52. *Rapport présenté à l'Assemblée générale des hommes d'affaires du département de la Seine, le 29 novembre 1876, par M. De Saine, secrétaire de la commission d'organisation, au nom de cette commission* (n.p., n.d.), 23.

53. "Pétition: Les notaires de l'arrondissement de Charleville (Ardennes), à MM. les membres de l'Assemblée nationale," *Mandataire du Notariat,* April 1, 1874, 3–4.

Notaries would continue this effort for the next several decades. See the reaction of the Syndicat professionnel des hommes d'affaires de France et des colonies in 1913: "Petition à Monsieur le Ministre de la Justice, à l'occasion d'un vœu émis par un groupe de notaires tendant à la suppression des actes sous-seing privé et à l'obligation de l'authenticité pour les ventes de toute nature," *La France Immobilière,* November 1–30, 1913. In the interwar period: "Le statut des agents immobiliers: Extrait du rapport de l'Assemblée générale de l'Association nationale des notaires de France," *Bulletin Officiel de la Chambre Syndicale des Agents Immobiliers de France* (hereafter *Bulletin des Agents Immobiliers*), no. 79 (July/August 1936). See also Archives de Paris (hereafter AP), Archives de la Chambre de Commerce et d'Industrie de Paris (hereafter CCIP), 2/ETP/3/4/13 8: "Réglementation de la profession de mandataire en vente de fonds de commerce et immeubles, Note, 16 octobre 1934."

54. *Enquête pour contribuer à l'étude du projet de réglementation de la profession d'agent d'affaires* (n.p., n.d [1907]), 3–4. On emulation and self-fashioning, see Carol E. Harrison, *The Bourgeois Citizen in Nineteenth-Century France: Gender, Sociability, and the Uses of Emulation* (Oxford: Oxford University Press, 1999).

55. For example, the real estate and property management firm of Langlois et Cie traces its roots to such a position at the end of the 18th century. Document, "Messieurs Langlois et Compagnie, bref portrait historique," communicated to the author by Jean-Pierre Langlois, May 2008.

56. "Agent d'affaires" and "Homme d'affaires," *Dictionnaire de l'Académie française,* 6th ed. (1832–1835), 39, 896.

57. Édouard Charton, *Guide pour le choix d'un état, ou Dictionnaire des professions* (Paris: Vve Lenormant, 1842), 4.

58. Émile Gazagnes, *Étude sur les agences d'affaires* (Paris: V. Giard et E. Brière, 1898), 71; Jeanne Fage, *Les agences d'affaires et le droit* (Tarbes: Éditions A. Hunault, 1928), 16.

59. The preferred status for *agents immobiliers,* no longer calling themselves agents d'affaires by the early decades of the twentieth century, was one of hire of services, which immunized their commissions from the arbitrary reductions imposed by commercial courts. These institutions preferred to classify the agent as a salaried representative throughout the nineteenth century and into the twentieth. See, for example, M. Millot, "Tribune libre: Le caractère juridique de la profession d'sgent immobilier," *Bulletin des Agents Immobiliers* 74 (February 1936): 2–3; "Agents d'affaires," in *Dictionnaire du commerce, de l'industrie et de la banque,* ed. Yves Guyot and Arthur Raffolovitch (Paris: Guillaumin et Cie, 1899–1901).

60. Suspicion of the estate agent was not isolated to France. See, for example, Alexander Rainy, *A Brief Exposition of Some Existing Abuses regarding the Transfer of Real Property by Public Auction and Private Contract* (London: n.p., 1838); and Alexander Rainy, *On the Transfer of Property by Public Auction and Private Contract: The Reciprocity or Allowance System, etc.* (London: n.p., 1845).

61. Balzac, *Code des gens honnêtes;* E. F. Vidocq, *Les voleurs, physiologie de leurs mœurs et de leur langage,* vol. 1 (Paris: Chez l'Auteur, 1837).

62. Gaetan Delmas, "Les agents d'affaires," in *Les Français peints par eux-mêmes* (Paris: L. Curmer, 1840), 3:137–159.

63. Charton, *Guide pour le choix d'un état,* 1–5.

64. Aurélian Scholl, *Fruits défendus* (Paris: Victor-Havard, 1885), 211, 213, 215.

65. The classic statement on this matter is David S. Landes, "French Entrepreneurship and Industrial Growth in the Nineteenth Century," *Journal of Economic History* 9, no. 1 (May 1949): 45–61. The development of the historiography on French economic development is traced in François Crouzet, "The Historiography of French Economic Growth in the Nineteenth Century," *Economic History Review* 56, no. 2 (2003): 215–242. For more recent work on the French path in industrial and commercial development, see the Introduction, note 20. On entrepreneurship more specifically, see Dominique Barjot, ed., *Les entrepreneurs du Second Empire* (Paris: Presses de l'Université de Paris-Sorbonne, 2003); and *Les patrons du Second Empire,* 11 vols. (Paris: Picard, 1991–2010); Hubert Bonin, "A Short History of Entrepreneurship in France (from 1780 up to Today)," in *Country Studies in Entrepreneurship: A Historical Perspective,* ed. Youssef Cassis and Ioanna Pepelasi Minoglou (Oxford: Oxford University Press, 2006), 65–97.

66. Sarah Maza, *The Myth of the French Bourgeoisie: An Essay on the Social Imaginary, 1750–1850* (Cambridge, MA: Harvard University Press, 2003).

67. Indeed, research on the eighteenth century highlights earlier, successful efforts to figure commerce as a patriotic undertaking. See John Shovlin, *The Political Economy of Virtue: Luxury, Patriotism, and the Origins of the French Revolution* (Ithaca, NY: Cornell University Press, 2006); James Livesey, "Agrarian Ideology and Commercial Republicanism in the French Revolution," *Past and Present,* no. 157 (November 1997): 94–121; Jay Smith, "Social Categories, the Language of Patriotism, and the Origins of the French Revolution: The Debate over *noblesse commerçante,*" *Journal of Modern History* 72, no. 2 (June 2000): 339–374. On France and economic liberalism, see Jean-Pierre Hirsch, "Revolutionary France, Cradle of Free Enterprise," *American Historical Review* 94, no. 5 (1989): 1281–1289; William M. Reddy, *The Rise of Market Culture: The Textile Trade and French Society, 1750–1900* (Cambridge: Cambridge University Press, 1984); Lucette Le Van-Lemesle, *Le juste ou le riche: L'enseignement de l'économie politique, 1815–1950* (Paris: Comité pour l'Histoire Économique et Financière de la France, 2004); David Todd, *L'identité économique de la France: Libre-échange et protectionnisme, 1814–1851* (Paris: B. Grasset, 2008).

68. Jean Garrigues, *La république des hommes d'affaires (1870–1990)* (Paris: Aubier, 1997). See also Richard Kuisel, *Capitalism and the State in Modern France: Renovation and Economic Management in the Twentieth Century* (Cambridge: Cambridge University Press, 1981), chap. 1; Michael S. Smith, *Tariff Reform in France, 1860–1900: The Politics of Economic Interest* (Ithaca, NY: Cornell University Press, 1980).

69. Timothy B. Smith, "The Ideology of Charity, the Image of the English Poor Law and Debates over the Right to Assistance in France, 1830–1905," *Historical Journal* 40, no. 4 (1997): 997–1032.

70. John Savage, "The Problems of Wealth and Virtue: The Paris Bar and the Generation of the Fin-de-Siècle," in *Lawyers and Vampires: Cultural Histories of Legal Professions*, ed. W. Wesley Pure and David Sugarman (Oxford: Hart, 2003), 171–210.

71. Christelle Rabier, ed., *Fields of Expertise: A Comparative History of Expert Procedures in Paris and London, 1600 to Present* (Newcastle, UK: Cambridge Scholars Pub., 2007).

72. Alessandro Stanziani, "Commerçant," in *Dictionnaire historique de l'économie-droit, XVIIIe–XXe siècles*, ed. Alessandro Stanziani (Paris: Maison des Sciences de l'homme, 2007), 49–58.

73. *Rapport présenté à l'Assemblée générale des hommes d'affaires . . . par M. De Saine*, 23.

74. Ibid., 24.

75. Bankruptcy records are held at the Archives de Paris, part of the archives of the Tribunal de Commerce, series D.11 U3. I consulted the files of any agents listed as property intermediaries (fifty) between 1870 and 1914.

76. Claude Nicolin (bankrupt: 1868; AP D.11 U3 593) worked as a tailor in Rouen, bankrupting himself twice, before coming to Paris and engaging in a commercial property sales business. Similarly, Claude Debray (bankrupt: 1870, AP D.11 U3 680) worked as a metalworker and dairyman before an expropriation indemnity allowed him to venture into the apartment rental business.

77. Bibliothèque Historique de la Ville de Paris (hereafter BHVP) Actualités Série 78, Logement: Claude Moreau, client solicitation letter (1906).

78. AP D.11 U3 593.

79. Jean-Laurent Rosenthal and Naomi Lamoreaux, "Legal Regime and Business's Organizational Choice: A Comparison of France and the United States during the Mid-Nineteenth Century," *American Law and Economic Review* 7, no. 1 (2005): 28–61.

80. AP D.11 U3 866, Rapport du Syndic.

81. AP D.11 U3 1397.

82. In 1875 the renowned firm of John Arthur et Cie drove one of its former employees, Daniel J. Costigan, bankrupt as he tried to defend his competing real estate agency from the 25,000 francs in damages his former employer demanded for the alleged violation of Costigan's hiring contract, which prohibited him from opening a similar business within seven years of leaving John Arthur et Cie. See AP D.11 U3 798.

83. E. Le Fur, "De la responsabilité et de la réductibilité du salaire de l'agent d'affaires et spécialement de l'intermédiaire en fonds de commerce" (doctoral thesis, University of Rennes Law School) (Lorient: Imprimerie du Nouvelliste, 1934).

84. *Rapport présenté à l'Assemblée générale des Hommes d'affaires . . . par M. De Saine,* 24.

85. Ibid., 25–26.

86. Ibid., 25.

87. Scholl, *Fruits défendus,* 216.

88. Randall Collins, "Market Closure and the Conflict Theory of the Professions," in *Professions in Theory and History: Rethinking the Study of the Professions,* ed. Michael Burrage and Rolf Torstendahl (London: Sage, 1990), 24–43.

89. Compagnie des Hommes d'Affaires du Département de la Seine, Statuts, 19 novembre 1876, article 28.

90. AP 1070W2 170 (Compagnie des Hommes d'Affaires de la Seine). Note, Préfecture de la Seine, Direction des Affaires Municipales, 29 novembre 1901.

91. "Courrier de Paris," *L'Illustration,* January 28, 1882.

92. On interwar regulatory plans, see articles in the *Bulletin des Agents Immobiliers:* Marcel Arnould, "Le projet de réglementation," no. 63 (January 1935); "Proposition de loi sur la réglementation de la profession d'agent immobilier," no. 80 (September/October 1936); "Assemblée générale extraordinaire: Rapport de M. Arnould," no. 81 (November 1936).

93. "Proposition de loi portant réglementation des agences d'affaires, présentée par MM. Borie, Vacher, Labrousse, Dellestalle, et Brugeilles, députés, le 28 octobre 1886," *JO,* annexe no. 1197 (April 29, 1887): 1003–1007.

94. Ibid., 1004.

95. The 1891 census counts 778 agents d'affaires in Paris with 369 employees, 50 of whom were women, compared to the only 21 female employees among the 2,241 employees that worked for the city's 747 officiers ministériels (a group that included notaries, bailiffs, and solicitors). Thirty-three out of the 778 agents d'affaires were recorded as foreigners, compared with only 15 of the 747 officiers ministériels; 5 percent of employees of agents d'affaires were of foreign origin, whereas only 1.8 percent of employees of officiers ministériels shared that status. See Préfecture de la Seine, Service de la statistique municipale, *Résultats statistiques du dénombrement de 1891 pour la Ville de Paris et le département de la Seine, et renseignements relatifs aux dénombrements antérieurs* (Paris: G. Masson, 1894), 170–171, 174–175.

96. The Syndicat Professionnel's administrative council was consistently staffed by agents identifying themselves primarily as property intermediaries.

97. "Bureau centralisateur du Syndicat professionnel des hommes d'affaires de France et des colonies," *La France Immobilière,* June 1908.

98. "Notre programme," *La France Immobilière,* June 15–30, 1897, emphasis in the original.

99. "Projet de Syndicat des hommes d'affaires de France," *La France Immobilière,* October 1897; "Assemblée générale du 9 avril 1899," *La France Immobilière,* May 15, 1899. The Syndicat Professionnel's proposal mirrored another unsuccessful

state effort from the previous year: "Proposition de loi tendant à réglementer la profession d'agent d'affaires, présentée par MM. Julien Goujon, Brindeau, vicomte de Montfort, Julien Rouland, Suchetet, comte de Pomereu, Bouclot, Rispal, Lechevallier, Quilbeuf, Leroy, Loriot, Guillement, députés, le 20 décembre 1898," *JO*, annexe no. 554, 570–571.

100. *Enquête pour contribuer à l'étude du projet de réglementation de la profession d'agent d'affaires: Poursuivie et présentée par le Syndicat professionnel des hommes d'affaires de France et des Colonies et la Compagnie des hommes d'affaires du département de la Seine* (Meaux: Imprimerie de Lalot, 1908).

101. Ibid., 2.

102. Similarly, the statutes of the short-lived Chambre Syndicale des Agents d'Affaires du Département de la Seine included as a goal of the association the pro bono representation of indigents before civil and commercial tribunals. This group was founded in 1893 and located at the Bourse de Commerce. It merged with the Compagnie des Hommes d'Affaires de la Seine in 1897. See AP 1070W9 809: Chambre Syndicale des Agents d'Affaires du Département de la Seine.

103. *Enquête pour contribuer à l'étude du projet de réglementation de la profession d'agent d'affaires,* 2.

104. Ibid., 4.

105. Ibid.

106. AP CCIP, 2/ETP/3/4/13 8: Chambre de Commerce de Beauvais et de l'Oise. Le Syndicat des Hommes d'Affaires, Rapport, 4 mai 1907, 3.

107. "Proposition de loi tendant à réglementer la profession d'agent d'affaires, 'directeur de contentieux,' mandataire en justice ou de justice, présentée par M. Jules Brunet (Dordogne), député, Session ordinaire du 3 mars 1913," *JO*, Chambre des Députés, annexe no. 2572, 105. See the discussion in the special issue of *La France Immobilière,* November 1913.

108. Jules Romains, *Les hommes de bonne volonté* (Paris: Flammarion, 1932), 4:20.

109. Ibid., 23.

110. Ibid., 25–26, 32.

111. Ibid., 26.

112. Ibid., 5:39.

113. "Programme de l'Agence Léon," *La Chronique Mobilière et Immobilière,* November 25, 1893.

114. "Un confrère," *La Chronique Mobilière et Immobilière,* May 25, 1894.

115. A. Aubert, "Aux propriétaires," *Moniteur de la Location,* February 20, 1881.

116. Hanotaux, *Du choix d'une carrière,* 111–112.

117. BHVP Actualités Série 78, Logement: Letters from C. Gosset, J.-B. Boisselot, the Agence Lagrange, William Tiffen of John Arthur et Tiffen, Charles Theuret, N. Keim & Fils, Edmond Largier of the Agence Largier, the Paris-New-York Agency

(ca. 1890–1914), and many more. AP D.18 Z1 Collection l'Esprit contains many similar solicitations from the interwar period.

118. AP VO NC 182: Lettre, Lescure à M. le Secrétaire général de la Préfecture de la Seine, 8 février 1887, and Lettre, Lescure à M. le Directeur des Travaux de Paris, 18 février 1887.

119. Romains, *Hommes de bonne volonté,* 4:34.

120. Ibid., 28.

121. Ibid.

122. Archives Nationales du Monde du Travail, 65 AQ I 31: Charles Paulet et Etienne Oudin, *Bourse immobilière: Projet de création* (Paris: A. Coulond, 1899), 1, 2.

123. Victor-Bénigne Flour de Saint-Genis, *Le crédit territorial en France et la réforme hypothécaire,* 2nd ed. (Paris: Guillaumin, 1889), li.

124. "L'épargne française et les placements immobiliers," *Le Reveil Immobilière,* April 1, 1893, 1.

125. "Pourquoi nous avons fondé *L'Annonce Immobilière,*" *L'Annonce Immobilière, Journal Hebdomadaire,* October 15, 1884, 3–4, emphasis in the original.

126. Mme Roch-Sautier patented the *Grand Journal Officiel* as a "publicity system" in 1885 (Patent 164,592, *Bulletin des Lois de la République Française* 31 [July–December 1885]: 929–930).

127. "La bourse des transactions immobilières," *Le Grand Journal Officiel des Locations et de la Vente des Terrains et Immeubles,* December 25, 1884, 25–26.

128. *Journal des Propriétaires, des Acquéreurs et des Locataires: Journal d'Annonces, Avis Divers,* January 5, 1891; *Le Guide des Locataires: Journal de l'Administration de la Bourse des Locations Immobilières,* May 1, 1874, emphasis in the original.

129. On the stock exchange as the definitive locus of modern capitalism, see Max Weber, "Stock and Commodity Exchanges [*Die Börse* (1894)]," trans. Steven Lestition, *Theory and Society* 29, no. 3 (June 2000): 305–338.

130. The Chambre Syndicale des Négociants en Immeubles de Paris, presided over by M. Sée and then Louis Deguingue, was also founded in 1919–1920 and collaborated closely with the Chambre Syndicale des Agents Immobiliers de France throughout the interwar period.

131. "Compte-rendu de l'Assemblée générale du 23 mars 1921: Rapport de M. Champonnois sur les relations réciproques entre confrères," *Bulletin des Agents Immobiliers,* 1 (July 1921).

132. Lucien Lagrave, "Pour un marché immobilier," *Le Figaro,* April 13, 1932.

133. "Assemblée générale du 27 février 1933," *Bulletin des Agents Immobiliers,* 47 (April 1933). See also "Assemblée générale extraordinaire: Rapport de M. Arnould," *Bulletin des Agents Immobiliers,* 81 (November 1936).

134. Agents were briefly regulated, along with most other occupations, under the 150 commercial and industrial committees created in 1940 by the Vichy regime. In

1943 the real estate agent was classified with "conseils et professions auxiliaires du commerce et de l'industrie." This regulation was done away with soon after the end of hostilities. *Guide professionnel des agents immobiliers et mandataires en vente de fonds de commerce de France* (Boulogne-sur-Seine: Société d'Édition des Guides Professionnels et de Publicité, 1947), 8–10. On the United States, see Hornstein, *A Nation of Realtors®*.

135. AP CCIP, 2/ETP/3/4/13 8: Rapport présenté, au nom de la Commission de Législation commerciale et industrielle par M. Godet, 26 juin 1913.

136. AP CCIP 2/ETP/3/4/13 8: Réglementation des agences de transactions immobilières. Epreuve réservée aux membres de la Commission du commerce et de l'industrie, 15 avril 1959.

137. J. M. F., "L'intermédiaire, son rôle, son utilité," *Le Fonds de Commerce: Organe Officiel de la Chambre Syndicale des Intermédiaires et des Mandataires en Vente de Fonds de Commerce et Industries* (n.d., ca. June 1914), 6–7.

138. *Affiches Parisiennes et Départementales: Journal d'Annonces Judiciaires et Légales et d'Avis Divers*, April 26, 1911.

139. J. Francès, *Affaires immobilières et publicité: Comment se créer une situation indépendante et de très grand rapport dans affaires immobilières et publicité avec capital restreint* (Bordeaux: n.p., 1925), 2.

140. Institut Foncier (Guinel et Cie), *Les affaires immobilières: Comment vous apprendrez et comment vous établirez, pour votre compte, une affaire permanente et excessivement lucrative, sans capital* (Nantes: Cottin, 1922), 4, 12, 16, 21.

141. See Lisa Tiersten, *Marianne in the Market: Envisioning Consumer Society in Fin-de-Siècle France* (Berkeley: University of California Press, 2001).

5. Marketing the Metropolis

1. Abel Lemercier, "De la crise locative et immobilière à Paris: Moyen d'y remédier," *Journal des Économistes*, January 1886, 85, 89.

2. Priscilla Parkhurst Ferguson, *Paris as Revolution: Writing the Nineteenth-Century City* (Berkeley: University of California Press, 1994); Peter Fritzsche, *Reading Berlin, 1900* (Cambridge, MA: Harvard University Press, 1996); Vanessa Schwartz, *Spectacular Realities: Early Mass Culture in Fin-de-Siècle Paris* (Berkeley: University of California Press, 1998).

3. Lisa Tiersten, *Marianne in the Market: Envisioning Consumer Society in Fin-de-Siècle France* (Berkeley: University of California Press, 2001), 150. See also Leora Auslander, *Taste and Power: Furnishing Modern France* (Berkeley: University of California Press, 1996).

4. Onésime Masselin, "Des effets du krach de la Bourse sur les opérations immobilières (suite)," *Le Foncier*, April 25, 1882, 1–2, emphasis in the original.

5. F. V., "Causerie foncière," *Grand Journal Officiel des Locations et de la Vente des Terrains et Immeubles*, October 1–15, 1884, 19, emphasis in the original.

6. Alexia Yates, "Selling *la petite propriété:* Marketing Home Ownership in Early-Twentieth-Century Paris," *Entreprises et Histoire,* no. 64 (September 2011): 11–40.

7. Thomas Piketty, Gilles Postel-Vinay, Jean-Laurent Rosenthal, "Inherited vs. Self-Made Wealth: Theory and Evidence from a Rentier Society (Paris 1872–1927)," *Explorations in Economic History* 51 (2014): 21–40.

8. This was true even for the early modern period. Annik Pardailhé-Galabrun's study of home life in early modern Paris notes that 77 percent of the individuals whose status was known (2,113 succession inventories) were renters. She observes that "even wealthy people possessing one or more houses that they had purchased or inherited might choose not to live in any of them themselves, preferring instead to keep them as rental properties." Annik Pardailhé-Galabrun, *The Birth of Intimacy: Privacy and Domestic Life in Early Modern Paris,* trans. Jocelyn Phelps (Cambridge: Polity Press, 1991), 41.

9. Préfecture de la Seine, Direction des Affaires Municipales, Service de la Statistique Municipale, *Résultats statistiques du dénombrement de 1891 pour la ville de Paris et le département de la Seine* (Paris: G. Masson, 1894).

10. The studies Octave Du Mesnil and Charles Mangenot carried out among the working classes in 1899 indicated that just over half of the families surveyed met this basic income requirement. See their *Enquête sur les logements, professions, salaires, et budgets (loyers inférieurs à 400 francs)* (Paris: Chaix, 1899), cited in Lenard Berlanstein, *The Working People of Paris, 1871–1914* (Baltimore: Johns Hopkins University Press, 1984), 39.

11. H. de W., *Le petit porte-bonheur domestique, ou le secret d'être heureuse: Dédié aux jeunes mariées, lettres à une élève* (Paris: Willemotte, 1885–1895), 2.

12. Percentages varied with class. François Robert and Loïc Bonneval calculate that 12 to 35 percent of a working-class budget was dedicated to housing in Paris between 1876 and 1908. The average rents for middle-class households were between 2,060 and 2,250 francs for the same period, representing 28 to 33 percent of income. See Loïc Bonneval and François Robert, *L'immeuble de rapport: L'immobilier entre gestion et spéculation (Lyon 1860–1990)* (Rennes: Presses Universitaires de Rennes, 2013), chap. 6.

13. Adeline Daumard, *Maisons de Paris et propriétaires parisiens au XIXe siècle (1809–1880)* (Paris: Éditions Cujas, 1965), 45–53.

14. Préfecture de la Seine, Direction des Finances, Service des Contributions Directes, *Les propriétés bâties de la ville de Paris en 1889 et en 1890* (Paris: Imprimerie Nationale, 1890), 47.

15. Maurice Halbwachs, *Les expropriations et les prix des terrains à Paris (1860–1900)* (Paris: Publications de la Société Nouvelle de Librairie et d'Édition, 1909), 385.

16. Tiersten, *Marianne in the Market,* chap. 5; Auslander, *Taste and Power,* pt. 3; Deborah Silverman, *Art Nouveau in Fin-de-Siècle France: Politics, Psychology, and*

Style (Berkeley: University of California Press, 1989), 75–106; Francesca Berry, "Designing the Reader's Interior: Subjectivity and the Woman's Magazine in Early Twentieth-Century France," *Journal of Design History* 18, no. 1 (2005): 61–79.

17. H. de W., *Le petit porte-bonheur domestique,* 3–4.

18. Émile Cardon, *L'art au foyer domestique (La décoration de l'appartement)* (Paris: Chaix, 1884), 44.

19. Yankel Fijalkow, "Surpopulation ou insalubrité: Deux statistiques pour décrire l'habitat populaire, 1880–1914," *Le Mouvement Social,* no. 182 (January–March 1998): 79–96; Fijalkow, *La construction des îlots insalubres: Paris, 1850–1945* (Paris: L'Harmattan, 1998); Roger-Henri Guerrand, *Les origines du logement social en France, 1850–1914,* new ed., preface by Annie Fourcaut (Paris: Villette, 2010); Monique Eleb and Anne Debarre, *L'invention de l'habitation moderne, Paris, 1880–1914* (Paris: Hazan, 1995).

20. Berlanstein, *The Working People of Paris,* 7, 9.

21. A. Dufrénoy, "Les habitations à bon marché: Concours ouvert par la Société de Passy-Auteuil," *Économiste Français,* December 17, 1881, 760. While the "employé" as discussed in the housing reform discourse was always a male, it should be noted that a large portion of growth in the white-collar sector was feminine; Berlanstein notes that women represented only 15 percent of employees in 1870, but nearly a third of all office and sales personnel forty years later (*Working People of Paris,* 7–8).

22. Paul Margueritte, *Jours d'épreuve: Moeurs bourgeoises,* 8th ed. (Paris: E. Kolb, 1889), 185–186.

23. Ibid., 186.

24. Berlanstein, *Working People of Paris,* 14.

25. Georges d'Avenel, "La maison parisienne," in *Mécanisme de la Vie Moderne,* 2nd ed. (Paris: Colin, 1903), 3:8–9, emphasis in the original.

26. Bibliothèque Historique de la Ville de Paris (hereafter BHVP) Actualités Série 78, Logement: "L'augmentation des loyers à Paris," *Paris Journal,* January 30, 1911. On height regulations and the preference of the wealthy for apartments, see "Rapport de [Joseph-Antoine] Bouvard, directeur administratif des services d'architecture . . . sur les conséquences du décret de 1902," Paris, June 23, 1909, cited by Gilles Ragache, *Histoire d'une famille d'architectes parisiens du Premier Empire à la Belle Époque* (Paris: Éditions Charles Hérissey/Airelles, 2003), 194.

27. Émile Rivoalen, "Promenades à travers Paris," *La Construction Moderne,* October 7, 1893, 1.

28. Ibid., 2.

29. "L'habitation ancienne et moderne," illustrated supplement to *Le Temps,* December 4, 1893.

30. E. Rivoalen, "À travers Paris: Première promenade," *Revue Générale de l'Architecture et des Travaux Publics* (hereafter *RGATP*), 39 (1882): 27.

31. E. Rivoalen, "Promenades à travers Paris: Maisons et locataires," *RGATP* 39 (1882): 260.

32. E. Rivoalen, "À travers Paris: Deuxième promenade," *RGATP* 39 (1882): 76.

33. Rivoalen, "À travers Paris: Première promenade," 34.

34. Leora Auslander, " 'National Taste'? Citizenship Law, State Form, and Everyday Aesthetics in Modern France and Germany, 1920–1940," in *The Politics of Consumption: Material Culture and Citizenship in Europe and America,* ed. Martin Daunton and Matthew Hilton (Oxford: Berg, 2001), 109–128.

35. Natacha Coquéry, *L'hôtel aristocratique: Le marché du luxe à Paris au XVIIIe siècle* (Paris: Publications de la Sorbonne, 1998), esp. pt. 2, chaps. 2 and 3.

36. David Garrioch, *Neighbourhood and Community in Paris, 1740–1790* (Cambridge: Cambridge University Press, 1986), 171–173.

37. Gérard Jacquemet, *Belleville au XIXe siècle: Du faubourg à la ville* (Paris: Éditions de l'EHESS, 1984), 34; Nicholas Green, *The Spectacle of Nature: Landscape and Bourgeois Culture in Nineteenth-Century France* (Manchester: Manchester University Press, 1990), 84–89.

38. Adeline Daumard, *La bourgeoisie parisienne de 1815 à 1848,* rev. ed. (Paris: Albin Michel, 1996), 480–489.

39. Jacquemet, *Belleville au XIXe siècle,* 37.

40. Alain Faure, "Villégiature populaire et peuplement des banlieues à la fin du XIXe siècle: L'exemple de Montfermeil," in *La terre et la cité: Mélanges offerts à Philippe Vigier,* ed. Alain Faure, Alain Plessis, and Jean-Claude Farcy (Paris: Créaphis, 1994), 167–194. See also Tyler Stovall, *The Rise of the Paris Red Belt* (Berkeley: University of California Press, 1990). For the first government-supported efforts for the elite of the working classes and the lower middle classes to become homeowners on the periphery, see Alain Faure, " 'Les couches nouvelles de la propriété': Un peuple parisien à la conquête du bon logis à la veille de la Grande Guerre," *Le Mouvement Social,* no. 182 (January–March, 1998): 53–78.

41. Piketty et al., "Inherited vs. Self-Made Wealth," 32.

42. Alain Plessis, *Régents et gouverneurs de la Banque de France sous le Second Empire* (Geneva: Droz, 1985), 211–217. Plessis draws additionally on a study by Adeline Daumard, *Les fortunes françaises au XIXe siècle: Enquête sur la composition et la répartition des capitaux privés à Paris, Lyon, Lille, Bordeaux et Toulouse d'après l'enregistrement des déclarations de succession* (Paris: Mouton, 1973).

43. Christophe Charle, *Les élites de la république, 1880–1900* (Paris: Fayard, 1987).

44. Ibid., 387–393.

45. Jean-Claude Farcy and Alain Faure, *La mobilité d'une génération de français: Recherche sur les migrations et les déménagements vers et dans Paris à la fin du XIXe siècle* (Paris: Institut National d'Études Démographiques, 2003), chaps. 8–10.

46. Adeline Daumard, *Les bourgeois et la bourgeoisie en France depuis 1815* (Paris: Aubier, 1987); Daumard, *La bourgeoisie parisienne.*

47. Anthony Sutcliffe, *The Autumn of Central Paris: The Defeat of Town Planning, 1850–1970* (London: Edward Arnold, 1970), 86.

48. Claire Lévy-Vroelant, "Un espace ouvert: Usages sociaux du logement en ville entre 1830 et 1880," *Recherches Contemporaines,* no. 3 (1995–1996): 63–90.

49. Documents generously communicated by Madame Marie-France Tiffen (hereafter Fonds Marie-France Tiffen): Fidus, "John Arthur," *L'Evénement,* December 16, 1890.

50. Archives Nationales du Monde du Travail, 65 AQ I 1163: *John Arthur et Tiffen, 1818–1968* (anniversary book, n.d.).

51. Fonds Marie-France Tiffen, "Un roi en exil: How the Ex-Monarch of the Rue Castiglione Crowned Himself," *Morning News* (n.d.).

52. "Art. 3072. Nom patronymique—Usage commercial—Abus—Concurrence déloyale—Maison de commerce—Emplacement," *Annales de la Propriété Industrielle, Artistique et Littéraire* 31, nos. 7/8 (July/August 1886), 193–221. Fonds Marie-France Tiffen, P. Blanc, "Rapport à Monsieur le juge d'instruction Brossard Marsillac, dans la procédure suivie contre John Arthur, inculpé d'abus de confiance" (handwritten document, 1893). Select articles from Fonds Marie-France Tiffen: "La ruine de John Arthur," *La Petite République Française,* December 7, 1890; "Tribunal de commerce de la Seine, audience du 19 décembre 1888: Faillite—Mise en vente du fonds de commerce—droits de l'acquéreur—droits du failli recommençant les affaires," *Le Droit: Journal des Tribunaux,* no. 305 (December 29, 1888).

53. *Factum: Cour d'appel de Paris, première chambre, audience du 26 novembre 1890; Affaire John Arthur (intimé) contre Comptoir Commercial et Immobilier (appelant)* (Paris: Imprimerie de C. Schlaeler, 1891), 2.

54. Colin Jones, "The Great Chain of Buying: Medical Advertisement, the Bourgeois Public Sphere, and the Origins of the French Revolution," *American Historical Review* 101, no. 1 (February 1996): 13–40.

55. *Gazette des Locations: Journal-Affiche des Propriétaires et des Locataires,* January 27, 1841.

56. *Le Vendeur,* August 19, 1838.

57. The contemporary reactions of Alexis de Tocqueville and Karl Marx to the 1848 revolution and resulting feelings of alienation are well known. See Alexis de Tocqueville, *Lettres choisies: Souvenirs, 1814–1859,* ed. Françoise Mélonio and Laurence Guellec (Paris: Éditions Gallimard, 2003); Karl Marx, "The Eighteenth Brumaire of Louis Bonaparte," in *The Marx-Engels Reader,* ed. Robert C. Tucker, 2nd ed. (New York: W. W. Norton, 1978). On 1848 and urban space specifically, see Françoise Paul-Lévy, *La ville en croix: De la révolution de 1848 à la rénovation haussmannienne* (Paris: Librairie des Meridiens, 1984). David Harvey's *Paris: Capital of Modernity* (New York: Routledge, 2003) also sees 1848 as a breaking point in the conceptual understanding of Paris; theses informing Harvey's own can be found in T. J. Clark,

The Painting of Modern Life: Paris in the Art of Manet and His Followers (New York: Knopf, 1984), and Ferguson, *Paris as Revolution.*

58. *Journal des Locataires et des Acquéreurs: Contenant l'Indication des Locations et des Ventes de Paris et des Départements,* January 1850.

59. Ibid.

60. A. de Lacroix, "Les appartements à louer," in *Les Français peints par eux-mêmes,* vol. *Prismes* (Paris: L. Curmer, 1840), 189–190.

61. *Journal des Locataires et des Acquéreurs,* January 1850, emphasis in the original.

62. Archives de Paris (hereafter AP) V.D6 733 no. 4: Les répertoires indicateurs universels de demandes et offres: Nouvelles petites affiches.

63. A letter from Haussmann to the director of the agency, A. Blanc Duquesnay, on June 25, 1868, congratulates the director and "sends wishes for the continued success of your ingenious enterprise" (AP V.D6 733 no. 4).

64. AP V.D6 733 no. 4: Modèle d'une formule d'adhésion, 1867, Administration des Répertoires.

65. Ibid.

66. Henri Lefebvre, *La proclamation de la Commune, 26 mars 1871* (Paris: Gallimard, 1965); Lefebvre, *La révolution urbaine* (Paris: Gallimard, 1970). See also Roger V. Gould, *Insurgent Identities: Class, Community, and Protest in Paris from 1848 to the Commune* (Chicago: University of Chicago Press, 1995); Kristin Ross, *The Emergence of Social Space: Rimbaud and the Paris Commune* (Minneapolis: University of Minnesota Press, 1988).

67. Clark, *The Painting of Modern Life.* Although it stresses that the emphasis on alienation that characterizes discussion of the Second Empire's renovations is overstated, Jeanne Gaillard's *Paris: La ville, 1852–1870* (Paris: Honoré Champion, 1977) suggests that Haussmann's projects created a passive urban populace, one that felt increasingly detached from its capacity to shape urban space. In Gaillard's eyes, this change was long-lasting: "Over time, the urban collectivity, having become passive, acquiesced to structures whose nature and meaning have not changed since Haussmann" (172).

68. Schwartz, *Spectacular Realities;* Gregory Shaya, "The *Flâneur,* the *Badaud,* and the Making of a Mass Public in France, circa 1860–1910," *American Historical Review* 109, no. 1 (February 2004): 41–77.

69. Alphonse de Calonne, "Domestic Architecture in Paris," *Littell's Living Age,* May 4, 1895, 300.

70. Sharon Marcus, *Apartment Stories: City and Home in Nineteenth-Century Paris and London* (Berkeley: University of California Press, 1999).

71. The first issue of the *Grand Journal Officiel des Locations et de la Vente des Terrains et Immeubles* noted in its "Avis aux lecteurs" that their enterprise "will be founded on one of the primary necessities of life: the 'Home,' or the *chez soi*"

(September 1–15, 1884). The use of the terms would not reappear. In the early twentieth century, the terms "home," "foyer," and "chez soi" begin to figure in the names of real estate development companies aimed at the working classes and associated with programs for low-income housing known as *habitations à bon marché* (HBM).

72. "Locations," *La Chronique Mobilière et Immobilière,* December 10, 1893.

73. Eugène Hatin, *Bibliographie historique et critique de la presse périodique française* (Paris: Didot Frères, 1866); Victor Gébé, *Catalogue de journaux publiés ou paraissant à Paris en 1874* (Paris: n.p., 1875); Émile Mermet and Henri Avenel, eds., *Annuaire de la presse française* (Paris: Mermet, 1880–1891); Paul Bluysen, ed., *Annuaire de la presse française et étrangère et du monde politique* (Paris: Annuaire de la Presse, 1907–1964).

74. The precise date of the beginning of this journal is unknown. The earliest located issues date from 1906, but one issue from 1913 states that the journal is in its thirteenth year, indicating that it may have been founded in 1900 or 1901.

75. The rental section of *La Presse* was very volatile and subject to frequent, short-lived efforts at reorganization. In the course of its long existence, the journal often carried rental notices, though these were limited in number and generally mingled with other commercial notices. The journal periodically created specialized rental sections, such as a short-lived rental service in coordination with an agency in 1839. *Le Temps* had also attempted to introduce a real estate listings section, run in coordination with a publicity agency, in 1862, though the venture was short-lived. Like *La Presse,* the journal ran periodic rental notices throughout this period.

76. BHVP Actualités Série 78, Logement: "Appartement à Louer, Le Supplément Spécial de l'Illustration" (ca. 1890).

77. See Chapter 6.

78. Archives du Crédit Agricole S. A. DEEF 29193: Études financières sur des sociétés immobilières.

79. The *Annuaire des Propriétaires* for 1910 indicates that insurance and property financing corporations owned approximately 2,500 apartment buildings in Paris at that time.

80. M. Drucker, "Les assurances des loyers, contre la perte des loyers et contre les réparations," in *Premier congrès international de la propriété bâtie: Exposition Universelle Internationale de 1900, à Paris* (Paris: Société des Publications Scientifiques et Industrielles, 1901), 100.

81. A. Aubert, "Chronique de la quinzaine," *Moniteur de la Location,* May 5, 1880.

82. F. V., "Causerie foncière," October 1–15, 1884, 19. Emphasis in the original.

83. "Causerie foncière," *Grand Journal Officiel des Locations et de la Vente des Terrains et Immeubles,* September 16–30, 1884, 15.

84. *Journal de l'Union des Propriétaires: Organe spécial de ventes et locations directes,* August 15, 1896.

85. A. Aubert, "Chronique de la quinzaine," *Moniteur de la Location*, January 5, 1880.

86. "A nos lecteurs," *Moniteur de la Location*, December 20, 1879.

87. "Pourquoi nous avons fondé L'Annonce Immobilière," *L'Annonce Immobilière: Journal Hebdomadaire*, October 15, 1884, 3–4.

88. Ads for apartment building sales in the *Grand Journal Officiel* included revenue figures "quart déduit," meaning that they took into account the customary quarter of revenues generally consecrated to maintenance and taxes, giving a more accurate picture of net returns.

89. Even though improved transportation networks increasingly facilitated travel across larger distances within (and outside) the capital, costs for such services were not insignificant; one historian estimates that in 1890 a return trip on an omnibus (including one transfer between routes) would have cost approximately a third of the daily salary of a worker. Dominique Larroque, "Le réseau et le contexte: Le cas des transports collectifs urbains (1880–1939)," in *Paris et ses réseaux: Naissance d'un mode de vie urbain XIXe–XXe siècles*, ed. François Caron, Jean Dérens, Luc Passion, and Phlippe Cebron de Lisle (Paris: Mairie de Paris, 1990), 299–341.

90. On the new import of visuality in psychological theories of the mind, see Silverman, *Art Nouveau*, 75–106; on the professionalization of publicity in France, see Marjorie A. Beale, *The Modernist Enterprise: French Elites and the Threat of Modernity, 1900–1940* (Stanford: Stanford University Press, 1999), introduction and chap. 1; Marie-Emmanuelle Chessel, *La publicité: Naissance d'une profession, 1900–1940* (Paris: CNRS Éditions, 1998); Gilles Feyel, "Presse et publicité en France (XVIIIe et XIXe siècles)," *Revue Historique*, no. 628 (2003–2004): 837–868; Marc Martin, *Trois siècles de publicité en France* (Paris: Odile Jacob, 1992).

91. "Avis aux lecteurs," *Grand Journal Officiel des Locations et de la Vente des Terrains et Immeubles*, September 1–15, 1884, emphasis in the original.

92. See the client solicitation letter from the Paris–New York Agency in 1907, BHVP Actualités Série 78, Logement.

93. For just a few examples of professional volumes, see César Daly, *Architecture de la vie privée au XIXe siècle (sous Napoléon III): Nouvelles maisons de Paris et des environs* (Paris: A. Morel et Cie, 1864); Théodore Vacquer, *Maisons les plus remarquables de Paris construites pendant les trois dernières années* (Paris: A. Coudrillier, n.d.); F. Barqui, *L'architecture moderne en France: Maisons les plus remarquables des principales villes des départements* (Paris: Librairie Polytechnique de J. Baudry, 1870–1875); Victor Calliat, *Parallèle des maisons de Paris construites depuis 1830 jusqu'à nos jours*, 2 vols. (Paris: B. Bance, 1850–1876); Besniée-Delahaye, ed., *Les nouvelles constructions*, 3 vols. (Paris: La Réforme du Bâtiment, 1899–1903). Pattern books for single-family homes would develop in the early twentieth century with the emergence of the movement (and government support) for *habitations à bon marché*.

94. "Publicité immobilière avec vues," *Le Reveil Immobilier,* November 1, 1893, 3.

95. Marc Martin, "L'affiche de publicité à Paris et en France à la fin du XIXe siècle," in *La terre et la cité: Mélanges offerts à Philippe Vigier,* ed. Alain Faure, Alain Plessis, and Jean-Claude Farcy (Paris: Créaphis, 1994), 373–387.

96. Sarah Howard, "The Advertising Industry and Alcohol in Interwar France," *Historical Journal* 51, no. 2 (2008): 421–455, quotation p. 428.

97. Jean Bastié, *La croissance de la banlieue parisienne* (Paris: Presses Universitaires Françaises, 1964); Alain Becchia, "Les lotissements du Comptoir Central de Crédit dans la commune d'Issy-Les-Moulineaux (fin XIXe–début XXe siècle)," *Mémoires de la Fédération des Sociétés d'Histoire de Paris-Ile de France* (1978): 267–295. On an earlier period, see Gérard Jacquemet, "Lotissements et construction dans la proche banlieue parisienne, 1820–1840," *Mémoires de la Fédération des Sociétés d'Histoire de Paris et de l'Ile de France* 25 (1974): 207–256; and on the interwar period, see Annie Fourcaut, *La banlieue en morceaux* (Paris: Créaphis, 2000).

98. Green, *Spectacle of Nature,* 75.

99. Michelle Perrot, "Les ouvriers, l'habitat et la ville au XIXe siècle," in *La question du logement et le mouvement ouvrier français,* ed. Jean-Paul Flamand (Paris: Éditions de la Villette, 1981), 17–39. See also Susanna Magri, "Le mouvement des locataires à Paris et dans sa banlieue, 1919–1925," *Le Mouvement Social,* no. 137 (October–December 1986): 55–76. Maurice Halbwachs pioneered this understanding of the working-class approach to housing in *La classe ouvrière et les niveaux de vie: Recherches sur la hiérarchie des besoins dans les sociétés industrielles contemporaines* (Paris: Alcan, 1912). Alain Faure's writings on property acquisition among the Parisian working and employee classes run counter to the notion that the working classes were indifferent to their housing conditions: Faure, " 'Les couches nouvelles de la propriété.' "

100. Marcelle Tinayre, "L'art de parer son foyer," *Femina,* April 1, 1910, 189–190; cited by Tiersten, *Marianne in the Market,* 151.

101. Etienne Rey, "Le home," *Fémina,* December 1921, 35.

102. Colette, *Trois . . . Six . . . Neuf . . .* (Paris: Corréa, 1946), 15.

103. Luc Passion's work on pedestrianism in Paris reminds us that alongside "badauderie, flânerie, tourisme, promenade, il y a aussi *le trajet* [the commute]." See Luc Passion "Marcher dans Paris au XIXe siècle," in Caron et al., *Paris et ses réseaux,* 27–43.

104. Émile Deschamps, "Les appartements à louer," in *Paris, ou le livre des cent-et-un,* 15 vols. (Paris: Ladvocat, 1831–1834), 8:66, 84.

105. Summarized in Paul Planat, "La maison de rapport," *La Construction Moderne,* April 27, 1907, 349–350; Mourey republished many of his observations in *Propos sur les beautés du temps présents* (Paris: P. Ollendorff, 1913).

106. "De la location," *La France Immobilière,* September 1910.

107. Jules Rengade, *Les besoins de la vie et les éléments du bien-être: Traité pratique de la vie matérielle et morale de l'homme* (Paris: Librairie illustrée, 1887), 84.

108. AP VO NC 182: Lettre, Henry Rozès (65 rue de Douai, Paris) à M. Alphand, Directeur des Travaux de Paris, 14 septembre 1889.

6. Districts of the Future

1. Archives de la Préfecture de Police de Paris (hereafter APP) BA 486: Rapport, Commissariat de Police du Quartier St-Ambroise, 25 juin 1882.

2. Patrice de Moncan, *A qui appartient Paris?* (Paris: Mécène, 1997), 39.

3. *Annuaire des propriétaires et des propriétés de Paris, des administrateurs d'immeubles, des architectes, et des fournisseurs de bâtiment,* 1910, 1932.

4. The Rente Foncière owned 150 buildings outright, and managed a further 50 in collaboration with the Société Générale Immobilière in the Quartier Marbeuf venture.

5. Archives du Crédit Agricole, DEEF 19377/2: Rente Foncière. Assemblée générale, 11 avril 1881. Rapport présenté au nom du Conseil d'Administration par M. le Baron Haussmann, président, 29; Archives Nationales du Monde du Travail (hereafter ANMT) 65 AQ I 102: Compte Rendu présenté au nom du conseil d'administration de la Compagnie Foncière de France, par M. Sauret, président. Exercice 1884, 14–15. Unless otherwise noted, all of the Compagnie Foncière de France's annual reports are found in this collection at the National Archives, and will be referenced hereafter simply by abbreviated report title.

6. Jean-Philippe Dumas, "Représentation et description des propriétés à Paris au XIXe siècle: Cadastre et plan parcellaire," *Mélanges de l'École Française de Rome, Italie, et Méditerranée* 111, no. 2 (1999): 779–793.

7. On the rarity and use of graphical representations in legal and bureaucratic spheres, see Robert Carvais, "Servir la justice, l'art et la technique: Le rôle des plans, dessins et croquis devant la Chambre royale des Bâtiments," *Société et Représentations* 18, no. 2 (2004): 75–96; and Daniel Lord Smail, *Imaginary Cartographies: Possession and Identity in Late Medieval Marseille* (Ithaca, NY: Cornell University Press, 2000).

8. Archives de Paris (hereafter AP) D.2 P4 49: Commission des Contributions Directes de la Ville de Paris, *Evaluation des propriétés bâties de la Ville de Paris effectuée en 1888 et 1889: Procès-verbal des opérations* (Paris, 1890), 5.

9. Many tenants whose leases were registered with the municipality, for example, do not appear on the *calepins.* For the 16th arrondissement, see AP D.Q7 26037–26042.

10. For a recent exploration of social relations inside fin-de-siècle Parisian apartment houses (though not necessarily speculative buildings), see Eliza Ferguson, "The Cosmos of the Paris Apartment: Working-Class Family Life in the Nineteenth Century," *Journal of Urban History* 37, no. 1 (January 2011): 59–67.

11. Carolyn Loeb, *Entrepreneurial Vernacular: Developers' Subdivisions in the 1920s* (Baltimore: Johns Hopkins University Press, 2001).

12. Onésime Masselin, *Formulaire d'actes et notice sur la législation et l'utilité des sociétés anonymes immobilières par actions* (Paris: Ducher et Cie, 1880), 7.

13. Monique Eleb-Vidal and Anne Debarre-Blanchard, *Architecture de la vie privée: Maisons et mentalités, XVIIe–XIXe siècles* (Brussels: Archives d'Architecture Moderne, 1989); Monique Eleb and Anne Debarre, *L'invention de l'habitation moderne: Paris, 1880–1914* (Paris: Hazan, and Archives d'Architecture Moderne, 1995).

14. Bibliothèque Historique de la Ville de Paris (hereafter BHVP) Actualités Série 78, Logement: Press clipping from the *Revue des Conférences* (n.d., n.p.). See also "Compagnie Foncière de France et d'Algérie," *La Réforme du Bâtiment,* July 17, 1881, 117–118.

15. CFF, Compte Rendu (Exercice 1881–1882), 5.

16. Ibid., 6–7.

17. Archives du Crédit Agricole, DEEF 29193: Études financières sur des sociétés immobilières, Compagnie Foncière de France (Juillet 1892), 23.

18. CFF, Compte Rendu (Exercice 1881–1882), 8.

19. The company's 1925 report said in summary: "The whole of your estate continues to be represented on the balance sheet for the amount of 57,943,709.99, a figure that represents the amount of debt engaged by the operations on the properties concerned, not the purchase price nor the building's estimated value." (CFF, Assemblée Générale Ordinaire du 24 juin 1925 [Exercice 1924], 5–6.)

20. Archives du Crédit Agricole, DEEF 29193: Compagnie Foncière de France, Étude, juillet 1892, 7.

21. CFF, Compte Rendu (Exercice 1884), 9, emphasis in the original.

22. Ibid., 11.

23. CFF, Compte Rendu (Exercice 1881–1882), 6–7.

24. O[nésime] Masselin, "Des effets du krach de la Bourse sur les opérations immobilières (suite)," *Le Foncier,* March 28, 1882.

25. Georges Grison, "Une cité ouvrière à Paris," *Le Figaro,* September 24, 1884.

26. César Daly, *Architecture de la vie privée au XIXe siècle (sous Napoléon III): Nouvelles maisons de Paris et des environs* (Paris: A. Morel et Cie, 1864), 25.

27. CFF, Assemblée Générale Ordinaire du 13 mai 1886 (Exercice 1885), 12.

28. CFF Assemblée Générale Ordinaire du 29 avril 1887 (Exercice 1886), 20.

29. Ibid.

30. Archives du Crédit Agricole DEEF 47354/1: Rente Foncière, Assemblée Générale du 27 avril 1896. Rapport présenté au nom du Conseil d'Administration par M. Coureau, vice-président, 14–15.

31. For example, AP D8U1 86 (Justice de Paix, 11e arrondissement, 1889–1890). Madame Mitrier was evicted by the Rente Foncière from 23 Rue Moret in April 1889

for 20 francs in missing rent payments; the CFF evicted Madame Collin from 8 Rue Chevreul in the same month for 90 francs in late rent.

32. Vacancy rates calculated from BHVP Actualités Série 78, Logement: Conseil Municipal de Paris, Rapport, présenté par M. Alfred Lamouroux, au nom de la 1re Commission, sur la valeur locative actuelle des propriétés bâties de la ville de Paris, en exécution de la loi du 8 août 1885 (Paris: 1888); and P. Simon, *Statistique de l'habitation à Paris* (Paris: Librairie Polytechnique Baudry et Cie, 1891).

33. CFF Compte Rendu (Exercice 1881–1882), 7.

34. CFF Compte Rendu (Exercice 1884), 13.

35. Archives du Crédit Agricole, DEEF 47354/1, Assemblée Générale du 27 avril 1896, Rapport présenté au nom du Conseil d'Administration par M. Coureau, vice-président, 12.

36. AP D.1 P4 98, rue des Belles Feuilles, 1876.

37. Tax evaluators noted the number of tenants already present in the firm's buildings on Rue des Belles Feuilles in the 16th arrondissement in January 1886, though the buildings had only been started in 1885 and were in various stages of development through 1888: five tenants in no. 19, four in no. 21, three in no. 23, four in no. 25, five in no. 39, and seven in no. 41. AP D.1 P4 98, rue des Belles Feuilles, 1876.

38. AP VONC 694: Direction des Travaux de Paris, 2e Division, 2e Bureau, Grande Voirie Répertoire (1881–1883).

39. Michel Pinçon and Monique Pinçon-Charlot, *Quartiers bourgeois, quartiers d'affaires* (Paris: Éditions Payot, 1992), chaps. 1 and 2.

40. AP VO11 949, rue du Débarcadère.

41. CFF Compte Rendu (Exercice 1883), 5.

42. The arrondissements with the highest densities were the 3rd (733 inhabitants/hectare), the 2nd (689), the 4th (613), the 11th (560), and the 10th (541). Commission des Contributions Directes de la Ville de Paris, *Les propriétés bâties de la ville de Paris en 1889 et en 1890* (Paris: Imprimerie Nationale, 1890).

43. AP D.1 P4 766, rue de Montreuil, 1876.

44. These new streets include: Rue du Trésor (4th arrondissement), Cité Vaneau (7th arrondissement), Rue Saint-Philippe du Roule (8th arrondissement), Rue Alfred Stevens (9th arrondissement), Rue Civiale (10th arrondissement), Rue Chevreul (11th arrondissement), Rue d'Alençon (15th arrondissement), and Rue de l'Amiral Courbet, Rue Gustave Courbet, and Rue Bosio (16th arrondissement).

45. The evaluations of municipal engineers show that for years after their construction, buildings belonging to the CFF were the only ones to enjoy adequate sidewalks on Rue des Belles Feuilles (16th arrondissement) and the western portion of Boulevard Pereire (17th arrondissement). See AP VO11 2629, boulevard Pereire, and AP VO11 261, rue des Belles Feuilles.

46. On Rue Simart in the 18th arrondissement, the buildings constructed by architect Paul Fouquiau and purchased by the Rente Foncière were provisioned with

full sidewalks immediately; the older portion of Rue Simart was still without full regulatory sidewalks in the late 1880s, despite negotiations between property owners and the city over their construction having begun in the late 1860s. AP VO11 3464, rue Simart.

47. AP VO11 3372, rue Saint-Philippe du Roule, Demande de Classement. Rapport, 9 février 1886.

48. AP VO11 2646, boulevard Pereire; Archives Nationales, Minutier Central des Notaires, ET/CIII/1490, Me. Latapie de Gerval, 27 et 29 juillet 1881, Vente par la Société Pereire à M. Minbielle; 27 et 29 juillet 1881, Vente par la Société Pereire à M. Deremble.

49. CFF Assemblée Générale Ordinaire du 21 mai 1889 (Exercice 1888), 5–6.

50. Émile Rivoalen, "Promenades à travers Paris," *Revue Générale de l'Architecture et des Travaux Publics,* ser. 4, vol. 10 (1883), 66; César Daly, *Architecture de la vie privée,* 1:16.

51. In referring to the story of a building, I use the vocabulary provided by the cadastral surveys that form the main source base for this chapter. The "entresol," located directly above the ground floor, would more commonly be referred to as the first floor, and the floor above it the second, rather than the first floor, and so on.

52. See AP VO11 3921, Boulevard de la Villette; AP D.1 P4 1199, Avenue Victor Hugo. The nearby "Belles Feuilles" group near the Lycée Janson had much smaller courtyards, reflecting its construction by several different architects and building entrepreneurs.

53. Daly, *Architecture de la vie privée,* 1:19. Buildings with service stairs included those upper-class buildings on Cité Vaneau (7th) and Rue Saint-Philippe du Roule and Rue du Faubourg Saint-Honoré (8th), buildings with one apartment per floor on Rue d'Alençon (15th), Rue de la Pompe (16th), and Rue de l'Amiral Courbet (16th), as well as the company's buildings on Boulevard Pereire and Rue du Débarcadère (17th).

54. This was the case for the houses on Rue de Montreuil (11th), Rue Civiale (10th), Rue du Mont-Cenis (18th), the building at 29 Rue Salneuve (17th), and for some buildings in the 16th arrondissement.

55. AP D.1 P4 525, rue Gustave Courbet, 1876.

56. "Rapport présenté par M. Muller, au nom de la 1re Sous-commission, relativement au projet de cahier des charges des travaux de construction des maisons à petits loyers . . . ," in *Monographies municipales: Les logements à bon marché; Recueil annoté, par Lucien Lambeau* (Paris: Imprimerie Municipale, 1897), 221–226.

57. "Formation d'une association syndicale pour la gestion et l'entretien en état de viabilité de la cité Vaneau: 4 mai 1900," *Recueil des Actes Administratifs, Bulletin Officiel d'Information de la Préfecture de Paris et de la Préfecture de Police* (1900), 362–370.

58. AP D.1 P4 262, rue Chevreul, 1876; AP D.1 P4 149, rue des Boulets, 1876.

59. Archives du Crédit Agricole, DEEF 19377/1, Crédit Foncier et Agricole d'Algérie, Assemblée générale du 28 mai 1887, Compte rendu, 28; DEEF 19377/2, Rente Foncière. Assemblée générale ordinaire et extraordinaire, 30 avril 1885, Rapport présenté au nom du Conseil d'Administration par M. Félix Thoureau, président, 20; DEEF 47354/1, Rente Foncière. Assemblée générale ordinaire, 7 avril 1892, Rapport présenté au nom du Conseil d'Administration par M. Félix Thoureau, président, 16.

60. This practice was known as "farming" in England; it generally involved several houses, and it was particularly associated with the management of working-class housing. See M. J. Daunton, *House and Home in the Victorian City: Working-Class Housing, 1850–1914* (London: Edward Arnold, 1983), 174–175.

61. Archives du Crédit Agricole, DEEF 47354/1: Rente Foncière, Assemblée générale ordinaire du 7 avril 1892, Rapport, 17.

62. On Rue des Boulets, houses on the even side of the road (nos. 4–12) were rented to Durand, who also leased nos. 3, 5, and 7, and possibly no.11, on Rue Chevreul. These buildings backed onto one another, sharing courtyard space. AP D.1 P4 149, rue des Boulets, 1876; AP D.1 P4 262, rue Chevreul, 1876.

63. AP D.1 P4 1199, avenue Victor Hugo, 1876.

64. AP D.1 P4 653, rue de Longchamp, 1876; AP D.1 P4 525, rue Gustave Courbet, 1876.

65. AP D.1 P4 336, rue du Débarcadère, 1876; AP D.1 P4 1167, rue d'Uzès, 1876.

66. Archives du Crédit Agricole, DEEF 47354/1: Rente Foncière Assemblée générale du 16 janvier 1897. Rapport du Conseil d'administration, résolutions de l'assemblée, 5–6.

67. On branding tactics for real estate investment corporations, see Russell James III, "Customer Satisfaction with Apartment Housing Offered by Real Estate Investment Trusts (REITs)," *International Journal of Consumer Studies* 33 (2009): 572–580.

68. Archives du Crédit Agricole, DEEF 47354/1: Rente Foncière Assemblée générale du 16 janvier 1897. Rapport, 5–6.

69. BHVP Actualités Série 78, Logement: Publicity flyer, Rente Foncière, n.d. (ca. 1900).

70. Archives du Crédit Agricole, DEEF 47354/1: Rente Foncière, Assemblée générale du 30 avril 1913, Rapport du Conseil d'administration, rapport des commissaires-censeurs, résolution de l'assemblée, 8.

71. Archives du Crédit Agricole, DEEF 47354/1: Rente Foncière, Assemblée générale ordinaire du 7 avril 1892, Rapport, 16, 17–18.

72. Archives du Crédit Agricole, DEEF 47354/1: Rente Foncière, Assemblée générale du 25 juillet 1896, Rapport du Conseil d'administration, rapport des commissaires-censeurs, résolution de l'assemblée, 19, 21.

73. CFF Assemblée Générale Ordinaire du 19 juin 1907 (Exercice 1906), 15.

74. CFF Assemblée Générale Ordinaire du 28 mai 1890 (Exercice 1889), 13. The Rente Foncière also converted many commercial rentals in the same period (Archives du Crédit Agricole, DEEF 29193: La Rente Foncière, Étude Avril 1892, Décembre 1894).

75. CFF Assemblée Générale Ordinaire du 17 juillet 1893 (Exercice 1892), 17.

76. "Déposition de M. Fernoux, architecte: Séance du 5 mars 1884," in Chambre des députés, "Procès-verbaux de la commission chargée de faire une enquête sur la situation des ouvriers de l'industrie et de l'agriculture en France et de présenter un premier rapport sur la crise industrielle à Paris," *Annales de la Chambre des Députés, Documents Parlementaires,* 12 (Paris, 1884): 112.

77. Archives du Crédit Agricole, DEEF 19377/2: L'Union immobilière des capitalistes, des constructeurs et des propriétaires fonciers, Conseil d'Administration, rapport, Assemblée générale 1er mai 1888, 13.

78. ANMT 65 AQ I 26: Compagnie du Parc de Bercy, Rapport du Conseil d'Administration à l'Assemblée générale des Actionnaires, 1880.

79. Leménil's firm had a stock capital of only 2.4 million francs, as opposed to the Rente Foncière's 22 million in 1887 and the CFF's 25 million in 1888; neither it nor the SA Compagnie du Parc de Bercy traded on the Bourse, though shares in Leménil's firm did trade on the unofficial exchange.

80. AP D.1 P4 8, rue d'Alençon, 1876; CFF Assemblée Générale Ordinaire du 21 mai 1889 (Exercice 1888), 14.

81. Alain Faure and Claire Lévy-Vroelant, *Une chambre en ville: Hôtels meublés et garnis à Paris, 1860–1990* (Paris: Créaphis, 2007), esp. pt. 2, "Le 'système du garni' parisien au XIXe siècle et dans le premier XXe siècle," by Alain Faure, 44–170.

82. Faure and Lévy-Vroelant, *Une chambre en ville,* 31, 36.

83. See a summary of jurisprudence on this topic in Félix Lebon and M. Hallays-Dabot, *Jurisprudence du Conseil d'État, statuant au contentieux pendant les dix dernières années* (Paris: M. D'Escrivan, 1859), 255–257.

84. See the entry "logeurs" in the Journal du Palais, *Répertoire général contenant la jurisprudence de 1791 à 1850* (Paris: Bureau du Journal du Palais, 1850), 9:173–174.

85. AP D.1 P4 336, rue du Débarcadère, 1876.

86. AP D.1 P4 98, rue des Belles Feuilles, 1876.

87. Ibid.

88. AP D.1 P4 900, rue de la Pompe, 1876.

89. Ibid.

90. AP D.1 P4 98, rue des Belles Feuilles, 1876.

91. AP D.1 P4 262, rue Chevreul, 1876.

92. AP D.1 P4 1199, avenue Victor Hugo, 1876.

93. Michele Perrot, "Le genre de la ville," *Communications,* no. 65 (1997): 149–163; Jean-Paul Barrière, "Les veuves dans la ville en France au XIXe siècle: Images, rôles, types sociaux," *Annales de Bretagne et des Pays de l'Ouest* 114, no. 3 (2007): 169–

194. On the clustering of widows in chic residential districts elsewhere, see Richard Wall, "Elderly Widows and Widowers and Their Co-residents in Late-Nineteenth- and Early-Twentieth-Century England and Wales," *History of the Family* 7, no. 1 (2002): 139–155.

94. *La Presse* ran a story in 1890 about a crime committed in a sublet apartment; the *principale locataire* was Mme Pusin, who let a ground-floor apartment in a building near her own residence on Rue d'Anjou, and explained, "During the Exhibition, I wanted to make money from this apartment and I hired an agency to find a sublessee for me." See "L'affaire Gouffé," *La Presse*, January 25, 1890.

95. AP D.1 P4 98, rue des Belles Feuilles, 1876.

96. Ibid.

97. AP D.1 P4 25, rue de l'Amiral Courbet, 1876.

98. AP D.1 P4 98, rue des Belles Feuilles, 1876. Technically, midwives were not supposed to be considered *loueurs* for such rooms, nor to be taxed for them.

99. Jean-Louis Deaucourt, *Premières loges: Paris et ses concierges au XIXe siècle* (Paris: Aubier, 1992), 63–66.

100. AP D.1 P4 25, rue de l'Amiral Courbet, 1876.

101. AP D.1 P4 653, rue de Longchamp, 1876.

102. Foreign travelers associated with the many embassies of the west end were also an important clientele. The Hotel Bradford, for example, was advertised in *La Revue Diplomatique* in 1906 as "First rate. Modern facilities. Highly recommended" (June 3, 1906).

103. One apartment in no. 39 Rue Simart was described as divided between two individuals (Perce and Dame Bitault) between 1893 and 1898; this apartment consisted of a kitchen, toilets, dining room, and three additional rooms, and cost 600 francs in rent (AP D.1 P4 1099, rue Simart, 1876).

104. AP D.1 P4 336, rue du Débarcadère, 1876; AP D.1 P4 1693, rue du Débarcadère, 1901.

105. Faure and Lévy-Vroelant, *Une chambre en ville*, 79–80.

106. See, for example, the rules established by the Société des Habitations Ouvrières de Passy-Auteuil, which prohibited families from giving into the "temptation to reduce their payments" by taking in a boarder (ANMT 65 AQ I 241: Émile Cheysson, "La Société Anonyme des Habitations Ouvrières de Passy-Auteuil: Communication faite à la Société d'Economie Sociale, dans sa séance du 23 avril 1882," 3). Alfred Leybach, *Les habitations à bon marché, la petite propriété, le bien de famille insaisissable* (Paris: Epinal, 1910), 161–162.

107. Decisions of the Cour de Paris (4th Chamber, June 25, 1857) and the Tribunal Civil de la Seine (5th Chamber, June 16, 1855), cited by Émile Agnel, *Code-manuel des propriétaires et locataires de maisons, hôteliers, aubergistes et logeurs* (Paris: Cosse et Marchal, 1874), 559.

108. Corliss L. Parry, "European Insurance Companies and Real Estate: With Particular Reference to Housing," *Journal of Land & Public Utility Economics* 16, no. 3 (August 1940): 294–305.

Epilogue

1. Lucien Lagrave, "L'évolution de la propriété immobilière et son avenir," *Revue de la Propriété Immobilière et de la Construction: Organe de l'Union Nationale des Propriétaires* (March 1932): 37–40.

2. Ibid., 38.

3. Alain Pottage, "The Measure of Land," *Modern Law Review* 57 (1994): 361–384, quotation at p. 382.

4. Tyler Stovall, *Paris and the Spirit of 1919: Consumer Struggles, Transnationalism, and Revolution* (Cambridge: Cambridge University Press, 2012), 36–45, 193–211; Susanna Magri, "Housing," in *Capital Cities at War: Paris, London, Berlin, 1914–1918,* ed. Jay Winter and Jean-Louis Robert (Cambridge: Cambridge University Press, 1997), 374–417; Susanna Magri, "Le mouvement des locataires à Paris et dans sa banlieue, 1919–1925," *Le Mouvement Social* 137 (October–December 1986): 55–76.

5. Law of October 23, 1919, articles 6 and 7. See Louis Bouzinac, *Les loyers: Le régime définitif des prorogations; La spéculation illicite; Analyse et commentaires de la loi du 31 mars 1922 et formulaire* (n.p., n.d.).

6. Archives de Paris, Archives de la Chambre de Commerce et d'Industrie de Paris, 2/ETP/3/4/42 1: J. Tchernoff, "La spéculation illicite," *Revue Pratique de Législation et de Jurisprudence du Tribunal de Commerce de la Seine* 22 (November 15, 1919), 91.

7. Alessandro Stanziani, ed., *Dictionnaire historique de l'économie-droit, XVIIIe–XXe siècles* (Paris: Maison des Sciences de l'Homme, 2007), 285–286.

8. Bibliothèque Historique de la Ville de Paris (hereafter BHVP) Actualités Série 78, Logement: Lauche, "La crise du logement," *L'Eveil des Locataires: Organe de la Confédération des Locataires de France et des Colonies,* May 10, 1919, 1.

9. Archives Nationales (hereafter AN) F7-13755: Lettre du Préfet de Police à Monsieur le Garde des Sceaux, Ministre de la Justice, 10 février 1919.

10. BHVP Actualités Série 78, Logement: Maurice Maurin, "Les offices municipaux de location," *L'Eveil des Locataires,* May 10, 1919.

11. AN F7-13756: Léon Osmin, "Rien à louer mais . . . on déménage," *Populaire,* June 21, 1922.

12. AN F7-13756: Henry Prete, "Allons-nous longtemps encore laisser agir librement les mercantis du loyer?," *Peuple,* October 15, 1923; Henry Prete, "On se demande pour quelles raisons la police tolère les agissements des escrocs du logement," *Peuple,* October 18, 1923.

13. AN F7-13756: "Se déciderait-on enfin à poursuivre les mercantis du loyer?," *Peuple,* November 4, 1923.

14. BHVP Actualités Série 78, Logement: Maurice Maurin, "Les offices municipaux de location."

15. BHVP Actualités Série 78, Logement: Henri Sellier, "La guerre a aggravé le problème des loyers," *L'Eveil des Locataires,* May 31, 1919.

16. Founded in 1921, the Chambre Syndicale des Agents Immobiliers de France has since been absorbed into FNAIM, the Fédération National des Agents Immobiliers.

17. "Pourquoi nous devons être unis," *Bulletin Officiel de la Chambre Syndicale des Agents Immobiliers de France* (hereafter *Bulletin des Agents Immobiliers*), July 1921.

18. Arthur Levasseur, "Une organisation à améliorer: Les offices municipaux," *Courrier des loyers,* reprinted as "Agences de locations—Régisseurs," *Journal de l'Homme d'Affaires,* April 15, 1921, 183.

19. "Comment la 'Chambre syndicale des agents immobiliers de France' a été constituée," *Bulletin des Agents Immobiliers,* July 1921, emphasis in the original.

20. "Compte-rendu de l'Assemblée générale du 23 mars 1921: Rapport de M. Esnault," *Bulletin des Agents Immobiliers,* July 1921.

21. "Rapport du Conseil d'Administration: Assemblée générale du 28 janvier 1922," *Bulletin des Agents Immobiliers,* April 1922. In 1929 the Association's president, Edmond Largier, now a deputy in the national legislature, succeeded in adding an amendment to the rental legislation of June 29, 1929, that penalized agents who accepted commissions before carrying out services for their clients, with fines of 1,000 to 5,000 francs. This amendment was an effort to moralize the profession in the eyes of consumers, as well as a means to strike against agents operating outside the boundaries of the Association. See Maurice Jacquault (président), "Mise au point rectificative," *Bulletin des Agents Immobiliers,* October 1931.

22. Law of April 1, 1926, article 25. Paul Colin, *Codes et lois pour la France, l'Algérie et les colonies. Supplément: Mise au courant à la date du 15 août 1927* (Paris: Librairie des Juris-classeurs, 1928), 147.

23. The leftist newspaper *L'Humanité* reported in the summer of 1926 on the complete absence of any kind of public registry of available housing in Paris. AN F7-13756: L. Dieulle, "Locataires—A quand l'établissement de la liste des locaux vacants?," *L'Humanité,* June 24, 1926.

24. Charles Brouilhet, "La propriété bâtie et la question du livre foncier," in *Congrès de la Propriété Bâtie de France* (Lyon: Imprimerie du Salut Public, 1894), 4.

25. Georges Dreyfus, *De l'exclusion des opérations immobilières du domaine du droit commercial* (Paris: Librairie nouvelle de droit et de jurisprudence, 1905), 53.

26. Marthe Torre-Schaub, *Essai sur la construction juridique de la catégorie de marché* (Paris: Librairie générale de droit et de jurisprudence, 2002), 28–29, 44–48.

27. Manual Aalbers, "The Financialization of Home and the Mortgage Market Crisis," *Competition and Change* 12, no. 2 (June 2008): 148–166; Kathe Newman,

"Post-industrial Widgets: Capital Flows and the Production of the Urban," *International Journal of Urban Research* 33, no. 2 (June 2009): 314–331.

28. "Jeudi 31 mai: La propriété bâtie et le crédit hypothécaire dans les différents états; Réponses de M. Baudelot (avocat à la Cour d'appel de Paris) et de M. Aubépin (avocat à la Cour d'Appel de Paris)," in *Premier congrès international de la propriété bâtie: Exposition Universelle Internationale de 1900, à Paris* (Paris: Société des Publications Scientifiques et Industrielles, 1901), 182.

29. Hernando de Soto, *The Mystery of Capital: Why Capitalism Triumphs in the West and Fails Everywhere Else* (New York: Basic Books, 2000).

Acknowledgments

This work could not have been completed without the help and generosity of many individuals and institutions. Crucial financial support came from the Social Sciences and Humanities Research Council of Canada, the Institut d'Etudes Politiques in Paris, the History Department and Division of Social Sciences at the University of Chicago, a Bourse Chateaubriand, and a Doris G. Quinn Foundation Dissertation Grant. The Society for French Historical Studies and Harvard Graduate School of Arts and Sciences provided travel funding at important points in the project.

Staff at numerous libraries and archives provided invaluable assistance over the course of this project: Roger Nougaret and Nancy Aravena at the archives of the Crédit Agricole, Odile Benedetti and Michel Terrioux at FNAIM-Ile-de-France, Andrée-Marie Dormion at the Archives Nationales du Monde du Travail in Roubaix, Olivier Accarie-Pierson at the Archives de la Préfecture de Police in Paris, the librarians at the Chambre de Commerce et d'Industrie de Paris, and Geneviève Morlet at the Bibliothèque Historique de la Ville de Paris. The president of the Chambre des Notaires de Paris, Christian Bénasse, graciously gave permission to consult the Chamber's library, and Alain Robert made my visits both enjoyable and productive. Conservators at the Archives de Paris and the Bibliothèque Nationale de France repeatedly granted me access to otherwise unavailable materials that proved crucial for this work. I am grateful to all these individuals for their professionalism and expertise.

Many individuals were also willing to share their time and knowledge of the Parisian real estate market with me. Foremost among these, I would like to thank MM. Francis and Jean-Philippe Beuchard, who responded enthusiastically to my requests for materials on the history of their agency (John Arthur et Tiffen). They were able to put me in touch with Marie-France Tiffen, who graciously opened her home and private archives to me. I would also like to extend my gratitude to Jean-Pierre and Thierry Langlois of Cabinet Langlois et Cie, who shared both their expertise and company archives with me.

My advisory committees, both formal and informal, have been unstinting in their enthusiasm for this project. For their sharp insights, challenging questions, and professional guidance, I am deeply grateful to Leora Auslander, Jan Goldstein, and Katherine Taylor. In particular, Leora's careful and engaged scholarship and teaching will long continue to be valued models for me. Patrick Fridenson at EHESS has gone above and beyond the call of duty, always making time in his impossibly full schedule for discussions that are as helpful as they are enjoyable. I am privileged to have benefited from his time and guidance. I am also thankful for wonderful instruction and encouragement from my undergraduate history teachers, Howard Nenner, Fred McGuinness, and Ernest Benz.

I have received support and camaraderie from a number of stellar academic communities. My fellow European history graduate students at the University of Chicago—Tom Dodman, Parker Everett, Sean Dunwoody, Venus Bivar, Erika Vause, Carolyn Purnell, and Tyson Leuchter—have been challenging and inspiring friends and colleagues. In Toronto, the French History Seminar offered a warm and vibrant community for a visiting scholar. At Harvard, the Center for History and Economics and the Prize Fellowship in Economics, History, and Politics are havens of rigorous interdisciplinary research, collegiality, and enthusiasm for all things touching on the history and practice of economic life. I am honored to have worked with the center's director, Emma Rothschild, and profoundly glad for—not to mention reshaped by—the insight and inspiration of my fellow Fellows. The University of Cambridge's Centre for Research in the Arts, Social Sciences, and Humanities has been an inspiring and deeply rewarding place to pursue this project and others.

Participants at annual meetings of the Business History Conference, the Society for French Historical Studies, the Western Society for French Historical Studies, the Urban History Association, and the Association of American Geographers offered valued opportunity for discussion and debate as my work progressed. I am also grateful to the organizers and participants of conferences held by the Hagley Museum and Library (Understanding Markets, 2009); the "History Takes Place" summer academy (Paris, 2010), funded by the ZEIT-Stiftung Ebelin und Gerd

Bucerius and Gerda Henkel Foundation; the Economic History Summer School "Echanges Marchands" organized by the Sorbonne and l'Institut Universitaire de France (Summer 2012); the Richard Robinson Business History Workshop at Portland State University (Spring 2014); and the National Endowment for the Humanities Summer Institute on "Meanings of Property" (Summer 2014). I extend deep thanks to the participants of the "Histories of Land and Power" conference and workshop, which I organized at the Center for History and Economics, Harvard University, in November 2012.

Andrew Kinney, the editorial staff, and anonymous reviewers for Harvard University Press have made the process of developing this book rewarding and exciting, and I am grateful for their work, insights, and improvements. For their toil with historical data to create wonderful maps, my thanks to Julie Roebotham and the Harvard Center for Geographic Analysis.

I have been lucky to develop particular friendships among some fellow travelers over the course of this project and my peregrinations. Ariel Beaujot, Jeff Bowersox, Elizabeth Everton, Valerie Deacon, Ruth Percy, Caitlin Rosenthal, and Valerie Wallace: for the example of their scholarship, and especially the strength and warmth of their personalities, I am singularly grateful. Heather Welland has moved beyond friend to personal hero.

Most importantly, I owe a profound debt to my family, upon whose unceasing love and support I am entirely reliant. My best friend and partner, Michael Pettit, deserves to be on every line of these acknowledgments, just as he is in every line of this book, and responsible for much more important and wonderful besides.

Index

abstraction, 12, 61, 77–80, 129–130
advertising: by speculators, 70–72, 78–79; legal controls, 142, 261; and urban space, 175–176, 182, 192, 195–197, 208–216; in sales and rental gazettes, 187–191, 193–195, 197–199, 204–207; by corporate owners, 244. *See also* advertising posters; floor plans
advertising posters, 206–207
Agence Lagrange, 168–169, 194, 195, 199, 324n117
Agence Largier, 193, 195, 196, 324n117
agents d'affaires, 7, 19, 135–137, 147–148; and officers of the court, 145–147; regulation, 146, 154–160, 170–171; representations, 148–150; typical practitioners, 152–154. *See also* real estate agents
Alphand, Adolphe, 25, 33, 34
Annonce Immobilière, 167, 197
apartment houses, 17, 21, 102, 123–124, 180–182, 199, 223, 226, 235–242, 256
architects, 18, 42, 62–68, 85–89, 104, 203, 232
associations, 51, 121, 150–151, 154–155, 172–173; and property owners, 99–100, 109–113, 117–119, 131, 133, 241, 263. *See also* Chambre Syndicale des Propriétés Immobilières de la Ville de Paris
auctions, 28, 30, 140–144, 158; of public land, 53–55
avenue Victor Hugo, 227, 230, 238, 240, 243, 245–246, 247, 249, 251

Blondel, Henri, 28–29, 31, 61, 67
Boulevard de la Villette, 232, 243
Boulevard Pereire, 232, 233, 235, 240, 245
Boulevard Voltaire, 111, 217
Brière de l'Isle, Georges, 232
building boom (1878–1884), 4, 38–42, 60–61, 72, 96, 174–177, 193, 217, 223–224; and municipal council, 49, 52–53; and notaries, 69–70
building entrepreneurs, 8, 20, 39, 42, 62–65, 174, 235, 279n44. *See also* municipal price series

building industry, 6, 8, 22, 30, 48, 56–57, 66–67, 73. *See also* building boom; municipal price series
building regulations, 44, 102–105, 108, 180, 235

capitalism, 5, 10, 11, 12, 36, 61, 264
Cernesson, Léopold-Camille, 35, 57
Chambre Syndicale des Agents Immobiliers de France, 170–171, 259–261
Chambre Syndicale des Propriétés Immobilières de la Ville de Paris: formation, 15, 100; on association, 110–111, 121–122, 131, 255, 263; campaign for 1865 law, 116–117, 133; on mobilizing property, 128, 129
cité Vaneau, 118, 232, 238, 241
commercialization, 256–257; and management, 7; and real property, 14, 77, 80, 102, 126, 131–132, 193–194, 262, 265–266; and urban landscape, 21, 175, 214, 223, 255; architects and, 63; civil code, 126–127; notaries and, 170
commercial object, 8, 10–11, 21, 61, 95–97, 121, 125–126, 255, 266
commercial selfhood, 5, 137–138, 150–151, 155, 172–173
Compagnie des Hommes d'Affaires du Département de la Seine, 136, 146, 150, 152, 154–159
Compagnie Foncière de France, 6, 7, 41, 67, 76–77, 118, 122, 141, 193, 218–219; operations, 223–225; portfolio, 227–230, 235–242; urban development, 232–235; marketing, 243; tenants, 226–227, 245–247. *See also* subletting
Compagnie Immobilière, 31, 41, 229, 280n55
consumption: and urban space, 17, 78, 95–96, 182–183, 191, 206, 214, 265; and real estate, 19, 65, 131–132, 168, 178, 200, 256; and apartment choice, 177–182, 212–214
corporate ownership, 21, 122, 132, 193–194, 217–219, 241, 246–247, 254–255, 263. *See also* Compagnie Foncière de France; Rente Foncière; Société des Immeubles de France
Crédit Foncier, 6, 40–41, 49, 66, 69, 82, 90, 127–128, 130, 141, 224, 262

Dauby, François, 67, 68, 232

embourgeoisement, 134, 240–242
entrepreneurial vernacular, 223, 248
entrepreneurs, 5, 138, 150, 152, 158
expropriation, 1, 29, 30, 31, 59, 83, 99, 103

Fernoux, Henri, 62, 67, 75
floor plans, 199–204, 215
Fouquiau, Paul, 1–5, 67, 73, 265; Montmartre development, 42–47, 96, 229; workers' housing project, 47–49; public lands, 53, 55; and notaries, 69; *Indicateur Général des Terrains et Immeubles à Vendre*, 70, 88
Fourmi Immobilière, 128, 254
freedom of enterprise, 122, 159, 171, 265

Grand Journal Officiel des Locations et de la Vente des Terrains et Immeubles, 168, 176, 186, 193, 194, 205, 210. *See also* floor plans; John Arthur et Tiffen Agency
Guyot, Yves, 35, 52, 113, 118

Halbwachs, Maurice, 59–60, 78, 91, 95, 115, 116, 178
Harvey, David, 12, 280n52
Haussmann, André, 81, 84–85, 90, 93
Haussmann, Georges-Eugène, 4, 21, 24, 110, 190; and the Rente Foncière, 25, 47, 69
Haussmannization, 6, 17, 52, 119–120, 191–192; legacies, 10, 24–25, 56, 57, 133; republic copying, 28–29, 32, 47
Haverkamp, Frédéric, 161–166
homestead law, 129, 130

housing, 17–18; workers' housing, 46–50, 53–55; consumer demand, 74–75, 85–88, 176–178; investors, 76–77, 217; renting, 86, 100, 177–182, 185, 208, 211–212; owning, 123–124, 182–184; and Great War, 171, 257–260, 261. *See also* advertising; commercialization

illicit speculation, 258
immovable property *(immobilier)*, 13, 15, 16, 78, 80, 101, 125–127, 130, 266
Indicateur Général des Terrains et Immeubles à Vendre. See Fouquiau, Paul
Indicateur illustré des appartements à louer, 78, 79, 200, 202
intermediaries. See *agents d'affaires;* notaries; real estate agents; solicitors

Jauffret, Antoine, 157
Jeannot, Joseph, 232
John Arthur et Tiffen Agency, 14, 96, 122, 181, 185–187, 195, 322n82, 324n117; *Guide Foncier*, 90, 93–95. See also *Grand Journal Officiel des Locations et de la Vente des Terrains et Immeubles*

La France Immobilière, 157–158
La Réforme du Bâtiment, 30, 31, 32, 48, 54, 88, 203, 223
Lagrave, Lucien, 170, 256–257
land: component of real estate, 10–11, 12; source of value, 15, 102, 114–116, 133; advertising, 70, 78; in development, 77–80, 89, 224; guides, 80–81, 90–95; auctions, 140–141. *See also livre foncier;* mobilization of property; municipal land
Langlois et Cie, 320n55
Largier, Edmond, 260, 324n117, 343n21
Laubière, Albert, 53, 67, 70, 71, 78, 80, 123, 265
Law of December 22, 1888, 109, 117–120, 133, 241, 309n63
Law of June 21, 1865, 16, 100, 112–113, 116–117, 133
Law of September 16, 1807, 113–114, 115, 119
Lazare, Louis, 23, 29, 98, 106–107, 108, 109
Le Foncier, 70, 73, 74, 80, 89, 125, 176, 231, 232
Lefebvre, Henri, 191, 211
Leménil, Emile, 245, 247
Leroy-Beaulieu, Paul, 15, 46, 53, 74–76, 115–116
Les Corbeaux, 138–139
lésion d'outre-moitié, 82–83, 257
Léveillé, Jules, 110, 129
limited liability joint stock corporation *(société anonyme)*, 1, 4, 15, 62; liberalization, 6, 41; in urban development, 6, 48, 65, 67–70, 122; mobilizing property, 7, 15, 124, 126, 127, 130, 132; opposition, 50–52, 56; commercial entities, 127, 265. *See also individual companies*
livre foncier, 128–130, 264

Manier, Joseph, 54, 55, 115
marketization, 11–12, 61, 137, 173, 262
Masselin, Onésime, 14, 65–67, 70, 72, 95, 176, 223
mobilization of property, 13–14, 102, 128–130, 132, 224, 263, 264, 266
movable property *(mobilier)*, 10, 13, 15, 16, 78, 80, 101, 125–127, 130, 142, 262, 266
municipal council: as elected body, 6, 24; prerogatives, 27, 37–38; public works, 28–30, 31–32, 39; borrowing, 32–33, 287n37; domain, 37; on housing, 47–50, 53; urban growth, 57–58; on expropriation procedures, 83; on *Guide Foncier*, 93–95; on property owner associations, 109, 112–113, 118. *See also* building boom; municipal land; municipal price series
municipal land, 30, 44–45, 53–55
municipal price series, 34–36

Napoleonic Code, 13, 102; civil and commercial codes, 121, 125, 127
notaries, 7, 136, 137–145, 170, 264; and development, 68–70; and *agents d'affaires,* 145–147, 152, 164, 171, 195
Nouveau Quartier des Martyrs, 111

papier-pierre, 15
Paris Commune, 1, 6, 10, 24–25, 56, 73, 100, 191–192
Parliamentary Commission on the Industrial Crisis (1884), 8, 14, 39, 51–52, 57–58, 77, 246
Pereire, Emile and Isaac, 41, 235, 280n55
Petibon, Maxime, 91–92, 137
Planat, Paul, 85, 87–88, 91, 96
price and value, 81–83
price guides, 80–81, 84–85, 89–95
principal tenants, 242–243
private roads, 98–99, 102–109, 118–119, 133, 241, 263
property management, 7, 10, 15, 122; management and municipal governance, 33, 53; corporate management, 193–194, 217, 219, 227–230, 243, 246, 254, 255. *See also* principal tenants
property owners, 15, 76, 182–184; ownership and work, 101, 120–125; prerogatives, 104–105, 133–134, 142. *See also* associations; Chambre Syndicale des Propriétés Immobilières de la Ville de Paris; corporate ownership
property registration, 140, 257, 316n17. See also *livre foncier*
public utility, 10, 27, 30, 42, 44, 58, 263; and property owner associations, 112–113, 117

Quartier Marbeuf development, 2, 4, 28–29, 32, 73, 244

real estate agents, 137; professional organization, 157, 159; business practices and attitudes, 163–164, 167–168, 172–173, 195, 214, 320n59. *See also* advertising; Agence Lagrange; Agence Largier; *agents d'affaires;* Chambre Syndicale des Agents Immobiliers de France; Haverkamp, Frédéric; John Arthur et Tiffen Agency
real estate markets, 8, 10–12, 60, 95, 144, 161, 166–171, 191, 258–260. *See also* auctions; price guides
real property, 10, 12, 14, 15, 60–61; and commerce, 13, 78, 82–83, 102, 121, 125–126, 169–170. *See also* auctions; *lésion d'outre-moitié;* mobilization of property
rent controls, 257–258
Rente Foncière, 6, 7, 25, 41, 67; Montmartre development, 4, 47, 252; portfolio management, 193, 219, 227, 229–230, 242–245. *See also* corporate ownership
residential mobility, 18–19, 184–185, 192, 207, 211–212
Réveil Immobilier, 167, 206
Rivoalen, Emile, 8, 18, 63, 96, 180, 181, 182
Roch-Sautier, Madame, 304n100, 325n126
Rue Chevreul, 234, 238, 241, 245, 249, 339n62
Rue Civiale, 236, 238, 243
Rue d'Alençon, 222, 241
Rue de l'Amiral Courbet, 231, 241, 243, 250, 251
Rue de la Pompe, 231, 243, 249
Rue de Longchamp, 231, 235, 239, 241, 243, 251
Rue de Montreuil, 233
Rue des Belles Feuilles, 227, 231, 232, 240, 241, 248, 249, 250, 251, 252, 337n37
Rue des Boulets, 234, 245, 246, 339n62
Rue du Débarcadère, 233, 243, 248, 249, 252
Rue du Mont-Cenis, 239
Rue du Trésor, 239, 243
Rue d'Uzès, 108, 232, 243
Rue Eugène Sue, 42, 252
Rue Gustave Courbet, 232, 243, 249

Rue Saint-Philippe du Roule, 106, 107, 235, 238, 251
Rue Simart, 42, 44, 252, 337n46

SA de Construction du Boulevard Pereire, 232
SA des Immeubles de l'Avenue Victor Hugo, 231, 241
SA des Immeubles du Boulevard Montparnasse, 241
SA des Terrains et Constructions de la Place d'Italie, 68
SA des Terrains et Constructions de la Porte Maillot, 233
SA du Quartier Marbeuf, 29, 122
SA Immobilière de Montmartre, 1, 45
SA Immobilière des Terrains et Constructions du Faubourg du Temple, 68, 236–237
Say, Léon, 30, 99, 109–110
Sellier, Henri, 260
shareholders, 4, 7, 128, 219, 225; reports, 21, 220, 229–230; building companies, 48, 67
Société des Immeubles de France, 67, 122, 219, 254
Société des Immeubles de Paris, 74, 286n31
solicitors, 7, 140, 149, 152, 166, 264
Songeon, Jacques, 29
Soty, E., 232
Sous-Comptoir des Entrepreneurs, 6, 40–41, 66, 96, 224
speculative building, 49–52, 80, 217, 230–235; leasing and sales options, 53–54, 77; buildings, 64–65, 235–242; risk-taking, 65–66; networks, 66–72; needs of the neighborhood, 88, 95–97, 227, 241. *See also* building boom; speculators
speculators, 59–61, 80, 264–265; architects, 62–63. *See also* Fouquiau, Paul; Laubière, Albert; speculative building
stock market (Bourse), 14–15, 77, 101, 130, 145; 1882 crash, 39, 156; and real property, 124–125, 145, 167–170, 262–263
street construction, 31, 42, 102–103, 233–235. *See also* private roads
subletting, 247–254
suburban development, 206–207
Syndicat Professionnel des Hommes d'Affaires de France et des Colonies, 146, 157–160, 214

tax evaluations, 220–223
Tiffen, William, 186. *See also* John Arthur et Tiffen Agency

unearned increment, 114–116, 131
urban growth, 23–24, 57–58, 59–60, 73–75, 84, 88, 112–113, 184–185

Vauthier, Louis-Léger, 29, 33, 88
Verdin, Berthe, 251